A Visual Feast

ARABELLA BOXER
TESSA TRAEGER

A Visual Feast

CENTURY
London Sydney Auckland Johannesburg

ACKNOWLEDGEMENTS

We would like to thank everyone at *Vogue*, where most of the
material in this book first appeared, and especially the
managing editor, Georgina Boosey.

First published in 1991 by Random Century Ltd,
Random Century House, 20 Vauxhall Bridge Road,
London SW1V 2SA

Random Century New Zealand Ltd,
9-11 Rothwell Avenue, Albany
Private Bag, North Shore Mail Centre, Glenfield,
Auckland 10 New Zealand

Century Hutchinson South Africa Pty Ltd,
PO Box 337 Bergvlei 2012 South Africa

British Library Cataloguing-in-Publication Data

Boxer, Arabella
A visual feast.
I. Title II. Traeger Tessa
641.5

IBSN 0 7126 4792 9

Origination by Colorlito, Milan

Printed and bound in Italy by Amilcare Pizzi SPA

'Eating books is bad for you,' announced Philip Howard in one of his entertaining and erudite essays in *The Times*, working himself into a positive frenzy about colour pictures ('emetic') and 'the revolting and embarrassing jargon on foodspeak'. Illustration and description of food can, like anything else, be carried to ridiculous extremes and in some examples of designer food, flavour, presentation and consumer seemed locked in terminal battle. One can only begin to imagine the secret fury of the chef as his masterpiece is demolished and devoured.

Designer food is the very antithesis of the Boxer/Traeger philosophy. In a collaboration that started in 1975 they brought to *Vogue* a rare blend of talents, both outwardly calm perfectionists, inwardly simmering with enthusiasms and adventure. They complemented each other by the apparent simplicity and traditional approach of the cook, the original and inventive strategies of the photographer.

Arabella Boxer made an immediate impact with the publication in 1964 of *First Slice Your Cookbook*. Mark Boxer conceived the idea of a Three Tier Menu Guide and 'he just wanted someone to write it', she says with habitual diffidence. The book was not intended for professionals but for amateurs who enjoyed cooking, and there were enough of them around to put it on the Best Seller List. It also propelled her on a career she might not otherwise have contemplated. Two years later she started contributing regularly to *Vogue*, twice winning the Glenfiddich Award for Cookery Writer of the Year.

Her outlook is more Chinese than European, 'the most simple foods prepared with loving care'. Rich surface effects are not in her vocabulary. One of her achievements has been to reawaken interest in herbs, salads and vegetables, vegetables not just as an accompaniment to a meal centred on meat, but as dishes in their own right. Gathering assurance and experience, with input from her travels round the world, she evolved from amateur to professional, informed, expert, but never dogmatic or pretentious.

Tessa Traeger invented a food iconography somewhere between photography and illustration which is intricate, witty and imaginative, drawing on visual references often with only oblique connections with food, everything to do with graphic surprise. At the Guildford School of Art she was taught by Ifor Thomas, a stickler for serious technical competence. 'There were no electronics then, you had to *know*...'

At *Vogue* she moved quickly from traditional food photography to a kind of *trompe l'œil*, deploying Victorian and primitive paintings as backgrounds that become an integral part of the design. She progressed to collages, endlessly imitated but never surpassed, to one dimensional images of herbs and vegetables reminiscent of medieval illustrated borders. Everything and everyone was grist to her mill, from Gauguin and surrealism to the vegetable faces inspired by the Italian Renaissance painter Arcimboldo. Raw materials, from a cabbage leaf to a collection of herbs, had to be in mint condition, each picture thought out to the last detail, nothing left to chance.

Cookery and gardening books can be an endless source of pleasure, not only for experts but, vicariously, for non-cooks and guess-work gardeners too. In the mind's eye, shaggy lawns and random shrubs become visions of paradise. In the kitchen, the lumpen sauce turns to nectar.

To a certain extent, *A Visual Feast* combines the two. In this context, *pace* Mr. Howard, eating books is very good for you.

Beatrix Miller
February, 1991

January

Stir-Fried Prawns
Mexican Beans
Potato and Lentil Cakes
Avocado Relish
Aigo Boulido
Grilled Chicken in Garlic Marinade
Roasted Squab with Garlic
Garlic Purée
Cheese Roulade with Garlic Filling
Hauser Broth
Ribollita
Warm Leeks with Iced Tomato Sauce
Cracked Wheat with Spinach
Meagadarra
Buckwheat Crêpes
Beef Stew
Braised Beef with Glazed Vegetables
Beef Olives
Sea Pie

According to Diana Kennedy, an Englishwoman who has spent much of her life in Mexico, and whose books on Mexican food are world famous, there are some 200 different sorts of chilli pepper, and roughly half of them grow in Mexico. Each has its own characteristics: its own shape and size, strength and flavour. The smaller and more pointed their shape, the hotter they tend to be, like the tiny bird, or bird's-eye chilli, while the larger blunt-ended *poblano* is mild, and can be stuffed and eaten whole, like an ordinary green pepper. The most often used in Mexico are probably the *serranos*, *jalapenos*, *poblanos* and *anaheims*. But their names are complex and confusing: when dried, the *poblano* becomes the *ancho*, while the *jalapeno*, after smoking and drying, is called the *chopotle*. Fresh chillies are usually green, while dried ones are always red. Like the sweet pepper, the chilli turns from green to red as it ripens, sometimes becoming yellow to brown along the way. In many parts of the world, red chilli peppers are threaded on string by peasant women, and hung in festoons, like giant necklaces.

The chilli pepper is a fruit, *Capsicum frutescens*. It is in no way related to black or white pepper, which are made from the berries of a climbing vine, *Piper nigrum*. The chilli is a tropical plant, unable to withstand frost, which grew originally in Mexico and in Central America, and was widely eaten by the Indians. It was discovered by Christopher Columbus in the late fifteenth century, and at some point in the next fifty years, during the era of the great voyages by Vasco de Gama and Ferdinand Magellan, it found its way to the Far East. It has been used there ever since, in India, China, Indonesia, Thailand and Japan. Eventually it reached Europe: in Spain, where 700 years of Arab domination had irrevocably altered the national palate, the chilli became popular instantly, and in Hungary, where the Turks imported chillies from Persia during their 150-year-long occupation, they acquired lasting popularity. By the time the Turks left, the slightly milder paprika pepper was firmly established at the heart of the national cuisine. But the chilli was too fierce for most Europeans, so a mild pepper was created, by crossing the chilli with the courgette. This produced the green, yellow and red pepper as we know it today, *Capsicum annum*, where the only trace of hotness lies in the seeds.

Today, chilli peppers figure highly in the cuisine of Mexico and south-western American states, the West Indies, Spain, Portugal and Hungary, the north coast of Africa, and parts of East and West Africa, India, parts of China, especially Szechuan, Hunan, Indonesia, Thailand and Japan. They are most highly valued in poor countries, where they help to lend interest to a bland diet. It was many years before I discovered the joys of cooking with chilli peppers. First a bottle of Tabasco found its way into my refrigerator, replacing the Worcester Sauce that my parents' generation relied on to hot up anything from a Bloody Mary to a devilled partridge. Then a friend brought me a jar of mixed red pepper flakes from Hong Kong, and I was hooked. I began using fresh chillies, albeit cautiously. I am still cautious, for I find that too much chilli deadens the palate. This has happened to me in Szechuan restaurants in London, although never in Szechuan, where I found the food totally delicious.

Chillies may be roasted and skinned before use. With some of the larger varieties, like the *poblano*, this is advisable, for their skins are tough and hard to digest. The roasting also imparts a delicious smoky flavour. All peppers are rich in vitamin C. I always discard the seeds, which contain much of the hotness but none of the flavour of the flesh. Fresh chillies can also be bought in tins – Old El Paso Jalapenos are a good example – or dried. Fresh chillies should be loosely wrapped in soft paper, not clingfilm, and stored in the bottom of the fridge. Alternatively they may be stacked upright in a jam jar and covered with olive oil. As well as preserving chillies, the oil makes a useful flavouring for stir-fried dishes, pizzas and pasta. The chilli also exists as chilli powder (sometimes blended with ground cumin and other spices), or cayenne, and its milder form, paprika. Then there are the thin hot sauces, such as Tabasco.

Chillies probably appear to their best advantage in sauces, for you can use them sparingly, to season food according to your taste. In Mexico and the bordering states of the USA, they make a wonderful uncooked sauce called *salsa*, of chopped tomatoes, onions and chillies, that they serve with just about everything, from fried eggs to stuffed tacos to grilled fish. There is an even better version made with green *tomatillos* instead of tomatoes. This little fruit is no relation to the tomato, but grows encased in a papery husk, like the Chinese gooseberry. Chillies also figure as a vital ingredient in *guacamole*, and in *ceviche*, while in Mexican bean dishes their dull earthy taste is spiked with fresh chillies, lime and coriander. It is probably in Mexico, where they first grew, that they are most highly prized, and their influence has spread into California, New Mexico and Texas. Even as far north as San Francisco, this sort of cooking, known as 'south-western', is popular: *guacamole* with tortilla chips, black bean soup with sliced chillies, lime and coriander, and oysters served on the half shell with *tomatillo salsa*.

Garlic is the most robust and vital of foods, closely linked with the earth, within the tradition of peasant cookery. It is probably in this context that its value is best appreciated, while its health-giving properties are most effective when treated as part of daily life, in all the traditional ways. It is also much loved by gourmets like Alice Waters, who holds annual 'Garlic Galas' at Chez Panisse, her restaurant in Berkeley, California. Alice is a true lover of garlic, and uses it almost daily, in dishes ranging from the sophisticated, like wine-based sherbet laced with garlic, to 'the ultimate in simplicity... good homemade bread, generously brushed with olive oil, grilled over charcoal, and then rubbed liberally with garlic.'

Garlic is an ancient food, once held in high esteem by such civilizations as the Egyptians, Greeks and Romans. Today, its greatest use lies probably in the countries of Southern Europe, along the shores of the Mediterranean. Garlic is an important crop in France, especially in Provence and the South West, where special garlic markets and fairs are held in summer. Two main varieties are grown: the white garlic which is ready for sale in June, and the pink which is harvested a month later. There are numerous subvarieties, many with romantic names like *jeunes filles en fleur: Violet de Cadours, Blanc de Lomagne* and *Rose de Lautrec*.

The other countries along the north shore of the Mediterranean also use garlic widely, although slightly more sparingly than the French. Almost all have one or two fiery sauces based on pounded cloves of raw garlic. Best known in Britain is the Genoese *pesto*, and its *Niçoise* variant, *pistou*. Then there is the Provençal *aiolli*, with its variations: the Spanish *ali-oli*, and the Greek *skordalia*. In some cases nuts are added, as in *bagna cauda*, *pesto*, and the Spanish *picada*. On the North African coast, fierce sauces are also popular, often served in conjunction with the bland couscous, but here the fiery element is supplied by chilli peppers instead of garlic. In Spain, as a result of centuries of Arab domination, both elements have been combined in a sauce called *romescu*, made with garlic, chillies, almonds and pine nuts.

I used to love such things when I was younger; now I prefer to eat garlic in other, gentler ways. The flavour of garlic that has cooked for a long time has little in common with the pungency of raw garlic. I roast whole cloves around a bird, then make a purée with the cooked garlic and incorporate it in a sauce. I bake whole cloves of garlic in the oven, then purée them and keep the resulting paste in jars in the refrigerator, like *pesto*, for adding to soups and sauces. A spoonful can be stirred into a purée of root vegetables, celeriac or parsnip, mixed with potato. It can be spread on slices of French bread dried in the oven and eaten as an aperitif, or floated on bowls of vegetable soup, or used as a base for roast squab or quail, or scrambled eggs. It can also be used as a medicament, as a last resort when laid low with colds, coughs, or influenza.

Another useful standby is garlic butter, sometimes called snail butter, or *beurre d'escargot*. This freezes well, and has a myriad uses. It can be dotted over steamed shellfish – scallops, mussels or clams – or cut in slices and laid over a grilled Dover sole, or over grilled tomatoes. Garlic butter is also excellent when added to a dish of cooked canellini beans, as is the garlic purée.

Garlic is a member of the *Allium* family, which includes the onion, leek and chives. There are three varieties on sale in the UK: the common garlic, with small cloves and white, papery skin; the pink or purple skinned variety, imported from Provence and Italy; and, in early summer, fresh garlic can be bought with giant cloves, plump and juicy. As it dries, the cloves shrink, becoming easier to peel, while the intersecting skin becomes dry and papery. Garlic is easily grown at home by planting the individual cloves two inches deep, in well-drained soil, but it will not have the same flavour as that grown in a hot region like the Midi. When grown under peach trees, it is thought to prevent leaf curl.

Garlic is one of the great health foods, although in India it is treated with caution. In the West, it is believed to possess many almost miraculous properties. It can help bronchial conditions and respiratory ailments; it benefits the circulation, at the same time lowering the blood pressure, and the level of cholesterol. It is held to stimulate the digestive system, and to act as a natural antibiotic and antisceptic. It can regulate disorders, whether an imbalance of intestinal flora, or a malfunction of the glands. Although it is rarely consumed in sufficient quantities to be significant, it is rich in vitamins B and C, and in potassium. For those who actively dislike the taste, it can be taken in capsule form; this is available in health food shops.

Most people realize that they should cut down on salt but few understand the sodium content of the food they eat. And it is not merely the sodium content that is important but the proportion of sodium to potassium within the foods. This is a delicate balance that has for centuries been regulated naturally by our own bodies. Nowadays it is upset by the use of artificial fertilizers and by a greater consumption of processed foods. Both these factors increase the sodium content of food to an unprecedented degree, making it impossible for our bodies to offset. Only by increasing our consumption of fresh vegetables, fruit, grain, nuts and seeds, grown wherever possible by organic methods, and some, at least, eaten raw, can we retain a healthy balance.

Although nutrition is a comparatively young science, with new discoveries constantly being made, some of the classic diet books published twenty or thirty years ago still make very good sense - more so, in fact, than many of the exaggerated and cranky newcomers that feature for a while in the best-seller lists before vanishing without trace. Max Gerson, a German doctor who suffered as a young man from severe migraines and managed to cure himself by a diet based largely on raw foods, went on to make a life study of diet as treatment for many illnesses, including cancer. (He treated Albert Schweitzer for diabetes by the same method; Schweitzer lived to ninety-two.) What interests me most about Gerson's work is not the cancer diet itself but his Diet for Good Health. Unlike the cancer diet, which is demanding in the extreme, his diet for general health is adaptable and remarkably undogmatic. Gerson claimed that if 75 per cent of the food consumed is 'chosen for the purpose of protecting the functions of the essential organs: liver, kidneys, brain, heart, etc, both by storing reserves and by avoiding putting unnecessary burdens on them,' the remaining 25 per cent can be personal choice. Gerson insisted that 'there must be more potassium than sodium in the organs in general, and that a certain relationship between potassium and sodium must be maintained.' Gerson believed that the starting point for all illness, cancer included, is an imbalance of sodium and potassium, usually too much sodium and too little potassium. This imbalance, he claimed, 'results in serious disturbance in body chemistry.'

A near contemporary of Gerson's was the Swiss physician Max Bircher-Benner, who was one of the pioneers of the use of diet for, as he put it, 'the healing of the sick and the prevention of disease'. Regarding the sodium/potassium balance, his daughter Ruth Bircher, writes: 'Sodium and potassium are so distributed in the body that potassium compounds predominate in the cells and blood corpuscles, and sodium compounds predominate in the blood fluid and tissues outside the cells. The more each group predominates in its own sphere the greater the tension between them, and the more powerful the functioning of the vital processes in the organism.' This is essential for optimum health. She goes on to explain how, when large amounts of sodium are consumed, a correspondingly high volume of water is retained in the body, in order to maintain the correct solution of salt in the body fluid. 'If conversely, the salt consumption is intentionally decreased by a salt-free raw diet, a corresponding elimination of water can be observed.'

A high-sodium diet has an effect on the blood pressure, as the quantities of sodium and potassium in the blood fluctuate constantly, and an excess of the one causes the other to be lost in the urine. Thus persons eating salt as they wished excreted nine times more potassium than when their salt intake was limited; and human volunteers kept on diets deficient in potassium retained so much salt that they developed high blood pressure.

Looking back at the work of the late Gayelord Hauser, I still find much to admire. He also understood the sodium/potassium balance, and his recipe for Hauser Broth, or Alkaline Broth, devised in 1922, based on principles laid down by Hippocrates, has become a standby in my kitchen. This delicious clear soup, quick and inexpensive to make, can be used as a pick-me-up, a substitute for mid-morning coffee, an accompaniment to a light meal, or a late-night drink.

One of the basics of all the above diets is the use of raw food, but I find recipes for uncooked dishes tedious to read. I will leave readers to work out their own combinations of raw vegetables and fruit, and simply suggest a few dishes using potassium-rich foods cooked in appropriate ways. I would also suggest using a low-sodium salt for cooking purposes, and a minimum of sea salt for adding at the table, when required.

When looking for sources of healthy dishes, I find myself turning yet again to the Middle East. By occasionally substituting brown rice for white, these healthy foods can be made even more nutritious.

Perhaps it is because I am now a granny, that I find the idea of 'granny food,' or *la cuisine de grandmère*, as always more elegant in French, so appealing. After years of living alone, pleasing oneself, cooking light meals for oneself and one's friends, gradually family meals start to happen all over again, with children and grandchildren, nephews and nieces and their children. As well as my own children, and those of my friends, I now have almost thirty nephews and nieces, counting their families, so that family meals are always appreciated, when one has the time and inclination to provide them.

Not far removed from the *cuisine de grandmère* is the *cuisine de terroir*. What both terms mean, gastronomically speaking, is going back to our roots, rediscovering and reassessing our inheritance. This can be done in different ways, depending on the individual. For some, it could mean studying old manuscripts, but for myself, whose approach is far from academic, and who has always preferred cooking and eating to talking about it, the concept takes on a more modest, practical form. I have gone back ten, twenty, even thirty years, sifting through dishes I used to enjoy, and remaking them. In so doing, especially with dishes I haven't cooked for over twenty years, I inevitably find things I want to change. Perhaps I want to use less cream than before, or reduce the fat content. I might want to shorten the cooking time, or introduce a new kitchen aid like the food processor, so that what was once a lengthy and troublesome dish now becomes, literally, a whizz. Whatever the outcome, I find that each of these dishes has given me much pleasure, both in memories of the past, and the joys of the present. It is a good idea from time to time to remind ourselves of our culinary inheritance, and to make a firm resolve to draw on this more often in the future, rather than looking elsewhere, in our desultory search for new experience.

I have a vague theory that grandmothers often play an important role in the formative years of great cooks. Not in my own alas - perhaps that's why I am not a great cook - for I don't think either of my grandmothers was specially interested in food. But again and again, in the reminiscences of chefs and food writers, I come across nostalgic references to their grandmothers.

It is not always the grandmother who plays this role; sometimes it is an aunt, or even a godmother, who initiated the child into the mysteries of the kitchen. In the case of Roger Vergé it was his aunt Celestine, who used to take her small nephew along on her weekly trips to market. He describes her haggling over the price of a fowl: ' "My poor woman," my aunt replied with an absolutely counterfeit air of profound commiseration, "your chickens ought to have stayed another week or two in the *epinette*. In any case at my table I can't serve birds that are nothing but skin and bone." With that, she began a false exit, knowing full well that the farmer's wife would do everything in her power to keep her from going. It was all part of an immutable ritual, without which, for the farmer's wife as well as for my aunt, the negotiation would have had no real interest.'

In the childhood memories of Nico Ladenis, living as a child in Tanganyika, now Tanzania, his memories are of his mother in this role. 'I have had an indelible image of my mother deeply imprinted on my mind. I picture her by our ancient, cast-iron woodburning stove. Wooden spoon in hand, her apron covered in flour, she would move around the kitchen, tugging at the dough to make filo.'

All this suggests that in mens' memories food is closely bound up with the women who produced it. In such countries as France, Italy, Spain and Greece, where extended families were the norm, it was as often as not the grandmother or aunt, as the mother, who was in charge of the kitchen, or who had time to share their work with the children. For this is without doubt women's cookery that we are dealing with. Some years ago on a trip to Anjou and Touraine, I interviewed a charming Frenchman, M. Albert Augereau, who spoke with feeling about '*la cuisine des femmes: moins elaborée que celui des hommes, mais fait avec beaucoup d'amour. Ça se passe de grandmère à fille: c'est l'origine de la cuisine régionale.*' ('Women's cooking: less elaborate than that of men, but done with love. It is handed down from grandmother to daughter: it is the origin of regional cooking.')

Not long ago, I watched Brian Sack, co-proprietor of Sharrow Bay, being interviewed on television. When he was asked 'What is the secret of becoming a great chef?', he replied emphatically: 'Mother's cooking professionally done, with an English emphasis.' And that, for Englishmen at least, is what it's all about. For this is how men's two basic hungers, for food, and for affection in the form of nostalgia, are satisfied together.

CHILLI PEPPERS

Stir-Fried Prawns

30 ml/2 tblsps sunflower oil
1 bunch spring onions, sliced
1-2 green chillies, finely chopped
7 ml/1½ tsps chopped root ginger
350 g/12 oz peeled prawns
juice of 1 Seville orange
(or ½ sweet orange and ¼ lemon)
15 ml/1 tblsp soy sauce
45 ml/3 tblsps chopped coriander

Heat a wok, or deep frying pan. Add the oil and heat again, then put in the sliced spring onions and toss for 30 secs, then the chopped chillies and ginger. Toss for another 30 secs before adding the prawns and stir-fry for 2 mins. Add the fruit juice and soy sauce and toss again, for about 1 min. Remove from the heat and stir in the chopped coriander. Serves 3, with boiled rice. (450 g/1 lb scallops, without their coral tongues, may be used instead of prawns. Cut them in half or quarters, depending on size.)

Mexican Beans

225 g/8 oz red or black kidney beans,
or borlotti or pinto beans
½ medium onion, chopped
2 cloves garlic, chopped
1 small bay leaf, crumbled
1-2 green chillies, finely chopped
sea salt and black pepper

garnish:
150 ml/¼ pt fromage blanc, or Jockey
2 limes (lemons), halved
90 ml/6 tblsps roughly chopped coriander

Soak the beans overnight, then drain them and put in a deep pan with 900 ml/1½ pts fresh cold water. Put over a moderate flame and, as they heat, add the onion and garlic, bay leaf and chilli. Let the water boil hard for 10 mins, then reduce the heat so that it simmers gently. Cook for 1½ hours, half covered, or until the beans are tender, testing them every 15 mins once the first hour is up. When they are ready, drain them in a colander standing over a bowl. Discard the bay leaf. Measure 300 ml/½ pt of the beans and put in a food processor with 150 ml/¼ pt of their liquid. Add sea salt and black pepper and process until roughly puréed. Mix the whole beans and the puréed ones in the saucepan, reheating them gently and adding more sea salt and black pepper. Cook gently, stirring often, for 3-4 mins, then tip into a serving dish. Serves 3-4, with the three garnishes in small bowls. They are good used as a filling for wholemeal pancakes, with the same garnishes.

Potato and Lentil Cakes

These little cakes are good with sausages, or with vegetarian meals, or with hard-boiled eggs.

225 g/8 oz freshly mashed potato
225 g/8 oz mashed cooked lentils
30 ml/2 tblsps sunflower oil
½ bunch spring onions, chopped
1-2 green chillies, finely chopped
5 ml/1 tsp ground cumin
5 ml/1 tsp ground coriander
sea salt and black pepper
30 ml/2 tblsps chopped coriander
1 egg, beaten
sifted flour
25 g/1 oz butter

Mix the mashed potato and lentils in a bowl. The lentils should be pushed through a coarse food mill, otherwise they will be too thin. Heat half the oil and cook the spring onions, adding the chillies after a moment. Add the cumin and coriander and cook all together gently for 2-3 mins, stirring. Then tip onto the potatoes and lentils and stir in, mixing well with a wooden spoon, and adding plenty of sea salt and black pepper. Finally add the chopped coriander. Form into small round patties, lay on a plate covered with clingfilm, and chill for several hours or overnight, to firm them up. Just before cooking, dip them in beaten egg and then in flour. Heat the butter with the remaining oil in a wide frying pan and cook them gently until brown on both sides, 4-5 mins. Makes 8 or 9 patties. Serves 4.

Avocado Relish

This is a cross between a *guacamole* and a *salsa*. It is half-way between a vegetable, a salad and a sauce, and I serve it with dry food like grilled steaks and chicken.

2 large ripe tomatoes,
skinned and seeded
½ bunch spring onions, sliced
1-2 chillies, finely chopped
22 ml/1½ tblsps lime juice
12 ml/¾ tblsp light olive oil
1 ripe avocado

The avocado should be added to the relish shortly before serving, but the rest of the ingredients can be prepared in advance. Chop the tomatoes and put in a bowl, adding the sliced spring onions and finely chopped chillies. Stir in the lime juice and olive oil and leave until just before serving. Then peel and chop the avocado, stirring it into the mixture, and serve within 30 mins. Serves 4.

GARLIC

Aigo Boulido

A Provençal soup, less austere than the Spanish *Sopa de Ajo*. Saffron makes it rich in flavour and very fragrant.

3 leeks, sliced
90 ml/6 tblsps olive oil
5 large cloves garlic, sliced
2 carrots, sliced
225 g/8 oz tomatoes, skinned and sliced
1.1 litres/2 pts light chicken stock
sea salt and black pepper
2 sprigs thyme
1 packet saffron
4-6 slices dry French bread, cut diagonally
4-6 eggs, 1 per person, poached

Cook the leeks slowly in the oil, until they start to soften. Add the garlic and continue to cook slowly. When all is lightly coloured, add the carrots and tomatoes. Stir for a moment, cover and cook gently for 5 mins. Then add the heated stock, salt and pepper, thyme and saffron. Bring to the boil and cook briskly, uncovered, for 15 mins. Toast the bread lightly in a low oven, and poach the eggs, keeping them hot in a bowl of hot water. Lift out the vegetables with a slotted spoon and divide them between heated soup bowls. Lay the toasted bread on this, with a poached egg on each slice. Discard the thyme, adjust the seasoning, and pour the soup gently over the eggs. Serve immediately. Serves 4-6.

Grilled Chicken in Garlic Marinade

1 large free-range chicken, cut in 8 joints

marinade:
15 ml/1 tblsp Dijon mustard
150 ml/¼ pt low-fat yoghurt
150 ml/¼ pt sunflower oil
12 g/½ oz root ginger, finely chopped
3 cloves garlic, finely chopped
1 small green chilli, finely chopped
(about 15 ml/1 tblsp)
juice of 1 lemon

garnish:
2 lemons, cut in quarters

Start a day in advance. Stir the mustard into the yoghurt, add the oil very slowly, literally drop by drop, as if making mayonnaise. Pound the ginger, garlic, and chilli together in a mortar until reduced to a paste, then stir into the yoghurt. Add the lemon juice. Skin the chicken joints and make a few small incisions in each joint with the point of a sharp knife. Paint all over with the marinade and lay them in a shallow dish. Cover with clingfilm and place low down in the refrigerator. Leave for 24 hours. To serve, heat the grill and lay the pieces on foil, skinned side down. When the grill is really hot, place them under it and cook until golden brown, turn over and grill the other side. Allow about 10 mins each side, then transfer them to a hot platter and serve as soon as possible, garnished with lemon quarters. Serve some fresh noodles, or rice, or new potatoes at the same time, with a watercress salad. Serves 4.

Roasted Squab with Garlic

Try to get the livers with the squab, if you can, otherwise substitute chicken livers.

4 squab, with livers
(50 g/2 oz chicken liver, if no
squab livers)
25 g/1 oz butter
45 ml/3 tblsps sunflower oil
15 cloves garlic, unpeeled
150 ml/¼ pt dry white wine
3 sprigs fresh thyme
1 shallot, chopped
30 ml/2 tblsps crème fraîche

garnish:
50 g/2 oz mâche

Brown the birds all over in 25 g/1 oz butter and 30 ml/2 tblsps oil in a casserole. Remove them and put in the whole cloves of garlic. Brown them gently in the butter and oil for 1-2 mins, pour on the wine and add the thyme. Bring to the boil, lay the squabs on the garlic and cover. Cook for 35-40 mins at 190ºC/375ºF/gas mark 5. Heat the remaining tablespoon of oil in a frying pan and cook the chopped shallot gently for 1-2 mins. Add the livers and cook briefly, until they are no longer pink. When the birds are cooked, transfer to a serving dish and keep warm. Push the garlic cloves through a food mill, with the livers and shallot. Mix with the juices from the casserole and reheat, adding salt and pepper if required. Serve the birds on a bed of *mâche*, with the sauce in a separate jug. Accompany them with fresh noodles, and wild mushrooms, when available. Serves 4.

Garlic Purée

8 whole heads garlic
2 small bay leaves
3 sprigs fresh thyme
6 black peppercorns
150 ml/¼ pt olive oil
2.5 ml/½ tsp sea salt

Break the heads up into cloves; do not peel them. Lay them in a shallow baking dish. Scatter the crumbled bay leaves, thyme, and peppercorns over; add the olive oil. Add 700 ml/⅓ pt water and cover the dish with foil. Bake for 1½ hours at 150ºC/300ºF/gas mark 2. Pour off the liquid, discard the herbs, and push the garlic cloves through a medium food mill. Stir in the sea salt, and pack into a screw-topped jar. Keep in the refrigerator and use as needed. Makes about 300 ml/½ pt.

Cheese Roulade with Garlic Filling

roulade:
40 g/1½ oz butter
45 ml/3 tblsps flour
300 ml/½ pt milk
75 g/3 oz grated Gruyère
sea salt and black pepper
grated nutmeg
4 eggs, separated
25 g/1 oz grated Parmesan cheese

filling:
225 g/8 oz fromage blanc
15 ml/1 heaped tblsp garlic purée
45 ml/3 tblsps chopped spring onions
45 ml/3 tblsps chopped basil or coriander, or parsley and chives
sea salt and black pepper
fresh tomato sauce (optional)

Oil a Swiss roll tin measuring 30 by 20 cm/12 by 8 ins, and line it with baking parchment or oiled greaseproof paper. Melt the butter, stir in the flour and cook for 1 min. Add the heated milk and stir until blended. Cook gently for 3 mins, add the grated Gruyère, stirring until it has melted. When all is smooth, add salt and pepper and grated nutmeg, to taste. Remove from the heat and beat in the (lightly beaten) egg yolks. Leave to cool for a few minutes, then fold in the stiffly beaten egg whites. Sprinkle the lined tin with the grated Parmesan and spread the roulade mixture over it using a palette knife dipped in hot water to even it. Bake for 12 mins at 200ºC/400ºF/gas mark 6, then remove from the oven. Lay a fresh piece of baking parchment, or greaseproof paper, on a flat surface, invert the tin over it, and remove the tin. Peel the first piece of paper off the roulade, and allow to cool slightly while you make the filling. Beat the *fromage blanc* until smooth, stir in the garlic purée, chopped spring onions and herbs. Add salt and pepper to taste, spread over the surface of the roulade, leaving 1 cm/½ in all round the edge uncovered. Then use the paper to roll it up, and slide onto a flat dish or board. Serve as soon as possible, alone, or with a sauce of puréed raw tomatoes. Serves 6, as a first course.

THE MINERAL BALANCE

Hauser Broth

This is Gayelord Hauser's famous alkaline broth, which I cannot recommend too highly. When tomatoes are cheap, I use freshly made tomato juice instead of tinned; at other times, I often substitute Campbell's V8. He wrote this recipe in 1922, when the food processor did not exist; nowadays the vegetables can be speedily prepared, using either the steel blade or the medium grating disc.

225 g/8 oz finely shredded celery, leaves and all
225 g/8 oz finely shredded carrots
50 g/2 oz shredded spinach
1.1 litres/2 pts water
300 ml/½ pt tomato juice
5 ml/1 tsp vegetable salt
5 ml/1 tsp honey or brown sugar
15 ml/1 tblsp chopped parsley or chives

Put all the shredded vegetables into the water. Cover and cook slowly for 30 mins. Then add thick tomato juice (or tomatoes), vegetable salt and honey or brown sugar. Let cook for 5 more mins. Strain and serve. A sprinkle of chopped parsley or chives will add vitamins, minerals and colour. Serves 4-6.

Ribollita

This Tuscan soup is made from the previous day's minestrone, but it is so good that it is well worth making specially. Instead of the white bread that is used in Italy, I sometimes use wholemeal, for added fibre.

100 g/4 oz cannelini beans
60 ml/4 tblsps olive oil
1 large onion, coarsely chopped
2 large carrots, chopped
3 stalks celery, chopped
1 head fennel, chopped
225 g/8 oz courgettes, unpeeled and coarsely chopped
225 g/8 oz tomatoes, skinned and coarsely chopped
2 cloves garlic, finely chopped
1.1 litres/2 pts chicken stock
sea salt and black pepper
450 g/1 lb chard, turnip tops, or spring greens
6 thick slices dry bread

Start some hours in advance, or the day before. Put the dried beans in a pan, cover with cold water, and bring to the boil. Turn off the heat once they reach the boil, cover, and leave for 1 hour. Heat the oil in a heavy casserole and cook the onion, carrots, celery, fennel, courgettes and tomatoes for 8-10 mins, stirring often. Add the garlic towards the end, then pour on the heated stock. Drain the beans and add to the pan. Bring to the boil and simmer for 1 hour, adding salt and pepper towards the end of the cooking. Then leave to cool. This is your basic minestrone, and some can be eaten the same day.

Next day, or the same evening, drop the chard, turnip tops, or spring greens into lightly salted boiling water and cook until just tender, then drain well and chop coarsely. Have six deep soup plates, lay a slice of bread in each one, and pile the chopped greens on the bread.

Re-heat the minestrone and pour over all. Serves 6, as a meal in itself; roughly 7 g/¼ oz fibre per serving. In Italy this is made with a purplish cabbage called *cavolo nero*, and it is served with a little fresh olive oil poured over each plate.

Warm Leeks with Iced Tomato Sauce

12 small thin leeks

sauce:
450 g/1 lb tomatoes, skinned
and quartered
1 bunch spring onions, sliced
30 ml/2 tblsps sunflower oil
5 ml/1 tsp chopped root ginger
30 ml/2 tblsps orange juice
30 ml/2 tblsps lemon juice

garnish:
30 ml/2 tblsps chopped chives

Make the tomato sauce ahead. Put the tomatoes in the food processor and process briefly. Cook the sliced spring onions in half the oil for 2 mins, then drain, and add to the tomatoes. Add the chopped ginger and process again. Add the remaining oil, orange and lemon juice and process once more very briefly, then pour into a bowl and chill for 2 hours.

One hour before serving, clean the leeks and cut in 2.5 cm/1 in slices. Drop into lightly salted boiling water, just enough to cover, and cook for about 8 mins or until just tender. Drain well, and leave for about 20 mins in the colander. Just before serving, combine them with the iced sauce, folding them in gently. Tip into a bowl and sprinkle with chives. Serves 4-6 as a first course, alone, or with other hors d'oeuvres. If not convenient to make as above, the leeks can be combined with the sauce ahead of time, and all chilled together.

Cracked Wheat with Spinach

225 g/8 oz spinach
30 ml/2 tblsps sunflower oil
1 small onion, chopped
225 g/8 oz cracked wheat
600 ml/1 pt chicken stock
sea salt and black pepper

Throw the spinach into lightly salted boiling water and cook for 4-5 mins; drain. When cool enough to handle, squeeze out excess moisture and chop roughly. Heat the oil in a sauté pan with lid, and cook the onion until it starts to colour. Then add the cracked wheat and cook gently for 2-3 mins, stirring. Add the chopped spinach, stirring to mix, then pour on the

heated stock. Cover, and simmer for 8-10 mins, or until all the stock is absorbed. Add salt and pepper to taste. Serves 3, or 4 with other dishes. About 5 g/⅕ oz fibre in each serving.

Meagadarra

This delicious Middle Eastern dish is made even more nutritious by substituting brown rice for white.

225 g/8 oz green lentils
100 g/4 oz brown rice
1.2 litres/2¼ pts water
1 large onion, sliced
45 ml/3 tblsps olive oil
a little sea salt
black pepper

Pick over the lentils and wash in a colander; wash the rice. Put both in a saucepan with the cold water. Bring to the boil and cook for 30-35 mins, until lentils and rice are tender and the water has been absorbed. Set aside. Fry the sliced onion in the olive oil until well browned. Turn the lentils and rice into a bowl, adding a little salt and pepper, then scatter the fried onions over the top. Leave to cool for about 45 mins before serving. Serve with warm hard-boiled eggs, or with a bowl of yoghurt. Serves 4.

Buckwheat Crêpes

75 g/3 oz strong white flour (bread flour)
75 g/3 oz buckwheat flour
2.5 ml/½ tsp sea salt
2 eggs
15 ml/1 tblsp light oil (or melted butter)
300 ml/½ pt milk and water mixed

Put the flour in a food processor or large bowl with the salt. Add eggs, oil or melted butter, and milk and water through the lid while processing. If making by hand, make a well in the centre of the flour and drop in the eggs. Beat by hand with a wire whisk, adding oil (or butter), and milk and water and continuing to beat until all is blended. If made in advance, process (or beat) again just before using. To make *crêpes*, grease a large hot frying pan so that it spreads evenly into a large thin *crêpe*. Cook until bubbles form on the top, about 2 mins, then turn and cook for another 2 mins. Serve warm, with *guacamole* or *ratatouille*.

CUISINE DE GRANDMERE

Beef Stew

1.2 kg/2½ lbs chuck steak,
or topside, sliced
1 large onion, sliced
300 g/1 oz butter

60 ml/4 tblsps olive oil
2 large carrots, cut in sticks
½ celeriac, or 3 stalks celery, cut in sticks
1 large parsnip, cut in sticks
2 large cloves garlic, crushed
seasoned flour, about 22 ml/1½ tblsps
300 ml/½ pt beef or chicken stock
300 ml/½ pt red wine
15 ml/1 tblsp tomato purée
juice of 1 orange
5 cm/2 ins by 1.25cm/½ in strip
orange peel
1 large bay leaf
3 shakes Tabasco
sea salt and black pepper
45 ml/3 tblsps coarsely chopped parsley

Trim the beef, removing all gristle and membrane, and cut it in neat rectangles. Cook the sliced onion gently in the butter and half the olive oil, for about 3 mins, then add the root vegetables which you have cut into strips like thick matchsticks, about 3.75 cm/1½ ins long by 1 cm/⅛ in square. Cook all together gently for about 5 mins, adding the crushed garlic half-way through. Lift out the vegetables with a slotted spoon, and put in the slices of beef which you have lightly coated with seasoned flour. (Do not do this far in advance.) Add the remaining 30 ml/2 tblsps olive oil to the pan, and brown the meat on both sides, doing it in 2 or 3 batches rather than altogether. Then remove the meat and put back the vegetables in the bottom of the pan. Heat the stock and wine together and pour into the pan slowly, stirring to blend with the flour. When all is smooth and bubbling gently, put back the beef and add the tomato purée, orange juice and peel, bay leaf and Tabasco. Add sea salt and black pepper, bring to the boil, then cover the pan and cook for 1 hour in a low oven 150°C/ 300°F/gas mark 2. (Up to this stage can be done in advance.) For the last half of the cooking, remove the lid and cook for another hour, basting the surface of the stew 2 or 3 times with the juice. (If cooking on 2 separate days, bring back to the boil on top of the stove before putting back in the oven for the final hour's cooking.) This somewhat unorthodox way of cooking a stew results in a truly excellent dish, for the sauce reduces until full of flavour, while the surface of the vegetables becomes caramelized and almost crisp. To serve, transfer the contents of the casserole to a serving dish – the casserole will have become discoloured during the second cooking – and scatter the chopped parsley over the top. Serves 6, with a purée of potatoes and a green salad.

Braised Beef with Glazed Vegetables

1.35 kg/3 lbs rolled rump, or topside,
larded whenever possible
1 large onion, sliced
2 large carrots, sliced
2 cloves garlic, peeled
2 bay leaves
2 sprigs thyme
1 bottle red wine
40 g/1½ oz butter
15 ml/1 tblsp olive oil
100 g/4 oz mushrooms, coarsely chopped
1 calf's foot, split in 4
sea salt and black pepper

garnish:
300 g/12 oz small onions, pickling
onions, or shallots, peeled
225 g/8 oz thin carrots, cut in 3
25 g/1 oz butter
15 ml/1 tblsp sugar
100-175g/4-6 oz chanterelles, when
available

Start a day in advance. Put the beef in a deep dish with the sliced vegetables, garlic and herbs scattered over it. Pour over the wine and leave overnight in a cool place, basting once or twice. Next day, drain the beef and wipe dry with kitchen paper. Strain the wine and reserve both it and the vegetables and herbs. Melt the butter and oil in an oval casserole and brown the meat all over. Then remove it and put the sliced vegetables in the pan. Add the chopped mushrooms and cook gently, stirring for 4 mins, then replace the beef with calf's foot tucked in around it. Heat the strained marinade and pour it over, adding sea salt and black pepper. Bring to the boil, then cover the pan and cook for 2½ hours in a low oven, 170°C/325°F/gas mark 3.

About 30 mins before the time is up, put the whole peeled onions and carrots cut in chunks in a small pan. (If baby carrots are available, they can be left whole.) Take about 300 ml/½ pt stock from the casserole, using a bulb-type baster, and pour over them. There should be enough almost to cover them. Bring to the boil and cook quite fast, covered, until the vegetables are tender, 15-20 mins, then drain, reserving any stock that remains, and put 25 g/1 oz butter and 15 ml/1 tblsp sugar in the pan. Put back 30 ml/2 tblsps of the same stock and cook all together gently shaking the pan from time to time, until the sauce has reduced to a sticky glaze and the vegetables have browned slightly.

If you have some chanterelles, put them in a small pan with a little of the stock from the vegetables, or from the main casserole. Cook gently, covered, until they have softened, about 6 mins, then set aside. When the meat is cooked, remove it and carve in fairly thick slices. Strain the stock and make a bed of the sliced vegetables on a shallow dish. Lay the slices of beef on this, and arrange the glazed onions and carrots along either side of the dish. Scatter the chanterelles over the meat, and moisten with a little of the stock from the vegetables. Remove as much of the fat as possible from the surface of the main body of stock, and reduce a little, if necessary, by boiling fast. Serve in a sauceboat, with the beef. This dish needs only a purée of potatoes, or some fresh noodles, to accompany it, with a green salad to follow. Serves 5-6.

Beef Olives

Your butcher will cut the beef for you if you ask him in good time. If you want to do it yourself, buy 900 g-1.2 kg/2-2½ lbs topside in a single piece, and chill it for 1 hour in the freezer, then cut it in thin slices, roughly 9 cm/3½ ins by 6.5 cm/2½ ins. They can be lightly beaten out, or rolled, between two slices of clingfilm.

6 thin slices topside, or buttock steak

stuffing:
25 g/1 oz soft white breadcrumbs
50 g/2 oz shredded suet
beef trimmings, finely chopped
2 rashers streaky bacon, chopped
15 ml/1 tblsp chopped parsley
2.5 ml/½ tsp finely chopped orange rind
sea salt and black pepper
2.5 ml/½ tsp chopped fresh thyme,
or 1.25 ml/¼ tsp dried thyme
1 egg, beaten
25 g/1 oz butter
15 ml/1 tblsp sunflower oil
1 medium onion, halved and thinly
sliced
1 medium carrot, thinly sliced
1 medium leek, thinly sliced
1 stalk celery, thinly sliced
7 ml/½ tblsp flour
300 ml/½ pt chicken or beef stock
30 ml/2 tblsps chopped parsley
potato purée

Beat out the slices of beef to the required thinness and trim them to a neat rectangular shape. Chop the trimmings and reserve for the stuffing. Put the breadcrumbs into a large bowl and mix with the shredded suet, chopped beef trimmings, chopped bacon, parsley and orange rind, sea salt and black pepper and thyme. Bind with a beaten egg, divide into 6 portions. Lay one on each piece of beef then roll up and tie with coarse thread, or fasten with a wooden toothpick.

Heat the butter and oil in a casserole and brown the sliced vegetables, stirring constantly. Then push them to one side, or remove altogether, and brown the beef olives all over. Remove them from the pan and sprinkle the flour into the pan. Stir till smooth, then pour on the heated stock, stirring till smooth, adding salt and pepper to taste. Put the sliced vegetables back in the pan and lay the beef olives over them. Cover with foil and the lid, then cook gently for 1½ hours, either on top of the stove, or in a moderate oven (170°C/325°F/gas mark 3). Towards the end of the cooking, make a creamy potato purée and spread it in a thick layer down the centre of a shallow (or flat) serving dish. When the olives are cooked, remove the thread or toothpicks, and lay them on the potato purée. Scatter the sliced vegetables over them, with the chopped parsley over all. Skim the fat from the surface of the sauce, and serve separately, or spoon some over the top if you prefer. Serves 6, with a green salad.

Sea Pie

This is a simplified version of beefsteak pudding, as given in an early edition of Mrs Beeton. It also appears in Alexis Soyer's *Modern Housewife*, first published in 1858, with 6 larks, trussed as for roasting, lying between the beef and suet paste.

900 g/2 lbs braising beef, sliced
2 medium onions, sliced
3 medium carrots, sliced
sea salt and black pepper

suet paste:
225 g/8 oz self-raising flour
100 g/4 oz shredded suet

Cut the sliced beef into pieces about 4 cm/1½ ins square, and lay them in a round casserole, or deep sauté pan with a lid. Scatter the sliced onion and carrot over the beef, and season with sea salt and black pepper. Pour on enough hot water, or light stock, to come level with the meat. Bring to the boil on top of the stove, then cover the pan and simmer gently for 30 mins. Towards the end of the cooking, make the suet paste. Sift the flour into a bowl and mix in the shredded suet. Rub lightly between the fingertips until blended, then add about 115 ml/4 fl oz cold water, gradually stirring with the blade of a knife, until you have the right consistency. Turn out onto a floured board and roll out until you have a circle about 2½ cm/1 in thick, roughly the same size as your pan. (You can use the lid of the pan as a guide.) When the 30 mins is up, remove the lid and lay the suet dough over the meat. Then replace the lid and continue to cook for another 1½ hours. To serve, cut the suet dough into 4 or 5 wedges and lift onto a plate. Transfer the meat and vegetables to a round serving dish and replace the wedges of suet paste over them. Serves 4-5, with a green vegetable.

February

When Pruniers first opened in Paris in the 1870s, it was a rule that no customer would be served unless he ate oysters. (The menu was restricted to oysters, snails and grills.) This was no hardship for the French, who have always prized oysters even more highly than the English. Today they consume 1,200 million a year, compared to the British 6 million.

There are three basic varieties of oyster being raised in the UK today. The most highly esteemed in Britain and in France, but now so rare as to be very expensive indeed, are the *ostrea edulis*. These are the flat oysters, the 'natives' of Kent and Essex, the Helford River oysters from the Duchy of Cornwall, the Irish natives of West Cork and Galway Bay, and the French *belons*.

As the oyster beds in England and France were gradually decimated by over-fishing, hard winters and disease, people began to lay down seed of a hardier oyster, *crassostrea angulata*. This was the cupped oyster, often called Portuguese. (*Portugaise* or *huître creuse* in France.) They had already become naturalized in France when a boat carrying a cargo of oysters from Portugal capsized off the Bay of Arcachon in 1868. Thinking the oysters had perished, the crew threw them overboard, whereupon some of the survivors proceeded to flourish. For many years the Portuguese oyster was farmed successfully in England and France, until both it and the native oyster fell prey to a disease called bonamia, for which there is no known cure.

In the seventies, a third oyster began to oust the Portuguese. This was *crassostrea gigas*, another cupped oyster of the same family as the Portuguese, often called the Pacific, or rock oyster, and *Japonaise* in France. Like the Portuguese, it has no closed season, since our waters are too cold for it to breed. It is oval, sometimes almost rectangular in shape, with a thickly encrusted shell. The oyster itself is very tender, softer than the native and, to some people, somewhat bland. But the oyster is an adaptable organism, and takes on many of the characteristics of its environment. Thus a cupped oyster raised in the same waters as the best natives can be very good indeed. Some of the most highly rated oysters in France are the *Portugaises* that come from the salt-water basins at Marennes, where a particular algae rich in iron causes them to turn green. These are the famous *verts de Marennes*, or *fines de claires*.

There are still a few wild oyster beds in existence, but any oysters you find for sale today will have been farmed, whether natives or cupped. In the UK the Pacific oyster has replaced the Portuguese, which is still farmed in large numbers in France. The Pacific oyster is ideally suited to farming, since it grows quickly, is resistant to diseases such as bonamia, and can withstand periods of exposure to the air without harmful effects, which renders transportation relatively easy. But native oysters are still being raised in the traditional places which have been famed for their oysters in the past, like Colchester, West Mersea and Whitstable, although at some point the beds may have been relaid with seed from France.

On the eastern seaboard of the US one variety of oyster is found, from Maine to the Gulf of Mexico. This is the *crassostrea virginica*, which varies widely in shape, size and flavour according to its environment. Among the most highly esteemed are those from Wellfleet, Chatham and Cotuit on Cape Cod, the Blue Points of Long Island, and the Chincoteagues of Chesapeake Bay. The picture differs on the West Coast, where the indigenous oyster, the famed Olympia, was virtually fished out during the improvident days of the Gold Rush. Pacific oysters were imported from Japan as early as 1902 and now predominate, although some flat oysters are raised from imported French *belons*.

One hundred years ago, the British consumption of oysters was 1,200 million, on a par with that of France today. These were native, of course, for neither of the cupped oysters had yet been introduced. They were widely loved by all strata of society, much as kippers are today. In eighteenth-century Edinburgh, which was a democratic place by any standards, there were wine bars called houghs where all and sundry sat down to enjoy oysters with their wine. Oyster lassies with baskets on their backs walked the streets calling their wares, but with the industrialization of the Firth of Forth towards the end of the last century the oysters were destroyed by pollution, and this rich source of supply dried up.

One man who would like to reverse this trend is John Noble of Loch Fyne Oysters. Living where he does, in a vast fairy-tale house built by Lorimer in 1906 on the very edges of Loch Fyne, he starts with many advantages. Loch Fyne is a sea loch sixty miles long and very deep, totally free from pollution, and fed by two rivers at its head: an ideal environment for the oyster, which enjoys a mixture of salt and fresh water, and the plankton which float down the rivers. Since the water is so pure, the oysters do not have to undergo the purification process that most others do, before being sold. Eleven years ago, Johnnie and his partner Andrew Lane, a biologist who had been working on a salmon farm in Loch Fyne, decided to have a go at oyster farming. Although he had never seen a live oyster in Loch Fyne, Johnnie had always been aware of their shells lying on the shore. 'My job as a tiny tot during the war was smashing up oyster shells to feed to the hens. Then Andy Lane told me that we could get seed oysters which I never knew, so I said "Let's start a business." The pilot scheme was a matter of a few hundred quid, and no one else was doing it. We copied French methods, adapting them with money from the Highlands and Islands Development Board. We started with *ostrea edulis*, the native flats, and there was a high mortality rate. We didn't quite know why. Soon after, we laid down *crassostrea gigas*, the cupped oyster, which is much tougher and very quick growing. And that is what we have majored on.' At present, they produce almost 1 million oysters a year. Johnnie is considering renting another two miles of foreshore from neighbouring cousins (he already owns four), and upping their production to 6 million, which is the total UK annual consumption.

During the last ten years, Loch Fyne Oysters have built up another business smoking local foods: fresh salmon, both wild and farmed, herrings and eels; and they make gravadlax and marinades of herring. They also sell fresh *langoustines* brought straight off the boats, and superlative scallops fished by divers in the Sound of Jura.

Perhaps the most difficult part of the whole operation has been breaking down the British restaurateur's resistance to the Pacific oyster. 'We were virtually thrown out of Rogano's, the old oyster bar in Glasgow. The manager was absolutely outraged by the very mention of the word *gigas*. Mind you they went up the spout soon after.... The old-fashioned oyster bars, the bastions of tradition, wouldn't consider anything but an enormous *edulis* (flat) oyster - and they are extremely supercilious about *gigas*. But the great British public couldn't care less, they just tuck in.'

In southern England most of the old-fashioned oyster bars tend to serve native, rather than Pacific oysters. Not being a a true oyster lover, I prefer the West Cork button, a small native no bigger than a large clam, easy to swallow and full of flavour.

Oysters are tricky to serve at home, unless you know how to open them. Luxurious without being rich, simple yet grand, they give an air of occasion while bringing a breath of the sea. To serve them raw, allow six to nine per person, open them fifteen minutes before serving and chill on a bed of cracked ice. Serve on cracked ice, with a few strands of seaweed for effect, and half a perfect lemon. Have a black pepper-mill, cayenne and a bottle of Tabasco on a small plate for those who like them.

The family of crustaceans includes the lobster, crab, spiny lobster, or crawfish, freshwater crayfish, all the various sizes of prawn, and shrimps. They are weird and fascinating creatures, with curious habits and an almost prehistoric appearance. Lobsters live to an immense age, as do crawfish. I was reminded of this as I watched these venerable creatures - some as much as sixty or seventy years old - wading mournfully round the holding tanks owned by the Cornish Fishermen's Cooperative at Padstow. Contrary to what you might expect, they do not deteriorate in flavour with age.

Lobsters have become so expensive as to be almost prohibitive, even in remote places. I bought two from a fisherman in the Hebrides last summer, and cooked the first according to RSPCA recommendations; by putting it in a pan of cold water and bringing slowly to the boil. This took so long that by the time I came to cook the second - the pan was not big enough to hold both at the same time - it was almost dinner time and I was forced to speed things up by dropping it into fast boiling water. The difference in flavour was remarkable: the second was better in every way. I buy lobsters so rarely now that all I ever want is to serve them soon after boiling, before they have quite cooled, with a bowl of mayonnaise. I sympathize with all the New Yorkers who spend their summer vacations on Cape Cod, and who rush out on their first evening to eat lobster in ultra-simple restaurants where the diners are wrapped in aprons and the lobster comes in a cardboard box. Because of its high price, lobster is usually treated - at least in Britain - as a luxury, but it is at its best served very simply.

Just as good as lobster, and slightly less expensive, is the spiny lobster, or crawfish, called *langouste* (as opposed to *homard*) in France. This is similar to the lobster except that it lacks the giant claws: the flesh is slightly less dense, and more delicate.

Crabs are also very good. I particularly like spider crabs, which I remember eating in a waterside restaurant in Portugal, where they serve them on thick boards, with a small wooden mallet to crack the claws. The famous soft-shell crabs of Chesapeake Bay in Maryland are blue crabs which, for two short days in May, live out a vulnerable existence between shedding their old shell and growing a new one. British green shore crabs, and the small swimming crabs, can be treated in the same way, but rarely are in this country. In Venice, however, they are kept in hatcheries so that they are ready for sale within hours of shedding their shells. In the Mediterranean,

especially around Marseilles, tiny crabs called *favouilles* are made into very good soups, or included in a *bouillabaisse*. I have eaten excellent crab in Japan, where much of the shellfish is already pink or red even when raw. There I saw a huge scarlet crab for sale in the market, for the equivalent of £200.

Freshwater crayfish live in streams in Britain, and are now being farmed in Dorset. This means that they can be bought live, unlike most salt-water prawns. The latter vary widely in size, from the giant Dublin Bay prawn, with claws like miniature lobsters, called *langoustines* in France, to the small deep sea prawns that come from the North Atlantic.

Unfortunately it is almost impossible to buy prawns in their natural state; the best are the large prawns that have been frozen in their shells while still at sea, uncooked. Also good are the smaller prawns that have been cooked at sea in sea water, then frozen in their shells. Those that have been cooked and shelled, then coated in ice glaze for freezing are almost tasteless.

Tiny brown shrimps are a rare treat, best enjoyed close to the sea. The deep sea shrimps from cold arctic waters are also delcious: the best I've ever had were in the Tivoli Gardens in Copenhagen, served very simply, piled on buttered rye bread, with chilled lager. In Skagen, in the north of Jutland, a restaurant called Plesner serves them mixed with *crème fraîche* and chopped chives, piled on toast and garnished with fresh lumpfish roe. At Ballymaloe, in West Cork in Ireland, Myrtle Allen serves the local shrimps from Ballycotton with hot buttered toast and hollandaise sauce with herbs.

One of my favourite dishes when I was growing up was Young's Potted Shrimps, always a sure-fire success with visiting Americans, who call prawns shrimps, and don't have real shrimps at all. A better alternative, and cheaper, is to make your own. A good prawn pâté can be made by putting freshly shelled prawns in a food processor with half their weight of butter, lemon juice and black pepper.

For a real treat, give me a plate of freshly caught, freshly cooked shrimps, served while still warm, with brown bread and butter, half a lemon, and a glass of white wine. Or a dish of large prawns, still in their shells, with a bowl of *aioli*, or sour cream and dill sauce. Or a freshly grilled crawfish with herb butter, or a small boiled lobster, barely cooled, with mayonnaise. Such things are rarely available at their best, nor are they easy to afford. More often, we have to make do with frozen produce, which is when recipes are needed to liven up their jaded flavours, and invigorate the imperfect creatures.

I had thought that brown pasta was a recent invention, a logical move towards healthy eating. On the contrary, like most good things it has been around for hundreds of years. The Venetians have been eating a wholemeal spaghetti called *biguoli* for centuries: as a lenten dish, with anchovies; or for feast days, with a rich duck sauce. The Japanese have a buckwheat noodle called *soba* whose origins are even more ancient, probably as old as pasta itself.

In Japan there are special noodle shops and restaurants serving nothing else. My favourite is one called Akura, near the entrance to the Kamigamo Shrine on the north-western outskirts of Tokyo. The building is a 300-year-old saké warehouse, which was moved here twenty years ago from its original site in Nara to avoid destruction, and rebuilt in a pretty garden with an old wooden watermill. The main room has a lofty ceiling with black beams; wooden buildings of this period were constructed entirely without nails. Here you sit on tatami mats around an open fire, enjoying their homemade noodles in the traditional ways. One of the most popular is *soba*, the flat buckwheat noodle, pale beige in colour, except when it has been made with green tea, when it looks like *tagliatelle verde*. *Soba* are served in a bowl of excellent thin broth; this is made with *dashi*, or *bonito* stock, flavoured with soy sauce, spring onions, peppers and horseradish. In hot weather *soba* are served iced, lying in a wooden box with a slatted base. These are accompanied by all the usual dipping sauces and condiments. The other basic noodle is called *udon;* these are made from wheat flour, round, white, and as fat as your finger. *Udon* are served in their cooking water, in the black iron pot they cook in. With them comes a bowl of soy-based dipping sauce which you flavour to taste with sliced spring onions, grated horseradish, and mixed pepper flakes.

Two or three years ago, London was dotted with shops selling freshly made pasta. Some sold wholemeal pasta, others made it to order. Sadly, almost all these shops have disappeared, and the dried wholemeal pasta sold in health food shops is unappealing: heavy and lacking in flavour. Buckwheat noodles are still around, thank goodness, and can be bought either in health food stores or in Asian supermarkets. They are pale khaki in colour, very thin and about six inches long. Buckwheat noodles go well with oriental flavourings: with spring onions, soy sauce, stir-fried vegetables, sesame seeds, and chilli peppers.

Now wholemeal pasta is so rarely sold fresh, the only answer is to make your own. This is easy with ICTC Pastamatic, which includes directions for making wholemeal and buckwheat pasta, as well as spinach and plain. Alternatively, you can mix the dough in a food processor and roll it out in a hand mill. This is lengthy, but enjoyable, especially if you have someone to help you. For real enthusiasts, it can be mixed by hand and rolled out on the kitchen table. Freshly made pasta freezes superbly, and it is worth making a lot at a time. I like to freeze it in small plastic bags, for one or two people.

Wholemeal pasta has its own character, quite distinct from white pasta, and from buckwheat. It has an affinity with mushrooms, spinach, flat parsley, garlic, shallots, olive oil and soft cheeses like ricotta, mozzarella and *fromage blanc*. It does not marry well with most of the things we associate with Italian pasta: the meat sauces, cream, butter or parmesan. (An exception is *spaghetti carbonara*, which is wonderful when made with brown noodles.) For a vegetarian dinner party, delicious dishes can be made with brown noodles and wild mushrooms, or brown lasagne, rolled very thin, and treated like a pancake. I like to fill a pudding basin with alternate layers of lasagne and two different fillings: one based on spinach and ricotta, the other of tomatoes and mozzarella. After baking briefly, turn the whole thing out on a flat dish and cover it with a creamy mushroom sauce, or one of mixed fresh herbs.

The most amazing exponent of pasta-making I have ever seen is Giovanni Bugialli, who has cookery schools in Florence and New York. He gave a demonstration in London a few years ago, to promote his book *A Taste of Italy*. Here he showed how to make *quadrucci:* a speciality of Puglia, whereby large sprigs of flat parsley are sandwiched between paper-thin sheets of lasagne, then rolled again through the pasta mill so that they stretch into delicate folds like silk scarves, with the parsley leaf shapes etiolated into shadowy silhouettes. They are later cut into squares and poached *in brodo*.

A loaf of freshly baked bread is a potent symbol of everything I love about cooking. It is the home cook's answer to the chef or restaurateur, for in this realm they cannot compete. Very few restaurants bake their own bread, and bought in bread, however good, just isn't the same as seeing a freshly made loaf on the table, chosen and made specifically for that meal. If I'm invited to dinner in someone's house, the nicest thing that can happen is to be greeted by the smell of baking bread. Anyone who is prepared to go to the trouble of making their own bread has their priorities in good order. They know how to exploit the difference between eating at home and in a restaurant.

I have experimented with sourdough starters as well as yeast when baking, and have made mixtures of rye and corn meal, flour and semolina. I have made breads that contain mashed potatoes, cooked grains, sprouted wheat, and also seed breads, muffin bread, corn bread and saffron bread. Every one was good: it seems hard to make a bad loaf, as long as you use good flour, and understand the basic principles.

On trips to Paris and San Francisco, I was struck by the sourdough bread. In Paris, the huge crusty round pale brown loaves of Lionel Poilane are everywhere. Sourdough bread is also very popular in San Francisco, to the point that some shops ration customers to two loaves each. Sourdough bread is made with a starter of fermented dough instead of yeast; sometimes a little yeast is also incorporated in the starter. It is probably best left to the commercial baker, for it is tricky, and should be made on a regular basis. The bread itself is full of character, dense and chewy, with a hard crust. It keeps well for up to a week in an airtight bread crock.

Before starting to make bread on a daily basis, it's good to make a shopping trip to lay in a store of ingredients. I buy two sorts of wheat flour: 100 per cent wholemeal and plain unbleached white. I don't bother with 85 per cent wheatmeal, since the same result can be achieved by mixing 100 per cent with white. Most of the bread flours I buy are mixed hard and soft wheat. Since English wheat is soft, and low in gluten, it is usually mixed with hard wheat from the US or Canada. Some purists claim that soft wheat gives the better flavour - the French have always made good bread with their own soft wheat - but commercial bakers insist on a proportion of hard wheat, since this absorbs more water and rises more, making it more economical.

The flours I buy are made with a mixture of wheat, some organically grown in England, some imported, and are for the most part stoneground. Rye flour has less gluten, and of an inferior sort, than wheat flour. For this reason, it is best combined with wheat flour. When used alone, it makes a heavy, dense loaf, hard to work, like pumpernickel, which I prefer to buy. Corn meal (also called maize meal, or *polenta*) lacks gluten, so that corn bread must be made with baking powder instead of yeast, which will only interact with gluten. But a small proportion of corn meal can be mixed with rye and wheat flour, or wheat alone, to make a delicious bread. Semolina also mixes well with wheat flour to make a lovely loaf, with a warm flavour and gritty texture that I find very pleasing.

I like to use fresh yeast whenever possible. I keep a supply of yeast in the freezer, cut in ½ oz squares and wrapped in clingfilm. Dried yeast works perfectly well, but it just isn't as much fun. Yeast now comes in a third form, usually called Easy Blend or Easy Bake. This is mixed directly with the flour, does away with proving, and only needs one rising. But I believe that bread benefits from slow rising, punching down, and rising again.

Other ingredients I use from time to time are granary (or malted wheat) flour, bran, wheat germ, flaked oats, molasses, honey, brown sugar, and spray-dried goats' milk. (Some American recipes call for dried milk, and this is the best solution I have found.) I also use cooked brown rice, cracked wheat, and mashed potatoes, having found that additions of cooked foods give a pleasant consistency and a nutty flavour to the finished product.

Practice will soon determine the most suitable place to put the dough for rising. I use the top oven, with the bottom oven at its lowest heat. The ideal temperature to aim for is that of a very warm room. If the dough doubles in volume - at the first rising - before one hour has elapsed, then it is too warm.

OYSTERS

Pierre Bruno's Grilled Oysters

Pierre Bruno is a Frenchman living in London, a cheese and *charcuterie* importer who is the distributor for Loch Fyne Oysters. He was kind enough to give me his own recipe for grilled oysters.

Open the oysters and strain off the juice into a small pan. Add some *crème fraîche* and white wine and boil up all together until reduced by about half. Pour over the oysters and grill for 1-2 mins, until they start to brown. Serve immediately.

Note: Unless you have special discs for holding shellfish level as they grill, make holes in thick slices of bread, or lay them in hollows in a bed of rock salt.

CRUSTACEANS

Cold Baked Eggs, with Prawns or Shrimps

6 g/¼ oz butter
4 eggs
sea salt and black pepper
60 ml/4 tblsps homemade mayonnaise
12 peeled prawns
or 20 shrimps

Butter 4 ramekins and break an egg into each one. Sprinkle with salt and pepper, stand them in a roasting tin half full of water, and bake for about 15 mins at 160°C/325°F/gas mark 3 or until the whites are just set. Err on the shorter time, as the eggs will go on cooking slightly as they cool. Take them out of the roasting tin and leave to cool. Then spread 15 ml/1 tblsp mayonnaise over each one, and lay the prawns (or shrimps) on top. Serve cold, but not chilled. Serves 4 as a first course.

Crab Vinaigrette

90 ml/6 tblsps light olive oil
45 ml/3 tblsps white wine vinegar
15 ml/1 tblsp capers, drained and chopped
15 ml/1 tblsp chopped gherkins
15 ml/1 tbsp chopped shallot
1 small clove garlic, finely chopped
15 ml/1 tblsp chopped parsley
sea salt and black pepper
1 large crab

Mix all the ingredients except the crab. Then stir in the white meat of the crab, coarsely chopped or shredded. Cover and chill for a few hours before serving. Serves 4 as a first course, or, with a green salad as a light main dish.

Devilled Prawns

60 ml/4 tblsps olive oil
1 clove garlic, finely chopped
2.5 cm/1 in square root ginger, finely chopped
1 small green chilli pepper, finely chopped
15 ml/1 tblsp chopped coriander
12 giant prawns, raw
50 g/2 oz butter

Mix the olive oil with the garlic, ginger, chilli pepper and coriander. Remove the heads from the prawns, also the legs, leaving the shells and tails intact. Pour the marinade over them and leave for 1-2 hours. Then lift the prawns out of the marinade and strain it, reserving the bits. Grill the prawns for 3-4 mins on each side, basting with the liquid marinade. (If using cooked prawns, allow 2-3 mins each side.) While the prawns are grilling, melt the butter and stir in the solid part of the marinade.

Lay the prawns on a flat dish to serve with the butter sauce poured over them.

Serves 3-4 as a first course or, with rice, as a light main dish. Crab claws can be used instead of prawns; allow 3 mins grilling on each side.

Grilled Giant Prawns

basting sauce:
100 g/4 oz unsalted butter
30 ml/2 tblsps lemon juice
freshly ground black pepper
12 giant prawns, raw
22 ml/½ tblsp chopped parsley
2 lemons, cut in quarters

Melt the butter, add the lemon juice and plenty of black pepper. Cut the heads and legs off the prawns, leaving on shells and tails. Lay them on the grill pan and brush with some of the basting sauce. Grill them gently for 4 mins on each side, turning once and basting once with the sauce.

Lay them on a flat dish to serve, with the remaining sauce spooned over them. Sprinkle with chopped parsley and garnish with cut lemons.

Serve alone, as a first course, or with boiled rice as a light main dish, or as part of a mixed array of shellfish. Serves 3, or 4 with other dishes.

Prawn Pâté

700 g/1½ lb unshelled prawns
approx 100 g/4 oz unsalted butter, at room temperature
30 ml/2 tblsps lemon juice
freshly ground black pepper

Shell the prawns and weigh them; you should have about 225 g/8 oz. Take half their weight in unsalted butter, cut it in bits, and put in a food processor with the prawns. Process into a sort of coarse paste, then add lemon juice and black pepper. Process again, then pile into a small dish, cover with clingfilm and chill for several hours or overnight.

Garnish with a sprig of parsley before serving, chilled, with toasted wholemeal bread. Serves 4, as a first course.

Spring Rolls 1

filling:
30 ml/2 tblsps sunflower oil
2 bunches spring onions cut in thin strips about 4 cm/1½ ins long
1 clove garlic, finely chopped
15 ml/1 tblsp finely chopped root ginger
225 g/8 oz mung bean sprouts
24 prawns, peeled
15 ml/1 tblsp soy sauce
15 ml/1 tblsp chopped mint
juice of 1½ limes when available, or
1 lemon

wrapping:
3-4 sheets filo pastry
40 g/1½ oz butter, melted

dipping sauce (optional):
45 ml/3 tblsps dry vermouth
45 ml/3 tblsps soy sauce
two 1cm/½ in squares root ginger, crushed

Thaw the filo pastry while you make the filling. Heat the oil in a wok or deep pan. Cook the spring onions for 1 min, tossing, then add the garlic and ginger. Toss for another 1 min, then add the sprouts which have been well drained. Toss all together for 2 mins, then add the whole prawns, soy sauce, and chopped mint. Toss the contents of the pan for 1 more min, then sprinkle with the lime juice, and set aside. To make into rolls, unwrap one sheet of filo at a time, keeping the rest covered with a damp cloth. Cut the first sheet in strips about 25 by 9 cm/10 by 3½ ins. Brush them with melted butter, then lay 30 ml/2 tblsps of the filling, including 2 prawns, across the end of each strip. Fold over the sides, then roll up to form rolls, sealing with melted butter. Lay them on an ungreased baking sheet and bake for about 12 mins at 190°C/375°F/gas mark 5 until they are light golden. Makes 12. Make the dipping sauce, if used, while they are baking. Mix the vermouth and soy sauce, then crush the ginger in a garlic press so that the juice runs into the sauce. These can be prepared in advance, laid on the baking sheet, then frozen for up to a week. Serve hot, as a first course, with the dipping sauce in tiny dishes. Serves 4. Alternatively, they may be served as part of a spread of dishes, without the dipping sauce.

Spring Rolls 2

Make the filling and dipping sauce as above. Instead of filo pastry, use lettuce leaves to enclose the filling. Have 8 medium-sized inner leaves, drop them in boiling water for 1 min, then refresh under the cold tap and drain. Divide the filling between them, making 8 slightly larger rolls than the pastry ones, and including 3 prawns in each roll. Serve soon after making, while they are still warm, with or without the dipping sauce. Serves 4 as a first course. While the filo pastry rolls may be eaten in the fingers, these must be eaten with a knife and fork and are no good as canapés.

Coral Mayonnaise

about 30 ml/2 tblsps roe from a hen lobster
200 ml/1/3 pt mayonnaise

Pound the roe in a mortar then add the mayonnaise bit by bit, continuing to pound. When all is blended, turn into a sauceboat and serve with cold boiled lobster. Serves 2-3.

BROWN PASTA

Wholewheat Pasta

225 g/8 oz wholewheat flour
100 g/4 oz plain flour
4 eggs
2.5 ml/1/2 tsp salt

Process all the ingredients at top speed, until they form a ball of dough (about 1 min). Knead on a floured board until well amalgamated, wrap in foil or greaseproof paper, and leave to chill in the refrigerator for 20 mins. Divide dough in half and knead separately for a few more mins. Set pasta mill to the widest opening and push the dough through. Fold it in three and put it through again (narrow end first). Repeat 7 or 8 times. This is a form of kneading and will make the dough smooth and more elastic. When a pretty smooth sheet of pasta comes out of the rollers, start reducing the width of the rollers and feed the sheet through (without folding), continuing down the scale until you have the required thickness.
This proportion of wholewheat to plain flour makes a fairly smooth but grainy textured pasta. You can, if you like, use a larger proportion of wholewheat flour to produce a rougher pasta.

Wholewheat Noodles with Grilled Aubergines

2 medium aubergines
30-45 ml/2-3 tblsps olive oil
350 g/12 oz wholewheat noodles
15 ml/1 tblsp sunflower oil
2 cloves garlic, finely chopped
sea salt and black pepper
60 ml/4 tblsps flat parsley, coarsely chopped

Cut the unpeeled aubergines into slices 1cm/1/2 in thick. Brush them with olive oil, then grill for 4 mins, until puffy and golden brown. Turn them, brush with more oil, and grill for another 4 mins. Leave to cool for a few minutes, then cut them in strips about 1.5 cm/3/4 in wide. Cook the noodles as usual, and drain in a colander. Warm the sunflower oil in a heavy pan and cook the chopped garlic for a moment, then add the drained noodles and toss them in the oil, adding a little sea salt and black pepper. Add the strips of aubergine and fold them in gently, adding most of the parsley. Turn into a warm bowl and scatter the rest of the parsley over the top. Serve immediately. Enough for 4.

Wholewheat Noodles with Wild Mushrooms

4 shallots, chopped
30 ml/2 tblsps olive oil
30 ml/2tblsps sunflower oil
2 cloves garlic, finely chopped
225 g/8 oz wild mushrooms, cut in slices
sea salt and black pepper
Maggi Liquid Seasoning
90 ml/6 tblsps flat parsley leaves, torn in pieces
350 g/12 oz wholewheat noodles

Cook the chopped shallots in the olive and sunflower oils for 2 mins then add the garlic and cook for another 1 min. Add the sliced mushrooms and cook, tossing frequently, until they have softened. While they are cooking, bring a pan of water to the boil for the noodles. Once the mushrooms have softened, add sea salt and black pepper, and a dash of Maggi Liquid Seasoning. Stir in the parsley and set aside. Cook the noodles as usual, drain in a colander, and turn into a heated bowl. Tip the mushrooms over them and toss, then serve immediately. Enough for 4 as a first course or light main dish.

Wholewheat Noodles with Avocado, Tomato and Basil

4 medium tomatoes, skinned
1 large avocado, peeled and stoned
60 ml/4 tblsps basil, torn in strips
350 g/12 oz wholewheat noodles
45 ml/3 tblsps light olive oil,
or sunflower oil
sea salt and black pepper

Bring a pan of water to the boil for the noodles while you prepare the vegetables. Chop the tomatoes quite finely, discarding seeds and juice. Chop the avocado likewise, and tear the basil into pieces, or cut in strips. Cook the noodles as usual, drain in a colander, then turn into a warm bowl. Stir in the oil, the chopped vegeta-

bles, and most of the basil, scattering the rest over the top. Season to taste. This simple dish can be served as soon as it is made, or left for a little, until cooled almost to room temperature. Serve with a green salad, as a light main dish. Serves 4.

Buckwheat Spaghetti with Stir-Fried Vegetables

90 ml/6 tblsps sesame seeds
350 g/12 oz buckwheat spaghetti
45 ml/3 tblsps sunflower oil
4 small carrots, thinly sliced
3 stalks celery, sliced
2 bunches large spring onions, sliced
sea salt and black pepper
Maggi Liquid Seasoning, or soy sauce

Toast the sesame seeds in a dry frying pan, turning them often so that they turn an even colour. Set aside. While the pasta is cooking, heat the oil in a wok, or deep round pan. Once it is hot, add the thinly sliced carrots and toss for 1 min, then add the sliced celery and toss for another min. Lastly, add the spring onions, and cook for 1 more min, adding salt and black pepper, and a few shakes of Maggi Liquid Seasoning, or soy sauce. When the pasta is cooked, drain it, and turn into a heated bowl. Tip the stir-fried vegetables over the top, put the sesame seeds in a small bowl, and serve. Serves 4.

Buckwheat Spaghetti with Mushrooms and Fromage Blanc

45-60 ml/3-4 tblsps sunflower oil
3 shallots, chopped
350 g/12 oz mushrooms, caps only, sliced
salt and black pepper
Maggi Liquid Seasoning
350 g/12 oz buckwheat spaghetti, or fresh brown noodles
90 ml/6 tblsps fromage blanc, or Jockey, or Quark
45-60 ml/3-4 tblsps chopped parsley, preferably flat

Heat the oil in a sauté pan and cook the chopped shallots for 2 mins. Then add the sliced mushrooms, and cook until they have softened, about 3 mins, stirring frequently. Add salt and pepper and a dash of Maggi Liquid Seasoning, then remove from the heat. Cook the buckwheat spaghetti, or brown noodles, as usual, then drain in a colander and turn into a heated serving dish. Reheat the mushrooms briefly, then stir in the *fromage blanc* and remove from the heat. Stir well, adding the chopped parsley, then pour over the pasta. Serves 4.

Brown Lasagne in a Bowl

Version 1 (serves 4-5)

225 g/8 oz brown lasagne
15 ml/1 tblsp olive oil
450 g/1 lb spinach
225 g/8 oz Ricotta
sea salt and black pepper
1½ Mozzarella cheeses
(about 225 g/8 oz)
tomato and pepper sauce (see below)

Version 2 (serves 6)

250-300 g/10-12 oz brown lasagne
15 ml/1 tblsp olive oil
450 g/1 lb spinach
225 g/8 oz Ricotta
sea salt and black pepper
2 Mozzarella cheeses
tomatoes, skinned
mushroom sauce (see below)

Version 1

Bring a large pan of lightly salted water to the boil. Drop in the lasagne, 4-5 sheets at a time, and cook until they are soft. This may take from 3-6 mins, depending on their thickness, and when they were made. Once they are ready, lift them out with a slotted spoon and drop into a large bowl of cold water with a tablespoon of oil in it. Leave them for a few moments, while the next batch cook, then transfer them to a cloth, to drain. When all are done, make the spinach filling. Drop the spinach into a large pan of lightly salted boiling water and cook for 4-5 mins, drain well. As soon as it is cool enough to handle, squeeze out excess moisture. Turn onto a board and chop roughly, by hand. Put it in a large bowl and add the Ricotta, mashing it all together with a wooden spoon. Add sea salt and freshly ground black pepper. (Do not use a food processor, as it will be too smooth.) Grate the Mozzarella, using a very coarse grater, or cut it in small thin slices. Butter a pudding basin or fireproof bowl holding about 1.05 litres/1¾ pints (slightly more for version 2). Put a layer of lasagne in the bottom, cutting the sheets to fit roughly, then cover with a layer of spinach and Ricotta. Cover this with another layer of lasagne, then some grated Mozzarella, adding salt and black pepper. When all is used up, finish with a layer of lasagne and rub the top surface with a few drops of olive oil. Cover with foil and bake for 35 mins at 180°C/350°F/ gas mark 5. (Or make in advance and bake for 45 mins.) While it is baking, make the Tomato Sauce (see below). When it is ready to serve, turn out onto a flat dish and spoon some of the sauce over it. Serve the remainder in a sauceboat. Serves 4-5.

Version 2

Make as above, putting the dried mushrooms for the sauce in to soak before starting. Slice the skinned tomatoes and lay them over the Mozzarella. Serve with Mushroom Sauce (see below). Serves at least 6.

Mushroom Sauce

15 g/½ oz dried mushrooms
300 ml/½ pt vegetable stock
225 g/8 oz flat mushrooms
salt and black pepper
60 ml/4 tblsps fromage blanc, Jockey or Quark
22 ml/1½ tblsps parsley, coarsely chopped

Soak the dried mushrooms in half the stock for 1 hour, then drain, reserving the liquid. Chop the mushrooms and set aside. Wipe the fresh mushrooms, chop the caps coarsely and slice the stalks. Put them in a saucepan and add the remaining vegetable stock and the liquid from soaking the dried mushrooms. Bring to the boil and simmer gently, half covered, for 10 mins. Then add the chopped dried mushrooms and cook for another 5 mins. Remove from the heat, add salt and black pepper, and leave to cool for a little. Then process briefly in the food processor, adding the *fromage blanc* (or Jockey or Quark). Process briefly, stopping before it is smooth, then pour into a pan and re-heat gently. Serve with noodles, or lasagne.

Tomato and Pepper Sauce

350 g/12 oz tomatoes, skinned
1 small red pepper
15 ml/1 tblsp sunflower oil
15 g/½ oz butter
½ bunch spring onions, sliced
sea salt and black pepper
a pinch of sugar (optional)

Chop the tomatoes. Grill the pepper, or hold over a gas flame, until the skin is charred evenly all over. Then scrape it away and chop the pepper. Heat the oil and butter and cook the sliced spring onions for 1-2 mins, then add the chopped tomatoes and pepper. Cook all together for 5-8 mins, depending on the ripeness of the tomatoes, adding salt and black pepper, and a little sugar if the tomatoes are at all unripe. Cool slightly, then process briefly, stopping before it becomes a smooth purée. Pour into a bowl and keep warm.

BREAD

Wheat and Molasses Bread

This is a delicious bread, one of my favourites, as made by Michel Stroot at Cal-a-Vie in California.

12 g/½ oz fresh yeast
250 ml/8 fl oz warm water
30 ml/2 tblsps safflower oil
60 ml/4 tblsps molasses
15 ml/1 tblsp honey
350 g/12 oz wholemeal flour
25 g/1 oz bran
60 ml/4 tblsps corn meal
50 g/2 oz dried milk (optional)
2.5 ml/½ tsp sea salt

Crumble the yeast into the warm water, then add the oil, molasses and honey and leave for 10 mins. Stir in the flour, bran and corn meal, with the dried milk and salt. Mix very well, either by hand or in a mixer. Put back in the clean bowl, rubbed with oil; cover and let rise for about 1 hour, until it has doubled in volume. Then punch down and knead. Form into a loaf shape and lay in a greased loaf tin. Cover and let rise until it has filled the tin, about 45 mins. Then bake for 1 hour at 180°C/350°F/gas mark 4. Cool on a rack.

Michel's Semolina Bread

This is the dough that Michel Stroot uses for pizzas. I find it delicious for bread also.

12 g/½ oz fresh yeast
225 ml/8 fl oz warm water
a pinch of sea salt
15 ml/1 tblsp honey
7 ml/½ tblsp virgin olive oil
200 g/7 oz semolina
125 g/5 oz wholemeal flour
75 g/3 oz unbleached white flour

Crumble the yeast into the water and leave for 10 mins, then add the salt, honey and oil and mix. Start adding the semolina and flours, mixing to make a firm dough. Knead for about 4 mins then return to the clean bowl which you have rubbed with oil. Cover the dough with a cloth and leave in a warm place until it has doubled in bulk, about an hour. Punch down, knead again briefly, and turn into a greased loaf tin. Cover again and leave until it has filled the tin, about 20 mins. Then bake for 50 mins at 180°C/350°F/gas mark 4, having dusted the top with semolina.

Brown Rice Bread

I based this on a recipe for rice bread made with white rice and unbleached flour in Elizabeth David's *English Bread and Yeast Cookery*, combining it with a modified sourdough technique. It makes an excellent loaf, and is very nutritious.

75 g/3 oz brown rice
175 ml/6 fl oz warm water
12 g/½ oz fresh yeast
250 ml/9 fl oz warm water
30 ml/2 tblsps safflower oil
7 ml/½ tblsp sea salt
15 ml/1 tblsp molasses
15 ml/1 tblsp honey
400 g/14 oz wholemeal flour

The day before baking, cook the rice in 175 ml/6 fl oz water, covered, for about 40 mins, or until all the water has been absorbed. Turn into a bowl and leave in a warm corner of the kitchen for anything from 12-24 hours. The next day, crumble the yeast into 250 ml/9 fl oz warm water and leave for 10 mins. Tip the cooked rice into a large bowl and stir in the oil, salt, molasses and honey. When the yeast has finished proving, add it to the rice mixture and mix well. Then start adding the flour, a large spoonful at a time, until all is used up and you have a soft dough. Turn out and knead for 4 mins on a floured surface, then return to the clean bowl, lightly oiled, and leave for 1½ hours, covered, until it has roughly doubled in size. Punch down, knead again briefly, then lay in an oiled loaf tin. Cover and leave for about 40 mins, until it has filled the tin. Then bake for 45 mins at 190°C/375°F/gas mark 5. Cool on a wire rack.

Saffron Bread

This is one of my favourite breads; it is almost best of all toasted.

12 g/½ oz fresh yeast
60 ml/4 tblsps warm water
150 ml/¼ pt milk
2 pkts saffron
2 eggs, beaten
450 g/1 lb unbleached white flour
5 ml/1 tsp sea salt

Crumble the yeast into the warm water and leave for 10 mins. Put the milk in a small pan and shake in the saffron. Heat until almost boiling, then cover and remove from the heat. Leave to cool, stirring occasionally. When it reaches blood heat, pour it onto the beaten eggs. (If in stamen form, pour through a strainer.) Then mix with the yeast in a large bowl. Start adding the flour and the salt, a cup at a time. Mix well, until the dough clings together. Turn out and knead for 4-5 mins on a floured surface, then put back in the clean bowl which you have rubbed with oil. Leave for 1-1½ hours in a warm place, until doubled in size. Punch down, turn out, and knead again briefly. Form into a loaf shape and lay in an oiled loaf tin. Cover and allow it to rise again for about 45 mins, until it has filled the tin. Bake for 40 mins at 190°C/375°F/gas mark 5. Cool on a wire rack.

Sour Corn-Rye Bread

12 g/½ oz fresh yeast
15 ml/1 tblsp brown sugar
100 ml/4 fl oz warm water
225 ml/8 fl oz buttermilk, or yoghurt

7 ml/½ tblsp sea salt
30 ml/2 tblsps safflower oil
7 ml/½ tblsp caraway seeds
200 g/7 oz wholewheat flour
175 g/6 oz rye flour
100 g/4 oz corn meal

Crumble the yeast and sugar into the warm water and leave for 10 mins. Warm the buttermilk (or yoghurt) until tepid, then stir in the salt, oil and caraway seeds. Mix this with the yeast in a large mixing bowl, then start adding the wholewheat flour, a cup at a time, stirring hard. When all this is incorporated, start to add the rye flour and corn meal. When you have a firm dough, turn onto a floured surface and knead for 4 mins, incorporating the rest of the corn meal and rye flour. Put back in the clean bowl which you have rubbed with oil, cover with a cloth, and leave to rise until doubled in volume, about 1½ hours. Then punch down, knead again briefly, and lay in a greased loaf tin. Cover and let rise again until it has filled the tin, about 40 mins. Then bake for 1 hour at 170°C/325°F/gas mark 3.

Potato Bread

This is an excellent bread, good to serve with soups or salads.

12 g/½ oz fresh yeast
30 ml/2 tblsps sugar
75 ml/5 tblsps warm water
100 ml/4 fl oz milk
75 g/3 oz butter
7.5 ml/1½ tsps sea salt
1 egg, beaten
75 g/3 oz freshly mashed potato
350 g/12 oz unbleached white flour

Crumble the yeast into a cup with 5 ml/1 tsp sugar and 75 ml/5 tblsps warm water. Put in a warm place for 10 mins. Heat the milk until lukewarm, then add the butter cut in small bits, off the heat. Pour the yeast into a large bowl, adding the milk and half melted butter. Stir in the remaining sugar, salt, and beaten egg. Then add the warm mashed potato, beating well. Add the flour, a cup at a time. When it all clings together, turn out on a floured surface and knead for 4-5 mins, adding the remaining flour as needed. When it is smooth, put it back in the clean bowl which you have rubbed with butter. Leave in a warm place, covered, for about 1½ hours, or until doubled. Punch down, turn out, and knead again briefly. Then lay in a buttered loaf tin and cover again, leave for about 45 mins, or until the dough has risen to fill the tin. Then bake for 45 mins at 190°C/375°F/gas mark 5. Cool on a wire rack before eating.

March

Mixed Fish Soup

Steamed Rock Shrimp with Ginger and Garlic

Steamed Fish à La Chinoise

Grilled Mahi Mahi with Coriander Sauce

Quails' Eggs on Sprouting Seeds

Stir-Fried Sprouting Seeds

Stir-Fried Sprouts with Noodles

Stir-Fried Sprouts with Steamed Brown Rice

Stir-Fried Vegetables with Vermicelli

Tartlets of Sprouting Seeds

Grilled Potatoes

Boiled Potatoes with Fromage Blanc

Gratin Dauphinois

Potato Salad with Truffle Oil

Potato, Tomato and Watercress Salad

Tandoori Chicken Strips

Poularde de Bresse à La Vapeur de Champagne

Poached Chicken in Vegetable Sauce

Poulet Noir aux Endives

Chicken, Tomato and Avocado Sandwich

Exotic fish are relative newcomers to our shores, coming as they do from such far away places as the Seychelles, the Maldives, Mauritius, the Indian Ocean, Hawaii, the Persian Gulf, Florida and the Caribbean. They first started to appear in the UK on a large scale relatively recently; before that, a few individual fishmongers had already been dealing in exotic fish for years, supplying Japanese restaurants. Now many fishmongers make a feature of exotic fish, and even supermarkets sell swordfish steaks. Their customers are beginning to grow familiar with these fascinating-looking creatures, and find they have much to recommend them. They are relatively inexpensive compared with our own fish, they are intriguing in appearance, and they are often as fresh, or fresher, than our native fish. Joe Fish of HJ Brunning explains that it is often cheaper to fly fish over from south Florida than it is to truck them down from the north of Scotland, and quicker too. 'When the clock is in our favour, ie when we are dealing with the West, we only have to order fish the evening before. Whereas if we want fish from Aberdeen, we have to order it the morning of the day before.'

At first, the picture is somewhat confusing, for there are so many varieties of these strange fish. But having made a few experiments, one soon begins to distinguish between them, and to rate their potential. In one way, they cannot compare with the best of our own fish like halibut and turbot, salmon and Dover sole, for I firmly believe that fish from cold northern waters have more flavour than, and a superior texture to, fish from warmer seas. Yet some of these semi-tropical fish are very good in their own right. They seem to fall into two distinct categories. There are those with soft, flaky flesh, roughly equivalent to our own bass and haddock, like the grouper, snapper, parrot fish, scabbard fish and bream. The others, with their dense, firm flesh that almost resembles meat, like swordfish, shark, pompano, bluefish, bonito and the various sorts of tuna, are usually cut in steaks for grilling.

The soft-fleshed group can of course be cooked in the same ways we cook our own fish, but it seems more appropriate, and more fun, to treat them in more exotic ways. I have spent several weeks testing and devising recipes, some my own version of classic dishes like fish soup, others borrowed from books on the subject, like Rick Stein's *English Seafood Cookery*. Alan Davidson's books are essential reading for the fish lover, and as he points out, most fish crop up all over the world, sometimes in slightly different species. The scabbard fish for instance, which I first remember seeing in the fish market at Setubal in Portugal, turns up – in slightly different forms – in both the Atlantic and Pacific Oceans, and in the Mediterranean, although not in English waters. Sylvain Ho Wing Cheong, chef of a French Mauritian fish restaurant in London, specializes in exotic fish. Chef Sylvain worked for several years in Paris, before coming to England, and when he arrived in London, he made a point of visiting Wheeler's fish restaurants, but he couldn't understand why they used so few sorts of fish. He decided to use a wide variety and, for reasons of cost, to concentrate on exotic fish. He believes that, since most of them are rather bland, they need strong flavours in the sauces. So he serves parrot fish with *aioli*, snapper with a sauce of green peppercorns, and grouper *à la Créole* with chilli peppers.

After experimenting with red bream, grouper, parrot fish, red emperor, snapper, scabbard fish, kingfish, swordfish, *mahi mahi*, mako shark and rock shrimp, I found I had clear preferences in each group. The fish that stood out among the soft-fleshed varieties were the grouper and the scabbard fish, while among the firm-fleshed fish I especially liked the *mahi mahi* and the kingfish. Best of all were the rock shrimp: fat, chunky, juicy prawns, sold shelled but uncooked, frozen but still full of flavour. I made a *ceviche* with some of them which was quite sensational: marinated in lime juice, with chopped shallot and coriander, and a dribble of oil. I steamed the rest of them with spring onions, ginger, and a dash of soy sauce, which was also excellent.

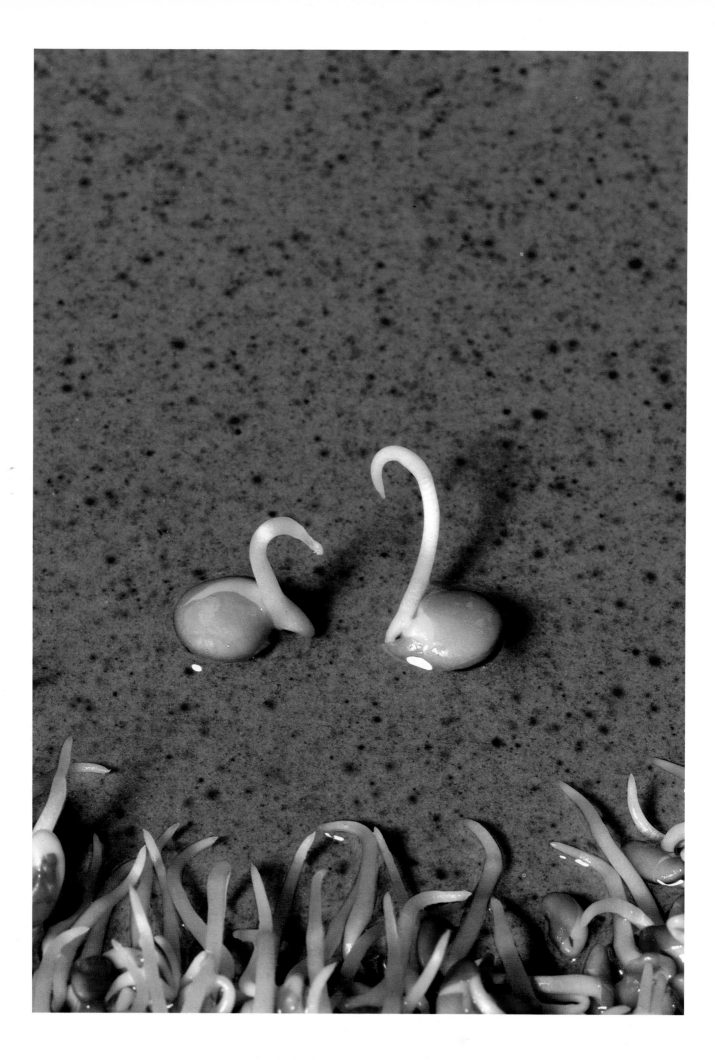

Sprouting seeds are a perfect symbol of healthy food, as far removed from junk food as it is possible to get. They are the freshest of fresh food, grown without fertilizers or pesticides in the safe environment of your own kitchen.

Some years ago, I had a letter for advice on healthy food to lay in for a fall-out shelter, in case of nuclear attack. I could not take the request seriously, but if I had, a supply of seeds for sprouting would have been the obvious answer. For anyone confined to the house, a stock of green or brown lentils, mung beans, sunflower seeds, alfalfa, mustard and cress can assure a varied supply of fresh food.

Supplying all the nutritional elements lacking in dried or otherwise preserved food, spouting seeds have long been recognized as invaluable for sailors. Visitors to Sir Francis Chichester's boat *Gypsy Moth*, in which he sailed round the world, may remember a special compartment for sprouting seeds was in the galley. According to Barbara Griggs' book *The Food Factor*, the true value of sprouting seeds was first assessed in 1912 by a colleague of the Norwegian scientist Axel Holst, who was researching means of preventing scurvy during long sea voyages. Their antiscorbutic properties had already been guessed at in the late eighteenth century, but it was not until the twentieth century that their use as a preventative for scurvy was generally accepted. Almost any dried vegetable, grain or seed can be sprouted, so long as it is whole (split peas and red lentils will not sprout). However, some are more suitable than others; my favourites are green and brown lentils and mung beans. For simple dishes, I use one of these on its own; for stir-frying I prefer to use a mixture, combined with additional vegetables for greater visual interest. The Chinese have used sprouting seeds for 3,000 years and their cuisine provides many possible combinations; spring onions, garlic, root ginger, chilli peppers, soy sauce and sesame oil complement all sorts of sprouting seeds and are well suited to stir-frying. I often add mustard and cress (the result of allowing the germinated seeds to grow one stage further until the first pair of leaves appears). This I usually buy, although it is easily grown from seed on pieces of flannel, or blotting paper, as many will remember from childhood.

Sprouted grains have an odd taste some of which I have not yet grown to like. Whole wheat, oats and rye can all be sprouted successfully, but they must be cooked briefly before using, either by steaming or stir-frying. They can also be chopped in a food processor and added to bread before baking. On the whole, I find commercially sold bean sprouts unsatisfactory except for use in Chinese dishes. Although grown from the same mung bean I sprout at home, they are taken much further, so that they are all sprout and no bean. The same applies to commercially sold alfalfa sprouts, which resemble a mass of fine hairy tissue, lacking in appeal. Much more to my taste are mixtures of green lentils, mung beans, chick-peas, aduki beans and fenugreek, which are ideal for stir-frying.

During the sprouting process, the dormant seed develops into a living organism and its food values multiply accordingly. A number of changes take place during germination: both B and C vitamins develop and continue to increase for several days; the starches are converted into sugar, the protein into amino-acids and the fats into soluble compounds. In this way, the seed is transformed into a valuable source of enzymes which can help compensate for the loss of nutrients in food which has been cooked. Enzymes are necessary to assist in a number of vital processes: the conversion of sugar, the digestion and the clotting of blood. The enzyme content of the sprouted seeds not only makes them more easily digestible than the original seed, it also helps those trying to lose weight. Sprouting seeds are a valuable source of protein, which complements that in non-sprouted grains and pulses. When combined with cooked grains like brown rice, or pulses like lentils, they constitute a nutritionally balanced dish.

It takes time and effort to become accustomed to the taste of sprouted seeds and to use them to their best advantage. I used to eat them occasionally without much enthusiasm – usually in salads in health food restaurants. Now, however, I have found ways of making them quite delicious. Wrapped in little rolls of filo pastry, like miniature spring rolls; used as filling for buckwheat pancakes; stir-fried and served over buckwheat spaghetti, egg noodles, or vermicelli; steamed over brown rice, or used as a filling for an omelette. A good salad can be made with sliced raw mushrooms, mixed with sprouted mung beans and mustard and cress.

Few people in this country, and this applies to greengrocers as well as the general public, seem aware just how many different sorts of potatoes there are. Some don't even realize the basic difference between floury and waxy potatoes. All new potatoes are by definition waxy, as anyone who has ever tried to make a purée with them knows to their cost, for something akin to wallpaper paste is the only possible result. As the potato matures, its true nature emerges, and it displays its potential: the floury ones, for making fluffy purées, melting baked potatoes, and tender roast potatoes; or the waxy ones, for making firm salads, delectable *gratins* and crisp pancakes.

In W Robinson's classic, *The Vegetable Garden*, published in 1905, he lists 194 different varieties of potato. The late Donald Maclean was cultivating more than 350 different sorts in Perthshire at the time of his death in 1988.

However, things are beginning to look up. Some supermarkets have started selling salad potatoes like Cara and La Ratte, in small packages. La Ratte and Charlotte are both waxy French potatoes and excellent for salads. One of the best potatoes I have eaten is Aura. To my mind this is even better than the much vaunted Pink Fir Apple, which I find almost too waxy. Aura is hard to find in Britain, since it is not on the national list, and cannot be imported from France without a permit. Another good potato is Wilja.

An invaluable work of reference for potato growers is *The Good Potato Guide*, by Lawrence D Hills for The Henry Doubleday Research Association. This leaflet is irreplaceable for the amateur grower, as it is packed with information not available elsewhere. It gives details of more than eighty varieties of potato, virtually all that are available to the small-scale grower, with details of their strengths and weaknesses, uses in the kitchen, and stockists. It is also full of interest, explaining how (and why) it costs so much to get an old variety back onto the national list, or to introduce a new potato. Its admirable aim is to encourage individuals to experiment with growing different varieties, especially the older ones, thus keeping them in general use and avoiding the danger of dying out, as so many would have, had it not been for Donald Maclean.

When I had a small vegetable garden attached to a cottage in the country, one of the few things I found worth growing were early new potatoes. They seemed the easiest of vegetables to cultivate, and very rewarding. Even with perfectly ordinary seed potatoes bought from the local town, the flavour was vastly improved when eaten the same day as dug, while with more interesting varieties the results were amazing.

Small new potatoes, boiled in their skins, are good enough to eat alone, and even better when accompanied with bowls of *fromage blanc*, chopped onion, and poppy seeds. They are also very good cooked in an earthenware lidded pot, or *diable*, without any liquid or fat added. This can be placed in the oven, on a gas or electric ring, or over an open fire. When used over heat, as opposed to in the oven, the pot must be shaken from time to time. Smallish new potatoes take about 45 minutes, and are good served with a dish of cold unsalted butter and sea salt. Potatoes are one of my favourite foods; like the other bland staples, the linchpins of our diet - bread, rice and pasta - I never grow tired of them. They are perfectly delicious eaten alone, yet they also make an exquisite background for other flavours. This applies both to luxury foods like caviar and black truffles and to homely things like sausages, bacon, grilled tomatoes, and dairy foods. One of my favourite places to eat in Paris is a small restaurant, modest in the extreme, attached to a cheese shop called La Ferme Sainte Suzanne, in the rue des Fossés Saint-Jacques, near the Panthéon. Here they specialize in cheese dishes, many of them based on an unbeatable combination of large waxy potatoes, simply boiled or steamed, with *fromage blanc*. They are served as part of a *raclette* - not a traditional *raclette*, but their own speciality - with thin slices of mountain ham laid over halved, boiled potatoes, under a bubbling layer of melted *raclette* cheese. The same potatoes are served with *fromage blanc* spooned over them, with garlic and chopped herbs, or, in season, with *vacherin*.

Almost the best waxy potato dish is a warm potato salad, made with plenty of chopped shallots, or sliced spring onions, extra virgin olive oil, a dash of white wine vinegar, and a thick sprinkling of chopped dill, or parsley. This is good on its own, or combined with other foods, such as salt herring, hard-boiled eggs, wilted endives, watercress. Waxy potatoes are also required for making a *gratin*, a classic dish of French provincial cookery. This exists in different forms: made with a mixture of thick cream and milk, or with thin cream alone, or with milk and eggs. Grated cheese is usually incorporated, although I tend to omit it when serving with meat, because I don't like meat and cheese together. An important factor is the size and shape of the dish, for this must be very wide and shallow, broad enough to hold the potatoes in a thin layer, so that the crisp, golden surface is high in proportion to the rest of the dish. This is the *gratin dauphinois;* the *gratin savoyard* is made with stock instead of milk or cream.

Keeping a few hens used to be common practice among country folk, but after the war the situation changed dramatically. With the advent of broiler houses and battery farms, new breeds of hen were developed for purely commercial ends, while the old breeds came close to disappearing. In the sixties, Peter Scott did a painting of some domestic breeds of poultry because he realized that they might soon become extinct, having outlived their usefulness to man. Now, however, the situation is changing again, and the old breeds are slowly regaining popularity. People are starting to keep poultry on a small scale again. There are poultry clubs and shows all over Britain; about thirty-five specific breeds of hen have their own society, while seventeen others are represented by the Rare Breeds Society. It's hard to specify exactly which are rare breeds, when even a well-known breed like Rhode Island Red is no longer common. As Fred Hams says in his delightful book *Old Poultry Breeds*, 'All breeds of large poultry can be considered rare, or at least potentially endangered.' He goes on to say that: 'The old breeds differ from their modern counterparts in that each has an individual characteristic.'

All breeds of hen are descended from jungle fowl, which still live wild in the forests of south-east Asia, where they are hunted like game. Until 1850, most British hens were crossbreeds, pecking around the farmyard. Then new breeds were brought from China; both Cochins and Light Brahmas were presented to Queen Victoria. These fluffy-legged birds laid brown eggs - a novelty at that time in Britain - and soon became very fashionable. People started to keep chickens in henhouses, which encouraged them to lay throughout the winter. In the second half of the nineteenth century, several breeds were introduced from the United States - Leghorns, Plymouth Rocks, Wyandottes and Rhode Island Reds - and the specialization and crossbreeding of the different strains began in earnest, and continued until 1940.

It has become very hard to make money out of breeding hens, since they are so undervalued. Tom Bartlett, a well-known breeder of waterfowl for conservation purposes, also breeds some chickens, but says he loses money on nearly every bird he rears. Anyone starting to keep chickens for the first time would be well advised to consult a knowledgeable but impartial person. You should choose a breed that appeals to you, on condition that it has a reasonably placid temperament. The old English breeds, the Dorkings, Sussex, Derbyshire Redcaps and Orpingtons, are all good dual-purpose birds, and relatively easy to raise. If you are interested in producing an exceptional bird for the table you could try raising two pure-bred lines and crossing them. This gives the best points of both parent birds, plus improved health, character, and drive: what is known as hybrid vigour. Thus an Indian Game Cock crossed with a Buff Orpington will give the broad, white breast of the Game Cock with the tender thighs and wings of the Orpington. The Mediterranean birds tend to be flighty and highly-strung, but they are good layers of predominantly brown eggs. The Leghorn, originally from Italy, holds the record for egg production, beating even the hybrid which was bred expressly for the purpose. The Italian Ancona and the Spanish Andalusian are excitable creatures, as are the French Houdan, Crève-Coeur and La Flêche. The Marran from north-west France is a more sensible choice, with a calm temperament and dark brown eggs. American birds tend to be lacking in interest, except for the decorative Wyandotte. The Silver-Laced Wyandotte is one of the prettiest of hens, like a black and white spotted party frock.

From China comes the Cochin, with fluffy fetlocks like miniature carthorses, and the exquisite Dark Brahma. This is a lovely bird, with feathers like soft herring-bone tweed in brown and black. One of my favourites is the Silkie, also from China. This is like a bundle of fluff in white, cream or black. Permanently broody, it is happy to hatch other birds' eggs as well as its own. Another of my favourites, also from China, is the Frizzle, now most often seen as a bantam. This looks exactly like a knitted tea cosy, with long, curly feathers, especially pretty in white.

Had it not been for the efforts of a handful of people over the past thirty years, many of these old breeds might have died out altogether. The Scots Dumpy, an amusing grey bird with almost non-existent legs, had in fact become extinct in this country, until Tom Bartlett re-introduced it from South Africa. Bantams have remained popular throughout, partly for reasons of space. Today, roughly five times as many people keep bantams as keep large fowl. A few bantams are true breeds in their own right, like the pretty Gold and Silver Sebrights and the Nankins, but most have been specially bred as miniaturized versions of large fowl, weighing about a quarter of their weight. Bantams are practical as well as ornamental, for their eggs are delicious, and the surplus cockerel also makes good eating. They are enchanting birds and one of the prettiest is the Silver-Spangled Hamburgh.

EXOTIC FISH

Mixed Fish Soup

It is best to choose three fish of varying texture for this soup.

700 g/1½ lbs mixed fish e.g.
225 g/8 oz each of grouper, kingfish and mako shark
60 ml/4 tblsps sunflower oil
2 bunches spring onions, sliced
3 x 2.5 cm/1 in squares root ginger, finely chopped
2 small chillies, seeded and finely chopped
2 cloves garlic, finely chopped
2 x 5 cm/2 in strips lemon rind
1.1 litres/2 pts light fish (or chicken) stock, heated
sea salt and black pepper
40 g/1½ oz rice, cooked
60 ml/4 tblsps chopped coriander

Skin and bone the fish and cut it in 4 cm/1½ in chunks. Heat the oil in a heavy pan and cook half the sliced spring onions for 2-3 mins. Then add the ginger, chillies, garlic and lemon rind and cook for another 2 mins. Then add the fish and stir around in the oil for 3 mins. Pour on the heated stock – a mild chicken stock is just as good as fish stock for this dish – adding salt and pepper to taste. Bring to the boil and cook for 4 mins, then remove from the heat. Lift out the pieces of fish with a slotted spoon and put them in a heated tureen. Pour the liquid soup through a strainer into a clean pan, and reheat, adding the cooked rice and the remaining spring onions. When it approaches boiling point remove from the heat and pour over the fish in the tureen. Sprinkle the chopped coriander over the surface of the soup and serve. Serves 5-6.

Steamed Rock Shrimp with Ginger and Garlic

Dublin Bay prawns can be substituted for rock shrimp, if you can find them uncooked.

sesame oil
450 g/1 lb rock shrimp
25 g/1 oz root ginger, finely chopped
2 cloves garlic, finely chopped
½ bunch spring onions, sliced
sea salt and black pepper
7 ml/½ tblsp soy sauce

garnish:
15 ml/1 tblsp chopped coriander, or parsley

dipping sauce:
30 ml/2 tblsps dry vermouth
30 ml/2 tblsps sunflower oil
15 ml/1 tblsp sesame oil
15 ml/1 tblsp soy sauce

Have 4 squares of foil rubbed with sesame oil, and divide the shrimp between them. Sprinkle them with the ginger, garlic and spring onions. Season with salt and pepper and a dash of soy sauce. Wrap up the foil packages and seal their edges by pinching them together. Steam for 6 mins over boiling water.
While they are cooking, mix the dipping sauce ingredients and whisk well. Pour into 4 small dishes and set one at each place. When the time is up, unwrap the packages carefully and slide them onto small plates. Sprinkle with coriander and serve at once. Serves 6-8 as a first course.

Steamed Fish à la Chinoise

1 grouper, or red snapper, weighing 700-800 g/1½ -1¾ lbs
5 ml/1 tsp sugar
5 ml/1 tsp sea salt
7 ml/½ tblsp sesame oil
7 ml/½ tblsp soy sauce
8 thin slices root ginger
2 large cloves garlic, thinly sliced
2 large, or 4 small spring onions, sliced

sauce:
30 ml/2 tblsps dry vermouth
30 ml/2 tblsps sunflower oil
15 ml/1 tblsp sesame oil
15 ml/1 tblsp soy sauce

garnish:
2 large, or 4 small spring onions

In order to make this dish successfully, you need either a fish kettle with adjustable tray, or a large wok with steaming rack and lid. Failing both, you can always bake the fish wrapped in foil for 20 mins in a moderate oven. Rub the fish inside and out with sugar and salt, sesame oil and soy sauce. Rub a large piece of foil with oil and lay half the sliced ginger, garlic and spring onions on it. Lay the fish on top, then cover with the remaining ginger, garlic and spring onions. Wrap the foil around the fish and seal tightly.
Bring some water to a fast boil in the fish kettle or wok. Lay the wrapped fish on the rack, cover with the lid, and steam for 25 mins. Replenish with more boiling water as needed; do not let the water go off the boil. While the fish is cooking, mix the 4 sauce ingredients in a small jug. Cut the remaining spring onions into thin strips about 5 cm/2 ins long. When the fish is done, unwrap it and pour the juices into the sauce. Slide the fish onto a flat dish, discarding the ginger, garlic and spring onion as much as you can. Remove the top skin and pour the sauce over it, after giving it a final whisk. Garnish with strips of spring onion over all, and serve. Serves 3-4 as a first course, or 2-3 as a main dish. It needs no accompaniment.

Grilled Mahi Mahi with Coriander Sauce

The *mahi mahi* is actually a fish called a dolphin, but in order to avoid confusion with the mammal dolphin, it is called by its Hawaiian name of *mahi mahi*. It is an excellent firm-fleshed fish, like a cross between swordfish and tuna.

4 mahi mahi steaks about 2.5 cm/1 in thick
olive oil

coriander sauce:
60 ml/4 tblsps olive oil
15 ml/1 tblsp lemon juice
45 ml/3 tblsps chopped coriander

garnish:
6 sprigs coriander

Rub the steaks with oil while the grill is heating. Grill them gently for 4-5 mins on each side, or until they are cooked through. While they are cooking, make the coriander sauce. Mix the oil and lemon juice together, whisking until they are blended, then stir in the chopped coriander. Serve in a small jug with the grilled steaks on a flat dish garnished with sprigs of coriander. Serves 4, with boiled potatoes and a green salad.

SPROUTING SEEDS

Quails' Eggs on Sprouting Seeds

12 quails' eggs
salt
30 ml/2 tblsps sesame seeds
225 g/8 oz mixed sprouting seeds
22 ml/1½ tblsps sunflower oil
2.5ml/½ tsp soy sauce, or Maggi Liquid Seasoning

Bring a small pan of lightly salted water to the boil and lower in the little eggs. Cook for 2 mins, then plunge them into cold water and shell them carefully, dropping each one into a second bowl of hot water once shelled. Heat a dry frying pan and add the sesame seeds. Toast them gently for 2-3 mins, shaking the pan now and then, until they start to turn colour and jump about. Set aside. Steam the sprouting seeds for 2½ mins over boiling water, then turn them into a bowl and stir in the sunflower oil and soy sauce, or Maggi. Make little mounds, like birds' nests, on 4 heated plates, and lay 3 quails' eggs on each one. Scatter the toasted seeds over each and serve as soon as possible. This quickly made first course serves 4.

Stir-Fried Sprouting Seeds

30 ml/2 tblsps sunflower oil
2 bunches spring onions
(50-75 g/2-3 oz after trimming),

cut in strips
1 large clove garlic, chopped
15 ml/1 tblsp chopped chilli pepper
15 ml/1 tblsp chopped root ginger
225 g/8 oz sprouting seeds, preferably mixed, i.e. green lentils, mung beans, aduki beans, sunflower seeds,
a few chick-peas
15 ml/1 tblsp soy sauce
a few shakes sesame oil
a few shakes Maggi Vegetable Seasoning
1 basket mustard and cress (optional)

Heat a wok or other deep round pan and add the oil. Heat again, then add the spring onions which you have finely cut into 4 cm/1½ in long strips. Stir-fry them for 1 min, then add the garlic, chilli pepper, and ginger, and stir-fry for another min. Add the mixed sprouts, which have been rinsed in fresh water and very well drained. Stir-fry all together for 2 mins, then add soy sauce, sesame oil and Maggi, and toss again for 30 secs. Remove from the heat and stir in the mustard and cress (only add this if the mixture is not going to be submitted to further heat.) Serves 3-4 as a side dish.

Stir-Fried Sprouts with:

1. Noodles

Make recipe as before adding mustard and cress, and serve piled on top of bowls of buckwheat spaghetti, Chinese egg noodles, or vermicelli. Serves 2-3. Very hard to eat with chopsticks.

2. Steamed Brown Rice

Make as before and serve either piled on a dish of brown rice, to serve 2-3, or as follows. Cook 175 g/6 oz brown rice; drain well. Make the stir-fried sprouts as above, and divide between 4 small bowls holding 300 ml/½ pt each, rubbed with oil, so that they are about ⅓ filled. Fill up with the brown rice, adding a few drops sunflower oil and Maggi Vegetable Seasoning or soy sauce. Cover with foil, and keep in the refrigerator until needed. Then steam for 12-14 mins over boiling water and serve, with one or two freshly cooked vegetables. This makes a useful standby and can be kept for several days in the refrigerator. The sprouts combine with the brown rice to make a perfect dish of balanced vegetable protein.

Stir-Fried Vegetables with Vermicelli

1 bunch spring onions, cut in 4 cm/1½ in lengths
175 g/6 oz mushrooms, caps only
175 g/6 oz mangetouts
225 g/8 oz vermicelli
30 ml/2 tblsps sunflower oil
15 ml/1 tblsp soy sauce
175 g/6 oz bean sprouts
30 ml/2 tblsps chopped coriander, or a few drops sesame oil

Cut the spring onions into thin slivers about 4 cm/1½ ins long. Slice the mushrooms, and cut each mangetout into 2 or 3 square pieces. Bring a large pan of lightly salted water to the boil and throw in the vermicelli. Cook for 5 mins, while stir-frying. Heat the oil in a wok and stir-fry the spring onions for 1 min. Add the mushrooms and mangetouts, and toss for 30 secs, then add the soy sauce and cook for another 2 mins. Then add the sprouts – bought ones do well for this dish – and continue to toss for another 1½-2 mins. Stir in the coriander, or sesame oil, and remove from the heat. By this point the vermicelli should be ready, so drain it well and tip into a shallow bowl. Pour the stir-fried vegetables over the top and serve immediately. Serves 4.

Tartlets of Sprouting Seeds

pastry:
225 g/8 oz flour
a pinch of salt
100 g/4 oz butter
a few drops sesame oil
60-75 ml/4-5 tblsps iced water

glaze:
1 egg yolk
7 ml/½ tblsp milk

filling:
175 g/6 oz mixed sprouting seeds
15 ml/1 tblsp sunflower oil
2.5 ml/½ tsp soy sauce, or Maggi Liquid Seasoning

garnish:
450 g/1 lb small mushrooms, button or flat, caps only
30 ml/2 tblsps sunflower oil
10 ml/2 tsps soy sauce, or Maggi Liquid Seasoning
60 ml/4 tblsps dry vermouth
a few drops sesame oil

alternative garnish:
50 g/2 oz peeled prawns
15 ml/1 tblsp sunflower oil
a few drops soy sauce, or Maggi Liquid Seasoning
22 ml/1½ tblsps chopped chives

another alternative:
6-12 quails' eggs

Make the pastry as usual, adding a few drops of sesame oil. Chill for 20 mins, then roll out and line 6 small tartlet tins, about 9 cm/3½ ins wide. Chill again for 10 mins, then line them with small pieces of foil, weighed down with a few beans. Bake blind for 6 mins, then remove the foil and brush them with egg yolk beaten with a little milk. Return to the oven and bake for another 6-8 mins, until golden brown.

While they are baking, make the filling. Steam the sprouting seeds for 2½ mins over boiling water, then turn into a bowl and stir in the sunflower oil and soy sauce. Toss the mushroom caps in sunflower oil for 2 mins, then add the soy sauce, vermouth and sesame oil and cover the pan. Simmer gently for another 2 mins, or until they are just tender. Fill the tarts with the seeds, allowing about 30 ml/2 tblsps each, then lay the mushroom caps over them, gills down, and sprinkle them with a little of the juice. Serve as soon as possible. Serves 6 as a first course, or 3 as a light main dish.

As an alternative to garnish, you can use a few peeled prawns, tossed briefly in sunflower oil and soy sauce, sprinkled with chives; or hard-boiled quails' eggs.

RARE SORTS OF POTATO

Grilled Potatoes

This unusual recipe is based on one I found in a cookery book published in the early thirties. It is quite delicious, and practical in that most of the cooking is done in advance.

4 large waxy potatoes, weighing about 175 g/6 oz each
90 ml/6 tblsps olive oil
1 small onion, finely chopped
25 g/1 oz butter
sea salt and black pepper

Boil the potatoes (whole) in their skins, then peel them as soon as they are cool enough to handle. Cut them in slices about 1 cm/½ in thick and lay them in a shallow bowl. Spoon over the oil and stir in the chopped onion. Leave for anything from 30 mins to 2 hours, stirring gently from time to time. Shortly before serving, drain off the oil and discard some of the chopped onion. Lay the potato slices on a baking sheet, side by side without overlapping; there is no need to oil the sheet. Put a tiny piece of butter on each slice and sprinkle them with sea salt and black pepper. Grill gently for 8-10 mins – there is no need to turn them over – until nicely browned and crisp. Slide onto a flat dish to serve. Serves 4. Excellent with roast and grilled meats.

Boiled Potatoes with Fromage Blanc

This is a good dish for gardeners, since it is the best way I know of appreciating freshly dug potatoes of a good firm variety like Aura, or Wilja. I found a version of this dish in an American cookbook published in 1941, where the hot boiled potatoes are served with bowls of cottage cheese, thick soured cream, chopped onion and caraway seeds.

freshly boiled potatoes in their skins
fromage blanc
sliced spring onions
poppy seeds
sea salt and black pepper

I usually make this when I am alone. I boil 4 or 5 medium-sized potatoes in their skins and drain them well. Then I skin them or not depending on how I feel, split them in half, and lay them on a hot plate. I then cover them with dollops of *fromage blanc* and scatter thickly sliced spring onions over them. I then sprinkle poppy seeds over all, with sea salt and black pepper. Serves 1.
If making for more than one person, I serve the potatoes, peeled or not, in a dish, with the *fromage blanc* and sliced spring onions in bowls, and the poppy seeds in an egg cup.

Gratin Dauphinois

This is the best possible accompaniment to a roast leg of lamb. I find it too rich when made with cream alone, and only add cheese when serving it alone, or with vegetable dishes.

1 clove garlic, halved and scored
12 g/½ oz butter
700 g/1½ lb waxy potatoes, peeled and thinly sliced
sea salt and black pepper
75 g/3 oz grated Gruyère, or some grated nutmeg
1 egg, beaten
300 ml/½ pt single cream
200 ml/7 fl oz milk

Choose a broad, shallow dish, wide enough to hold the potatoes in two, or at most three, layers. Rub it with the clove of garlic, then with the butter. Arrange the sliced potatoes in overlapping layers, sprinkling each layer with salt and black pepper, and grated cheese or nutmeg. Use the uneven shaped slices in the bottom layer, keeping the best ones for the top. (The slices may be round or semi-circular, depending on the size of the potatoes.) When all are done, beat the egg with the cream and milk, adding more salt and pepper, and pour over the potatoes. There should be enough to come almost level with the top layer. Bake for 1½ hours at 180°C/350°F/gas mark 4 until the top has browned. Serves 4-6.

Potato Salad with Truffle Oil

Potato salad incorporating sliced black truffles is a luxury few can afford, but a more modest dish can be made with olive oil flavoured with truffles. The somewhat less expensive oil flavoured with *funghi porcini* can be used instead of the truffle oil; this can be bought at good Italian delicatessens.

700 g/1½ lb new potatoes, unpeeled
3 large shallots, finely chopped
90 ml/6 tblsps extra virgin olive oil
15 ml/3 tsp truffle oil, or porcini oil
45 ml/3 tblsps white wine vinegar
sea salt and black pepper
chopped parsley

Boil the potatoes in their skins until just tender; drain well, and shake over low heat until they have dried out. As soon as they are cool enough to handle, peel them and slice thickly into a shallow bowl. Scatter the chopped shallots over them, then pour on the olive oil, lifting them gently to mix without breaking up. Then add the truffle (or *porcini*) oil, cover with a cloth, and leave for 20-30 mins. Then add the vinegar and mix gently, adding sea salt, black pepper and chopped parsley. Serve soon after making; serves 4.

Potato, Tomato and Watercress Salad

This excellent dish is based on one in Dorothy Hartley's *Food in England*. I like to serve it alone, as a first course.

700 g/1½ lb waxy (or new) potatoes, freshly cooked
100 ml/4 fl oz single cream
sea salt and black pepper
450 g/1 lb tomatoes, skinned and sliced
½ bunch watercress, tender sprigs only
30 ml/2 tblsp olive oil
15 ml/1 tblsp white wine vinegar

Peel the potatoes while they are still hot, then slice them thickly and drop into the cream, in a bowl. Add sea salt and black pepper, and mix gently. Then spread evenly on a flat dish and cover with a layer of thinly sliced tomatoes. Sprinkle with more salt and pepper, then lay the watercress sprigs over the tomatoes. Mix the olive oil and vinegar and pour over all. Serves 3-4.

RARE BREEDS OF FOWL

Tandoori Chicken Strips

This is best for an informal meal since it must be assembled at the last moment.

4 (boneless) chicken breasts, skinned and cut in strips about 1 cm/½ in thick

marinade:
300 ml/½ pt yoghurt
15 ml/1 tblsp Dijon mustard
12 g/½ oz root ginger, grated
2.5 ml/½ tsp cumin seeds, roughly crushed
2.5 ml/½ tsp coriander, roughly crushed
2.5 ml/½ tsp ground turmeric
30 ml/2 tblsps sunflower oil
30 ml/2 tblsps lemon juice

garnish:
2 pitta bread
2 handfuls rocket, or 2 bunches watercress, tips only
2 large, or 4 small tomatoes, skinned and cut in strips
2 avocados
sea salt and black pepper

dressing:
30 ml/2 tblsps olive oil
7 ml/½ tblsp white wine vinegar
7 ml/½ tblsp lemon juice

Lay the chicken strips in a shallow dish. Put the yoghurt in the food processor with the mustard, grated ginger, cumin and coriander – which have been lightly crushed in a mortar – and turmeric. Process until blended, then add the oil and lemon juice slowly, through the lid while continuing to process. Pour over the chicken strips and leave for anything from 6-24 hours under refrigeration.
Shortly before serving, heat the grill. Lift the chicken strips out of the marinade and lay them on a grill pan which you have lined with foil. Grill them for 8-10 mins, until nicely browned, turning them over half-way through.
While they grill, prepare the pitta. Toast them, then split into flat halves and lay on warmed plates. Cover with the rocket, or watercress, and lay tomato strips along one side of each plate. Slice the avocados and lay along the opposite side of the plates. Sprinkle tomatoes and avocados with sea salt and black pepper to taste, and a little dressing, then lay the grilled chicken strips over the rocket, or watercress. Serve immediately; it needs no accompaniment. Serves 4.

Poularde de Bresse à la Vapeur de Champagne

I watched Michel Lorain preparing this dish in the kitchens of Le Meridien, and ate it later in the Oak Room restaurant, with its lovely Venetian chandeliers. It is an exquisite dish: pure, delicate and very simple. I make a modified version at home, using a good white wine instead of Pommery champagne, and it is still very good.

1 poularde de Bresse (about 1.4 kg/3 lbs)
1 carrot, chopped
1 onion, chopped
½ leek, chopped
1-2 cabbage leaves
1 bottle of champagne

sauce:

chicken stock
350 ml/12 fl oz fresh double cream
diced vegetables (carrots, peas, etc.)
already cooked
sea salt and black pepper

Place a plate upside down inside a large earthenware casserole and put the chicken on top. Place the chopped carrot, onion and leek around the plate. Blanch the cabbage leaves to soften them, and then use them to cover the breast of the chicken. Pour about 500 ml/18 fl oz of champagne with a little water into the casserole. (It is important to ensure that the liquid does not touch the chicken, as it is to be steamed.) Place the lid on the casserole and seal the edge with a paste made from flour, water and salt rolled out into a long strip. The dish is now hermetically sealed and if the lid does not have a small hole in the top, as a traditional French *marmite* does, it is necessary to introduce a small air hole which can be done by inserting a small piece of macaroni through the paste. Cook in the oven at 220°C/425°F/gas mark 7, for between 1-1¼ hours.

To make the sauce, reduce the rest of the champagne with an equal amount of chicken stock (a stock cube can be used to make the stock) and then add the double cream, taking care that the two do not separate. The mixture should cook long enough to achieve a consistency which will coat the back of a spoon evenly. Add the diced vegetables and seasoning to taste.

Poached Chicken in Vegetable Sauce

This is my latest variation on that old favourite, chicken in white sauce with rice. It is surprising how good these dishes can be, despite the fact they are pale in colour, and verging on the bland.

1 free-range chicken
1 onion, cut in quarters
1 large leek, thickly sliced
1 large carrot, cut in quarters
1 bay leaf
3 stalks celery, halved
1 bay leaf
3 stalks parsley
sea salt and black pepper

sauce:

40 g/1½ oz butter
45 ml/3 tblsps flour
150 ml/¼ pt single cream
100 g/4 oz fennel, weighed after trimming, cut in 1cm/¼ in slices
100 g/4 oz courgettes, cut in 1 cm/¼ in slices
1 bunch watercress, leaves only

Start 1 day in advance. Cut off the lower leg joints and wing-tips and put them in a pressure cooker with the neck and giblets – all except the liver. Add the onion, leek, carrot, celery, bay leaf and parsley. Cover with 1.2 litres/2 pts cold water, add salt and black pepper, and bring to the boil. Cook for 1 hour under pressure (or 3 hours in an ordinary pan). Strain and cool, then chill overnight, or for several hours. Next day remove the fat from the surface of the stock and pour stock over the chicken in a deep pan. Bring to the boil and simmer for 1-1¼ hours, depending on the size of the bird, then remove it and keep it warm. Strain the stock and remove the fat once more. In a clean pan, reduce it to 450 ml/¾ pt by fast boiling, then set aside. Melt the butter, add the flour and cook for 1 min, stirring. Then add the hot stock, stirring constantly, and the cream. Season to taste and simmer gently for 4 mins, stirring often. Then set aside to cool for a little.

Cook the sliced fennel in lightly salted water for about 8 mins, or until tender. Then lift it out with a slotted spoon and cook the sliced courgettes in the same water for 5 mins, adding the watercress leaves for the last minute, then drain. Put the cooled *veloute* sauce in the food processor with the cooked fennel, courgettes and watercress. Process till blended, then pour into a clean pan and reheat, adjusting the seasoning to taste. Carve the chicken into joints and lay in a shallow dish. Pour some of the sauce over and serve the rest in a sauceboat. Accompany with boiled rice and a green vegetable; broccoli is a good choice. Serves 4.

Poulet Noir aux Endives

This recipe can also be made with a free-range or corn-fed chicken, or a guinea fowl.

1 poulet noir, cut in quarters and trimmed
1 small onion, halved
½ leek
1 carrot, halved
1 stalk celery, halved
½ bay leaf
25 g/1 oz butter
15 ml/1 tblsp sunflower oil
700 g/1½ lbs chicory, cut in eighths lengthwise
30 ml/2 tblsps orange juice
15 ml/1 tblsp lemon juice
sea salt and black pepper

Put the trimmings of the chicken – backbone, leg-ends, wing-tips, neck, skin, etc – in a pressure cooker with the onion, leek, carrot, celery and bay leaf. Add about 450 ml/¾ pt cold water, bring to the boil, and cook under pressure for 1 hour (or in an ordinary pan, covered, for 2½ hours). Strain, cool, and remove the fat. Measure 150 ml/¼ pt of the resulting stock. Heat the butter and oil in a heavy casserole and brown the chicken pieces on both sides, then remove them and put the chicory into the pot. Stir around for about 5 mins, then add the stock and orange and lemon juice. Lay the chicken pieces on the chicory, sprinkle with sea salt and black pepper, and cover with foil and the lid. Cook for 40 mins in the oven at 180°C/350°F/gas mark 4. Take the chicken pieces out and keep warm, covered. Lift out the chicory with a slotted spoon, leaving the liquid in the casserole, and lay it on a shallow serving dish. Keep warm. Boil up the liquid until it is reduced to 75-90 ml/5-6 tblsps, being careful it does not burn. Then lay the chicken pieces on the chicory and pour the reduced juices over them. Serve with a purée of potatoes – I like one made with olive oil and hot milk – and a green salad.

Serves 4. (If using a guinea fowl, it is best simply cut in half, to serve two.)

Chicken, Tomato and Avocado Sandwich

This makes a good light meal, ideal for watching TV. I use the rest of the bird for making chicken noodle soup.

2 chicken breasts
2 large tomatoes, or 4 small ones, skinned
1 large avocado, peeled and stoned
a few drops lemon juice
12 large slices dry white bread
150 ml/¼ pt mayonnaise, preferably homemade
sea salt and black pepper

garnish:

6 Little Gem lettuce leaves
6 cherry tomatoes, halved

Slice the chicken breasts about 1 cm/¼ in thick. Slice the tomatoes, discarding seeds and juice. Slice the avocado and sprinkle with lemon juice. Toast the bread, and lay the sliced chicken on half the slices. Dab with mayonnaise and sprinkle with salt and pepper. Cover with sliced tomatoes, and more mayonnaise, salt and black pepper. Then lay the sliced avocados over the tomatoes. Cover with the rest of the toast, then cut off the crusts. Lay the sandwiches on a dish, and garnish with lettuce and tomatoes. Serves 4.

April

I had planned to write a worthy piece about yoghurt, detailing its beneficial qualities, its ability to promote healthy bacteria in the organism, its use as an aid to longevity, and so on. Then I changed my mind. Sitting in my flat on a sunny afternoon, I found myself thinking back to holidays abroad, and all the delicious varieties of yoghurt I had enjoyed over the years, in many different countries.

Yoghurt plays no part in my childhood memories, for it was unknown at that time in Scotland, where dairy food (during the war years at least) consisted of milk, butter and cheese. Nor did yoghurt figure later at an English boarding school, where the only addition to an even more narrow range of dairy food was Wall's ice-cream in two colours - I won't use the word flavours, for that would be inappropriate. My first experience of yoghurt came when I was just sixteen, having already left school - somewhat prematurely it now seems - in order to spend a year living with a French family in Paris. Our weekly diet turned out to follow a set pattern that never varied, and yoghurt was the order of the day for Thursday lunch, eaten as a dessert. It came in little glass pots, and we ate it sprinkled with sugar. I hated it on sight, although looking back I feel sure it was delicious.

Soon after my return to London, aged seventeen, I was taken out to lunch at The White Tower, in Percy Street. Here I ate Greek yoghurt for the first time, and began to like it, in my cautious way, although I would probably still have preferred junket given the choice, for in those days I still thought of yoghurt as a sweet dish. I next encountered it in semi-liquid form, when we went to Ibiza the year we married. We used to drink it in glasses in our favourite café in Santa Eulalia, filling in the long hours before the Spanish consider it fitting to dine, and we grew greatly attached to it. But it was not until the first of our trips to stay with relatives in the Middle East that its true significance became apparent. For there in Beirut, in those carefree days before the war, I learnt to appreciate yoghurt not just as a dessert, or a drink, but as a sauce, marinade, salad and - drained - as a soft cheese eaten for breakfast, with little dishes of wild thyme, sesame seeds and olive oil. I quickly grew to love the Lebanese foods: the aromatic dishes of grilled fish and meat, fried aubergines and peppers, flat breads, pinenuts and sesame seeds, and exotic spices like sumac and zaatar.

Like countless other Anglo-Saxons before me, I responded to the clean, tart tastes and the smoky scents that make you want to sniff the air and smack your lips. When my niece, Joumana, came to live in London a few years later, I remember her sighing for what she used to call the 'juicy' tastes of Lebanese food, and lamenting the dry, stodgy quality - if it can be called a quality - of most English food.

By 1970 yoghurt had become fairly easy to buy in southern England, but the choice was limited. With the growing interest in health foods in the early seventies, yoghurt began to assume a new importance. I remember my friends were growing their own brand of yoghurt, using a starter that had been brought out of Russia. This was very sharp and strong, good for serving as a sauce with grilled lamb or diluting as a drink, but too intense to eat alone. By 1974, when I wrote a book on cooking with vegetables, yoghurt was in common use. But as I travelled more, to Greece, Turkey, Spain, Yugoslavia, India, Egypt and Denmark, I found more and more yoghurts that I loved, while those I could buy at home had little appeal. I began to make my own, using my preferred brand as a starter, experimenting with different methods, ranging from the modern, like electric yoghurt-makers, to the ancient, like basins wrapped in bath towels overnight.

Today there is a wide range of yoghurt in the shops, with new brands appearing all the time. The fact that the great majority are sweetened fruit yoghurts prove that it is still used mainly as a dessert. In the past few years Greek 'strained' yoghurt has become very popular. I do not much care for these, finding them too sharp and concentrated in flavour, and too thick and smooth in consistency. The Greek yoghurts I like best unfortunately do not seem to be exported. I prefer the milder yoghurts from Germany and France, or the excellent yoghurts now being made in Britain from ewes' and goats' milk. Most of the low-fat yoghurts seem similar: perfectly acceptable in cooked dishes, but dull on their own. When using yoghurt in cooked dishes, some recipes stipulate 'stabilizing' it beforehand to prevent it separating. This can be done in various ways, by the addition of cornflour or egg white, but it does alter the character of the yoghurt. I prefer to use it without stabilizing, adding it at the end of the cooking, and being careful to keep the finished dish warm, rather than hot. Since many Middle Eastern dishes are served warm, this is not hard to do.

All eggs are edible, and have probably all been eaten at one time or another. Swans' eggs were once used for wedding cakes, while plovers' and quails' eggs have been considered a delicacy in this country for hundreds of years. All domestic birds' eggs may be eaten; this includes those of geese and ducks as well as hens. Duck eggs are supposed to be especially good for making cakes, while guinea fowl eggs are an unknown quantity, at least to me. Pullets' eggs, like those of bantams, are full of flavour despite their small size. Quails' eggs have become fashionable in restaurants over the past decade, just as they were sixty years ago. They are usually sold raw, a dozen at a time, in tiny boxes. Simply hard-boiled and shelled, they make an excellent canapé, served with a larger (hen's) egg shell filled with celery salt. They are almost always served boiled, either hard or soft, and are often used as a decorative garnish. They can also be bought smoked.

Doves' eggs were once much used, for the dovecote was not merely a decorative addition to a country house, but had a sound practical value. With all the facilities of modern life we tend to forget the exigencies of feeding large families through the winter months. With a dovecote, a supply of fresh eggs and the occasional bird was assured. Dovecotes were never filled by man; they were simply built and left empty, whereupon flocks of wild doves would arrive, on the principle of the nesting box. Nowadays their eggs are protected, with the exception of the collared dove in Scotland.

Almost all wild birds' eggs are now protected by law, with a few exceptions. The eggs of the lapwing, or green plover, may be gathered from the nest, but only up until April 14th, and then only for home consumption; their sale is prohibited. Those of the black-headed gull fetch high prices in the shops during their short season in late May and early June, but those of the black-backed gull, the herring gull and the common gull are not good enough to eat, except in dire emergency. Pheasants' eggs are supposed to be very good, but are too valuable to be eaten.

It comes as a surprise to see just how much eggs vary in size, shape, and colour. The owl's egg, like the dove's, is so spherical as to be almost round, while the guillemot's eggs are long and pointed, like an avocado pear. This is a form of protection, for the guillemot often lays its eggs on precipitous ledges on cliffs; when caught by the wind, this egg swings round on its axis to face into the wind.

Although English cookery books from the fourteenth century onwards contain many recipes for cooking eggs, in pastry, with vegetables, in omelettes, fritters and custards, they are rarely mentioned in accounts of meals. Perhaps they did not figure in the grand meals that were considered worthy of recording, but they were certainly used in large numbers in puddings, both savoury and sweet, in sauces and in stuffings. Up until the seventeenth century, hard-boiled egg formed the basis of most stuffings in the way that breadcrumbs do today. Yet I can find only two mentions of egg dishes as part of a meal. The first was an account of a grand dinner given in 1730; among a list of sixty-eight dishes was a reference to a roast pheasant dressed with its eggs, another to a dish called Portugal Eggs. Thirty years later, in *The Diary of a Country Parson*, Parson Woodforde records a simple dinner consisting of roast mutton, veal cutlets, a selection of cold meats and eggs boiled in their shells; this was followed by a plum pudding.

In the nineteenth century the egg made its first appearance at the breakfast table. Until then a heavy meal of meat dishes with cheese and beer had been the custom among country folk, while more sophisticated people had taken to a light breakfast of rolls with hot chocolate. Now the traditional English breakfast as we know it became established: a meal consisting of porridge, eggs and bacon, and fish, followed by toast and marmalade, accompanied by coffee or tea.

Our consumption of eggs in this country doubled just before the First World War; then it doubled again shortly before the Second World War. It seems that the restrictions inevitable in wartime interrupted what would otherwise have been a pattern of steady growth. In the interwar years, for the first time in hundreds of years, the English started to eat less. The heavy meals of the eighteenth and nineteenth centuries gave way at last to a totally new approach to food, encouraged by the emergence of smaller households, with fewer children and servants alike. In this era of lighter meals the egg took on new importance. Certainly by the 1920s and 1930s an egg dish was considered acceptable as the first course for luncheon, while some years later it would be thought of as a possible meal in itself. Nowadays egg dishes have become almost a way of life, especially for people living on their own. As Cole Lesley recorded in his biography of Noël Coward, all the Master wanted to eat in the evening was 'a little eggy something on a tray'.

Coriander is part of the carrot family, and so like flat-leafed parsley in appearance that the only way I can tell them apart is by surreptitiously pinching a leaf and smelling it. For whereas parsley has virtually no smell at all, coriander has a most weird smell which gave rise to its name, derived from the Greek word *koris*, meaning bedbug. (I didn't realize that bedbugs smelt, but the Greeks knew better.) This somewhat fetid smell put me off for years, but now I don't even notice it. It did put me off trying to grow it myself, however, for when I tried in the dense clay soil of Sussex the smell was truly unpleasant.

Coriander was brought to Britain by the Romans during the first century AD, and it was one of the bitter herbs ordained to be eaten at the Passover. Yet in the detailed list of salad leaves and herbs in John Evelyn's *Acetaria*, published in 1699, I can find no mention of it. It may be that its use in Britain died out after the Romans left, and was not revived until comparatively recently. In W Robinson's classic horticultural book *The Vegetable Garden*, published in 1905, he includes coriander in his list of herbs with the comment: 'Some writers say the leaves are used for seasoning, but this statement seems odd, as all the green parts of the plant exhale a very strong odour of the woodbug, hence the Greek name of the plant.'

If we want to find coriander foliage in daily use - the berries are another matter, for they are widely used and appreciated - we must look to India, China and Thailand, also to Mexico, the countries of Latin America, the Caribbean and the south-western states of the United States, where it is called cilantro. The only European countries to use it are Portugal and Cyprus. It is used for the most part as we use parsley: the leaves are used whole, torn in pieces, or roughly chopped. They are usually added to dishes towards the end of their cooking, as a flavouring and as a garnish. The stalks are tough and should not be eaten, although they can be used as a flavouring for soups and stews, as they are in China and Thailand, where the roots are also used as flavouring.

I was finally converted to coriander in California, where many good restaurants specialize in a variant of Mexican food. A number of restaurants in and around San Francisco serve delicious things like crab cakes with *salsa*, grilled rabbit with coriander and mustard seeds, mesquite-grilled chicken marinated in lime juice with chillies and coriander, and *tortillas* filled with black beans liberally garnished with sour cream and coriander. I was also intrigued by a fresh tomato and chilli pepper sauce that appeared on the table at almost every meal, including breakfast. This was the ubiquitous but delicious Mexican *salsa*, which goes with just about everything, and is served almost as often as salt and pepper. There are several variations: the most usual is *salsa fresca*, a hash of raw (unskinned) tomatoes with chopped onion, chillies, coriander and lemon juice. There is another version, made with grilled (skinned) tomatoes and chillies, with a smoky taste and thinner texture. Best of all, but sadly not available in Britain, is the *salsa* which is made with the little *tomatillo*. This looks like a green cherry tomato encased within a papery husk like a Chinese gooseberry. I ate this with pan-fried oysters in San Francisco and it was delicious.

The coriander berry has a totally different taste from the leaf, and one which is widely appreciated. Ground coriander is used in curry powder, although it is not hot, and combines very well with ground cumin in varying proportions. It has a gentle, warm flavour, and goes well with bland foods like lentils. I sometimes use it together with its leaf, as in spiced lentils with coriander, and coriander steaks.

Fresh coriander can be bought fairly easily now in large towns, in supermarkets and Greek Cypriot shops, where it is known as Greek parsley. It can also be grown at home by sowing the whole seeds in fine friable soil. After buying it, I cut off the roots and stand it in a jug of water, like a bunch of flowers. Most people advocate standing it in water in the refrigerator with a plastic bag over the leaves, or wrapped in damp newspaper, but I prefer my own method. Out of sight, out of mind tends to be my motto in the kitchen.

All in all, coriander is a wonderful discovery, a totally new taste for many people, one which goes remarkably well with meat and fish, eggs and vegetables, pulses and grains. It is particularly welcome after Christmas, for it has a pleasantly astringent, cleansing quality that seems appropriate after several days of over-eating. It may take a while to grow to like it, but once the taste has been acquired, you will never tire of it. Its complementary flavours are garlic and ginger, spring onions and shallots, chilli peppers, and the juice of limes and bitter oranges.

Milk fresh from the cow has a universal appeal, and cows were kept in London until quite recently. Apparently there was a herd of cows in Peckham Rye as late as 1959, while in the 1920s milk was wheeled through the streets in giant churns and ladled into housewives' jugs. In earlier times, the cow itself was brought to the door and milked before the customers' eyes, to prove the freshness of the milk.

There is something magical and mysterious about dairy processes, as anyone who has seen Polanski's *Tess* is aware. An image that remains in the eye is the cheeses in their muslin bags, dripping in cacophony through the night while everyone in the farmhouse is sleeping. Consternation ensues when the butter fails to 'take', probably because all the dairy maids are in love with the dread Angel Clare. Yoghurt making is equally uncertain: often for no apparent reason the yoghurt does not set. Milk has a primaeval quality about it; perhaps because it is the first food that we experience, it has a special significance, an almost mystic property.

Although the English tend to think of milk as cows' milk, in other countries this is often rare to the point of non-existence, and the milk of sheep, goats, water buffalo, even mares, is commonly used. Some of my favourite cheeses are made from ewes' milk: the little *banon*, a Provençal cheese wrapped in chestnut leaves, or, alternatively, flavoured with *poivre d'âne* – the wild savoury that grows on the hills – and the creamy *brousse*, a large white cheese made in and around Arles. *Feta*, the salty white Greek cheese that goes so well with tomatoes, is also made from ewes' milk, while the many delicious French *chèvres* are, of course, made from goats' milk. In the south of Italy, the milk of water buffalo was formerly much used for making the *mozzarella*; nowadays these are more often made with cows' milk, but the best *mozzarella di buffala* are still made in the old way and are not cheap.

Goats' milk is also excellent for cooking, for its characteristic flavour only develops during cheese-making; when used fresh, it is mild and delicious, with no 'goat' taste whatsoever. Since it does not have to be pasteurized (assuming it comes from one's own goats), it is richer in thiamin and vitamin C.

A fermented mares' milk called *kumiss* is very popular in Russia. During the nineteenth century, it was widely regarded as a cure for tuberculosis. Tolstoy became an enthusiastic follower of the *kumiss* treatment, and went many times to the Steppes of Samara, where he lived in a felt tent among the Bakshir nomads, living entirely on *kumiss* and mutton. He became so dependent on the regime, although its good effects never survived his return to Yasnaya Polyana, that he eventually bought a large tract of land near Samara, with a dilapidated wooden house. On at least two occasions his whole family, complete with children, governesses and servants, went with him to partake in the cure. He hired a family of Bakshirs to pitch their tents nearby, with their mares and foals, to supply the *kumiss*. The veiled women milked the mares twice a day – the foals were tethered to keep them away from their mothers – and prepared the *kumiss* hidden behind curtains. Tolstoy's daughter, Tatyana, in her book *Tolstoy Remembered*, describes it: 'First, the mares' milk was poured into long leather containers made out of horses' skins, then some already fermented liquid was poured in to start the fresh milk fermenting, and finally the liquid had to be stirred with long sticks. The more thoroughly it was stirred, the better it was...'

Yoghurt is easily made at home, but our western yoghurt is very different from that of Russia and the Balkans. This must be made again each day, so that there is always plenty of yoghurt. It is much stronger than ours, thick and full of flavour; it is excellent for eating with meat or vegetables, but too strong for eating with fruit, at least to my mind. It makes a refreshing summer drink, called *ayran* in Turkey, where it is very popular in the cafés of Istanbul.

Buttermilk can also be made at home, and is becoming easier to buy. Originally, the liquid left in the churn after making butter, commercial buttermilk is different in that it is made from skimmed milk with an added culture. Its nutritional content is less than that of whole milk, since its fat content is lower. It is much used in Ireland for making soda bread and scones; its fresh tart flavour also makes delicious cold soups and sauces. Simple curd cheeses are easily made at home. When using fresh milk or cream, these must be artificially soured since, due to pasteurization, they will not sour naturally but go 'off'. A starter can be added, or simply some lemon juice or vinegar; in the case of yoghurt or bought buttermilk this is not necessary, as they already contain their own culture. They are first gently heated, then poured into muslin and left for some hours to drain. They are then shaped in moulds and drained again, standing on bamboo or rush mats. Later they are turned out, with the imprint of the muslin still on them. They are delicious eaten with salad, or with soft fruit, cream and sugar, or with a fruit jelly and water biscuits. Alternatively, they may be coated with chopped fresh herbs, or with dried herbs and sesame seeds.

YOGHURT

Leyla Soup

This is my slightly adapted version of a delicious soup, perfect for summer, as made by the painter Derek Hill's housekeeper and cook, Gracie, and printed in *The Picnic Papers*, edited by Susanna Johnston and Anne Tennant.

12 g/½ oz butter
15 ml/1 tblsp flour
1.1 litres/2 pts good chicken stock
2 eggs, beaten
juice of 1½ lemons, strained
600 ml/1 pt yoghurt
30-90 ml/2-6 tblsps tomato juice, freshly made if possible (optional)
sea salt and white pepper
45 ml/3 tblsps roughly chopped mint

Melt the butter and add the flour; cook gently for 1 min, then add the heated stock. Bring to the boil, stirring, and cook gently for 3 mins. Beat the eggs until frothy, then add the lemon juice, still beating. Add a little of the boiling soup while continuing to beat, then tip the contents of the bowl back into the saucepan. Stir over very gentle heat until almost boiling, then remove from the heat. Cool for a little, then pour into a food processor, and add the yoghurt and tomato juice. (If you have a juice extractor and can make your own, add as much of the tomato juice as you like, tasting as you do so. I think 90 ml/6 tblsps is about right. If using tinned tomato juice it is probably best to stick to 30 ml/2 tblsps.) Add salt and pepper to taste, and the roughly chopped mint. Process until blended and perfectly smooth, then chill for several hours, or overnight. Serve in chilled cups. Serves 6-8. Alternatively, leave out the mint and scatter 5 ml/1 tsp mint, cut in thin strips, over the surface of each cup before serving. When made with freshly crushed tomato juice, this is a fabulous soup, a lovely pale pink in colour. I like to serve it with crisp pitta bread, split and lightly buttered, then baked for about 15 mins at 180°C/350°F/gas mark 4, until golden brown. Serve warm, or after cooling.

Fried Aubergines in Garlic Sauce

I like to serve this dish soon after making, so that the warm vegetables contrast with the chilled sauce.

2 aubergines, sliced 0.5 cm/¼ in thick
sea salt
light olive oil, or sunflower oil
25 g/1 oz butter
2 beefsteak tomatoes, sliced as above

yoghurt sauce:
450 ml/¾ pt yoghurt, chilled
1 clove garlic, crushed
sea salt

garnish:
30 ml/2 tblsps basil, or mint, or coriander, cut in thin strips

Salt the sliced aubergines in layers in a colander and leave for 30 mins. Then rinse off the salt under the cold tap and pat dry with kitchen paper. Heat some light oil in a large frying pan, preferably non-stick. When it is very hot, put in 4-5 aubergine slices and fry until golden brown, turning them round from time to time. Then turn and fry the other side, adding more oil as needed. As each lot are done, drain on kitchen paper while frying the next batch. When all are done arrange them in a concentric circle in a shallow earthenware dish. Add a little butter to the oil remaining in the pan and fry the tomato slices briefly, just long enough to soften. To make the sauce, beat the yoghurt until smooth, then stir in the crushed garlic and salt to taste. Spoon a layer of the sauce over the aubergines, lay the tomato slices on top, and cover with the rest of the yoghurt. Scatter the herb over the top. This simple dish may be served at any temperature, with some warm pitta bread, preferably as a first course.

Aubergine and Yoghurt

Aubergines and yoghurt have a special affinity, as is demonstrated in this excellent Turkish *meze*.

2 large aubergines
2 cloves garlic, finely chopped
sea salt and black pepper
30 ml/2 tblsps virgin olive oil
30 ml/2 tblsps lemon juice
175 ml/6 fl oz yoghurt

Bake the aubergines for 50-60 mins at 190°C/375°F/gas mark 5, until they are soft in the centre. Turn them over halfway through the cooking. Leave until cool enough to handle, then split them in half and scoop out the insides with a spoon. Chop roughly with a large knife, then turn into a shallow dish and mash with a fork. (On no account use a food processor, as the purée should not be too smooth.) Mash in the chopped garlic, season, then add the oil and lemon juice. Finally, beat in the yoghurt and chill for a couple of hours before serving. Serves 3 as a first course, with warm pitta bread, or 4 with one or two other dishes.

Variation:
While the aubergines are baking, grill 1 green pepper and 1-2 beefsteak tomatoes, turning them constantly until the skins have charred evenly all over (or, stick on skewers and lay over a gas flame). Once they are cool enough to handle, skin and chop them, then add to the purée with the garlic. Serves 4.

Asparagus and Egg Salad

This excellent recipe, which I have slightly adapted, comes from one of my favourite cookbooks on food from the Caucasus, called – rather misleadingly – *The Best Foods of Russia*, by Sonia Uvezian.

700 g/1½ lbs asparagus, tender parts only

yoghurt sauce:
1 large clove garlic
1.25 ml/¼ tsp sea salt
300 ml/½ pt yoghurt

garnish:
1 hard-boiled egg, chopped
1 tblsp chopped chives

Use ½ - ⅔ of the asparagus stalks, wash and drain them, then cook in lightly salted boiling water until tender. Drain well, then lay them neatly piled up on a flat dish. Make the sauce: crush the garlic and mash with the salt, then add the yoghurt and beat well. When the asparagus has cooled, spoon the sauce over, then scatter the hard-boiled egg over the top. Finally, sprinkle the whole thing with chopped chives. Serve soon after making, if possible while the asparagus is still just warm. Serves 4.

Yoghurt Picnic Sauce

This is a wonderfully versatile sauce, ideal for picnics, since a whole meal can be built around it. Meatballs, fishcakes, grilled sausages, shellfish, new potatoes cooked in their skins, hard-boiled eggs, cherry tomatoes, celery stalks, raw carrots, and pitta bread all go well with this.
Mix equal parts yoghurt, *tahini*, and homemade mayonnaise. Thin with half a part lemon juice, and chill.

Lentil and Spinach Soup

This is an example of a truly successful combination of flavours, where the lentils and the spinach seem to merge totally, forming a completely new taste.

175 g/6 oz green or brown lentils
sea salt
225 g/8 oz spinach, sliced
black pepper
1 medium onion, chopped
30 ml/2 tblsps light olive oil
2 cloves garlic, chopped
225 g/8 oz Greek yoghurt
a little milk, or buttermilk
juice of ½ a lemon

Wash and drain the lentils, then put them in a pan with 1 litre/1¾ pts cold water and bring slowly to the boil. Cover and cook gently until almost tender, about 35 mins, adding sea salt towards the end. Wash and drain the spinach, then cut it across in 2.5 cm/1 in slices. Add to the lentils when their time is up, and cook for another 10-15 mins until both are soft, adding more sea salt and pepper.

Cook the chopped onion in the oil for 5 mins, then add the garlic and cook for another 5 mins, watching carefully to see they don't burn. When both onion and garlic are soft and golden remove them from the heat. When the lentils are cooked, stir in the fried onions and their oil and leave to cool. Later, purée in the food processor, adding the yoghurt and more seasoning as required. If it seems too thick, thin a little with milk, or buttermilk if you have it. Stir in the lemon juice. Serve chilled or at room temperature. Serves 4-6.

Fresh Cream Dishes

Various combinations of low-fat dairy products with cream make good accompaniments for fruit compôtes, lighter and less rich than cream alone. Unlike soft cream cheeses, these do not have to be drained, but are best made shortly before serving.

1

150 ml/¼ pt yoghurt
150 ml/¼ pt double cream
5 ml/vanilla or castor sugar

Beat the yoghurt until smooth, and the cream until fairly thick. Fold the 2 together, adding sugar if you wish. Made with vanilla sugar, this is good with fresh or dried apricots.

2

As above, with the addition of 1 stiffly beaten egg white, folded in at the last. Sweeten slightly with vanilla sugar to serve with apricots, otherwise I prefer unsweetened.

3

150 ml/¼ pt fromage blanc, or Jockey
150 ml/¼ pt double cream, partly whipped

Fold the 2 together and pile in a bowl. Good with all dishes.

E G G S

Cuban Eggs

175 g/6 oz rice
1 large onion
75 g/3 oz butter
sea salt and black pepper
4 rashers streaky bacon
2 bananas
4 eggs

Cook the rice until just tender in boiling salted water and drain well. Chop the onion and cook slowly in 45 g/1½ oz butter until pale golden. Add the rice and stir around until coated with butter, well mixed and heated. Add sea salt and black pepper. Pour onto a shallow dish and keep hot. Cut the bacon in strips, about 3 to each rasher, and fry until crisp. Drain and lay on the rice. Cut bananas in half horizontally, then in half across. Fry in 15 g/½ oz butter until lightly browned. Lay round the edges of the dish. Fry the eggs in 15 g/½ oz butter. Drain on soft paper and lay in the centre of the rice. Serve with Fresh Tomato Sauce (see below). Serves 4.

Eggs in Green Peppers

4 green peppers
40 g/1½ oz butter
1 medium onion, chopped
150 g/5 oz rice
sea salt and black pepper
4 eggs
Fresh Tomato Sauce

Drop the peppers into a large pan of boiling water and cook for 20-25 mins, until soft. Lift out carefully, drain and cool slightly. Cut off the tops and scoop out the seeds with a teaspoon. Melt the butter and cook the chopped onion until golden. Boil the rice until almost tender, drain and add to the onion. Stir around for a few minutes until well coated with fat. Season well with salt and pepper and continue cooking for a few moments until soft. Spoon into the peppers and break an egg into each. Sprinkle with salt and pepper and bake for about 12 mins at 180°C/350°F/gas mark 4 until the whites are just set. Serve with Fresh Tomato Sauce (see below). Serves 4.

Eggs with Potatoes and Leeks

700 g/1½ lbs potatoes
450 g/1 lb leeks
50 g/2 oz butter
300 ml/½ pt milk
sea salt and black pepper
4 freshly poached eggs

Boil the potatoes. Chop the leeks coarsely and cook gently in the butter in a sauté pan. After 8-10 mins, heat the milk and pour on about half. Cover the pan and cook for another 10 mins or until the leeks are soft. Mash the potatoes and stir in the leeks with their juices, and enough of the remaining milk to make a fairly thin purée. Season well with sea salt and black pepper. Pour into a dish, or divide between 4 plates, and lay the poached eggs on top. Serves 4.

Eggs in Nut Sauce (cold)

6 eggs
heart of a Webb's lettuce
½ cucumber
3 stalks celery
30 ml/2 tblsps lemon juice
30 ml/2 tblsps chopped almonds
150 ml/¼ pt single cream
sea salt and black pepper

Hard-boil the eggs; cool and shell. Chop the heart of the lettuce, the cucumber and the celery. Mix together in a layer on a flat dish. Lay the whole eggs on it. Stir the nuts and the lemon juice into the cream and add salt and pepper to taste. Pour some of the sauce over each egg. Serves 6 as a first course.

Egg Sauce

2 eggs
300 ml/½ pt milk
½ bay leaf
1 slice onion
1 clove
50 g/2 oz butter
22 ml/1½ tblsps flour
a pinch of ground mace or nutmeg
sea salt and black pepper
30 ml/2 tblsps chopped parsley

Hard-boil the eggs and shell. Heat the milk in a small pan with the bay leaf, onion and clove. When simmering point is reached, turn off the heat, cover the pan and leave for 20 mins to flavour the milk. Melt the butter, stir in the flour and cook for 1 min. Discard the bay leaf, onion and clove, and pour on the heated milk. Stir until blended, add a pinch of mace or nutmeg, some sea salt and black pepper and simmer for about 4 mins. Chop the eggs and stir in, adding the chopped parsley also. This sauce can be enriched by the addition of cream but I prefer it without. It is delicious with poached white fish – turbot, halibut, haddock or cod, also with hot boiled bacon, cauliflower or broccoli. Serves 4.

Fresh Tomato Sauce

450 g/1 lb tomatoes, skinned and cut in quarters
½ bunch spring onions, bulbs only, sliced
15 ml/1 tblsp sunflower oil

Put the tomatoes in a food processor and process until reduced to a chunky purée. Cook the sliced spring onions in the oil for 2 mins, then add to the tomatoes and process again briefly, just until reduced to a coarse purée. Tip into a small saucepan and warm gently. This useful sauce may be served warm, at room temperature, or chilled. Serves 4.

Egg Croquettes

300 ml/½ pt milk
½ bay leaf
a pinch of mace, or nutmeg
1 small onion, chopped
25 g/1 oz butter
30 ml/2 tblsps flour
6 eggs, hard-boiled
30 ml/2 tblsps chopped parsley
sea salt and black pepper
flour
1 egg, beaten
dry (white) breadcrumbs
frying oil

Start 1 day, or several hours, in advance. Heat the milk with the bay leaf and mace, or nutmeg. When it reaches the boil, cover the pan and remove from the heat; stand for 15 mins, then discard the bay leaf and reheat gently. Cook the onion gently in the butter until lightly browned, about 4 mins. Then stir in 2 tblsps flour and cook for 1 min, stirring. Pour on the reheated milk and bring to the boil, stirring. Cook gently for 3 mins, then remove from the heat. Chop the hardboiled eggs coarsely and stir into the sauce, with the chopped parsley and plenty of sea salt and black pepper. Turn into a shallow dish which you have rubbed with butter, and chill overnight, or for several hours, in the refrigerator, to firm. When ready to cook, use a dessertspoon to form oval shapes, like eggs, or rolls like large corks. Roll them lightly on a floured board, then dip first in beaten eggs and then in flour. Fry in a 1 inch layer of frying oil until golden brown, turning once. They will take about 2-3 mins on each side. Drain on soft paper before serving, with Tomato and Pepper Sauce (see page 39) Serves 4 as a first course, or 3 as a light main dish, with a green salad.

Catalan Eggs

60 ml/4 tblsps olive oil
½ large Spanish onion, cut in 1 inch squares, then separated into layers
225 g/8 oz red peppers, cut in strips
225 g/8 oz courgettes, cut in ½ inch slices
225 g/8 oz tomatoes, skinned and roughly chopped
sea salt and freshly ground black pepper
3 ml/½ tsp sugar
22 ml/1½ tblsps chopped mint
22 ml/1½ tblsps chopped parsley
4 large eggs, beaten

Heat the oil in a large heavy frying pan with a lid. Fry the onion squares for about 10 mins over a gentle heat, until softened but not browned. Add the red pepper strips and fry for a further 10 mins, stirring from time to time. Add the sliced courgettes and continue to cook for a further 10-15 mins, stirring now and then. Add the chopped tom-atoes, salt and pepper, sugar and chopped herbs. Cover the pan and simmer for 10 mins, then remove from the heat and leave to cool for 3-4 mins. Then add the beaten eggs and stir constantly over a gentle heat for 3-4 mins, until the eggs have set, and slightly thickened the juices. Turn off the heat and stand, covered, for 5 mins before serving. This simple dish is best served straight from the pan, with crusty French bread, as a first course or light main dish. Serves 4 as a first course, or 3 as a main dish, with a green salad.

Avgolemono Soup

This Greek soup must be made with a good chicken stock, thickened with egg yolks and flavoured with lemon juice.

40 g/1½ oz rice
1.2 litres/2 pts good chicken stock
sea salt and white pepper
2 eggs, beaten
juice of 1 large lemon (45-60 ml/3-4 tblsps)

Boil the rice for 10 mins in lightly salted water, then drain. Heat the stock, adding salt and pepper to taste. When it reaches the boil, add the rice and cook for 5 mins. Beat the eggs in a bowl, adding the lemon juice. Pour a ladleful of the boiling soup onto them, continuing to beat, then tip the contents of the bowl back into the pan of chicken soup and cook over a very gentle heat for 3-4 mins, stirring constantly. It must be kept just under boiling point or the eggs will cook in little shreds, instead of (slightly) thickening the soup, like an egg custard. Serves 6.

Eggs Soubises

2 Spanish onions, halved and thickly sliced
40 g/1½ oz butter
30 ml/2 tblsps flour
1.8-2.4 litres/¾ pt chicken stock
150 ml/¼ pt single cream
25 g/1 oz grated Gruyère or Emmental
sea salt and black pepper
1.25 ml/¼ tsp ground mace, or nutmeg
6 hard-boiled eggs, shelled

Cook the sliced onions slowly in the butter, allowing about 10 mins for them to soften without allowing them to brown. Then add the flour, stirring, then add the heated stock and the cream. Stir until it reaches the boil, then simmer gently for 15 mins, half covered. Then add the cheese, stirring till it has melted, with sea salt and black pepper to taste, and the ground mace, or nutmeg. Cut the eggs in halves or quarters and fold gently into the sauce. Pour into a shallow dish which has been well buttered, and brown quickly under the grill. Serves 4-6 as a first course, or 3 as a main dish.

Poached Eggs on Celeriac Purée

1 celeriac, peeled and cut in chunks
350 g/12 oz potatoes, peeled and halved
75 ml/3 fl oz cream
50 g/2 oz butter
sea salt and black pepper
4 eggs, poached
45 ml/3 tblsps grated Gruyère

Put the celeriac in a pan, cover with lightly salted cold water, and bring to the boil. Cook until just tender when pierced with a skewer, then drain very well and dry out over gentle heat. Repeat the process with the potatoes, then push both vegetables through a medium food mill into a clean saucepan. Stir over low heat until well dried out, then add the cream and butter which you have warmed together, gradually, stirring as you do so. Season with plenty of sea salt and black pepper, then tip into a shallow dish and lay the poached eggs on it. Sprinkle the grated cheese over the surface of the dish and brown quickly under the grill. Serves 4 as a first course, or 2 as a light main dish, with a green salad.

Crème Brûlée

1.8-2.4 litres/¾ pt double cream
½ vanilla pod
6 eggs
22 ml/1½ tblsps vanilla sugar, or castor sugar

crust:
castor sugar, or brown sugar

Start a day in advance. Heat the cream with the vanilla pod in a small pan. Stop just before it reaches boiling point and remove the pod. Beat the eggs in a bowl, add the vanilla (or castor) sugar, and pour on the hot cream beating steadily. Stand the bowl over a pan of simmering water, making sure the bottom of the bowl does not touch the water. Stir the custard constantly until it has thickened very slightly, just enough to coat the back of a wooden spoon. This may take 7 or 8 mins. Remove from the heat and pour into a fire-proof dish, or 6 small soufflé (or *oeuf en cocotte*) dishes. Put in the oven for 5-10 mins (depending on the size of the dish), at 150°C/300°F/gas mark 2. Then remove and cool. To make the crust, spread an even layer of castor sugar, or light brown sugar, about ⅟₁₆ in thick over the surface of the cream. Heat the grill to its highest, then place the dish(es) under it, turning them as they cook so that the top browns evenly. Leave to cool, then chill for several hours before serving.

Variation:
A layer of peeled, halved and seeded white grapes can be put in the dish(es) before pouring in the cream.

Soufflé Omelette

4 eggs, separated
30 ml/2 tblsps cold water
5 ml/1 tsp castor sugar
6 g/¼ oz unsalted butter
22 ml/1½ tblsps apricot jam, warmed

Beat the egg yolks with the water, adding the sugar. Beat the whites until stiff, then pour the beaten yolks over them, stirring gently until they are incorporated. Heat an omelette pan and add the butter. Once it is hot, and starting to brown, turn down the heat and pour in the eggs. Let them cook without stirring. Once the surface has become puffy, with little bubbles bursting on the surface, spoon the warmed jam over the omelette. Fold it over and slide onto a dish. Serve at once, with cream. Serves 2.

CORIANDER

Scalloped Crab

25 g/1 oz butter
1 small onion, chopped
25 g/1 oz soft white breadcrumbs
450 g/1 lb white crabmeat, fresh or frozen, flaked
2 eggs, beaten
100 ml/4 fl oz single cream
15 ml/1 tblsp lemon juice
sea salt and black pepper
45 ml/3 tblsps coarsely chopped coriander
30 ml/2 tblsps dry breadcrumbs

Melt the butter in a heavy pan, add the chopped onion and cook for 1 min, then add the breadcrumbs and cook for another 3 mins. Then remove from the heat. Stir the flaked crabmeat into the onion and breadcrumbs, mixing well. Then beat the eggs and cream together and stir into the crab mixture, adding lemon juice and sea salt and black pepper to taste. Finally, stir in the chopped coriander and turn into a shallow gratin dish (a round china dish with crinkled edges works well; it should be about 20.5 cm/8 ins wide). Sprinkle the dry breadcrumbs over the top and bake for 30 mins at 180°C/350°F/gas mark 4. Serves 4, with a green salad and possibly one of tomatoes also.
Crab cakes are made with the same basic mixture; but in a slightly drier form, with one beaten egg, and 30 ml/2 tblsps cream. After mixing, chill overnight. Form into cakes about 7.5 by 2.5 cm/3 by 1 ins. Dip them in 1 egg beaten with 15 ml/1 tblsp milk, then in 25 g/1 oz dry breadcrumbs. Shallow fry them for 4-5 mins on each side in butter and oil. Makes about 6 cakes. Serve with Salsa (see page 73). Serves 3-4.

Ceviche

An unusual *ceviche* can be made in the months after Christmas, when the bitter Seville oranges come into the shops. A firm white fish like bass can be substituted for the scallops.

8 large scallops (or 450 g/1lb bass fillet) and 4 shells
150 ml/¼ pt fresh lime or lemon juice
150 ml/¼ pt bitter orange juice (when bitter oranges are not available, use equal parts lime or lemon juice and orange juice)
15 ml/1 tblsp finely chopped onion
1 green chilli, seeded and finely chopped
22 ml/1½ tblsps chopped coriander
15 ml/1 tblsp sunflower oil

Wash the scallops, discarding the orange tongues. Cut them in round slices horizontally, about 1 cm/½ in thick. (If using bass fillets, skin and cut in 1 cm/½ in cubes.) Put in a bowl and pour over the fruit juices. Stand overnight in the refrigerator, covered with clingfilm. Shortly before serving, drain off the juice and stir in the chopped onion, chilli, coriander, and oil. Spoon on scallop shells to serve. Serves 4 as a first course.

Spiced Lentils with Coriander

175 g/6 oz brown lentils
100 g/4 oz small green lentils
2.5 ml/½ tsp black peppercorns
2.5 ml/½ tsp black mustard seeds
2.5 ml/½ tsp sea salt
45 ml/3 tblsps olive oil
2 bunches large spring onions, sliced
2 cloves garlic, finely chopped
2.5 ml/½ tsp ground coriander
2 pieces root ginger, 4 cm/1½ ins square
30 ml/2 tblsps chopped coriander
zest of 1 lime
juice of 2 limes

Cook the lentils as usual, separately, until tender but not mushy, then set aside. Crush the peppercorns, mustard seeds and salt in a mortar. Heat the olive oil in a heavy pan and cook half the sliced spring onions until they start to colour, then add the chopped garlic and cook for another 1 min. Then add the crushed spices and the ground coriander and cook gently for another 3 mins. Then drain the lentils, reserving their stock, and add them to the pan. Cook gently for 5 mins, stirring now and then. If the mixture seems dry, moisten with a little lentil stock, but this probably won't be necessary, in which case the lentil stock can be used for soup. Then crush the ginger in a garlic press and stir the juice into the lentils. (If you don't have a garlic press, the ginger can be finely chopped and added with the garlic.) Remove the pan from the heat and leave

to cool for 30 mins, then stir in the remaining sliced spring onions and the coriander, keeping back a little of each as a garnish. Lastly, mix in the finely chopped zest of 1 lime and the juice of 2. Just before serving, turn into a serving dish and scatter the reserved spring onions and coriander over the top. This delicious dish is best served warm, or at room temperature. It goes with almost everything: game, duck, smoked meat, fish, hard-boiled eggs, rice, and vegetables. Serves 4-5, but can easily be made in double or even treble quantities.

Warm Pasta Salad with Coriander

1 medium aubergine
1 yellow pepper
1 beefsteak tomato, skinned
60 ml/4 tblsps olive oil
30 ml/2 tblsps lemon juice
350 g/12 oz thin egg noodles
sea salt and black pepper
45 ml/3 tblsps roughly chopped coriander

Bake the aubergine for 50 mins, lying on the bars of the oven at 180°C/350°F/gas mark 4, turning it over from time to time. Then remove from the oven and leave for a little to cool. Grill the pepper slowly, turning often, until the skin is charred and blackened. Allow to cool slightly. When the aubergine is cool enough to handle, cut it in half lengthwise and scoop out the interior. Chop it with a large knife, or mash it with a fork. Skin the pepper and dice it. Take large thin slices from the skinned tomato until you have cut off all the outer layer; discard the centre with juice and seeds. Dice the outer flesh, like the pepper. Mix the vegetables together, adding olive oil and lemon juice. Then cook the pasta as usual and drain. Turn into a large bowl. Mix with the sauce, adding salt and pepper and 30 ml/2 tblsps chopped coriander. Turn into a serving dish and scatter the reserved coriander over the top. Serves 4.

Steak au Coriander

This is a variant on steak *au poivre.*

15 ml/1 tblsp whole coriander seeds
5 ml/1 tsp black peppercorns
7 ml/1½ tblsp black mustard seeds
5 ml/1 tsp sea salt
2 sirloin steaks
12 g/½ oz butter
15 ml/1 tblsp sunflower oil

Put the coriander seeds in a mortar with the peppercorns, mustard seeds and sea salt. Crush them all together roughly, then use to coat the steaks on each side. Leave for 1 hour, then heat the butter and oil in a heavy frying pan and fry the steaks briefly on each side. Serve with Salsa, (see below) in a small bowl, and a green salad. Serves 2.

Coriander Pesto

This is a version of the famous Ligurian sauce using coriander instead of basil. It can be made either in a mortar or in a food processor.

450 ml/³/4 pt coriander leaves; loosely packed
1 large clove garlic, roughly crushed
60 ml/4 tblsps pine kernels
175 ml/6 fl oz extra virgin olive oil

If using a mortar, chop the coriander leaves roughly by hand then pound them in the mortar. When all are crushed, add the garlic and pound again. Then add the pine kernels and continue to pound. Lastly, add the olive oil drop by drop, as if making a mayonnaise, stirring with a wooden spoon. When all is absorbed, the sauce is ready. It may be served in the mortar, or in a bowl. If making in a food processor, simply process the coriander leaves, garlic and pine kernels all together until reduced to a fine hash. Then start to add the oil drop by drop through the lid, while continuing to process. This sauce is excellent with freshly boiled vegetables which are still warm, boiled new potatoes in their skins, grilled or poached fish, cold poached chicken, or added to minestrone.

Coriander Butter

75 g/3 oz butter
45 ml/3 tblsps chopped coriander
1 clove garlic, crushed (optional)
15 ml/1 tblsp lemon juice
sea salt and black pepper

Cream the butter in a mortar, or in a food processor, adding coriander, garlic (if used), lemon juice, and salt and black pepper to taste. Wrap in clingfilm and chill for 20-30 mins, until firm. Then form into an even roll about 3 cm/1¼ ins wide and 0.8 cm/⅛ in thick. Excellent with grilled steaks or hamburgers, grilled tomatoes or mushrooms. Served with grilled fish, it is better made without the garlic. Can be stored in the freezer.

Corn Soup

600 ml/1 pt chicken stock
4 ears corn, cut off the cob,
or 450 g/1 lb frozen corn
40 g/1½ oz butter
1 bunch spring onions, sliced
1-2 green chillies, finely chopped
7 ml/½ tblsp flour
sea salt and black pepper
150 ml/¼ pt single cream
37 ml/2½ tblsps chopped coriander

Heat the stock, add the corn, and bring to the boil. (If using frozen corn, thaw it first.) Cook for about 4-5 mins, or until tender. (This will be less in summertime, if it is homegrown and fresh.) Then set aside to cool slightly. Pour into the processor, and process briefly, without attempting to make it smooth.
Heat the butter in a large saucepan and cook the sliced spring onions, adding the minced chilli(es) after 1 min. Cook gently, stirring, for 2-3 mins, then add the flour and cook for another min or two. Then pour on the processed corn and stock and bring to simmering point. Cook gently for 2 mins, adding sea salt and black pepper to taste. Then lower the heat and add the cream. Reheat, without allowing it to boil, then pour into a soup tureen and stir in the chopped coriander. Serves 4.

Salsa

2 ripe beefsteak tomatoes, or 4 regular ones
1 small onion, finely chopped
2 green chillies, very finely chopped
22 ml/1½ tblsps finely chopped coriander
a pinch of sea salt
15 ml/ 1 tblsp lemon juice

Cut the (unskinned) tomatoes in quarters and remove the central core, then chop quite finely. Mix with the chopped onion. Slit the chillies, scraping out the seeds. Chop very finely and add to the tomatoes with the chopped coriander, salt and lemon juice. Rest for 30 mins before serving. This Mexican sauce is delicious served with dry fried foods like croquettes and fritters, fried fish and fish cakes, grilled steaks and sliced avocados.

Guacamole

This wonderful Mexican dish is made with the same ingredients as Salsa (see above), with 2 mashed avocados added at the last moment. Make the Salsa as above, then cover with clingfilm and leave for 1-2 hours. Just before serving, mash the avocados roughly with a fork and stir into the Salsa. Serves 4 as a first course, or 6 as a dip with tortilla chips.

Courgette and Coriander Purée

2 bunches large spring onions, bulbs only, sliced
50 g/2 oz butter
700 g/1½ lbs courgettes, unpeeled, roughly chopped
1 large bunch coriander, leaves only, roughly chopped (40 g/1½ oz)
450 ml/¾ pt good chicken stock; heated
50 g/2 oz rice
sea salt and black pepper
100 ml/4 fl oz double cream

Cook the spring onions in the butter for 2 mins, then add the courgettes and coriander. Cook all together for 5 mins, stirring now and then, and add the heated stock. Bring to the boil, add the rice, and cook for 20 mins, half covered, adding salt and pepper to taste. Cool slightly, drain off any remaining stock, and put the contents of the pan in a food processor. Blend thoroughly, adding the cream, and extra salt and pepper as needed. Reheat, and serve with veal escalopes, roast pork or chicken. This purée has a subtle flavour, and needs no other vegetable. It also makes a good base for poached or soft-boiled eggs, and freezes well. Serves 6.

Cold Curried Soup

30 ml/2 tblsps sunflower oil
2 shallots, finely chopped
1 cm/½ in square of root ginger, finely chopped
1 clove garlic, finely chopped
5 ml/1 tsp curry powder
2.5 ml/½ tsp ground coriander
15 ml/1 tblsp flour
900 ml/1½ pt chicken stock
30 ml/2 tblsps lemon juice
150 ml/¼ pt single cream
sea salt and black pepper
30 ml/2 tblsps chopped coriander

Heat the oil in a heavy pan and cook the chopped shallots gently for a couple of mins, then add the ginger and garlic. Cook for another 2 mins, then add the curry powder, ground coriander and flour. Cook gently, stirring, for 1 min then add the heated stock. Bring to the boil, stirring, then lower the heat and simmer for 4 mins. Add lemon juice and cream and season to taste with sea salt and black pepper. Tip into a large bowl and stand in a sink half full of very cold water. Stir now and then, to prevent a skin forming, while it cools. When it has cooled to room temperature, put in the refrigerator for several hours, or overnight. The next day process in a food processor, then serve, chilled, in cups or bowls, sprinkled with chopped coriander. Serves 4.

Coriander Chutney

900 g/2 lb cooking apples, peeled, cored and chopped
450 g/1 lb onions, coarsely chopped
2 cloves garlic finely chopped or crushed
1 green pepper, chopped
1 red pepper, chopped
900 ml/1½ pt red wine vinegar
450 g/1 lb brown muscovado sugar
7.5 ml/½ tblsp coriander seeds
6 allspice berries
6 black peppercorns
15 ml/1 tblsp sea salt

50 g/2 oz root ginger, bruised
60 ml/4 tblsps chopped coriander
30 ml/2 tblsps chopped mint

Put the chopped fruit and vegetables in a heavy pan, add the vinegar and bring to the boil. Simmer for about 30 mins, until soft. Then add the brown sugar, coriander, allspice and peppercorns, sea salt and whole bruised ginger tied in a small piece of muslin. Reheat gently until the sugar has melted, then simmer until thick; this may take up to 1 hour. When it is done, remove from the heat and stir in the chopped herbs. Spoon into hot sterilized jars and seal. Fills two 5 kg/11 lb jars.

DAIRY FOOD

Cold Carrot Soup

350 g/12 oz carrots, sliced
25 g/1 oz butter
350 g/12 oz tomatoes, skinned and chopped
450 ml/³/4 pt chicken stock
sea salt and black pepper
2.5 ml/¹/2 tsp sugar
450 ml/³/4 pt buttermilk
22 ml/1¹/2 tblsps chopped parsley

Cook the carrots gently in the butter, adding the chopped tomatoes after 2 mins. Cook all together for another 3 mins, then add the heated stock, sea salt, black pepper, and sugar. Cover and simmer gently for 35-40 mins, until quite soft. Cool, then put in a food processor, adding the buttermilk. When blended, chill and serve cold, sprinkled with parsley. Serves 6.

Yoghurt

900 ml/1¹/2 pts long-life milk
30 ml/2 tblsps yoghurt

Heat the milk to boiling point, then cool to between 38-48°C/100-120°F so that you can keep your little finger in it without pain while you count up to ten. Stir in the yoghurt, using one that you like, for it will give its flavour to your yoghurt also. Pour into a wide-mouthed Thermos jar which has been rinsed out with hot water, cover closely, and stand for 8 hours, by which time it should have set to a firm yoghurt. Turn into a bowl and chill in the refrigerator. The use of a Thermos makes the finding of a place at exactly the right temperature unnecessary. I find the long-life milk gives a firmer yoghurt with less chance of failure than ordinary milk; if using fresh milk, I usually add 60-75 ml/4-5 tblsps instant dried milk to thicken it, while it is cooling and before stirring in the yoghurt. This gives a different consistency which some people may prefer.

Cream Cheese

600 ml/1 pt single cream
300 ml/¹/2 pt soured cream
15 ml/1 tblsp yoghurt, or buttermilk

Heat the 2 creams together until about 38°C/100°F, just over blood heat. Remove from the heat and stir in the yoghurt or buttermilk. Cover and stand in a warm place, as if making yoghurt, for 8-10 hours, or overnight. Next day, spoon the curds into muslin as for making Labneh (see below), and leave to drain for 2 hours. Then place in a mould for another 2 hours, before turning out. This makes a rich creamy cheese with a slightly tart flavour, good for serving either with fresh berries, or with water biscuits and a fruit jelly such as quince or medlar. Serves 4.

Buttermilk Cheese

900 ml/1¹/2 pts buttermilk

Heat gently until approximately 38°C/100°F (just over blood heat). Then tip into muslin, exactly as for making Labneh (see below), and drain for 2 hours. Then untie the muslin bag and place in a round mould, made by taking the bottom out of a round tin – a 450 g/1 lb coffee tin for example. Stand on a bamboo mat, or other form of draining surface, for another 2-3 hours in a cool place, or in the refrigerator. This allows it to drain further, and to take on the shape of the mould. Later, turn out of its muslin onto a flat plate. Serve, either with biscuits, sea salt and black pepper or with sugar and soft fruit. Alternatively, cover with a thick layer of coarsely chopped fresh herbs: parsley, dill, chervil and/or tarragon. Serves 4.

Labneh

900 ml/1¹/2 pts firm yoghurt
15 ml/1 tblsp sesame seeds
15 ml/1 tblsp dried wild thyme
a little olive oil

Have a strainer lined with muslin standing in a bowl; tip the yoghurt into it, and tie the muslin with string to form a bag, leaving long ends. Place the bowl under a chair with a cane seat, and tie the ends of the string through the cane, so that the muslin bag is suspended over the bowl. Remove the strainer and leave to drip overnight. Alternatively, tie the bag to the taps over the kitchen sink. Next day, turn out the drained yoghurt onto a dish. Toast the sesame seeds in a dry frying pan, turning them over and over with a spatula until they are lightly coloured. Tip into a mortar, and add the wild thyme. Pound together until roughly crushed, then tip into a small bowl and serve with the Labneh and a little jug of olive oil. Each

person helps himself to the cheese, sprinkles it with the herb mixture, and dribbles a little olive oil over it. (Alternatively, the little cheese may be coated with the thyme and sesame seeds). Serves 4.
In the Lebanon, this is served for breakfast, but is equally good for lunch. I made a delicious yoghurt cheese recently, using goats' milk yoghurt from Neal's Yard Dairy. I coated the finished cheese with chopped tarragon leaves.

Caramel Blancmange

50 g/2 oz sugar
30 ml/2 tblsps water
600 ml/1 pt milk
50 g/2 oz cornflour

Put the sugar in a heavy pan with the water and heat slowly, watching carefully to see that it doesn't burn. At the same time, heat 150 ml/¹/4 pt of the milk almost to boiling point, and when the caramel has turned a pale golden, pour on the very hot milk gradually, stirring hard. The two substances should be as near the same temperature as possible, or they will not blend. If they refuse to amalgamate, simply pour off into a bowl and leave to cool. Mix the cornflour to a paste with 150 mi/¹/4 pt of the remaining milk and beat well to mix. Heat gently until it thickens and boils, stirring constantly to prevent lumps forming. Pour into a mould that has been rinsed with cold water, and leave to set. (If using an elaborate china mould, it is advisable to brush it first with a tasteless oil.) Leave overnight to set, then turn out to serve. Serves 4-5.

Crème Caramel

caramel:
75 g/3 oz sugar
60 ml/4 tblsps water

crème:
600 ml/1 pt milk
¹/4 vanilla pod
45 ml/3 tblsps castor sugar
4 eggs

Heat the sugar together with the water in a heavy pan until it forms a light golden syrup. Pour quickly into a soufflé dish, and turn it round and round so that it is evenly coated with caramel. Put the milk in a pan with the vanilla pod, bring slowly to boiling point, then remove from the heat. Stand for 15 mins, then bring back to the boil and remove the pod. Add the sugar and stir until it has melted. Cool in a sink half full of cold water until it is lukewarm. Beat the eggs thoroughly in a large bowl, and stir in the milk. Pour into the caramel-lined dish, and bake for 40 mins at 150°C/300°F/gas mark 2, standing in a roasting tin half full of water. Cool, then chill before serving. Turn out to serve. Serves 4.

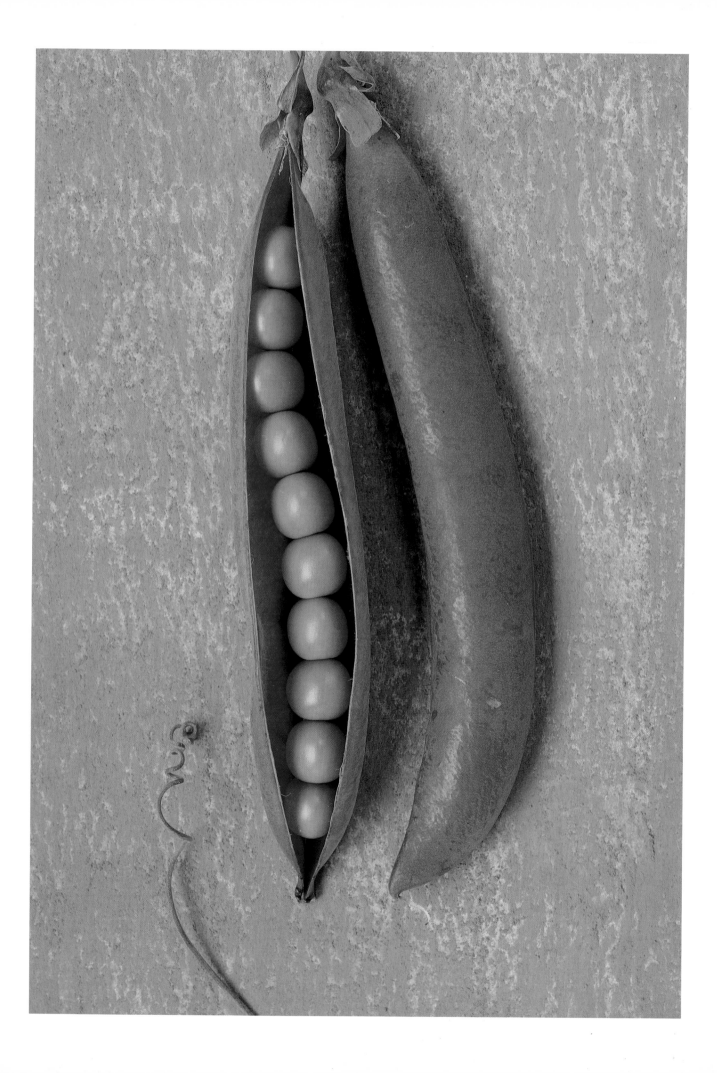

May

Fresh Pea Soup

Mangetout Soup

Oeufs St Germain

Tartlets of Peas

Couscous with Green Peas

Green Pea Moulds

Mixed Green Salad

Risi e Bisi

Fish Terrine with Purée of Green Peas

Green Pea Timbale with Tomato Sauce

Green Pea Sandwiches

Kipper Pâté

Smokie Pâté

Smoked Salmon Rolls with Mackerel Pâté

Baked Smoked Haddock

Smoked Haddock with Eggs

Scrambled Eggs with Smoked Salmon

Horseradish and Watercress Sauce

Marinated Kipper Fillets

Smoked Haddock Mousse

Smoked Haddock Soufflé

Game Birds Wrapped in Cabbage Leaves

Leek (or Mushroom) Pudding

Steamed Vegetables in Cabbage Leaf

Vegetable Couscous

Gentleman's Pudding

Steamed Scallops

Stuffed Cabbage Leaves (cold)

Chervil Soup with Dumplings

Tarragon Soufflé

Stuffed Eggs

Eggs in Dill Sauce

Onion Purée with Sage

Fried Potatoes with Rosemary

Vegetable Marrow with Mint

Sage and Apple Sauce

Dill Sauce with Mustard

Mint Chutney

Grapefruit and Mint Sorbet

Ginger and Watercress Consommé

Watercress Frittata

Purslane Salad

Peas are thought to have originated in western Asia, where they grew wild. This was the field pea, *Pisum arvensis*, rather than the garden pea we know today. Field peas are still grown for drying and for feeding livestock. They were well known in the ancient world and have been found in Swiss lake dwellings dating from the Bronze Age. Peas were used by the ancient Greeks, Romans, Persians and Chinese. They were probably brought to Britain by the Romans around the birth of Christ.

The garden pea, *Pisum sativum*, was developed by Italian gardeners in the sixteenth century. It reached France in 1660, when Audiger, author of *La Maison Reglée*, brought green peas back with him from Genoa, and presented them to Louis XIV at Versailles. They instantly became fashionable, though they were expensive since they had to be imported from Italy. Thirty years later they were being grown in France, and their popularity had not abated. Mme de Maintenon, writing to the Cardinal de Noailles in 1696, tells him: 'At court, the chapter of peas continues. Impatience to eat them, pleasure in having eaten them, and joy in the knowledge that we would soon be eating them again, formed the subject of discussion among our princes during the last four days. Some ladies, having supped, and supped well with the King, go home, and at the risk of being made ill, eat more green peas. They are the fashion and the passion of the day.'

Garden peas seem to have reached England earlier than France, for they are mentioned in cookery manuscripts dating back to Elizabethan times. At first they were imported from Holland, but by the middle of the seventeenth century they were being cultivated in England. The field pea, called grey or blue peas at that time, retained its popularity, as shown by such English dishes as pease pudding and pea soup. The garden pea has many different subspecies. In W Robinson's *The Vegetable Garden*, first published in 1905, there are no less than 197 varieties of pea listed. Some, called marrowfat, have large peas with wrinkled skins, while others, like the French *petits pois*, are small and tender. Yet another, *Pisum sativum var. macrocarpum*, has pods without an inner lining, so that they can be eaten in their entirety, when the peas have barely formed. This is the mangetout, sugar or snow pea, which has been much used in Chinese cookery, and has become very popular in Europe during the last fifteen years. The asparagus pea does not belong to the pea family, nor does the chick pea.

Green peas have always been treated rather differently in France and England. In France, they are never served as they are here: simply boiled and drained, with butter. The French tend to stew them gently in butter, with scraps of raw ham, small onions, and strips of lettuce. When Elizabeth David's *Summer Cooking* came out, I remember reading her assessment of the different ways of cooking duck with peas. 'A *caneton aux petits pois* and a duckling with green peas are not so alike as they sound. The two dishes demonstrate one of the fundamental differences between the cooking of France and England. The English dish consists of a roast duckling served with boiled and buttered green peas, and there the matter ends. In the French version, the peas are added to the duck while it is still cooking, with little pieces of smoked bacon and small onions, good stock is added, all is simmered together sufficiently long for the peas to absorb the stock and some of the fat from the duck.'

Here I cannot help disagreeing with the implication that the French method is superior, for I actually prefer the English version, where the different foods are cooked separately and only meet, as it were, for the first time on the plate. The green pea has such a delicate flavour that it quickly becomes overshadowed by the French garnishes, the bacon, onions and stock, to say nothing of the duck.

The great sadness is that since the freezing industry took over most of our pea harvest, it has become very hard to buy young green peas. They should be in season from June till September, yet I rarely see them for more than a couple of weeks in the shops, and seldom at their best. The frozen pea has distorted our image of what a pea ought to be, for even freshly picked peas are never as soft and delicate and bright emerald green as frozen *petits pois*; the only thing these lack is flavour.

Smoking was originally a method of preserving food, usually pork or fish, during the winter months. Over the past forty years the process has changed radically. For one thing, the traditional smokery was a home-based operation which did not lend itself to expansion; for another, the mechanization of the wood industry made finding suitable fuel an acute problem. The smokeries had grown up side by side with the ship-building yards and carpentry shops, which kept them supplied with oak sawdust, an ideal fuel for smoking. With the centralization of the wood industry the sawdusts became mixed, and were no longer so suitable for smoking. This caused the emphasis to change, and smoke itself became of secondary importance. It was discovered that the effects of smoke could be achieved more simply by other means. The preservation was more easily effected by refrigeration, the colouring by dyes, and the flavour by brief periods of curing and smoking, or by merely painting the food with liquid 'smoke flavour', a concentrate of distilled smoke. The result was inevitably a different article, for it had been smoke-flavoured rather than smoke-cured.

Defendants of modern methods claim that the stronger flavours of traditionally smoked fish would not appeal to the modern palate, which has become accustomed to milder flavours. This is true up to a point; certainly so in extreme cases like the red herring, which was so strongly cured and smoked that it could be kept from one season to the next without benefit of refrigeration.

There are many small smokeries dotted around the UK, some operating commercially, others privately. Some farmers have started smoking their own products; some fishermen do the same. Some use the electrical equipment recommended by the Ministry of Agriculture, Fisheries and Food; others have developed their own methods. I spent a most instructive day some years ago with the late Mr Pinney of the Butley-Orford Oysterage: a fascinating man who had made a prolonged study of smoking, and who had worked out his own method of producing traditional results. Mr Pinney died in 1989, but his widow Mathilde and his son William still carry on the business. Other smokers, like Hugh Forestier-Walker of Minola Smoked Products, in Gloucestershire, learnt their trade from Mr Pinney, and use his methods with great success.

Mr Pinney was a remarkable man, with a gift for lateral thinking. Once, on holiday in Portugal, he found time lying heavy on his hands and proceeded to build a portable smokehouse on the beach. He then set about smoking the local seafood and selling it to the nearest hotel. In the sixties, faced with the difficulty of finding an adequate supply of oak sawdust, Mr Pinney took the nearest equivalent in the form of small oak logs, and set about inventing a stove which would burn them in such a way as to produce smoke without much heat.

Smoking by traditional methods is a fairly primitive process, except for the smoke production which is very precise. When wood is heated, a succession of different vapours are released, each at a different temperature. The most suitable vapours for smoking are those released at a low heat, as they get progressively more acid. While the first smoke is sweet, and hazy blue in colour, the smoke which is produced at higher temperatures is acrid, rank and yellowish grey in colour.

The main virtue of oak sawdust as a fuel is that it will not burn naturally at a high temperature, because the minute particles restrict the oxygen intake. Most modern smoking equipment subjects the sawdust to a forced draught, thus raising the temperature. In some cases, moisture is added, thus introducing steam which had no place in the original smoking process. Mr Pinney was doubtful about both these refinements, and proceeded to develop his own stove, which by a degree of oxygen control allowed him to retain carbon dioxide around the unburnt logs, causing them to smoke without allowing them to burn. In this way the wood was converted into charcoal, which was then used for the second process.

There are two stages in smoking: cold-smoking and hot-smoking. Most fish undergo both processes, except salmon and kippers which are cold-smoked only. Many commercial smokeries refrigerate their fish after smoking, but to Mr Pinney this was unthinkable because it arrests the natural process of maturation.

Before smoking, the food is subjected to the preliminary process of curing, or salting. This is done mainly by salt, either dry or in brine. Sugar is added, and other flavourings such as fennel, cloves, or coriander if desired. Mr Pinney used only salt and sugar, but many smokers have their own secret recipes for cures. Both salt and brine have their respective merits: dry salt preserves the food better, while brine causes less weight loss, and imparts a nice sheen to the surface.

Mr Pinney's smokehouses were built like sentry-boxes, standing back to back. The salmon were first split and packed in dry salt for eight hours. Then they were rinsed and hung on hooks inside the smokehouse, where they were then cold-smoked for twenty-four hours. They were ready for eating a few days after cooling.

Until recent times, steaming played little part in the English kitchen. Even the steamed puddings which seem a part of our heritage were not steamed at all until the Victorian era, but boiled in a cloth. In my youth, steamed food was considered fit only for invalids or for babies. I remember steaming fillets of Dover sole in a spoonful of milk between two enamel plates laid over a pan of boiling water, for convalescents and tiny children. I found them delicious: 'very delicate', as Antonio Carluccio says when I present him with some bland English dish, his innate courtesy triumphing over his preference for robust Mediterranean flavours...

Twenty years ago I had just one steamer in my kitchen. It was a beautiful object, a French potato steamer in glazed china, a rich, glossy brown like a ripe chestnut, bought from Elizabeth David's shop in the happy days when she still owned it, and often worked in it herself: a challenging presence, enough to keep lazy shoppers on their toes.

It never occurred to me to use my potato steamer for anything other than potatoes. For we were very hidebound in those days, when kitchen practice was still regulated by strict rules of conduct. It was not until much later that things became free and easy in the kitchen, as the amateurs took over and Jack Lemmon drained spaghetti on his tennis racket.

Things changed in 1977 with the publication of Michel Guèrard's *Cuisine Minceur*, when steaming suddenly became fashionable. For it was perfectly suited to the precepts of healthy cooking since it used no fats of any kind and the minimum of nutrients was lost. It is also well suited to *haute cuisine* with its emphasis on presentation, for fragile foods are left intact without being buffeted about by boiling water. Yet its disadvantages must not be forgotten, for steaming is an art that requires full attention. Food that has been overcooked by steam is the worst thing imaginable: devoid of flavour, colour and texture.

Steaming is carried out, for the most part, over plain, unsalted water. It is only when cooking absorbent food such as rice or couscous that there is much point in using stock. Nor is there any sense in salting the water, for the salt is not transformed into steam. Indeed, salt is hardly used in steaming, which worries me not at all since I use very little now and prefer to add it at the table. In most cases, the food to be steamed is laid on a perforated surface and cooked literally surrounded by steam. With foods like fish, chicken, game or meat, it may be best to lay them on a plate to catch the juices that exude as they cook, but there must be room for the steam to rise around the edges of the plate. With fragile food like fish, it is sometimes helpful to wrap it in a cloth for easy lifting in and out. Steaming is a very quick method of cooking, just as fast as boiling, and most foods cook in a matter of minutes. Those that require long cooking, like suet puddings, are not allowed to come into contact with the steam for they would become waterlogged. In fact, they are rarely cooked 'in steam' at all, since few domestic steamers are tall enough to accommodate a pudding basin. Instead, they are cooked inside lidded saucepans, with boiling water coming halfway up the sides of the bowl, which is in its turn closely covered.

Steaming has always been widely used in the East, especially in China, where it is used to cook meat, fish, vegetables, rice and even bread. According to Ken Lo, one of the reasons steaming has always been popular in China is economic. Since vast amounts of rice are always on the boil in the average Chinese kitchen, it costs no more to cook other foods in the steam thus generated. This is especially true in the case of *congee*, the rice porridge which uses five times its weight in water, and takes up to two hours to cook. This accounts for the tiers of wicker baskets that are used in the home, and the perforated metal trays used in the restaurants.

There are two methods of steaming used in China: fast steaming, as described above, where the food cooks rapidly in the steam; and slow steaming, where the food is enclosed in the container, like our own steamed puddings, and cooks slowly in heat generated by steam. Today I have four steamers in my kitchen, and would like to acquire a fifth, if I had room to store it. Yet none is essential, and I still cook couscous in a colander suspended over a stockpot, as I have done for years. But for those with the inclination to buy one, there is a wide range of steamers in the shops. Cheapest of all are probably the wicker baskets from Chinese supermarkets, so long as you have a wok to pile them in. If your wok has a lid, you need only buy a very inexpensive metal or wooden rack to lay in it, to support a plate for steaming whole fish. Less satisfactory, though still inexpensive, are the metal expandable steamers shaped like the petals of a flower, for their legs are too short to allow much room for boiling water. Very good value are the large round metal two-tier steamers made in Taiwan.

The earliest herb gardens on record in England were those attached to monasteries during the thirteenth century. These, in their turn, were based on the Roman gardens of many centuries previously, and were made up of formal beds edged with box. Although herbs were already well known to the Druids in pre-Roman times, the Church destroyed all records of their pagan practices, and established itself as the authority on herbs and their uses. During the fourteenth and fifteenth centuries, herb gardens spread to private houses, but were still modelled on those of the monasteries. They were rectangular in shape, and were often enclosed within a thick bank, covered with a carpet of herbs. Inside, herbs grew in profusion, habitually mixed with certain flowers, including gillyflowers (border carnations), roses, lilies, and marigolds.

During the sixteenth century, a fashion spread for knot gardens and mazes, which were already much in vogue in France and Italy. A knot, according to Dr Johnson's dictionary published in 1750, is 'any figure of which the lines intersect each other frequently.' The most usual patterns were geometric, intricate designs of squares, circles, triangles and arcs subtly inter-woven. A few were closer to topiary work, featuring animals, or even heraldic coats of arms. Most of the knot gardens were non representational, and were probably based on designs taken from oriental carpets. The carpets themselves were close to patterns used in ancient Moorish gardens, like that of the Alhambra in Granada, Spain. Here the rigid design had two purposes; the first was visual, in keeping with the Islamic aesthetic which forbids any representation of the human form, thus encouraging the use of pattern in all the visual arts. The second was utilitarian, for the divisions between the straight-edged beds were used for channels of running water, necessary in the dry Arab countries to irrigate the plants.

When similar gardens were introduced into Italy and France, during the late fifteenth century, water was not needed, since there was enough rain to water the plants, and the place of the rivulets was taken by low hedges, borders and paths. The French word for gardens of this sort was *parterre*, and the concept is close to that of a carpet. In order to be seen properly, the knot garden must be viewed from above, so it was usually planned in conjunction with terraces. In England, its popularity continued throughout the seventeenth century, but declined during the eighteenth century, when a move towards more natural planning transformed the English garden, creating a soft-edged effect.

The formal knot garden demands almost daily care during the growing season. Nothing looks worse than a garden of this sort that has been neglected, and many herbs grow at a vigorous rate. In *Richard II*, the Queen compares England to a neglected garden of this sort: 'our sea-walled garden, the whole land, is full of weeds, her fairest flowers choked up, her fruit trees all unpruned, her hedges ruined, her knots disordered, and her wholesome herbs swarming with caterpillars.'

The early knot gardens were planted much more sparsely than our modern gardens. Each knot usually contained just one variety of plant, while the smallest knots were left empty. The design was emphasized by the use of different materials covering the surface of the soil: red and silver sand pebbles of varying colours, chips of coal and even of glass were used to make colour contrasts and in the case of glass, to reflect the light. The lines of the design were usually traced in herbs - germander, thyme and hyssop were often used for this purpose - but sometimes flat stones, boards, slates, or bones of sheep or pigs were used. Low hedges surrounding the beds were made with box lavender, rue or santolina.

The choice of herbs appears to have been made for purely decorative reasons. Herbs had many uses in the large households of Elizabethan and Stuart times: for a start they took the place of vegetables in a diet based mainly on meat, and they were also used for medicinal purposes and for strewing, while the poisonous varieties were used as a defence against pests.

After the decline in popularity of the formal *parterre* style of garden in the eighteenth century, English gardens developed more and more along their own lines, diverging totally from other European countries. The first enthusiasm for landscape gardening, at which the English excelled, led to such refinements as the wild, or woodland garden, which developed during the nineteenth and early twentieth centuries.

Treatment of herb gardens developed in the same way. The intricacies of the knot garden were rarely revived, probably because they demanded such an investment in terms of labour. Another sort of herb garden grew into being: this was the romantic garden, often laid out on a formal plan but loosely planted, to give an effect of carelessness. Such a garden is the herb garden at Sissinghurst, where the herbs appear to grow totally at will, creating an effect of peace and tranquillity.

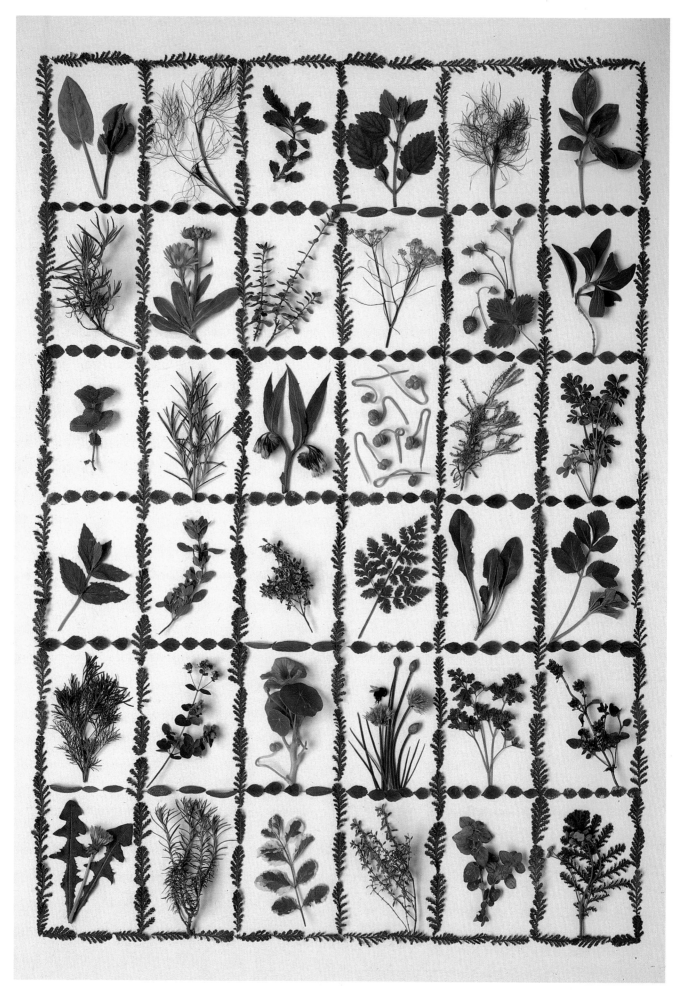

GREEN PEAS

Fresh Pea Soup

450 g/1 lb shelled peas (fresh or frozen)
300 ml/½ pt chicken stock
300 ml/½ pt single cream
sea salt and black pepper
a little lemon juice

Cook the peas as usual, in 200 ml/7 fl oz lightly salted water. When they are soft, do not drain but put them in a food processor with their liquid. Keep back a few whole peas as garnish. Heat the stock and cream together and add to the peas in the processor. When all is smooth, return to the pan and add sea salt and black pepper to taste, and a little lemon juice. Reheat, pour into cups, and serve with a few whole peas in each one. For a cold soup, simply chill for several hours in the refrigerator before serving. Serves 5-6.

Mangetout Soup

225 g/8 oz potatoes, peeled and sliced
900 ml/1½ pts light chicken stock
40 g/1½ oz butter
1 small onion, finely chopped
225 g/8 oz mangetouts, trimmed and cut in 2 or 3 pieces
150 ml/¼ pt single cream
a pinch of sugar (optional)
sea salt and black pepper

Put the potatoes in a pan with the stock. Bring to the boil and simmer for 20 mins, or until soft. Melt the butter in a sauté pan, add the onion and cook gently for 3 mins, then add the peas. Cook altogether, stirring often, for 5 mins, then add to the potatoes. Bring back to simmering point and cook gently for another 5 mins, no longer. Push through a coarse sieve, or food mill. Reheat gently, adding the cream, sugar, if used, and salt and pepper to taste. Serves 6. This soup is also good served chilled.

Oeufs St Germain

1.6 kg/3½ lbs peas in the pod, or
450 g/1 lb shelled peas
300 ml/½ pt good chicken stock
25 g/1 oz butter
30 ml/2 tblsps double cream
sea salt and black pepper
4 eggs

sauce:
12 g/½ oz butter
15 ml/1 tblsps flour
150 ml/¼ pt single cream
45 ml/3 tblsps grated Parmesan
sea salt and black pepper

Cook the shelled peas in the stock until just tender. Drain, reserving the stock. Put the peas in a food processor with half the stock and process until reduced to a purée. Tip the purée into a clean pan and stir in the butter and cream over gentle heat and season to taste. Drop the eggs into boiling salted water and cook for exactly 5 mins, then transfer them to a bowl of cold water; shell and keep warm. Then make the sauce; melt the butter in a clean pan, stir in the flour and cook for 1 min. Then stir in the remaining chicken stock and the single cream and simmer for 4 mins, stirring until smooth. Add the Parmesan, adding sea salt and black pepper to taste. To serve, lay the eggs in shallow individual bowls and spoon the pea purée over them. Dribble a little of the cream sauce over each one. Serves 4.

Tartlets of Peas

pastry:
175 g/6 oz flour
a pinch of salt
75 g/3 oz butter
1 egg yolk

filling:
350 g/12 oz shelled peas, fresh or frozen
12 g/½ oz butter
7.5 ml/1½ tsps flour
150 ml/¼ pt good chicken stock
150 ml/¼ pt single cream
sea salt and black pepper

Make the pastry as usual, using the flour, salt, butter and a little iced water. Wrap in clingfilm and chill for 30 mins, then roll out thinly and line 6 small tins. Prick them here and there with a fork, and line with a small piece of foil weighed down with a few dried beans. Bake for 5 mins at 190°C/375°F/gas mark 5. Then remove the foil and brush the pastry with beaten egg yolk. Replace in the oven for another 5 mins, remove and keep warm.
While the tarts are baking, make the filling. Cook the peas in a little salted boiling water, then drain. Melt the butter in a clean pan, stir in the flour, and cook for 1 min, stirring. Heat the stock and cream together, then add to the roux, stirring until blended. Simmer gently for 3 mins, then add the peas, with sea salt and black pepper to taste. Pour into the pastry cases and serve immediately.

Couscous with Green Peas

225 g/8 oz couscous
900 ml/1½ pts chicken stock
450 g/1 lb shelled or frozen peas
50 g/2 oz butter
sea salt and black pepper

Put the couscous in a bowl and pour 300 ml/½ pt cold water over it. Leave for 10 mins, then heat the chicken stock in the bottom half of a steamer. When it boils, tip the soaked couscous into the top part of the steamer. (If you don't have a proper steamer, use a strainer suspended over a deep pan.) Steam for 40 mins, then turn the couscous into a bowl and break up any lumps that may have formed with a fork. Cook the peas in lightly salted boiling water until just tender, then drain. Mix them with the couscous, adding the butter, cut in small bits, and salt and pepper to taste. Serves 6.

Green Pea Moulds

These little moulds make a good first course, served with a Wild Mushroom Sauce (see page 196), Tomato and Pepper Sauce (see page 39), or Mushroom Sauce (see page 39). You will need some small metal dariole moulds holding about 150 ml/¼ pt each.

450 g/1 lb shelled green peas, fresh or frozen
60 ml/4 tblsps double cream
60 ml/4 tblsps fromage blanc
2 large eggs, separated
salt and freshly ground black pepper
butter, for greasing moulds

Cook the peas briefly, in the minimum of lightly salted water. Drain them, then process briefly in a food processor. Add the cream and *fromage blanc* and process again, then turn the mixture into a bowl. Beat the egg yolks lightly and stir into the mixture, adding salt and pepper to taste. Beat the egg whites and fold into the mixture. Divide between 6 well-buttered dariole moulds. Do not fill them to the brim, as they need a little room to rise. Stand them in a roasting tin half full of hot water, and bake for 35 mins at 180°C/350°F/gas mark 4, until risen and firm. Make the sauce of your choice while they are cooking. To serve, cut a thin slice off the top of each mould to make a flat base, then invert onto individual plates. Spoon the sauce over or around them. Serve immediately. Serves 6.

Mixed Green Salad

1 round lettuce
1 cucumber, peeled
700 g/1½ lbs peas in the pod, or 100 g/4 oz frozen peas
olive oil

dressing:
sea salt and black pepper
2.5 ml/½ tsp sugar
1.25 ml/¼ tsp Dijon mustard
7 ml/½ tblsp white wine vinegar
7 ml/½ tblsp lemon juice
30 ml/2 tblsps olive oil
30 ml/2 tblsps single cream

Wash the lettuce and drain well, using the tender inner leaves only. Cut the peeled cucumber in 5 cm/2 in sections, then divide each one into 9 strips. Shell the peas, if fresh, and cook briefly until just tender. Drain well, then moisten with a little olive oil. Lay the lettuce leaves in a bowl with the strips of cucumber lying on it, then scatter the peas over all. Put the seasonings in a small bowl and mix until blended with the vinegar and lemon juice. Then add the olive oil, and lastly the cream, mixing well until blended. Pour over the dressing at the last moment and toss lightly. Serves 4-6.

Risi e Bisi

The Venetians make this dish in early summer, with the first of the young green peas. It is more moist than a *risotto*, and is eaten in soup plates with a spoon and fork.

1 small onion, chopped
75 g/3 oz butter
50 g/2 oz chopped prosciutto (optional)
900 g/2 lb (unshelled) green peas
225 g/8 oz risotto rice (arborio or superfino), washed
900 ml/1½ pts good chicken stock
sea salt and black pepper
25 g/1 oz freshly grated Parmesan

Cook the chopped onion in 50 g/2 oz butter until it starts to change colour, then add the chopped *prosciutto*, if used. (It is often made with peas alone.) Cook for 2 mins, stirring once or twice, then add the shelled peas. Cook gently for 4 mins, covered, then add the rice and cook for another 2 mins, stirring. Heat the stock and add to the pan. Stir well, add sea salt and black pepper, and cover the pan. Cook for about 15 mins, until the rice and peas are tender and all the stock has been absorbed. Stir once or twice towards the end of the cooking, then at the very last stir in the grated cheese and the remaining 25 g/1 oz butter. Serve immediately. Serves 4 as a first course, or 3 as a light main dish. It needs no other accompaniment.

Fish Terrine with Purée of Green Peas

450 g/1 lb haddock fillet, skinned
2 egg whites, lightly beaten
100 g/4 oz fromage frais
150 ml/¼ pt double cream
5 ml/1 tsp sea salt
freshly ground black pepper
butter

purée of green peas:
225 g/8 oz shelled peas, fresh or frozen
30 ml/2 tblsps double cream
2 eggs, lightly beaten
sea salt and freshly ground black pepper

Chop the haddock fillets coarsely and put them in a food processor. Process until reduced to small pieces, then add the egg whites and process again until blended.

Then add the *fromage frais*, cream, salt and pepper, and process for a third time, until smooth. Turn into a bowl, cover with clingfilm, and chill for 1-2 hours.
Cook the peas briefly in lightly salted boiling water, just until tender. Drain and put in the food processor. Add the cream and process until blended, then add the beaten eggs and process again, adding salt and pepper to taste. Pour into a fireproof bowl and cover with foil.
Butter a loaf tin holding 750 ml/1¼ pt and turn the fish mixture into it. Cover with foil, stand in a baking tin half filled with boiling water side by side with the pea purée in its bowl, and cook for 45 mins in the oven at 180°C/350°F/gas mark 4, or until the terrine is firm when pressed. Unmould to serve. Spread the pea purée over it, and cut in thick slices. Serves 6.

Green Pea Timbale with Tomato Sauce

450 g/1 lb shelled peas, fresh or frozen
60 ml/4 tblsps soft white breadcrumbs
30 ml/2 tblsps milk
50 g/2 oz butter, softened
sea salt and black pepper
3 eggs, separated

sauce:
1 small onion, chopped
25 g/1 oz butter
300 g/12 oz tomatoes, skinned and chopped
sea salt and black pepper
2.5 ml/½ tsp sugar (optional)

Cook the peas as usual, in the minimum of lightly salted boiling water. Drain well and push through a medium food mill. Soak the breadcrumbs in the milk for 4 mins, then squeeze dry and add to the mashed peas. Beat with a wooden spoon to mix, adding the softened butter and sea salt and black pepper to taste. Beat the egg yolks and stir in, then fold in the stiffly beaten egg whites. Turn into a buttered bowl and cover loosely with a piece of foil. Stand the bowl on an upturned saucer inside a saucepan, with boiling water coming halfway up the sides of the bowl. Steam, covered, for 1 hour, replenishing the water as needed.
Cook the chopped onion gently in the butter until golden, then add the chopped tomatoes and stew them slowly for about 8 mins, adding sea salt and black pepper. If the tomatoes are not fully ripe, add a pinch of sugar. The sauce may be pushed through a coarse food mill, or puréed briefly in a processor, or left as it is. In any case, it does not want to be a smooth sauce. To serve, unmould the timbale onto a flat plate, and serve the hot sauce with it, in a bowl. Serves 3-4, as a first course, or 2-3 as a light main dish.

Green Pea Sandwiches

This unusual idea for a sandwich was popular in the 1920s. Make a purée of fresh green peas, adding a pinch of sea salt and black pepper, and use to make sandwiches, with thinly sliced brown or white bread. 200 g/8 oz peas make 3 rounds, or 12 small sandwiches.

SMOKED FISH

Kipper Pâté

1 plump kipper
50 g/2 oz Philadelphia cheese
50 g/2 oz butter
15 ml/1 tblsp lemon juice
black pepper

Cook the kipper as usual (I cover it with boiling water, then leave for 10 mins). Scrape all the flesh away from the skin and bones and weigh. You should have 100-150 g/4-5 oz. Chop it finely, then pound in a mortar; if you have no mortar, it should be pushed through a sieve or food mill. Beat in the cream cheese and butter, cut in small pieces, and add the lemon juice and black pepper to taste. Pile into a small dish and chill in the refrigerator until quite firm. Serve very cold, with wholemeal toast and lemon quarters. Serves 3-4.

Smokie Pâté

1 large smokie
50 g/2 oz Philadelphia cheese
15 ml/1 tblsp soured cream
15 ml/1 tblsp lemon juice
sea salt and black pepper
1 sprig parsley

Take the flesh off the smokie and weigh it. You should have 90-100 g/3½-4 oz. Chop it finely and pound in a mortar or push through a sieve or food mill. Beat in the cheese (I use a German cream cheese called Quark). Continue to beat, adding the soured cream, lemon juice and a little sea salt if needed. Add plenty of black pepper and chill in a small dish until quite firm. Serve with brown toast. Serves 3-4. Garnish with a small sprig of parsley.

Smoked Salmon Rolls with Mackerel Pâté

2 fillets smoked mackerel
50 g/2 oz Philadelphia cheese
15 ml/1 tblsp soured cream
15 ml/1 tblsp lemon juice
black pepper
6-8 small slices smoked salmon

Take the flesh away from the skin and weigh it. You should have 100-150g/4-5 oz. Chop it finely and either pound in a mortar or push through a sieve or food mill. Add the cream cheese and the soured cream, beating with a wooden spoon until all is incorporated smoothly. Add the lemon juice and black pepper to taste. Serve with toast. Serves 3-4.

Take small slices of smoked salmon and roll each one around a spoonful of smoked mackerel pâté. Serve with lemon quarters.

Baked Smoked Haddock

900 g/2 lb smoked haddock
4 large tomatoes
50 g/2 oz butter
150 ml/1/4 pt milk
150 ml/1/4 pt single cream
black pepper
30 ml/2 tblsps chopped parsley

Cut the smoked haddock in large pieces (either whole fish or fillets can be used). Lay in a shallow fireproof dish. Skin the tomatoes and chop them coarsely. Soften briefly in the butter, then pour with their juice over the fish. Heat the milk and cream together and pour over all. Sprinkle with plenty of black pepper and bake for 20 mins at 180°C/350°F/gas mark 4. Sprinkle with chopped parsley before serving. Serve with plain boiled rice and a green salad. Serves 4.

Smoked Haddock with Eggs

2 smoked haddock
300 ml/1/2 pt milk
4 freshly poached eggs
black pepper

Cut each haddock in half and wash well. Put the pieces in a broad pan and pour over the milk. Add about the same amount of water, so that the fish is half covered. Bring to the boil, cover the pan and simmer gently. After 12 mins lift out the fish and drain. Lay on a shallow dish. Place a poached egg carefully on each piece of fish, sprinkle with black pepper, and serve. Alternatively, the fish can be flaked and piled on 4 rounds of hot buttered toast. The eggs are then laid on top of the fish, after sprinkling with black pepper. Serves 4.

Scrambled Eggs with Smoked Salmon

6 eggs
sea salt and black pepper
25 g/1 oz butter
100 g/4 oz smoked salmon trimmings

Beat the eggs, adding salt – only a little – and pepper. Melt the butter in a heavy sauté pan and pour in the eggs. Cook slowly, using a metal spoon to scrape the egg from the bottom as it sets. When the eggs are half cooked, stir in the smoked salmon trimmings which you have cut in small strips. Continue to scrape the scram-bled eggs, folding in the smoked salmon, until nearly set, then pour immediately onto a warm dish and serve. Serves 3.

Horseradish and Watercress Sauce

150 ml/1/2 pt double cream
22 ml/1 1/2 tblsps watercress, leaves only
25 g/1 oz butter
20 ml/1 1/2 tblsps flour
200 ml/7 fl oz fish stock
30 ml/2 tblsps grated horseradish
10 ml/2 tsps Dijon mustard
5 ml/1 tblsp orange juice
sea salt and black pepper

Put the cream and watercress in a food processor and process until the watercress is very finely chopped. Melt the butter in a small pan and stir in the flour. Cook for 1 min, stirring, then remove from the heat and bring to the boil, stirring, then sim-mer gently for 3 mins. Then add the horseradish, mustard and orange juice. Cook for 1 min, then add the watercress and cream. Reheat gently, then pour into a heated sauceboat. Serve with poached smoked haddock. Serves 4.

Marinated Kipper Fillets

3 kippers
1/4 mild Spanish onion, thinly sliced
90 ml/6 tblsps olive oil
30 ml/2 tblsps lemon juice
freshly ground black pepper
15 ml/1 tblsp finely chopped parsley

Start 1 day in advance. Fillet the kippers, lifting the 6 fillets off the bone and away from the skin. Lay the fillets in a shallow dish and scatter the onion rings (or quar-ter rings) over them. Pour the olive oil and lemon juice over all, and sprinkle with freshly ground black pepper. Leave in a cool place, or the bottom of the refrigera-tor, overnight, basting once or twice. Lift the fillets onto a clean dish to serve at room temperature, scattered with a few of the onion slices and a little chopped pars-ley. Serves 4 as a first course, with brown bread and butter.

Smoked Haddock Mousse

2 large smoked haddock
1 onion, sliced
1 carrot, sliced
1 leek, sliced
1 stalk celery, sliced
3 stalks parsley
1 bay leaf
6 black peppercorns
12.5 g/1/2 oz gelatine
30 ml/2 tblsps lemon juice
freshly ground black pepper
a pinch of cayenne
300 ml/1/2 pt double cream

Cut the haddock into quarters. Put the sliced vegetables, herbs and peppercorns in a broad pan with enough water to cover the fish; don't put in the fish yet. Bring slowly to the boil and simmer for 30 mins. Then put in the fish and poach gently for 12 mins. Lift out the fish and drain in a colander. Reduce the stock by fast boiling, tasting to make sure it does not get too salty. Then strain it, and measure 300 ml/ 1/2 pt. Pour 60 ml/4 tblsps into a cup and dissolve the gelatine in it. Flake the fish, discarding skin and bone, then put it in a food processor with the measured fish stock and the dissolved gelatine. Process till amalgamated, then add the lemon juice, black pepper and cayenne to taste. No salt will be needed. Turn into a bowl and fold in the lightly whipped cream. Spoon into a soufflé dish and chill for 2-3 hours before serving, (or overnight). Serves 4, as a first course.

Smoked Haddock Soufflé

200-250 g/8-10 oz smoked haddock
200 ml/7 fl oz milk
40 g/1 1/2 oz butter
30 ml/2 tblsps flour
45 ml/3 tblsps freshly grated Parmesan
freshly ground black pepper
4 eggs, separated

Put the smoked haddock in a pan and pour over the milk, adding enough water to barely cover the fish. Bring to the boil and simmer gently for 12 mins, then lift out the fish and strain the milky fish stock. Measure 300 ml/1/2 pt and set aside. Flake the fish, discarding skin and any bone. Chop the flakes quite finely. Melt the but-ter, add the flour and cook for 1 min, stir-ring. Then add the measured fish stock and bring to the boil, stirring. Cook for 3 mins, adding 30 ml/2 tblsps of grated Parmesan and lots of freshly ground black pepper – no salt. Lastly, stir in the chop-ped fish. Remove from the heat and stir in the egg yolks, one by one. Cool for a little, then fold in the stiffly beaten egg whites. Turn into a buttered soufflé dish and scat-ter the remaining grated Parmesan over the top. Bake for 25 mins at 180°C/350°F/ gas mark 4. Serve immediately.

STEAMING

Game Birds Wrapped in Cabbage Leaves

2 grouse, or 4 partridges
1 green (or Chinese) cabbage
900 ml/1 1/2 pts game or chicken stock
25 g/1 oz butter
sea salt and black pepper
1 egg yolk
15 ml/1 tblsp lemon juice

If using grouse, cut wings and breasts off each bird, making 4 pieces in all. (The backs etc. can be used for making the stock.) If using partridge, leave the breasts and wings in one piece, cutting away the legs and back, for stock. Blanch 4 large cabbage leaves by dropping into a pan of boiling water for 2 mins, then drain and cool. Wrap each one around a piece of game and lay in the top part of the steamer over game or chicken stock (or a mixture of the two). Bring to the boil, covered, and cook 20 mins for grouse and 30 mins for partridge. Chop the rest of the cabbage coarsely and cook in lightly salted boiling water, just until tender. Drain well, chop more finely, then reheat with a little butter, sea salt and black pepper. When the birds are cooked, transfer them to a serving dish, laying them on top of the chopped cabbage, and keep warm. For the sauce, measure 300 ml/½ pt of the stock and heat in a small pan. Beat the egg yolk with the lemon juice. When the stock boils, pour 30 ml/2 tblsps of it on to the egg yolk, beating, then tip the contents back into the rest of the hot stock. Stir constantly over the lowest possible heat for a few minutes, until it has slightly thickened. Serve in a small jug, with the birds. Serves 4. Pigeons can be treated like partridge but will take longer, depending on their age. Allow 45-60 mins, adding more stock to prevent it boiling dry.

Leek (or Mushroom) Pudding

350 g/12 oz self-raising flour
a pinch of salt
175 g/6 oz shredded suet
6 medium leeks, trimmed and sliced 2.5 cm/1 in thick (or 350 g/12 oz shaggy field mushrooms, cut in pieces)
sea salt and black pepper
300 ml/½ pt chicken stock, (or game stock with the mushrooms and lemon juice to taste)

Sift the flour with the salt into a large bowl. Stir in the shredded suet with the blade of a knife, adding just enough cold water to make it cling together. Form into a ball and knead lightly, just once or twice, on a floured board. Divide it into 2 pieces, one twice as large as the other. Roll out the larger piece into a sort of pouch shape, and lay it in a buttered pudding basin holding about 900 ml/1½ pts. Fill with the sliced leeks sprinkled with salt and pepper, and add the chicken stock. Roll out the remaining dough and lay over the leeks. Dampen the inner edges and press to seal, then trim with a knife. Cover with a large piece of buttered foil and tie the whole basin in a cloth, tying the 4 corners in knots to form a handle. Lower into a saucepan of boiling water, with an up-turned cake ring, or cold saucer, in the bottom. Have the water coming half-way up the sides of the bowl. Cover and boil steadily for 2½ hours, checking the level of the water every 20-30 mins. Serve with a beef stew. Serves 4-6.

To make with mushrooms: use shaggy field mushrooms cut in large pieces and game stock, if you have it, and a squeeze of lemon juice. This is also excellent served with a beef stew, or braised oxtail.

Steamed Vegetables in Cabbage Leaf

An ideal recipe for a gardener living alone, as it is a perfect way to enjoy the first fruits of the vegetable garden.

1-2 large cabbage leaves and as many of the following as are available:
2-3 baby carrots
2-3 small turnips, halved or quartered
2-3 tiny beetroot, halved or quartered
2-3 large spring onions, or shallots
50-75 g/2-3 oz mangetout
6 g/¼ oz butter
sea salt and black pepper
7 ml/½ tblsp chopped parsley

Bring some water to the boil in the bottom half of a steamer. Lay a large cabbage leaf in the top part, and lay the little vegetables on it. Try to have at least 2 or 3 different sorts. Wrap the leaf around them if it is large enough, or cover them with a second leaf. Steam over rapidly boiling water for 10 mins, then test to see if they are tender. When done, lift them on to a hot plate using a fish slice and spatula. Lift off the top leaf and dot the vegetables with butter. Sprinkle with sea salt, freshly ground black pepper, and chopped parsley. Replace the top leaf and eat right away. Delicious. Serves 1.

Vegetable Couscous

350 g/12 oz couscous
1.5 litres/2½ pts chicken or vegetable stock
6 small onions, peeled
4 leeks, thickly sliced
4 carrots, thickly sliced
2 stalks celery, thickly sliced
4 courgettes, thickly sliced
6 small tomatoes, skinned
1 pckt saffron
sea salt and black pepper
225 g/8 oz chick peas, cooked or tinned (optional)

hot sauce:

5 ml/1 tsp ground cumin
5 ml/1 tsp ground coriander
2.5 ml/½ tsp chilli powder
2.5 ml/½ tsp celery salt
30 ml/2 tblsps tomato purée

Put the couscous in a large bowl and pour over it 450 ml/¾ pt cold water. Leave for 10 mins, by which time it will have been absorbed. Put the stock in a *couscousière*, or deep stock pot. Add the whole onions and bring to the boil. When it boils, add the leeks, carrots and celery. Put the soaked couscous in the top half of the *couscousière*, or in a strainer that fits nicely inside the pot, lined with muslin. Set over the simmering stock, cover, and boil steadily for 30 mins. Then lift the top part with the couscous in it, and add the courgettes to the stock. Cook for 5 mins. Then remove the couscous and tip onto a large shallow dish, breaking up any lumps. Add chick peas, if used, with saffron and salt and pepper to taste. Reheat, then stand beside the heat for 5-10 mins before serving, while you make the hot sauce.

Mix the spices with the tomato purée in a small bowl, then add 30 ml/2 tblsps of the hot vegetable stock from the bottom half of the *couscousière*, or stock pot. Stir until smooth, then tip into a tiny dish and set on the table. To serve, lift the vegetables out of the stock with a slotted spoon and pile on the couscous. Pour the stock into a large tureen, and serve all together. each person should have a deep soup plate, knife, fork and spoon. The hot sauce should be added very sparingly, in tiny dabs, at the last. Serves 6.

Gentleman's Pudding

This recipe is a good example of a steamed sponge pudding – that is to say, one made without suet or breadcrumbs. It is light, delicate in flavour, and has an unusual sauce based on a zabaglione.

150 g/5 oz butter
60 g/2½ oz castor sugar
150 g/5 oz self-raising flour
3 large eggs
45 ml/3 tblsps raspberry jam

sauce:

2 egg yolks
15 ml/1 tblsp caster sugar
60 ml/2½ fl oz dry sherry
22 ml/1½ tblsp raspberry jam

Cream the butter and sugar, then add the sifted flour and eggs (one at a time), alternately. Beat well, then add the jam. Turn into a buttered bowl, cover, and steam for 1½ hours. Turn out and serve with the sauce. Whip the egg yolks with the sugar over hot water. Add the sherry then the jam. Serve hot, either poured around the pudding, or separately, in a sauceboat. Cream may be served as well, if you wish. Serves 6.

Steamed Scallops

12 large scallops, with 4 curved shells
a few drops sesame oil

12.5 g/½ oz root ginger, finely chopped
1 large clove garlic, finely chopped
4 large, or 6 small spring onions cut in
3 cm/1½ in lengths
sea salt and black pepper
1.25 ml/ ¼ tsp soy sauce

sauce (optional):

22 ml/1½ tblsp dry vermouth
7 ml/½ tblsp sunflower oil
7 ml/½ tblsp sesame oil
15 ml/1 tblsp soy sauce

Rub 4 squares of foil with a few drops of sesame oil. Cut the scallops across into 2 or 3 rounds, depending on size, leaving the coral whole. Lay them on the foil and scatter the chopped ginger and garlic over and among them. Cut the lengths of spring onion into thin slivers. Reserve half, and mix the rest with the scallops. Fold the foil into neat packages, sealing the edges tightly.

Steam the packages for 8 mins over boiling water. Try to have them layed out in one layer, rather than piled on top of each other. While they are steaming, mix the sauce ingredients (if used), in a small bowl. When the scallops are done, unwrap the foil and tip the juices into the sauce. Discard most of the spring onions and lay the scallops in the curved shells. Mix the sauce well and pour over the scallops, then scatter the fresh spring onions. Serves 4.

Stuffed Cabbage Leaves (cold)

Chinese leaves
100 g/4 oz rice, washed
50 g/2 oz pine kernels, or nibbed almonds
200 g/8 oz tomatoes, skinned and chopped
1 bunch spring onion, sliced
120 ml/8 tblsps chopped flat parsley
sea salt and black pepper
900 ml/1½ pt light chicken stock
2-3 lemons

Separate the Chinese leaves and choose 12 large ones. Drop them into a large pan of boiling water and cook for 1 min, then drain in a colander. Put the drained rice in a bowl and add the pine kernels (or almonds), chopped tomatoes, sliced spring onions, and chopped parsley. Season to taste with sea salt and black pepper, mixing well. Open out the cabbage leaves carefully on a flat surface and stuff each one with about 22 ml/1½ tblsps of the rice mixture. Roll them up with care and lay them, side by side, in the top half of a steamer. Put the chicken stock in the bottom half of the steamer and bring to a boil. Lay the cabbage leaves over it, cover, and boil steadily for 30 mins. Remove the stuffed leaves and lay them on a flat dish. Sprinkle generously with lemon juice and leave to cool. Serve at room temperature, garnished with lemon wedges. Serves 3-4, as a first course, or part of a spread of veg-etable dishes. When Chinese leaves are not available, you can use leaves of Cos lettuce, or spinach beet.

HERB GARDENS

Chervil Soup with Dumplings

900 ml/1½ pts chicken or veal stock
30 ml/2 tblsps chopped chervil
sea salt and pepper

dumplings:

50 g/2 oz self-raising flour
a pinch of salt
12 g/½ oz butter
1 large egg, beaten
15 ml/1 tblsp chopped chervil

Heat the stock in a saucepan and while it is heating pound the chopped chervil in a mortar to bruise it thoroughly. When the stock boils, add 150 ml/¼ pt of it to the mortar, continuing to pound. Stand for 5 mins, then pour back into the pan with the rest of the stock, adding sea salt and pepper to taste. To make the dumplings, sift the flour into a food processor, adding the salt and the butter in small bits. Process briefly, then add the beaten egg with the chopped chervil mixed into it. Process again. (If making by hand, simply sift the flour into a bowl and cut in the butter in small bits. Beat the egg with the chervil and stir into the flour, beating until smooth.) Drop small teaspoonfuls of the batter into a broad pan of simmering lightly salted water. Simmer for 10 mins, covered, turning them over half-way through. Serve the soup in plates, with 3 dumplings in each one. Serves 4.

Tarragon Soufflé

40 g/1½ oz butter
30 ml/2 tblsps flour
200 ml/7 fl oz milk
sea salt and black pepper
2.5 ml/½ tsp Dijon mustard
50 g/2 oz grated Gruyère cheese
15 ml/1 tblsp chopped tarragon
3 egg yolks
4 egg whites

Melt the butter, stir in the flour, and cook for 1 min, stirring. Heat the milk and add to the roux. Cook gently for 3 mins, then add salt and pepper to taste, mustard, grated cheese, and tarragon. Cool for a little, then stir in the lightly beaten egg yolks. Beat the whites until stiff, then fold in. Tip the mixture into a buttered soufflé dish and bake for 20 mins at 200°C/400°F/ gas mark 6. Serve alone, or with a Fresh Tomato Sauce (see page 70). Serves 4.

Stuffed Eggs

6 eggs
sea salt and black pepper
30 ml/2 tblsps soured cream
30 ml/2 tblsps chopped chives
15 ml/1 tblsp chopped dill
15 ml/1 tblsp chopped chervil
12 tiny springs dill

Boil the eggs for 12 mins, cool and shell. Cut them in half lengthwise and scoop out the yolks with a teaspoon. Mash them with a fork, adding salt and pepper to taste. Stir in the soured cream and the chopped herbs, then pile into the egg whites, laying a tiny sprig of dill around each one. Serves 4 as a first course.

Eggs in Dill Sauce

1 cucumber
40 g/1½ oz butter
5 ml/1 tsp flour
150 ml/¼ pt chicken stock
7 ml/½ tblsp chopped dill
sea salt and black pepper
60 ml/4 tblsps double cream
4 hard-boiled eggs, freshly boiled

Peel the cucumber and chop it coarsely. Melt the butter and cook the chopped cucumber gently for 5 mins, stirring occasionally. Remove from the heat, and shake in the flour. Stir until blended, and replace over gentle heat. Cook for 1 min, then add the heated stock. Stir until blended, then simmer very gently for 10 mins. Add the chopped dill, salt and pepper and the cream. Put a hot egg in each of 4 bowls, and pour the cucumber over them. Serves 4 as a first course.

Onion Purée with Sage

700 g/1½ lbs onions
25 g/1 oz butter or beef dripping
100 g/4 oz carrots, thinly sliced
150 ml/¼ pt chicken stock
sea salt and black pepper
15 ml/1 tblsp chopped sage
a dash of lemon juice
30 ml/2 tblsps soured cream

Skin the onions and slice evenly. Heat the fat in a sauté pan and cook the onions slowly until they start to colour. Add the sliced carrots, and, a few mins later, the heated stock. Simmer for 15 mins, covered, stirring occasionally. Cool, then purée in a food processor or blender. Pour back into the pan and re-heat, adding salt and pepper, chopped sage, lemon juice, and soured cream. If necessary, add a very little extra sage, but be careful as it can be overpowering. Serve with roast duck, roast pork, veal or sausages. Serves 4.

Fried Potatoes with Rosemary

700 g/1½ lbs potatoes
45 ml/3 tblsps olive oil
1 clove garlic, crushed
2 sprigs rosemary
sea salt and black pepper

Boil the potatoes in their skins until three-quarters cooked. Cool slightly, then skin and cut in thick slices. Heat the oil in a heavy frying pan and add the sliced potatoes, together with the crushed garlic. Pull the leaves off the rosemary and scatter them over the potatoes. Cook gently for 15-20 mins, turning over and over until nicely browned. Sprinkle with sea salt and black pepper before serving. Serve with roast or grilled lamb, steaks or pork chops. Serves 4.

Vegetable Marrow with Mint

1 medium vegetable marrow, about
900 g/1½ lb
sea salt and black pepper
40 g/1½ oz butter
60 ml/4 tblsps orange juice
30 ml/2 tblsps chopped mint

Peel the marrow, taking off a thicker layer than just the dark green skin. Cut in 2 cm/¾ in slices, then in sections, discarding the seeds. Sprinkle with salt and leave to drain for 25 mins. Pat dry on paper towels. Heat the butter in a sauté pan and put in the marrow. Cover and cook gently for about 8 mins, stirring from time to time. Test with a skewer; when it is just soft, add sea salt and black pepper, orange juice and chopped mint. Serve with roast or grilled chicken, roast lamb, or veal escalopes. Serves 4.

Sage and Apple Sauce

2 Bramleys, peeled and cored
2.5 ml/½ tsp sugar
black pepper
5 ml/1 tsp chopped sage

Cut the apples in thick slices and put in a small pan with just enough water to cover the bottom. Stew gently until soft. Add the sugar and a little black pepper. Stir in the chopped sage and stand, covered, for 5 mins before serving in a sauceboat. Serve with roast duck, roast pork, or coarse pork sausages. Serves 4-5.

Dill Sauce with Mustard

7 ml/½ tblsp Dijon mustard
7 ml/½ tblsp olive oil
60 ml/4 tblsps yoghurt
juice of ½ lemon
30 ml/2 tblsps chopped dill

Put the mustard in a bowl and stir in the oil, drop by drop, as if making a mayonnaise. When they are amalgamated, stir in the yoghurt. Add lemon juice to taste, and stir in the chopped dill. (If it should separate at any stage, emulsify in a food processor or blender.) Serve (cold) with grilled chicken, pork or lamb, barbecued spare ribs, or white fish. Serves 4.

Mint Chutney

900 g/2 lbs cooking apples, peeled, cored
and sliced
450 g/1 lb onions, chopped
2 cloves garlic, crushed
1 green pepper, chopped
1 red pepper, chopped
900 ml/1½ pts red wine vinegar
450 g/1 lb brown sugar
7 ml/½ tblsp whole coriander seeds
6 black peppercorns
6 whole allspice
15 ml/1 tblsp sea salt
50 g/2 oz root ginger, bruised
60 ml/4 tblsps chopped mint

Put the apples, onions, garlic, and peppers in a heavy pan with the vinegar. Bring slowly to the boil and simmer until soft, about 30 mins. Add the sugar, coriander, peppercorns, allspice, salt and the ginger, which you have tied in a small muslin bag. Heat gently until the sugar has melted, then simmer until thick; this may take as long as 1 hour. When done, remove the ginger and stir in the chopped mint. Spoon into hot clean jars, and leave to cool. Seal. Makes about 900 g/2 lbs.

Grapefruit and Mint Sorbet

4 sprigs mint
50 g/2 oz castor sugar
juice of 2 pink grapefruit
1 egg white, stiffly beaten

Pick 4 tiny leaves off the mint and set aside. Wash the rest, and pat dry in a cloth. Boil the sugar with 150 ml/¼ pt of water until the sugar has dissolved, then add the mint. Cover, remove from the heat, and leave for 20 mins to infuse. If the flavour is weak, boil up once more and infuse for another 10 mins. Strain and cool. Add the grapefruit juice and freeze until mushy – about 1 hour. Then fold in the stiffly beaten egg white and freeze for another hour, or until firm. Serve in glass goblets, with a mint leaf on top of each. Serves 4.

Ginger and Watercress Consommé

1 duck, pheasant, or chicken carcass
1 onion, unpeeled, cut in quarters
1 large leek, halved
1 large carrot, halved
1 stalk celery, halved
1 bay leaf
5 ml/1 tsp sea salt
6 black peppercorns

garnish:
22 ml/1½ tblsps finely chopped root
ginger
12 small sprigs watercress

Put the carcass into a large pan with the onion, carrot, leek, celery, bay leaf, salt and peppercorns. Pour on 1.5 litres/2½ pts cold water; bring slowly to the boil, skimming often. When the surface is clear, cover and simmer for 2½ hours. Strain and measure the liquid. If there is over 900 ml/1½ pts, tip back in the cleaned pan and boil rapidly to reduce. Leave to cool, then chill overnight.
Next day, remove the fat from the surface. Reheat gently, adjusting the seasoning as required. Just before serving, bring to the boil and add the ginger. Simmer gently for ½ min, then pour into individual bowls, or a tureen, and garnish with the watercress. Serves 4.

Watercress Frittata

A *frittata* is an Italian omelette: a flat version of the French omelette, and firmer in consistency. Purslane (see below) can be substituted for watercress.

40 g/1½ oz butter
1 bunch watercress, tender sprigs only
(or purslane)
5 eggs, beaten
sea salt and black pepper

Melt the butter in a frying pan and spread the watercress evenly over the bottom of the pan. Fry over a moderate heat for 3 mins, until the watercress has wilted. Beat the eggs with salt and pepper and pour over the watercress. Once the edges start to set, lift with a spatula to allow the liquid egg to run underneath. Cook for 2-3 mins, until the *frittata* is well set. Slice onto a heated dish and serve immediately. Serves 2, as a light main course, with a tomato salad.

Purslane Salad

Purslane can be bought in Greek Cypriot shops where it is known as 'Greek watercress'. (In French it is called *pourpier*). It is easily recognized by its plump fleshy stalk with a rosette of leaves, like small *mâche* leaves, at the top.

1 bunch purslane
sea salt and black pepper
15 ml/1 scant tblsp lemon juice
15 ml/1 scant tblsp white wine vinegar
45-60 ml/¾ tblsps virgin olive oil

Pinch the top 2 inches off the purslane stems, wash quickly and pat dry, then pile loosely in a salad bowl. Put the salt and pepper in a small bowl, add lemon juice and white wine vinegar, then add olive oil and beat till blended. Pour over the purslane and toss just before serving. Serves 4.

June

Purée of Peas and Beans
Mushroom Purée
Purée of Spring Greens
Watercress Purée
Grilled Aubergine Purée
Grilled Tomato Purée
Marinated Salmon
Salmon Pie with Cucumber Sauce
Salmon Fish Cakes
Grilled Halibut with Sauce Dugléré
Herrings in Oatmeal
Soused Herrings
Salt Herring Fillets
Marinated Herrings 1
Marinated Herrings 2
Sauce Diable
Sauce Ravigote
Grilled Mediterranean Fish with Oil and Lemon
Potato Purée with Olive Oil
Artichokes à La Barigoule
Broad Beans with Dill
Onion Tart with Olive Oil Pastry
Flavoured Olive Oil

A vegetable purée is the most adaptable of dishes, one that can be altered to suit the season, and the occasion. Its character can stretch from the homely to the elegant, and it can range from the lightest of calorie-controlled dishes to one that is both rich and sumptuous. Although purées are not cheap - the high water content of vegetables means that it takes a large amount to make a relatively small dish - they do have many advantages. They are practical, in that they can be made well in advance, and often seem to benefit, as a soup does, from having time for their flavour to develop. They are easy to reheat and need little last-minute attention, especially when reheated in some form of *bain marie*. They freeze well, and make a useful standby. A large carton of frozen vegetable purée can be used as the basis for an unplanned meal, serving not only as a vegetable, but also as a hot or cold soup, a base for soft-boiled eggs, or an addition to a spread of *mezes*.

Each vegetable requires its own special treatment to bring out its best points, both in the choice of other ingredients, and in the method used. Some, like broccoli, I find best served very simply, finely chopped and without cream. Others, like watercress or mushrooms, seem better incorporated within a sauce, to give them body. Sometimes a special flavour is achieved by the preliminary cooking: grilling aubergines and peppers, for instance, contributes a delicious smoky taste to the finished dish.

I usually make a good chicken stock to use as the base for vegetable purées. This is not essential, but it does give a fuller flavour to the dish, enabling it to stand alone. The last-minute additions, usually in the form of dairy food, vary according to the richness you desire, and the temperature at which the dish will be served. *Crème fraîche* or sour cream may be added to a purée of mushrooms, while yoghurt is good in oily dishes of grilled aubergines and peppers which are served cold. Low-fat dairy foods like *fromage blanc* are useful in that they add a creamy texture to hot or cold dishes without the fat content of cream.

A purée can vary both in consistency and texture: those which are almost liquid can double as a sauce for eating with dry foods. Almost all purées are at their best served with fairly solid food; they go well with potentially dry birds like guinea fowl and pheasant, with fried dishes like veal escalopes, and with grilled foods like chicken wings, lamb cutlets, pork chops and steaks. They also help to moisten dishes made with minced meat: meat loaf, meat balls, and dishes of stuffed cabbage. They do not only complement meat dishes; a mushroom purée is excellent as an accompaniment to brown rice, or pasta, or a vegetable terrine, while the cold purées of aubergine and tomatoes go well with salads and *mezes*, especially when accompanied by hot pitta bread. Some of the most delicious purées are made from winter vegetables, for then we have the old floury potato, and all the root vegetables whose sweet nutty flavours are ideally suited to dishes of this sort. A well-made potato purée, where hot milk and melted butter are beaten together into the floury mass, together with plenty of sea salt and black pepper, is one of the world's great dishes. An unusual version, extra nutritious, can be made with baked potatoes, using yoghurt instead of milk, with the purée piled back into some of the potato skins for serving. Potato combines well with other root vegetables, and helps to dry out purées of turnip, celeriac and parsnip, which tend to be watery. All the root vegetables make good purées, either alone, or mixed. One of my favourites is made with equal parts of carrots, parsnips and swedes, stewed first in butter, then in beef stock, with lots of chopped parsley added at the last minute. A mixture of celeriac and potato, turnip and leek makes the perfect accompaniment to a roast leg or shoulder of lamb, or a dish of braised beef. Purées of root vegetables are unfailingly delicious with game birds, hare, or venison, for their earthy quality goes well with autumnal foods.

Dried vegetables also make good purées, and their bland character lends itself to exotic flavourings like garlic and ginger, chillies and coriander. These complex dishes fit well into a vegetarian meal, served warm, or at room temperature, while the more basic purées of lentils or split peas are good served with pork sausages, bacon or ham.

Kitchen equipment comes into its own when making purées. While the fibrous root vegetables demand a good vegetable mill, most of the summer vegetables are tender enough to be puréed in a food processor, or chopped by hand, or even mashed with a fork. The texture is important, and variable: often a slightly lumpy consistency is more desirable than a smooth cream. Potatoes are best pushed through a medium food mill, for the food processor will turn them into a gluey paste.

For an elegant meal, two or three vegetable purées may be served, in contrasting colours, to accompany a dish like grilled chicken breasts. For a simple meal, on the other hand, what could be nicer than a soft-boiled egg, lying in a shallow bowl on a bed of watercress purée?

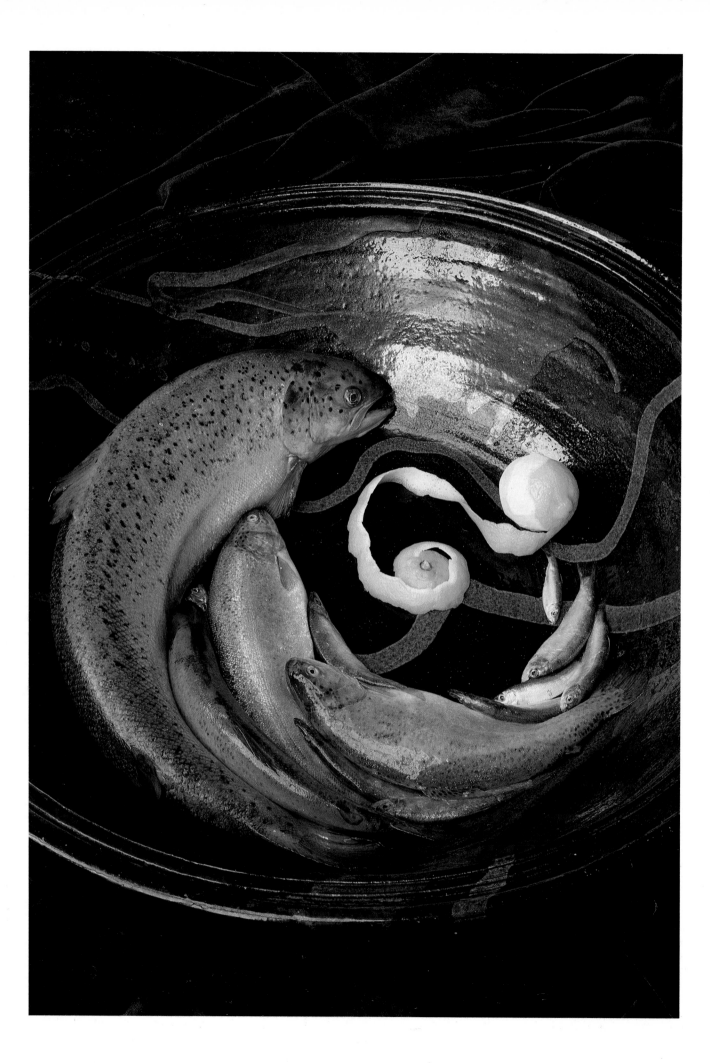

The wild salmon lives a split existence: half in fresh water, half in salt. Its strange life cycle starts and ends in the rivers of northern Europe, Russia, Canada, and Iceland. The best are believed to be those from Scotland, Ireland, and Norway. The Pacific salmon is smaller in size and inferior in every way; this is used mostly for canning, and for smoking.

The salmon is hatched from spawn lying on the river bed, and it grows slowly. Along the road to maturity, it is called progressively alevin, fry and parr. These stay in the river for anything from one to three years; two is the average. When the time for migration to the sea approaches, the parr changes perceptibly, both inside and out. It loses its black 'parr' markings, its tail grows longer and more forked, and its respiratory system adapts itself for living in salt water. The fish is now called a smolt, and it starts its long voyage to the sea, often travelling literally thousands of miles. Most of the salmon from our rivers feed off the coast of Greenland for one to three years. While living in the sea, the salmon feeds on larvae and minute crustaceans, whose caryatid pigment makes the salmon flesh turn pink. In farmed salmon, this is achieved by adding a colouring agent to the feed. When the salmon reaches full maturity, it returns to its birthplace to breed. The fish that returns after one year in the sea is called a grilse; this weighs from 2 to 8 lbs, and makes excellent eating. Those that stay longer in salt water are fully grown salmon weighing up to 20 lbs.

In some mysterious way, the salmon finds its way back to its birthplace; not only the same river, but the self-same tributary, or stream. Alan Davidson suggests in *North Atlantic Seafood* that it may be guided by the taste of the water. The salmon is at its prime as it moves back up the river in spring and early summer, well-fed and full of vigour after its months at sea. It does not feed again while it is in the river, and grows progressively weaker. After spawning, the salmon is called a kelt; after returning to the sea, which some do, it becomes a mended kelt. Most of them die after their first spawning, but some survive to make a second, and even a third trip back to their feeding grounds in salt water.

Salmon used to be plentiful in the UK, and were considered a food of the poor, almost like herring. This gave rise to the oft-repeated tales of working men and women refusing to eat salmon more than two or three times a week. In the early nineteenth century, ice houses were built along the banks of the principal salmon rivers in Britain, so that the salmon could be packed in ice immediately after catching, for transporting to the capital. As the nineteenth century progressed, however, over-netting of the rivers combined with pollution to make the salmon a rare fish. The same thing happened in France: the Loire was once full of salmon, now there are few left.

Like other oily fish, the wild salmon is immensely valuable for our health. These oily fish contain a group of unsaturated fatty acids called Omega-3s, which have a remarkable effect in reducing the risk of heart disease and thrombosis, and lowering the blood pressure. Far from raising the level of fat in the body, they appear to reduce it, at the same time as increasing the brain power.

From a health-conscious point of view, the farmed salmon is less appealing. Not only are they fed artificial colouring agents to make the flesh pink, some are also given antibiotics on a routine basis to prevent the outbreak of disease. Bearing this in mind I feel that it is worth paying extra for the wild fish when it is at its best. The wild salmon season runs from February to the end of August, and the fish are at their best until the end of June. In July and August the flesh starts to become slightly flabby.

The halibut is another oily fish which I value highly. This massive creature, up to 7 ft in length and largest by far of the flatfish, lives in cold northern waters and is never found south of Scotland. Unlike other flatfish which tend to be lazy creatures, the halibut is a fast moving fish. Its flesh is excellent, firm and full of flavour: ideal for grilling and baking. Its liver is rich in nutrients, and haliveroil has been given to babies for decades.

At the other end of the financial scale are herrings and mackerel. Fifteen years ago our average consumption was one herring per person per year, and I don't believe that it has risen much since.

In Victorian times the herring was enormously popular at all levels of society. While the poor bought fresh herrings, six for a penny, from barrows in the street, the rich men enjoyed fried herrings for breakfast, and pickled herrings at lunchtime, in their clubs. In Scotland they were split open and dipped in coarse oatmeal, then fried in bacon fat or dripping: an excellent breakfast dish. Herring roes, both hard and soft, were popular as a savoury, served on toast. There are countless different sorts of pickled herrings, as anyone who has visited Scandinavia knows. They may be pickled fresh or after salting, raw or cooked in their marinade, flat or rolled up. The silvery mackerel is a beautiful fish, also cheap, and very nourishing. It is only good when very fresh. I prefer it simply grilled, served with a sharp sauce, or with lemon wedges.

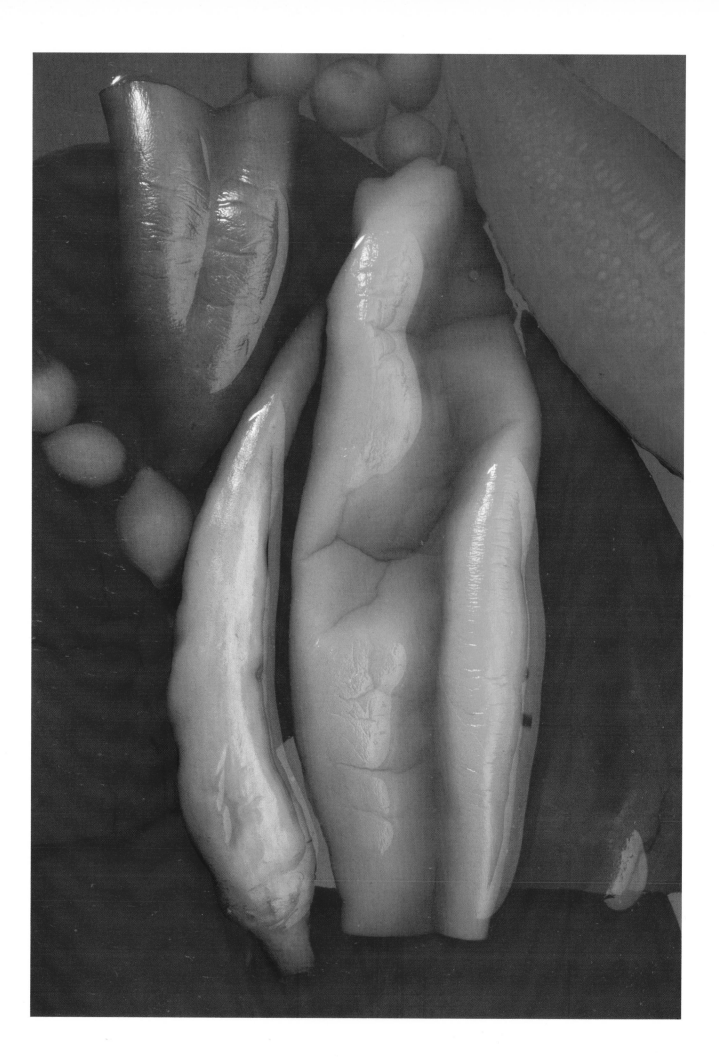

'Malt vinegar,' says the French culinary bible, *Larousse Gastronomique*, 'particularly popular in Britain, is obtained from malt barley.' Can it be true that such an assault on the senses is particularly popular in Britain, or is this just another French put-down? I've never found any culinary use for malt vinegar. Vinegar is basically soured alcohol, and the alcohol in question may be obtained from various sources, usually different types of wine, or ale. The souring process is achieved by the action of bacteria on the surface of the spirit; here the bacteria cling together to form a spongy substance which is called the vinegar 'mother'. Once obtained, this may be divided into pieces and reused.

The best French vinegar is made at Orléans, or at Bordeaux. It is not cheap, for the Orléans method is a lengthy one. In and around Orléans, it is made in the following fashion: three parts of red or white wine are mixed with two parts of vinegar in a barrel, and injected with the vinegar 'mother'. The barrel is left open and a skin forms on the surface; this must not be allowed to prevent the air getting through. When it is ready, the vinegar is drawn off by a tap and more wine is added.

The same method can be followed at home, by obtaining a piece of vinegar 'mother'. Red or white wine is then poured over it. This is one way of using the ends of good bottles; the better the wine, the better the vinegar will be. I tried making it once, but since I only use vinegar in minute quantities it soon became a nightmare, as such home-based operations often become, whereby 'mothers' and sourdough or yoghurt 'starters' are shouting out for more wine, flour and milk, while the kitchen slowly fills up with more vinegar, bread or yoghurt than any one family could possibly eat. Many people make great claims for cider vinegar on health grounds, but it has a curious honey-ish taste that I find unappealing. An excellent sherry vinegar is made at Jerez, in Spain, which is full of character, with a rich brown colour and oaky flavour. In California two years ago I discovered champagne vinegar; there they use it in *sauce mignonette* which they serve with oysters. It has now become available in the UK, imported by Taylor & Lake. But the most exciting new arrival on the scene is balsamic vinegar which has been made for centuries in Modena, in Italy. According to Anna del Conte's *Secrets from an Italian Kitchen*, this exists in two forms. One, called simply *aceto balsamico*, is usually about five years old, and relatively inexpensive. *Aceto balsamico tradizionale*, must be more than ten years old by law, and is often fifty years old or more. It is made on a very small scale in Reggio Emilia and Modena, from the cooked and concentrated must of white Trebbiano grapes, and aged in kegs of many different woods in succession: oak, birch, juniper, chestnut and mulberry.

When *nouvelle cuisine* burst upon the scene, fruit-flavoured vinegars became all the rage. What was basically a good idea was taken too far, not by the originators themselves but by their imitators, and before long we were all as heartily sick of raspberry vinegar as we were of kiwi fruit. In fact, flavoured vinegar was no new invention. In a section on the dressing of salads in John Evelyn's *Aceteria*, published in 1699, he asks that 'the vinegar be of the best wine vinegar and impregnated with the infusion of clove gilliflowers, elder roses, rosemary, nasturtium and thus enriched with the virtues of these plants.' One hundred years later, the French firm of Maille, now merged with Grey-Poupon, was making no less than sixty-five different vinegars. Some of the most popular at the time were those made with raspberries, elderflowers, tarragon, truffles, and *fines herbes*. In *The Cook's Oracle*, by William Kitchiner, published in 1817, there are recipes for making vinegars flavoured with basil, cucumber, tarragon, burnet and elderflower. Basil vinegar is recommended for adding to mock turtle soup.

At some point, probably during the latter half of the Victorian era, a sort of bland miasma overlaid British cuisine, and strong sharp tastes were laid aside. This did not happen in France and Italy, where the use of vinegar is still widespread. In French regional dishes it turns up again and again, in marinades and sauces, stews and casseroles. In the game season especially, it is valued for its rich, sharp flavour and its tenderizing properties. The French have an excellent range of piquant sauces, like *sauce diable*, *sauce Ste Ménéhould*, *sauce ravigote*.

In Italy, vinegar is used constantly, most often in dishes of pickled vegetables served as *antipastos*. In the countries of northern Europe, vinegar is highly valued because of their love of pickled herrings. The love of pickles, although not necessarily fishy ones, extends through Turkey to the Middle East. Visitors to Istanbul may remember the stalls selling glasses of pickled vegetables as 'street food', and just how popular they are, especially in hot weather. In China, and in Japan, pickled vegetables are central to the diet, and are eaten with rice. Here the vinegar is made from fermented rice; the Japanese one is better than the Chinese. Rice vinegar is mild and slightly sweet: either balsamic vinegar or champagne vinegar make a good substitute.

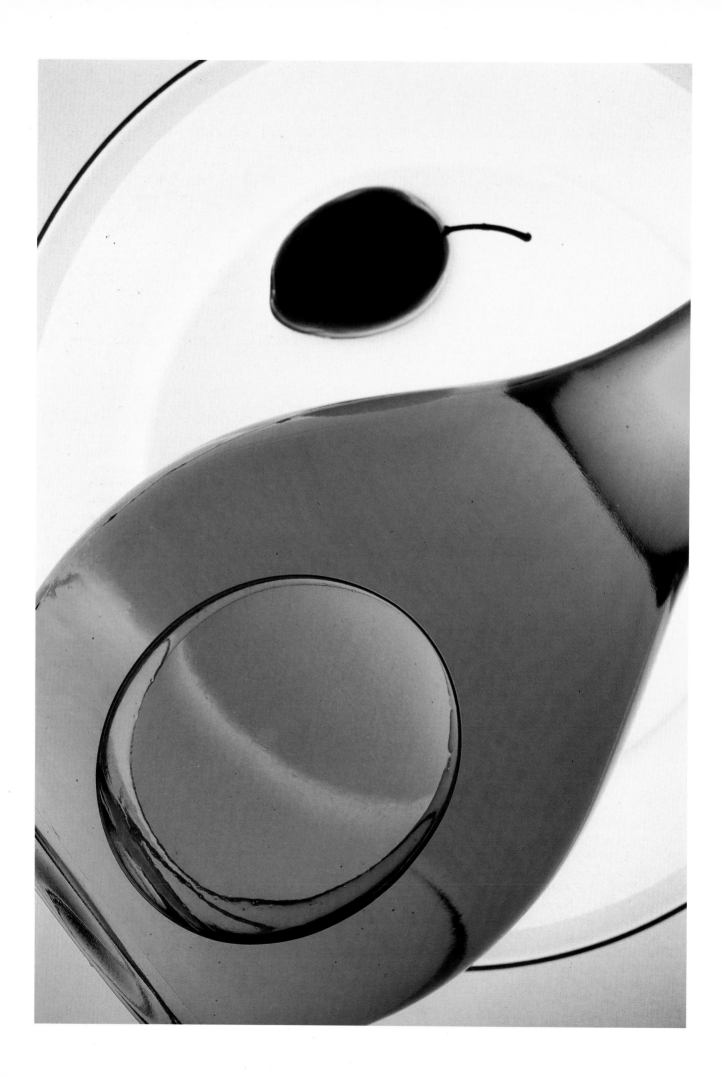

Olive oil has been made since biblical times, yet it is only in the last decade that we have come to value it in Britain. To pay the equivalent of £15 for a bottle of extra virgin Tuscan olive oil would have seemed unthinkable a few years back. Before the war, a refined olive oil was used for salad-dressings, and little else. Virgin oil was unheard of. When my mother returned to Scotland from a trip to Greece, bringing with her a bottle of the first pressing of a friend's olives, everyone was aghast, for they found it quite inedible: 'like engine oil, and a terrible colour'. Today it would probably seem quite delicious.

During the war, olive oil was virtually unobtainable, and many people made cooked dressings for their salads. These were cold sauces made with vinegar and milk, thickened with flour, or an egg. By the time that Elizabeth David's *A Book of Mediterranean Food* came out in 1950, 'commodities like olive oil, rice and imported pasta [were] no more than exotic memories.' But when I started to cook, two years later, olive oil was obtainable, if you knew where to look for it, but there was no variety. Under the David influence we began to use it - albeit gingerly - in cooking. In the sixties and seventies, Provençal oil was thought to be the ultimate. My favourite was Plagniol, in its pretty bottle, which I used to buy at Elizabeth David's shop.

Olive oil can be divided into three catagories. Best of all is the estate-bottled extra virgin oil. This is made from the first cold pressing of the olives, unrefined. It must by law contain less than 1 per cent oleic acid. (Virgin oil must have less than 4 per cent.) Next comes the commercial extra virgin (or virgin) oil. This is also unrefined, and made for the most part from the first pressing, but it may be made with a mixture of olives, or oils, from different places, even different countries.

Any oil with more than 4 per cent oleic acid must be refined before being sold. This accounts for the third category, 'pure olive oil'. This is a blended oil that has been chemically refined, then mixed with some virgin oil to give flavour. (Refined olive oil is virtually tasteless, like the oil you buy from the chemist for medicinal purposes.) These oils can vary widely, and are something of an unknown quantity, since the proportion of virgin to refined oil is not stated on the label. Plagniol is one of the best 'pure' olive oils, but it's also one of the most expensive because it contains more virgin oil than most. One man who has done much to promote interest in olive oil in recent years is Charles Carey, who specializes in importing olive oil from Italy, France, Greece and Spain. He started with an Italian oil, and this is where his preference still lies. 'I like the slightly more elegant peppery taste of Italian oil. If I had to take one to a desert island I'd probably take a Tuscan oil.' These are much the most expensive. The Italians spend more on packaging than the French, often using elegant flasks or square bottles, and on promotion. But they have had a hard time in recent years, due to freak weather conditions. Since the frost of 1985, which killed off most of the olive trees in Tuscany, many of the estates have still not recovered, and are having to buy in oil to supplement their own. Just like wines, the estate-bottled oils vary from year to year. In Tuscany they harvest all the olives together, and press them together, so that the lack of one olive can upset the balance. On the Colonna estate, further south, in Molisse, they grow four or five different varieties in separate groves, and harvest and press them separately. At the start of the bottling season in early December, an analyst checks the quality of each of the oils for flavour, acidity, colour, and suggests a blend, so that they end up with a perfectly balanced oil. So, in a year that is bad for the rest of Italy, the Colonna oil will be better than the others.

Charles Carey would like to encourage people to have at least two olive oils open at any one time: a 'pure olive oil' for general purposes, and an estate-bottled extra virgin oil for special dishes, although he himself, like most keen cooks, would prefer to have three. For general purposes, and for making mayonnaise, he would choose Plagniol. 'There is nothing to beat handmade mayonnaise, but an estate-bottled virgin oil would be too assertive.' He would choose a good commercial extra virgin oil like A L'Olivier for most purposes, 'pouring over new potatoes and other cooked vegetables, and giving a final basting to roast lamb, so that you've got the flavour of the oil as a base for making the gravy. I always pour some over game before I roast it, and often add a slice of bacon. After roasting I take the bird out of the pan and pour in a few drops of wine and balsamic vinegar, bubble them away for a bit, and then add a little bit of stock if needs be: and that makes a wonderful gravy, slightly sweet and sourish, for game.' For his estate-bottled oil, Carey would choose Colonna. 'I use oil of this quality where oil is the dominant flavour, like *bruschetta*, or over a green salad - just that, and maybe a squeeze of lemon. But if you like a thick mustardy vinaigrette, as I sometimes do, then I'd use the cheaper A L'Olivier.' He doesn't recommend using oil of this quality for cooking, although 'a delight on a Sunday morning is to have an egg fried in the most expensive oil!'

VEGETABLE PUREES

Purée of Peas and Beans

1.4 kg/3 lbs broad beans
900 g/2 lbs green peas
2 bunches large spring onions, bulbs only,
thickly sliced
25 g/1 oz butter
sea salt and black pepper
100 ml/4 fl oz double cream

Cook the shelled beans and peas separately, in lightly boiling water, until just tender. Drain well. Push the broad beans through a coarse vegetable mill, to get rid of the outer skins. (If you don't have one with really coarse holes, oval rather than round, you will have to remove the outer skins by hand.) Put the resulting purée in the food processor with the peas. Cook the sliced spring onions in the butter for 4 mins, covered, stirring now and then. Then add them with their juices to the peas and beans and process all together. Add sea salt and black pepper to taste, and the cream. Then reheat and serve. Serves 4-6. Good with chicken or veal, lamb cutlets, or as a base for soft-boiled eggs.

Mushroom Purée

25 g/1 oz dried mushrooms
300 ml/½ pt chicken stock
50 g/2 oz butter
450 g/1 lb flat mushrooms, caps and
stalks, roughly chopped
sea salt and black pepper
grated nutmeg
15 ml/1 tblsp flour
150 ml/¼ pt crème fraîche, or soured
cream
15 ml/1 tblsp lemon juice

Soak the dried mushrooms in the stock for 30 mins, then drain them, reserving the stock. Squeeze out the soaked mushrooms and chop roughly. Heat the butter in a heavy pan and cook the chopped fresh mushrooms for 10 mins, stirring often. Then add the chopped soaked mushrooms and their stock. Bring to the boil and cook all together for 5 mins, adding sea salt and black pepper and grated nutmeg to taste. When the time is up, stir the flour into the *crème fraîche*, or soured cream, until you have a smooth paste. (A Multipractic hand blender is useful for getting rid of any lumps.) Stir the cream gradually into the mushrooms, and cook gently for 3 mins, adding the lemon juice. Serves 6. This delicious purée is almost like a sauce, and goes exceptionally well with dry birds like guinea fowl. Also good with meatballs or meatloaf, stuffed cabbage leaves, or fresh pasta.

Purée of Spring Greens

This transforms spring greens, which I have never much liked, into a delicious dish.

450 g/1 lb spring greens
450 ml/¾ pt chicken stock
50 g/2 oz butter
sea salt and black pepper
60 ml/4 tblsps double cream (optional)

Cut the greens across in 2 cm/¾ in slices, after washing and draining. Heat the stock until boiling and pile in the sliced greens, packing them down well. Cook for 8-10 mins, covered, or until they are just tender, then drain, reserving the stock for another dish. Melt the butter in a heavy pan and add the greens. Cook gently, half covered, for 5 mins, adding sea salt and black pepper, and stirring now and then. Cook for a few mins, then put the contents of the pan into the food processor. Process briefly, until finely chopped. Either serve as it is, after reheating, or add cream and process again. It is good either way, depending on the dish it is to accompany. Made without cream, this goes well with sausages, piled on rounds of buttered toast. Made with cream, it goes well with roast beef or lamb. Serves 4.

Watercress Purée

This is a thin purée, almost more of a sauce than a vegetable dish.

4 bunches watercress
300 ml/½ pt good chicken stock, heated
2 bunches large spring onions,
bulbs only, sliced
25 g/1 oz butter
30 ml/2 tblsps flour
sea salt and black pepper
60 ml/4 tblsps crème fraîche, or double
cream
15 ml/1 tblsp lemon juice, if using
double cream

Trim the watercress, wash and shake dry, and throw into the boiling stock. Cook for 5 mins, covered, then cool for a few mins. Cook the sliced spring onions in the butter for 2 mins, then remove from the heat and stir in the flour. Stir until blended, then cook for 1 min. Process the watercress with its stock, then pour onto the onions. Bring to the boil, stirring, and cook for 4 mins, adding sea salt and black pepper. When the time is up, stir in the *crème fraîche*, or double cream and lemon juice. Serves 3-4. This is very good poured over a dish of soft-boiled eggs.

Grilled Aubergine Purée

This unusual purée made with grilled aubergines is one I first had in Turkey, many years ago. It has a subtle and delicious flavour, and can be used in many different ways.

1.1 kg/2½ lbs aubergines
juice of 1 large lemon
15 ml/1 tblsp olive oil
40 g/1½ oz butter
30 ml/2 tblsps flour
300 ml/½ pt good chicken stock, heated
sea salt and black pepper

Grill the aubergines, turning them often, for about 30 mins, until the skin is blistered all over and the interior is soft when pierced with a skewer. Cool for a little, then cut them in half and scoop out the insides. Squeeze out excess moisture with the hands, then chop roughly and put on a flat dish. Mash them with a fork, without trying to make it too smooth, then stir in the lemon juice and olive oil. The aubergines may be prepared in advance up to this stage, then kept, covered, in the refrigerator.
Later, melt the butter, add the flour, and cook for 1 min, stirring. Add the heated stock and bring to the boil. Simmer for 3 mins, stirring often. Then stir in the aubergine pulp and mix well. Reheat gently, adding sea salt and black pepper to taste. Aubergine purée is excellent served with grilled chicken or lamb. Serves 6.

Grilled Tomato Purée

3 large beefsteak tomatoes
(700-900 g/1½ – 2 lbs)
45 ml/3 tblsps olive oil
1 large red pepper
2 bunches large spring onions, bulbs only,
thinly sliced
2 cloves garlic, chopped
5 ml/1 tsp chopped root ginger
sea salt and black pepper
2.5 ml/½ tsp sugar, if needed
15 ml/1 tblsp chopped coriander
60 ml/4 tblsps yoghurt (optional)

Cut the tomatoes in half and brush the cut surfaces with a little of the oil. Grill them until they are well cooked, slightly blackened on the surface. Set aside, then grill the red pepper. (First cut off the top and bottom, and open out into a flat rectangle.) When the skin is charred all over, remove and leave to cool. Cook the sliced spring onions in the remaining oil (about 30 ml/2 tblsps) for 2 mins, then add the chopped garlic and ginger and cook for another min. Then set aside to cool for a few mins. Scoop the tomato pulp out of the skins and put in the food processor. Scrape the burnt skin off the red pepper, chop roughly, and add to the tomatoes. Then pour in the onion mixture and process all together, adding salt and pepper, a little sugar if the tomatoes are not sweet enough, and the coriander. Process briefly, leaving it still slightly lumpy. Add yoghurt if used. This depends on how you plan to serve it; it is good either way. Chill well before serving. Serves 6.

This cold purée can be used in many different ways: as a dip with *crudités* or hot pitta bread, as a filling for avocados, or spooned on to grilled mushrooms, fried aubergine slices, or poached courgettes.

SALMON AND OILY FISH

Marinated Salmon

If I had to choose just one dish from all those that have been developed in the past twenty years, this would be it. Fresh-tasting and nutritious, sustaining without being rich, simple to prepare yet elegant enough for the most formal dinner: this is a truly faultless dish. Allow about 75 g/3 oz salmon per head, and slice it as thinly as you can. When making this on a small scale, I buy a good-sized piece of salmon and freeze the remains of the fish for another time.

900 g/2 lb piece of salmon fillet, unskinned
22 ml/1½ tblsps extra virgin olive oil
45 ml/1½ tblsps lemon juice
sea salt and freshly ground black pepper
22 ml/1½ tblsps chopped dill

The salmon fillet is half the fish, split horizontally, with the bone removed. Some fish shops now sell it like this; in others, you will have to buy a whole piece of salmon and ask them to fillet it for you (or do it yourself). If you have a longish piece, start slicing it from the middle, cutting outwards in each direction. Do not worry if you cannot get large pieces; simply lay them neatly on 4 plates until the surface of each plate is covered with a thin layer. Brush them all over with the olive oil and lemon juice, scatter some sea salt and ground black pepper over the surface, then sprinkle the dill over all. Stand for 3-4 mins before serving. This amount of fish will serve 4 people on 2 separate occasions, if the remainder of the fish is wrapped in foil and frozen. It is also easier to cut while still chilled, about 1 hour after taking out of the freezer.

Salmon Pie with Cucumber Sauce

700 g/1½ lbs salmon
salt and black pepper
200 g/7 oz long grain rice
30 ml/2 tblsps chopped dill
2 eggs, lightly beaten
225 g/8 oz filo pastry
50 g/2 oz butter, melted

glaze:
1 egg yolk
15 ml/1 tblsp milk

Start 1 day in advance. Put the fish in a pan that fits it as closely as possible and cover with lightly salted cold water. Bring slowly to the boil and simmer for 3 mins, then turn off the heat, cover the pan, and leave to cool overnight.

Next day, boil the rice and drain well, then leave to cool. Flake the salmon into a bowl, discarding all skin and bone. Add the rice and mix well, adding plenty of sea salt and black pepper, and the chopped dill. Stir in the beaten eggs and set aside while you make the cucumber sauce.

1 hour before serving, turn on the oven to 180°C/350°F/gas mark 4. Have ready a rectangular baking sheet measuring roughly 25 by 20.5 cm/10 by 8 ins. Brush it with melted butter. Lay a sheet of filo in it; trim it with scissors to fit the dish exactly on the longer sides, and to overlap the short sides by about 5 cm/2 ins. Brush with melted butter, then lay another sheet of filo in the dish so that it fits the short sides exactly and overlaps the long sides by 5 cm/2 ins. Brush this also with melted butter, then cover with 3 more sheets, trimming them to fit exactly within the baking sheet, and brushing each one with melted butter. Spread the salmon filling over the filo, and cover it with 2 more sheets cut to fit exactly, and brushed with butter. Then fold the overlapping edges over the top sheet of filo, brushing them down with more butter. Then cut 3 broad strips of filo and lay them across the pie, overlapping slightly. Trim them so that there is just 1 cm/½ in left to tuck down the sides of the dish. Brush the top surface with the egg yolk beaten with milk, and score a large diamond pattern with the point of a knife, or a pastry wheel. Bake for 35 mins, or until golden brown. Serve hot, with the cold cucumber sauce. (It is also good served alone.) Serves 6.

cucumber sauce:
½ large cucumber, peeled and coarsely grated
150 g/5 oz Greek yoghurt
150 ml/¼ pt single cream
sea salt and white pepper

Put all the ingredients in a food processor, adding salt and pepper to taste. Process briefly, so that bits of cucumber are left intact within the sauce. Pour into a bowl and chill. One hour before serving, take out of the refrigerator and serve at room temperature. Serves 6.

Salmon Fish Cakes

Good for breakfast, or indeed at any time of day, salmon fish cakes are one of my favourite dishes.

225g/8 oz flaked salmon, free from skin and bone

100 g/4 oz freshly cooked and mashed potato
12 g/½ oz butter, at room temperature
30 ml/2 tblsps chopped parsley
sea salt and black pepper
1 egg, beaten
dry white breadcrumbs
frying oil

Mix the flaked fish with the warm mashed potato, beating well with a wooden spoon. Beat in the butter in small bits, the chopped parsley, and plenty of sea salt and black pepper. Chill the mixture for a few hours, or overnight, if convenient. Then form into round cakes, flattening them slightly on a floured board. Dip them in beaten egg and breadcrumbs. Heat a 2.5 cm/1 in layer of oil in a broad frying pan, then fry the cakes until golden on both sides. Makes 4 large fishcakes, or 6 smaller one. Serves 3-4. If serving at lunch or dinner, they can be accompanied by a parsley sauce and a green vegetable. They also freeze well, before frying.

Grilled Halibut with Sauce Duglére

4-6 halibut steaks
olive oil
sea salt and black pepper

sauce duglére:
1 shallot, finely chopped
25 g/1 oz butter
2 tomatoes, skinned, seeded and finely chopped
15 ml/1 tblsp flour
150 ml/¼ pt dry white wine
150 ml/¼ pt fish stock
sea salt and black pepper
150 ml/¼ pt double cream
7 ml/½ tblsp each finely chopped chervil, chives and parsley

Brush the halibut steaks with olive oil and sprinkle with sea salt and black pepper. Set aside while you make the sauce. Cook the shallot in the butter for 3-4 mins, then add the chopped tomatoes and cook for a further 2 mins. Add the flour, cook for 1 min, stirring, then add the white wine and fish stock which you have heated together. Bring to the boil and simmer for 4 mins, stirring now and then. Add salt and pepper to taste. Lastly, add the cream and cook for another 1-2 mins, then remove from the heat. Stir in the chopped herbs and pour into a sauceboat. Keep warm while you cook the fish.

Grill the steaks slowly, allowing about 6 mins on each side, then serve with the *Sauce Duglére*. Serves 4-6.

Herrings in Oatmeal

These are an old-fashioned breakfast dish, but I often have them for lunch or supper, with some sliced leeks. Traditionally fried in dripping or bacon fat, I prefer them grilled.

4 herrings, skinned and filleted
90 ml/6 tblsps milk
about 100g/4 oz coarse oatmeal
40 g/1½ oz butter

Rinse the herrings and pat them dry. Remove any stray bones, then dip each fillet first in milk then in oatmeal, patting it on well with a palette knife. Dot with butter and grill, inner side up, for 3 mins. Then turn them over and grill for another 3 mins. These are delicious served alone, or with mustard sauce, or with a green vegetable. Serves 4 as a light main dish.

Soused Herrings

These are my favourite of all the pickled herring dishes. My Scottish grandmother used to eat one for breakfast every morning.

6 herrings, skinned and filleted, without their roes

marinade:
225 ml/8 fl oz dry white wine
225 ml/8 fl oz white wine vinegar
1 small onion, cut in thin rings
1 carrot, thinly sliced
3 stalks parsley
2 bay leaves, crumbled
1 sprig thyme
7 ml/½ tblsp sea salt
8 black peppercorns
3 cloves
1.25 ml/¼ tsp ground mace, optional
1.25 ml/¼ tsp ground allspice (optional)

garnish:
1 small carrot
15 ml/1 tblsp finely chopped parsley

Put the wine and vinegar in a pan with the sliced onion, carrot, herbs and spices. Bring slowly to the boil and simmer for 20 mins, half covered. Have the filleted herrings lying in a rectangular dish and pour the hot marinade over them. Cover loosely with foil and bake for 10 mins at 180°C/350°F/gas mark 4. Remove from the oven and leave to cool, then chill until needed. Take out of the refrigerator at least 1 hour before serving. Lift the fillets onto a clean dish and spoon a little of the marinade over them, just enough to moisten. For the garnish, cut 4 or 5 grooves down the side of the carrot with a canelle knife, then cut it in slices about 3 mm/⅛ in thick. Cook the flower-shaped slices in lightly salted boiling water for 2 mins, then drain under the cold tap. Scatter a few over the herrings, with a little finely chopped parsley over all. Serves 6, as a first course. These keep well for 3 or 4 days in the refrigerator.

VINEGAR

Salt Herring Fillets

6 large herrings, filleted
1½ bay leaves
75 g/3 oz coarse salt

I prefer to skin the herrings, but this is optional. Rinse them under the cold tap, then lay them in a rectangular dish and scatter the crumbled bay leaves over them. Put the salt in a jug and pour on a little very hot water. Stir until the salt has dissolved, then make up to 900 ml/1½ pts with cold water. Pour over the herrings and weigh them down with a plate so they are completely submerged. Place in the refrigerator for 24 hours, then drain them and throw away the brine. Makes 12 fillets.

Marinated Herrings 1

12 salt herring fillets
300 ml/½ pt white wine vinegar
100 g/4 oz sugar
6 black peppercorns
3 bay leaves, crumbled
2 medium onions, sliced in rings
15 ml/1 tblsp chopped parsley

Lay the fish fillets in a shallow dish. Mix the vinegar with the sugar, peppercorns and crumbled bay leaves. Pour over the fish, and scatter half the sliced onion over the surface. Put in the refrigerator overnight. To serve, discard the sliced onion and lay the fish fillets on a clean dish. Moisten with a little of the marinade, and scatter freshly sliced onion rings over the top, with chopped parsley. Serves 4 as a first course, with buttered rye bread, or pumpernickel.

Marinated Herrings 2

1 large onion, halved and sliced
1 large carrot, halved and sliced
12 salt herring fillets
6 small sprigs parsley
1 bay leaf, crumbled
6 black peppercorns
200 ml/7 fl oz dry white wine
200 ml/7 fl oz white wine vinegar
15 ml/1 tblsp finely chopped parsley

Make a layer of half the sliced onion and carrot in a shallow rectangular dish. Lay the herring fillets on this, and cover them with the remaining sliced vegetables, parsley, bay leaf and the black peppercorns. Mix the wine and vinegar – there should be just enough to cover the fish – and pour it over. Cook for 30 mins at 180°C/350°F/gas mark 4, then remove and leave to cool. Once cool, it may be stored in the refrigerator for up to a week, or eaten the following day. To serve, lift the fillets out

of their marinade and lay on a flat dish. Moisten with a little of the marinade, and scatter a few slices of onion and carrot over them. Sprinkle with a little freshly chopped parsley. Serves 4 as a first course, with rye bread and butter, or pumpernickel.

Sauce Diable

This sauce is excellent served with bland fatty foods like pig's trotters, grilled pork chops, or braised and grilled breast of lamb.

40 g/1½ oz butter
1 small onion, chopped
2 shallots, chopped
50 g/2 oz bacon, chopped
175 ml/6 fl oz dry white wine
60 ml/4 tblsps white wine vinegar
150 ml/¼ pt chicken stock, heated
5 ml/1 tsp tomato purée
¼ bay leaf
sea salt and black pepper
a pinch of cayenne
10 ml/2 tsps flour

Heat 25 g/1 oz of the butter in a small pan and cook the chopped onion and shallots until they start to soften. Then add the chopped bacon and continue to cook, stirring often, for another 3-4 mins, until all is lightly coloured. Heat the wine and vinegar together and add to the pan. Bubble away for a few mins until it has reduced by about a quarter, then add the heated chicken stock, tomato purée, bay leaf, salt and pepper and cayenne. Simmer for another 5 mins. Mix the remaining 12 g/½ oz butter with the flour in a cup, beating until you have a smooth paste. When the sauce has finished cooking, drop the paste in by degrees, stirring until each addition has melted smoothly into the sauce. Continue to cook very gently for another 3 mins, then pour into a heated sauceboat to serve. Serves 4.

Sauce Ravigote

This sauce is good served with hot or cold boiled beef, boiled tongue or cold roast pork.

200 ml/7 fl oz olive oil
52 ml/3½ tblsps white wine vinegar
30 ml/2 tblsps Dijon mustard
15 ml/1 tblsp finely chopped shallot
15 ml/1 tblsp finely chopped gherkin
15 ml/1 tblsp finely chopped parsley
15 ml/1 tblsp finely chopped chervil
15 ml/1 tblsp finely chopped chives
1 hard-boiled egg, chopped

Mix the olive oil, vinegar and mustard, whisking well until they have amalgamated. Then stir in the other ingredients. Serve at room temperature, with hot or cold meats. Serves 4.

Grilled Mediterranean Fish with Oil and Lemon

All along the shores of the Mediterranean, fish are very simply grilled. In France, olive oil alone is used to baste the fish and keep it moist, while in Italy, Greece, Turkey and the Middle East a mixture of oil and lemon juice is usual. Some of the best Mediterranean fish for grilling are bass, dentex, sea bream, sole and red mullet. Mackerel and sardines are also good, as is the bluefish of the Bosporus. Steaks of halibut and turbot may be used in the same way, but must be even more carefully basted, as the cut surface does not have the skin to protect it.

oil and lemon sauce:
90 ml/6 tblsps olive oil
45 ml/3 tblsps lemon juice
sea salt and black pepper
15 ml/1 tblsp chopped herbs (optional)
parsley, chervil, or dill

Beat the oil and lemon juice together, using a wire whisk, until they have amalgamated, then stir in the salt and pepper. Use about half the sauce to baste the fish while grilling, basting once or twice on each side. Pour the rest of the sauce over the fish before serving, adding herbs if used. Do not use the basting juices.

Potato Purée with Olive Oil

I use a fairly strong-flavoured oil like the Greek Sparta to come through the bland mass of potato, and I mix it with an equal quantity of milk to thin the finished purée. Serve it with robust dishes like spicy sausages, or rabbit or oxtail stew.

900 g/2 lbs floury potatoes
sea salt and black pepper
60 ml/4 tblsps virgin olive oil
60 ml/4 tblsps milk

Boil the potatoes in lightly salted water until just tender, then drain well and dry out over gentle heat. Push through a medium food mill into a clean pan. Warm the oil and milk together over gentle heat, then beat into the purée, adding plenty of sea salt and black pepper. Turn into a dish to serve. Enough for 4.

Artichokes à la Barigoule

Olive oil and wine vinegar together are used in this Provençal dish of stewed artichokes.

4 artichokes
½ lemon
75 ml/5 tblsps olive oil
1 onion, coarsely chopped
2 carrots, diced

sea salt and black pepper
225 ml/8 fl oz dry white wine
2 cloves garlic, peeled
sprig of rosemary

Trim the artichokes down to their base and rub all over with the lemon to stop them discolouring. Heat the oil in a heavy pan and add the onion. Cook for 2-3 mins, then add the carrots and stir to mix with the onion. Lay the artichokes on top, adding salt and pepper. Cover and cook gently for 5 mins, then add the wine, garlic, and rosemary. Cover again and cook over a low heat for 30 mins, or until the artichokes are tender when pierced with a skewer. Lay them on a serving dish and spoon the onions and carrots over them, with their juices, discarding the rosemary. Serves 4, as a first course.

Broad Beans with Dill

This is a Greek dish, and is made with the very young pods of broad beans, before the beans have formed. We can rarely get them this young, but the recipe also works with shelled broad beans.

110 ml/4 fl oz virgin olive oil
2 bunches large spring onions, sliced
1.2 kg/2½ lb broad beans, shelled or
700 g/1½ lb young bean pods
37 ml/2½ tblsps chopped dill
sea salt and black pepper

Heat the oil in a heavy pan and cook the sliced spring onions gently, until they start to colour. (If using the young bean pods, cut them in 2.5 cm/1 in pieces.) Add the shelled beans (or pods) to the pan and cook gently for 2-3 mins, then add enough hot water to come level with the beans. Add dill, salt and pepper and cook gently, covered, until the beans are tender. In Greece this is sometimes served with a bowl of yoghurt. Serves 4-5.

Onion Tart with Olive Oil Pastry

pastry:
225 g/8 oz flour
a pinch of salt
75 ml/5 tblsps olive oil
75 ml/5 tblsps tepid water
1 egg, lightly beaten

filling:
1 Spanish onion (or 450 g/1 lb), thinly sliced
90 ml/6 tblsps virgin olive oil
2 cloves garlic, finely chopped
5 anchovy fillets
30 ml/2 tblsps milk
6 black olives

First make the pastry. Sift the flour with the salt into a food processor. Mix the olive oil and water in a jug, beating them with a wire whisk. Process the flour,

adding the beaten egg through the lid, then the oil and water. Turn the dough onto a floured piece of clingfilm and refrigerate for 30 mins, while you make the filling.

Cook the sliced onions in 60 ml/4 tblsps olive oil in a broad heavy pan, covered. Cook them gently, stirring occasionally, for 15 mins, then add the garlic and cook for another 15 mins. While they cook, soak the anchovy fillets in the milk for 10 mins, then rinse in cold water and pat dry. When the pastry has finished chilling, partly unwrap it and lay in an oiled flan ring 22.5-25 cm/9-10 ins wide. With the clingfilm lying over it, flatten the dough, pushing it out from the centre with your knuckles until it fills the tin. Then remove the clingfilm and chill again until the filling is ready. Then fill the pastry case with the onions and lay the anchovy fillets over the top. Dot with the olives, and dribble the remaining 30 ml/2 tblsps olive oil over the surface. Bake for 40-45 mins at 190°C/375°F/gas mark 5. Serve hot, or warm. Serves 4-5 as a first course, or 3-4 as a light main dish.

Flavoured Olive Oil

A bottle of good extra virgin olive oil with various aromatic herbs and seasonings floating in it is a pretty sight, and makes a good present.

600 ml/1 pt French or Italian extra virgin olive oil
2 sprigs rosemary
6 sprigs thyme
1 large clove garlic, peeled and cut in half
1 green chilli pepper
5-6 small red chilli peppers
6 black peppercorns
6 juniper berries

Put the oil in a glass bottle. Wash the herbs and pat them dry. Push them into the bottle, with the garlic and chillies, peppercorns and juniper berries. Cork, and keep for 2 weeks before using. It can then be used for cooking, or for adding to cooked dishes.

July

Tarragon Chicken
Grilled Duck Breasts
Glazed Duck
Grilled Tomatoes and Mozzarella
Horseradish and Apple Sauce
Melon and Feta with Black Olives
Compôte of Peaches
Compôte of Fresh Apricots
Compôte of Mixed Soft Fruit
Compôte of Rhubarb with Ginger
Petits Pots de Crème
Soft Cream Cheeses
Fennel Mousse with Mustard Sauce
Broccoli Mousse with Wild Mushroom Sauce
Courgette Mousse with Tomato and Pepper Sauce
Apple Mousse with Blackberry Sauce
Cold Mango Mousse with Passion Fruit
Sole Meunière
Chaudfroid of Sole
Sole Florentine
Saffron Sauce
Fried Parsley

Pairs of foods that complement each other perfectly make an interesting study. Each country has its own classic combinations, and each individual his own variations. In *My Gastronomy*, Nico Ladenis lists twenty-six of his preferred combinations, which he calls 'marriages made in heaven'. Some seven or eight overlap with my own, while others are perhaps inevitably outside my range of experience, like *foie gras* with Sauternes. I have chosen to stick to more modest ingredients, but the problem here is that many simple foods make such good foils for other foods that it is hard to choose their opposite number. What goes best with lentils, for instance? Game, or duck, or hard-boiled eggs? And what is the ideal vehicle for mayonnaise? Cold lobster is Nico's choice, but even better to my mind is a fairly solid white fish like bass, poached or baked in foil, and served at room temperature. Yet new potatoes, freshly cooked in their skins and served when still warm, are also utterly delicious with mayonnaise, as are hard-boiled eggs. And who's to say what goes best with bread? A wedge of unpasteurized brie, or a ripe tomato, or a slice of raw ham, or homemade greengage jam, or just butter alone?

Many of the best combinations do not even need cooking, like the radishes and butter that are the prelude to so many good meals in simple French country restaurants, or the Marie biscuits and bitter chocolate that Elizabeth David cites in *Summer Cooking* as a good conclusion for a picnic; advice that I have followed many times. Other food combinations are the by-products of cooking that seem to occur naturally, as a bonus for the cook. One such is a hot boiled potato, cut in slices and eaten with wedges of cold butter straight from the fridge. I eat this while making a potato purée, just before pushing the hot potatoes through the food mill. Other delicious conjunctions of taste occur naturally, on the plate, like a lettuce salad immediately after a roast chicken, on the same plate, with the remains of the gravy. (The same principle applies to other roast meats, and even to a beef stew.)

Trying to analyze what makes a perfect combination, I come to the conclusion that it's usually to do with contrast, either of taste, texture or temperature. The bland mozzarella paired with the acidity of the tomato; the peppery bite of the radish with the cool smoothness of butter; and the crisp juicy sweetness of melon with the dry salty flavour of Parma ham. Sometimes however, the pairings transcend such limitations. Eggs, for instance, that go well with assertive foods like bacon and ham are also well matched with the bland potato. Some of my favourite dishes fall in this category: fried eggs with hashed brown potatoes, poached eggs on potato purée, and that old favourite, egg and chips.

Some foods go so well together that it seems hardly worth eating one without the other. The prospect of eating gooseberry pie without cream, for instance, or plum pudding without brandy butter, is hardly worth considering. Everyone must remember a picnic where the vital ingredient has been forgotten, so that one is left with gulls' eggs but no celery salt, or sausages but no mustard.

Many of our feelings for complementary foods are based on national or even regional features, others on childhood associations. For this reason it is not always easy to appreciate foreign food combinations that lie outside our own experience. Some, like the Scandinavian use of horseradish with fish, or dill with potatoes, have an instant appeal, while others, like the Dutch Christmas dish of cold poached liver eaten on slices of fruit bread, seem merely bizarre. Even the most sophisticated foreigners' tastes seem surprising at times, like the late Baron Phillipe de Rothschild, who liked to eat poached haddock with marmalade for luncheon at the Savoy, on his visits to London.

As for childhood tastes, my own seem to have been based almost entirely on sugar, and white sugar at that. White bread and butter spread with sugar, lettuce leaves sprinkled with sugar, and an orange with a sugar lump forced into a hole cut in the top. Later, at boarding school, I came to love eating fried bread spread with marmalade, sometimes with a thin layer of Marmite in between.

My tastes changed, thank goodness. The last food combination that really pleased me was one I happened to chance upon a year ago, returning from a trip to Paris with three jars of flower jelly from Hediard: orange blossom, rose petal, and jasmine. Remembering a dish I used to eat many years ago in New York, of guava jelly with cream cheese and water biscuits, I tried eating them with *fromage blanc* and small Carr's Table Water Biscuits, and found myself hooked. Served at the end of a meal, instead of cheese or dessert, the three disparate elements seem to blend together into a harmonious whole: a combination of flavour and fragrance.

A well-made compôte is a delicate and elegant dish, redolent of summer luncheons at The Ritz. Far removed from the dreary stewed fruit of the English provincial hotel, it is transformed by the details that go to make a pleasing dish: the care in execution, the subtlety of flavouring, and the style with which it is served. The syrup is prepared first, in generous amounts. It may be composed of water mixed with wine, or water alone: it may be flavoured, or not, with such things as lemon rind, vanilla pod, or cinnamon stick. The fruit is left whole in most cases, merely skinned where desirable, and dropped into the boiling syrup to poach very gently, half covered, until soft. (The fruit for a compôte is best used when slightly underripe.) Once cooked, it is lifted out with care and the syrup is reduced by fast boiling until it has reached the desired amount, and is of a good flavour, when it is poured back over the fruit, and left to cool. A few drops of Kirsch, or a fruit-based *eau-de-vie*, may be sprinkled over the dish once it has cooled. Compôtes are usually served at room temperature, but in some cases they are good served warm, or chilled in hot weather.

A classic compôte, made of whole peaches or pears, halved apricots, golden plums, greengages, or morello cherries makes an appealing dish, served at the end of a simple meal, accompanied by a jug of cream or a bowl of yoghurt. But this is only the starting point, for a compôte can be used as the basis of a more elaborate dessert. I like to cook two or three different fruits one after another, using the same syrup, which becomes progressively more delicious. At the Hotel Royal in Evian-les-Bains, compôtes of peaches, pears, and bitter cherries appear on the *chariot des desserts*, served with a bowl of *crème fraîche*, and gigantic *tuiles d'amandes*. At a small hotel in Trouville, the dessert consisted of a tray of yellow Provençal earthenware casseroles which was brought to the table. Five contained compôtes and purées of fruit - apples, pears, rhubarb, dried apricots and prunes - while the sixth was piled high with *fromage frais*. Yet compôtes are rarely seen in England, either in restaurants or private houses. Old-fashioned hotels like Claridges usually have one or two, and I fall on them with delight whenever I see them.

Autumn fruiting cultivars of strawberries, raspberries and gooseberries can be combined with fruit from your freezer to make late summer compôtes. Blueberries and raspberries make a good combination, as do red and blackcurrants, raspberries and loganberries, blueberries, cherries and strawberries.

With these small fruit, the method is quite different. Only a small amount of water is needed - just enough to cover the bottom of a heavy pan - and only sugar is added. Once the sugar has melted, the currants, blueberries, or cherries are dropped in, and cooked very gently for 2-3 minutes, while the strawberries or raspberries sit in a deep bowl beside the cooker. Once the brief cooking time is up, the cooked fruit is poured, still boiling, over the soft berries, cooked merely by contact with the boiling syrup. A dash of Framboise, Myrtille, or other fruit-based *eau-de-vie* may be added after cooling. These compôtes are delicious served still slightly warm with soft cream cheeses, *petits pots de crème*, *fromage blanc* or yoghurt.

For family meals, dried fruit make excellent compôtes, either alone or combined: very good for breakfast, with homemade muesli and yoghurt. They may be made more interesting by careful use of flavourings: I use a mixture of jasmine tea and white wine to cook dried apricots, and scatter toasted pine nuts over the top. Even the familiar prune can be surprisingly good when cooked in China tea, and lifted with a dash of brandy, Calvados or marc. Flaked toasted almonds may be scattered over the top, before serving with *fromage blanc*. Other good compôtes can be made with whole apples - dessert apples are better for this than Bramleys - or with rhubarb cooked with sliced ginger.

There is a whole range of sauces and creamy dishes that go divinely with compôtes of fruit. White peaches can be served with a *coulis* of fresh raspberries and a bowl of whipped cream lightened with *fromage blanc*. *Sauce à la vanille*, the true custard, is unbeatable with cooked fruit: for a special occasion, it can be enriched by folding in equal parts (or less) of lightly whipped cream, soon after cooling. Homemade vanilla ice cream is excellent served with a warm compôte of cherries, currants, or berries. *Petits pots de crème* are rich and delicious, eaten with a compôte of mixed soft fruit. Soft cream cheeses like *petits suisses* and *coeurs à la crème* are often served with raw berries, but I like them even better eaten with a juicy compôte.

For a dinner party, I might make a few biscuits to serve at the same time. *Tuiles* made with almonds or hazelnuts go well with fruit, as do ginger thins, and lacy oatmeal biscuits. Best of all are the little almond cakes called *financiers*. I ate these for the first time in Paris, and fell for them instantly. Not unlike a *madeleine*, both in appearance and texture, they are even more delicious, since two-thirds of the flour is replaced with ground almonds, and only the whites of eggs are used.

There are few sensations more lowering than leaving a dinner party weighed down with indigestible food, dreading a sleepless night and a bad day to follow. Years ago, I remember a friend telling me she felt so well leaving our house after dinner that she walked the two miles home. I took this as one of the greatest compliments.

It is not easy to keep within the bounds of a healthy regime when entertaining, but if one is accustomed to eating healthy food, anything in the nature of a blow-out is far from enjoyable. There are many appealing dishes, pretty enough for a dinner party and yet low in fat. An obvious first course is salad: raw spinach and prawns dressed with olive oil and lemon juice; sliced avocado, tomato and low-fat mozzarella sprinkled with strips of fresh basil, olive oil and freshly ground black pepper; or a variety of green leaves topped with a lattice of strips of grilled red and yellow peppers. Soups are also good, hot or chilled: variations of *vichyssoise*, using *fromage blanc* or yoghurt instead of cream; thin purées of broad beans or green peas; salad-type soups such as *gazpacho*; clear consommés, hot, chilled or jellied. Alternatively, a simple vegetable, perfectly cooked: asparagus or artichokes, served warm, with a choice of a yoghurt-based herb sauce or vinaigrette; a large dish of French beans or mangetout, broccoli or young cauliflower, served warm, with a dressing of good olive oil and lemon juice.

A more unusual first course is a hot vegetable mousse, made with the minimum of egg and dairy products; these have the appeal of a soufflé without the fat content. Baked in small moulds and turned out, with a contrasting sauce or garnish, they make an attractive opening to a light meal. I use dariole moulds (the ones used for castle puddings in the bad old days), tiny pudding basins and oval *oeufs en gelée* moulds, in sizes ranging from 4 to 6 fl oz. The shapes look pretty turned out, either together on one large flat dish or on individual plates, with the sauce over or around them, or handed separately. Mixtures too soft for turning out are better baked in small soufflé dishes. If in fact they seem firm enough to unmould, you then have the option. Firmer mousses, such as broccoli, may be baked in a narrow loaf tin and sliced, perhaps with a wild mushroom sauce spooned over. Fennel mousse is delicious with mustard sauce, courgette looks pretty with a sauce of chopped tomatoes and grilled red peppers, while carrot is best left in its dish (unless deftly turned out right way up so that its crust of grated Parmesan remains on top) with a garnish of sliced mushrooms with chervil.

After a hot vegetable mousse, a cold main course is perfectly acceptable: chicken salad with a curry-flavoured dressing; shellfish salad served with hot pitta bread. If a hot dish seems appropriate, it could be a light dish of steamed scallops with boiled rice or poached fish with new potatoes and a light sauce, both served with a green salad.

If starting with salad or soup, a hot fruit mousse makes a rather special pudding. I have had excellent results with mango, made in a small soufflé dish and served with a raspberry sauce; and apple, served with a hot blackberry sauce. Citrus fruits make better cold mousses, using gelatine as the setting agent. Tropical fruit mousses can be garnished with sliced fresh fruit or served with a fruit sauce, preferably in a contrasting colour.

Flatfish are fascinating creatures. Like other fish, they start life perpendicularly but as they grow they flop on to one side. This enables them to lie flat on the bed of the sea and bury themselves in the sand. The underside becomes white, while the upper side turns anything from greyish beige to brownish black, often spotted or mottled according to the species, matching the sea floor as nearly as possible. As they mature, the eyes migrate: the eye on the underside, together with the nostril, moves round to join the other eye on top of the head, since an eye buried in the sand is useless.

Flatfish with their eyes on the left are called sinistral; this group consists of the family called *Bothidae*, which includes the turbot and brill. Those with their eyes on the right, called dextral, cover two families: the *Pleuronectidae*, which includes the halibut, flounder, plaice, lemon sole and dab, and the *Soleidae*, which includes the Dover sole. This quirk of nature allows the fish to swim in one direction only, the dextral flatfish can only swim from left to right, and the sinistral group only vice-versa. Occasionally a fish develops in a perverse way: this is called a reversal. The mind boggles at the thought of a lonely sinistral flounder, forced to swim all its life in the opposite direction to its dextral relatives.

The naming of the Dover sole is misleading, since this fish exists throughout the eastern part of the Atlantic and in the Mediterranean, not just in the Channel. However, it is not found on the American side of the Atlantic and Americans have to use flounder for our sole recipes. I have always found Mediterranean sole just as delicious as English ones but this may be because the ones I have eaten were very fresh. The little wooden fish restaurants built out over the sea on stilts along the north coast of the Mediterranean just do not exist here.

The Dover sole is God's gift to chefs, since it combines delicacy of flavour with firmness of texture in a unique way. Its shape is ideal, for frying, grilling whole and for easy filleting. Wheelers base their whole menu on Dover sole; they buy some 5,000 1 lb soles each week and have no less than twenty-three sole dishes on the menu. I have a fondness for Wheelers based largely on nostalgia; for me it represents some thirty years of eating out. As a teenager, my two favourite dishes were *Sole Veronique* and *Sole Florentine*; both are still on the menu. When I make the same dishes at home, I present them slightly differently, with sauce - much less of it - served underneath the fish, instead of masking it. However, I admire Wheelers for ignoring the passing fashion. *Sole Dugléré*, as served at the Savoy, is a cold dish but is delicious hot, if made at home. I tend to think of these as restaurant dishes but they are just as suitable for home cooking. Sole is quickly cooked and at its best eaten within seconds, rather than minutes. It makes a perfect dish for light meals, luncheons or late suppers. What could be nicer for supper after the theatre than *Sole à l'Indienne* - little strips of sole served in a lightly curried sauce, with chopped onions and apple? The sauce can be made in advance, the rice cooked and kept hot. At the last minute, while the sauce reheats, the strips of fish are poached for 2 minutes, added to the sauce and simmered for another minute.

Once you get in the habit of cooking flatfish, it is almost as easy as boiling an egg. Having the right tools helps; a fish kettle is not required but an oval frying pan is ideal, both for cooking whole fish and fillets. A special saucepan, kept just for making fish stock and for poaching fillets, is another luxury worth having, for the smell of fish does tend to hang about the pan it is cooked in. An alternative to poaching is steaming over fish stock; this can be done on a simple metal rack, kept for the purpose, that fits inside a wok. Most important of all is a good fishmonger; not only do they sell the freshest fish but they will prepare it for you exactly as you want.

Plaice or lemon sole can be substituted for Dover sole and are much less expensive. They are best cooked on the bone, however, since the flesh is soft and tends to disintegrate, especially when cut into goujons. A whole fried plaice is an excellent dish, as I learnt on a visit to Denmark. There it is served with grated horseradish or with a mustard sauce; both somewhat surprising to an English palate but extremely good with fish. Ever since, I add a little mustard to a sauce mornay for serving with fish, while mustard or horseradish combined with watercress, make a good peppery sauce for poached fish.

MARRIAGES IN HEAVEN

Tarragon Chicken

Tarragon and chicken are a classic combination, and this simple recipe is a good way of using them. A regular chicken, free-range if possible, is better for this dish than the yellow corn-fed one.

1.6 kg/3½ lb roasting chicken
75 g/3 oz unsalted butter
2 pckts tarragon, leaves only, chopped
sea salt and black pepper
2.5 ml/½ tsp flour
150 ml/¼ pt double cream

Stand the chicken on a piece of foil large enough to enclose it completely. Melt the butter, adding half the chopped tarragon, and pour some of it over the chicken so that the whole of its upper surface has been anointed. Then sprinkle the bird inside and out with sea salt and black pepper, and wrap the foil around it, sealing the edges so as not to allow any butter to run out. Lay on its side in a roasting tin and roast for 20 mins at 190°C/375°F/gas mark 5, then turn it on its other side for another 20 mins. Turn it right side up and roll back the foil. Pour some more tarragon butter over the breast and roast for a further 35-40 mins, basting once or twice. When the time is up, take out of the oven and pour the juices through a strainer into a small pan. Stir the flour into the cream, beating until smooth. Then heat the butter gently, adding the thickened cream. Stir constantly until boiling point is reached, then simmer gently for 2-3 mins, adding the rest of the chopped tarragon. I usually serve the chicken whole, on a dish, with the tarragon sauce in a small jug. If you prefer, you can carve the chicken and pour the sauce over it. Serve with new potatoes, rice or noodles, and a green salad. Serves 4.

Grilled Duck Breasts

Many butchers sell gigantic French duck breasts, packaged in pairs. They are not cheap, but good value in that there is no wastage, and they are quick and easy to cook.

2 large duck breasts
15-30 ml/1-2 tblsps sunflower oil

Rub the breasts on both sides with oil, then place them, skin side up, under a pre-heated grill. Cook for 6-8 mins on the first side, then turn and cook for another 4-5 mins on the second side. Remove from the heat and leave to cool. When they have cooled to room temperature, cut them in fairly thick slices diagonally, and lay on a flat dish. Serve at room temperature with Spiced Lentils with Coriander, (see page

72), or with a green salad, or watercress and tomatoes. Serves 4-6.

Glazed Duck

Excellent small French duck called *Croisé* are a cross between a wild duck and a domestic one, like the English Gressingham duck. They have much less fat than the domestic duck, and one makes a good meal for 2 people. Serve with Spiced Lentils with Coriander (see page 72).

2 Croisé or Gressingham duck
30 ml/2 tblsps clear honey
60 ml/4 tblsps fruit jelly:
crab apple, rowan, redcurrant
juice of 1 orange
juice of 1 lemon
90 ml/6 tblsps port

Lay the two birds right side up on a roasting rack. (If using ordinary duck, roast them upside down for the first 30 mins.) Put the honey and the fruit jelly in a small bowl over a pan of boiling water. When it has melted, add the fruit juices and port and remove from the heat. Spoon some of the glaze over the duck, then put them in the oven and cook for 45-55 mins at 200°C/400°F/gas mark 6. Baste with the glaze 3 or 4 times during the roasting. When the time is up, take them out of the oven and cut each bird in half. Serve on a platter, with the hot spiced lentils in a separate bowl. This needs little else in the way of accompaniment, except perhaps some grilled tomatoes. Serves 4.

Grilled Tomatoes and Mozzarella

This is best done for 2 people as it must be served immediately.

a few inner leaves of Cos lettuce
1 beefsteak tomato, halved
1 bunch spring onions, coarsely chopped
10 ml/2 tsps chopped basil
black pepper
10 ml/ 2 tsps olive oil
30 ml/2 tblsps orange juice
1 Mozzarella

This is best served on individual plates as it is hard to lift the melted cheese. Prepare 2 plates with a layer of lettuce leaves cut across in 4 cm/1½ in pieces. Scrape out the seeds of the halved tomato with a tiny teaspoon, and fill the cavities with the chopped spring onions, so that the entire surface of the tomato is covered. Scatter the chopped basil over the top and sprinkle with black pepper – I don't find salt necessary. Dribble the olive oil over each one, then lay them in a baking dish and pour the orange juice over them. Bake for 20 mins at 180°C/350°F/gas mark 4. 5 mins before the time is up, cut the Mozzarella in thick slices (about 0.5 cm/¼

in), and lay them on a greased baking sheet. Put on the top shelf of the oven, above the tomato, and bake for 5 mins, by which time the cheese should just be starting to melt. Using a broad palette knife, transfer the cheese onto the lettuce leaves, lay half a tomato on each plate, and serve immediately as a first course. Serves 2.

Horseradish and Apple Sauce

This may sound odd, but it works very well indeed. In Scandinavia, it is served with cold roast pork, duck, or veal, while in Austria it is one of the traditional accompaniments to hot boiled beef.

2 Bramleys, peeled, cored and thickly sliced
75 ml/3 fl oz mayonnaise
75 ml/3 fl oz soured cream, fromage blanc, or yoghurt
45-60 ml/3-4 tblsps grated horseradish
lemon juice to taste

Cook the apples with 30 ml/2 tblsps water – no sugar – until soft, and push through the food mill to make a thick purée. Leave to cool, then stir in the other ingredients, tasting as you add the horseradish until the 2 flavours are nicely balanced. Add a little lemon juice to taste. Serve cold, with cold duck, pork, veal or beef. Serves 4-6.

Melon and Feta with Black Olives

Watermelon and Feta cheese are a Middle Eastern combination of tastes, surprisingly successful and delicious as a snack or salad, especially in hot weather. I've added black olives partly because they look so pretty.

For each person, as a first course, allow:

75 g/3 oz watermelon, without rind, cut in large cubes
40 g/1½ oz Feta, cut in large cubes
3 black olives

dressing (optional):
10 ml/2 tsps light olive oil
5 ml/1 tsp lemon juice

Cut the melon in cubes or rectangles about 4 by 2.5 cm/1½ by 1 in, and the Feta slightly smaller, about 2.5 cm/1 in. Lay them side by side on a small flat plate, with the olives among them. I like to eat this absolutely plain, but a light dressing may be spooned over them if you prefer. Don't try to toss them in a salad bowl however, or they will look messy and lose their charm. This can also be served in double quantities as a substitute for a meal.

FRUIT COMPOTES

Compôte of Peaches

When made with white English hot-house peaches, this is the most delicious of all compôtes. It is also good with yellow peaches.

100 g/4 oz sugar
300 ml/½ pt white wine
6 peaches, very slightly underripe
15 ml/1 tblsp eau-de-vie, eg Framboise (optional)

Put 900 ml/1½ pt water in a broad saucepan and add the sugar. Bring to the boil and cook for 5 mins, then add the wine. Bring back to the boil, then prepare the peaches. If hard to skin, drop them in the boiling syrup for 1 min, then lift out and cool under the cold tap. The skin will peel away easily. Drop the peeled peaches into simmering syrup and poach gently, half covered, until they are soft. This may take anything from 5-25 mins, depending on the degree of ripeness. Once they are soft, lift them out carefully with a slotted spoon, and lay in a shallow dish. Boil up the syrup until it has reduced to about 225 ml/⅓ pt, and pour back over the peaches. Leave to cool, serve at room temperature, or chilled. A dash of fruit-based *eau-de-vie* may be added after cooling if you like. The compôte can be served alone, or with cream, or with a fresh raspberry sauce. It is also good served with one or two other compôtes. Serves 6.

Compôte of Fresh Apricots

700 g/1½ lb fresh apricots
1 vanilla pod
60 ml/4 tblsps vanilla sugar, or castor sugar

Cut the apricots in half and remove the stones. Put 600 ml/1 pt water into a broad pan and add the vanilla pod and the sugar. Bring to the boil and cook for 3 mins, then drop in the apricots. Bring back to the boil and cook very gently, covered, until they are soft, checking frequently. This may take only 3-4 mins if they are ripe. Once they are soft, lift them out with a slotted spoon and lay in a shallow bowl. Boil up the syrup until it is reduced by about half, remove the vanilla pod, and pour over the apricots. Leave to cool. Serve at room temperature, with a bowl of whipped cream mixed with yoghurt, sweetened with a little vanilla sugar. Or, with creamed rice, *fromage blanc* or thick cream. Serves 5-6.

Compôte of Mixed Soft Fruit

This can be made with the last of the late summer fruit combined with frozen fruit that has not been long in the freezer.

700 g/1½ lbs mixed soft fruit, fresh and frozen: red and blackcurrants, raspberries, loganberries, blueberries, strawberries, cherries, etc
75 g/3 oz sugar
15 ml/1 tblsp eau-de-vie, eg. Framboise or Kirsch

Divide your fruit into 2 bowls: those that require a few minutes cooking, like red and blackcurrants, blueberries, and cherries, and those that only need immersing in the boiling syrup, like strawberries, raspberries, and loganberries. In a broad heavy pan put enough water to come 1 cm/½ in deep, and add the sugar. Bring to the boil, then add the firmer fruit. Bring back to the boil and cook gently, covered, for 2-3 mins, until just softened. Then remove from the heat and pour the boiling fruit over the berries. Leave to cool for a while before adding the *eau-de-vie*.
This is delicious served warm, with vanilla ice cream, or *sauce à la vanille* with whipped cream folded into it, or chilled, with *cœur à la crème*. Serves 5-6.

Compôte of Rhubarb with Ginger

700 g/1½ lb rhubarb
60 ml/4 tblsps sugar
1 piece preserved ginger, about 22 ml/1½ tblsps chopped
15 ml/1 tblsp ginger syrup

Trim the rhubarb and cut in 2.5 cm/1 in chunks. Put them in a broad heavy pan and add 90 ml/6 tblsps water and the sugar. Bring slowly to the boil and cook very gently, covered, until the rhubarb is soft, checking often as it disintegrates very suddenly. When it is hot, tip into a bowl and leave to cool. After about 10 mins, stir in the chopped ginger and the ginger syrup, taken from the jar of preserved ginger. Serve at room temperature with *fromage blanc*. Serves 4-5.
Instead of preserved ginger, you can use fresh root ginger. Peel a piece about 2.5 cm/1 in square and cut in thin slices. Cook with rhubarb, then stir in 15 ml/1 tblsp orange juice after it has cooled.

Petits Pots de Crème

These little baked custards are very rich, but delicious for a treat. They are especially good served with a compôte of soft fruit, berries, currants, or cherries.

300 ml/½ pt single cream
300 ml/½ pt double cream
1 vanilla pod
3 egg yolks
37 ml/2½ tblsps vanilla or castor sugar

Start 24 hours in advance. Heat the cream together with the vanilla pod. Stop just before it reaches boiling point, cover the pan, and remove from the heat. Stand for 20 mins to infuse, then remove the pod and reheat slowly. Beat the egg yolks with the sugar and pour onto the cream when almost boiling. Mix well, then pour through a strainer into 6 small flame-proof dishes – *oeuf en cocotte*, or tiny soufflé dishes are best. Stand them in a baking tin half full of hot water. Bake for 35 mins at 150°C/300°F/gas mark 2, or until just set. Cool, then chill overnight. Serve the little dishes on a flat plate, with a compôte of black cherries, or mixed soft fruit. Serves 6.

Soft Cream Cheeses

Cœur à la crème, Cremets d'Anger, Fontainebleau: all are versions of the same dish, ideal accompaniments to a compôte of mixed soft fruit. Once the basic formula is understood you can make your own version, depending on what dairy products are easily available.

1 part low-fat dairy product, ie fromage blanc, Jockey, Quark, yoghurt, Ricotta, curd cheese
1 part full-fat dairy product, ie crème fraîche, double cream, full-fat cream cheese
15-30 ml/1-2 tblsps vanilla or castor sugar (optional)
1-2 egg whites (optional)

The two dairy products are beaten separately, until smooth; *crème fraîche* and double cream are beaten longer, until thickened without being stiff. The two are then mixed together, and sugar added to taste, if used. (I used to add sugar, but now prefer it without.) If using egg whites – they give a lighter crumbly texture – beat them until stiff, allowing 1 per 300 ml/½ pt, and fold into the mixture. Have a suitable porous mould prepared, lined with a piece of muslin. Heart-shaped china moulds can be bought in kitchenware shops, but a simple round shape is just as pretty, with the imprint of the muslin still on the surface of the cheese. I use a small strainer, or a large carton pierced with holes, or one of the tiers of my seed sprouter. Turn the cheese into its container and stand in a dish in the refrigerator overnight, pouring off the water that collects in the dish from time to time. Turn out on a flat dish to serve, lifting off the muslin carefully. Serve with a compôte of blueberries and raspberries, or other soft fruit. This must be made 24 hours in advance, and eaten within 24 hours.
For 2 people, I sometimes use 150 ml/¼ pt Jockey mixed with 150 ml/¼ pt semi-whipped cream, without either sugar or egg whites: the simplest dish imaginable.

MOUSSES

Fennel Mousse with Mustard Sauce

550 g/1¼ lbs fennel, trimmed weight,
plus leaves
600 ml/1 pt chicken stock
75 g/3 oz fromage blanc, or Jockey
sea salt and black pepper
2 large eggs, separated

mustard sauce:

40 g/1½ oz butter
30 ml/2 tblsps flour
300 ml/½ pt fennel stock
150 ml/¼ pt yoghurt
10 ml/2 tsps lemon juice
5 ml/1 tsp Dijon mustard
5 ml/1 tsp horseradish
sea salt and black pepper

garnish:

22 ml/1½ tblsps chopped fennel leaves, or
dill

Cut the fennel in chunks and cook in the stock until tender, about 20 mins, covered. Drain, reserving the stock. Put the fennel in the food processor with the *fromage blanc* and process until smooth, adding salt and black pepper to taste. Add the lightly beaten egg yolks and process again. Then tip into a bowl and fold in the stiffly beaten egg whites. Spoon into greased moulds holding 100-150 ml/4-5 fl oz, and bake in a roasting tin half full of hot water, allowing 35 mins at 180°C/350°F/gas mark 4. While they are cooking, make the sauce. Melt the butter, add the flour and cook for 1 min, stirring. Add 300 ml/½ pt of the strained fennel stock. Simmer for 3 mins, stirring often. Cool slightly, then put in the food processor with the yoghurt and lemon juice, and process until smooth. Add mustard and horseradish and process again briefly. Tip into a small pan and re-heat gently, without allowing it to boil, or it will separate.

When the mousses are cooked, remove from the oven and stand for 3 mins before unmoulding. Then turn them out onto a large dish, or individual plates if you pre-fer, and spoon the mustard sauce over and around them. Scatter the chopped fennel, or dill, over all and serve immediately. Serves 5-6.

Broccoli Mousse with Wild Mushroom Sauce

450 g/1 lb broccoli, trimmed weight
100 g/4 oz fromage blanc, or Jockey
salt and black pepper
2 large eggs, separated, plus 2 egg whites

wild mushroom sauce:

2 shallots, finely chopped
15 ml/1 tblsp sunflower oil
100 g/4 oz wild mushrooms, thickly sliced
1 clove garlic, finely chopped
150 ml/¼ pt chicken stock, heated
salt and black pepper
100 ml/4 fl oz thick yoghurt
30 ml/2 tblsps chopped chervil, or flat
parsley

Steam the broccoli until just tender, drain well and cut in pieces. Cool slightly, then put in the food processor with the *fromage blanc*, salt and black pepper. Process until roughly blended, then tip into a bowl. Stir in the lightly beaten egg yolks, and fold in the lightly beaten whites. Spoon into a greased loaf tin holding about 900 ml/1½ pts and bake, standing in a roasting tin half full of hot water at 180°C/350°F/gas mark 4, for about 45-50 mins, until firm. While it bakes, make the sauce. Cook the chopped shallots in the oil for 2 mins, then add the sliced mushrooms and the garlic. Cook gently for 4-5 mins, until the mush-rooms start to soften. Then add the heat-ed stock and simmer gently for 10 mins, half covered, adding salt and black pepper. Cool slightly, then process with the yo-ghurt in a food processor. Adjust the sea-soning, and stir in the chopped chervil. Keep warm until ready to serve. If it has to be reheated, be careful not to boil, or it will separate. To serve, turn out the broc-coli mousse onto a flat dish and cut in thick slices. Put one slice on each plate, and spoon the sauce over it. Serves 5-6.

Courgette Mousse with Tomato and Pepper Sauce

550 g/1¼ lbs courgettes, unpeeled and
coarsely grated
75 g/3 oz fromage blanc, or Jockey
salt and black pepper
a pinch of nutmeg
2 large eggs, separated

First make the sauce (see page 39). The sauce can be made in advance and reheat-ed before serving; it wants to be warm rather than hot.
Put the grated courgettes in a bowl and pour boiling water over them. Leave for 1 min, then drain and rinse under the cold tap. Squeeze dry, then mix with the *fromage blanc*, adding salt and pepper and a pinch of nutmeg. Stir in the lightly beaten egg yolks, and fold in the stiffly beaten whites. Spoon into small greased moulds holding 100-150 ml/4-5 fl oz and bake for 35 mins at 180°C/350°F/gas mark 4, standing in a roasting tin half full of hot water. When they have finished cooking, take them out of the oven and stand for 3 mins before turning out. This allows them to firm up, and to sink slightly, making them easier to unmould. Turn them out, either on indi-vidual plates, or onto a large dish, and serve with the Tomato and Pepper Sauce poured over and around them. Serves 5-6.

Apple Mousse with Blackberry Sauce

700 g/1½ lbs Bramleys, peeled, cored and
thickly sliced
30 ml/2 tblsps sugar
90 ml/6 tblsps fromage blanc, or Jockey
2 large eggs, separated, plus 1 egg white

blackberry sauce:

225 g/8 oz blackberries
30 ml/2 tblsps sugar
15 ml/1 tblsp vodka

Cook the sliced apples with 45 ml/3 tblsps water and the sugar. When soft, push through a food mill and leave to cool. Then put in the food processor with the *fromage blanc* and process until blended. Then add the lightly beaten egg yolks. Turn into a bowl and fold in the stiffly beaten egg whites. Spoon into small soufflé dishes and bake for 35 mins at 180°C/350°F/gas mark 4. While they are baking, make the sauce.
Cook the blackberries for about 3 mins with the sugar, in 30 ml/2 tblsps water. Cool slightly, then process to a purée and rub through a sieve to catch the pips. Pour into a bowl, and serve, warm, with the hot mousses. Serves 4-6.

Cold Mango Mousse with Passion Fruit

3 limes
45 ml/3 tblsps castor sugar
1½ pckts gelatine
2 large ripe mangoes
5 passion fruit
50 g/2 oz fromage blanc, or Jockey

garnish:

225 g/8 oz green grapes, or 1 mango, or
4 kiwi fruit

Pare the rind of the limes and put it in a small pan with the sugar and 75 ml/5 tblsps water. Bring to the boil and cook gently until the sugar has melted, then turn off the heat, cover the pan, and stand for 10 mins. Then lift out the rind with a slotted spoon and reheat the syrup. When almost boiling, remove from the heat and shake in the gelatine. Leave to dissolve, then stir in. Cut the mangoes in pieces and put in the food processor. Cut the passion fruit in half, scoop out the insides, and add to the mangoes. Squeeze the juice of the 3 limes and add. Process briefly, then add the *fromage blanc* and process again, until smoothly blended. Pour in the gelatine through a strainer, process, then pour into small moulds and chill for several hours, or overnight. Turn out on individual plates to serve, with a garnish of green grapes, peeled, seeded and sliced. Alternative gar-nishes: small slices of fresh mango, or semi-circular slices of kiwi fruit. Serves 4-6.
Note: I like the black seeds of the passion fruit showing through the translucent

mousse, but if you do not like them, you can pass the fruit purée through a coarse sieve after processing, before adding the *fromage blanc*.

FLATFISH

Sole Meunière

Like all fried or grilled sole dishes, this is best made for 2 or even one. When eaten almost straight from the pan, it is delicious.

2 Dover sole, or lemon sole
a little milk
seasoned flour
50 g/2 oz butter
22 ml/1½ tblsps chopped parsley
15 ml/1 tblsp lemon juice

To be correct, the fish should be skinned but I prefer to leave the skin on. Ask the fishmonger to trim the side fins and remove the head and tail. Wash the fish and pat dry; dip them first in milk, then in seasoned flour. Heat half the butter in a frying pan – an oval one if possible – and put in your fish, white side down. (If the pan is not big enough to hold two, you will have to do one after the other, adding a little fresh butter for the second one.) Fry for 5 mins on each side, then transfer, white side up, on to the serving plate. Add the remaining butter to the pan; if the first lot has blackened, throw it out and add 50 g/2 oz instead of 25 g/1 oz. When it has melted, add the parsley and lemon juice and swirl round for a moment or two, then pour over the fish. I like this best served alone or with some plain boiled or steamed potatoes. The white skin becomes deliciously crisp, while the black skin is left on the plate.

Chaudfroid of Sole

3 Dover sole, skinned and filleted into 12 fillets, with bones, skins, etc.

vegetable trimmings:

½ small carrot and onion, sliced, and ends of leek and celery
½ bay leaf
1 stalk parsley
salt and 6 black peppercorns
75 ml/3 fl oz white wine
1 pckt gelatine
300 ml/½ pt double cream
2-3 sprigs tarragon
a small bunch chives

Put the fish bones, skins, etc in a saucepan with the vegetable trimmings, bay leaf, parsley, salt and black peppercorns. Add the wine and enough cold water just to cover. Bring to the boil and simmer for 25 mins, then strain. Return to the cleaned pan and bring back to the boil. Put in the fish fillets, adjust the heat so that it barely

simmers and poach for 4 mins; drain and leave to cool. Strain the stock and measure; you only need 300 ml/½ pt, so if it is much more, pour into a clean pan and boil up to reduce. Pour 60 ml/4 tblsps stock into a cup and cool quickly over ice. Soak the gelatine in this after it has cooled, then reheat, standing in a pan of hot water to dissolve the gelatine. Mix with the rest of the stock, straining once more if necessary. Stand the bowl over ice and leave to cool, stirring as it approaches setting point. When it is about to set, beat the cream until semi-thick, and fold into the stock. Continue to stir over ice until about to set again, then use to coat the fish fillets. Have them laid out, close together but not quite touching, on a baking sheet. Spoon the *chaudfroid* over them, leave to set, then make a second layer, smoothing with a palette knife dipped in hot water. Chill in the refrigerator for 1 hour minimum, to set firmly, then trim round each fillet and lift on to the serving dish. Decorate with tarragon leaves and chives. Serve with hot new potatoes and a green salad. Serves 4, as a light main course.

Sole Florentine

2 Dover sole, lemon sole (or plaice), skinned and filleted, with bones

vegetable trimmings:

½ small carrot and onion, sliced, and ends of leek and celery
½ bay leaf
1 stalk parsley
salt and 6 black peppercorns
75 ml/3 fl oz white wine
225 g/8 oz frozen leaf spinach (or 450 g/1 lb fresh spinach)
40 g/1½ oz butter
22 ml/1½ tblsps flour
150 ml/¼ pt single cream
5 ml/1 tsp Dijon mustard
50 g/2 oz grated Gruyère or Emmental

Put the fish bones, skins, etc. in a saucepan with the vegetable trimmings, herbs, salt and peppercorns. Add the wine, and enough cold water just to cover. Bring to the boil and cook for 25 mins, then strain into a clean pan. While the stock simmers, cook the spinach and drain well. Keep hot. Bring the fish stock back to the boil and drop in the 8 fish fillets. Poach gently for 4 mins, then lift them on to a plate and keep warm. Boil up the stock to reduce, until it has a good flavour. Measure 200 ml/7 fl oz. Melt the butter, stir in the flour and cook for 1 min. Add the hot stock and cook, stirring, for 3 mins, then add the cream, mustard and grated cheese. Stir until all is smooth, adding salt and pepper to taste. To serve, lay half the fish fillets upside down on a plate and make a thick layer of leaf spinach over them. Cover

with the remaining fillets, right side up, to make a sort of fish sandwich. Pour the sauce on to a shallow serving dish, keeping back a little if you like. Lay the fish on the sauce and serve as it is, or with a little sauce dribbled over the top. Serves 4 as a first course or light main dish, with a few boiled or steamed potatoes.

Saffron Sauce

1 egg yolk
1 pckt powdered saffron
1.25 ml/¼ tsp ground cumin
1.25 ml/¼ tsp ground coriander
150 ml/¼ pt sunflower oil
7.5 ml/1½ tsps white wine vinegar
7.5 ml/1½ tsp lemon juice
150 ml/¼ pt yoghurt

Put the egg yolk in a bowl and stir in the saffron, cumin and coriander. Add the oil, drop by drop, beating with a wooden spoon until each addition is absorbed. When half is amalgamated, it can be added more quickly. When all is absorbed, stir in the vinegar and lemon juice and finally the yoghurt. Spoon into a clean bowl and serve with grilled sole or poached fillets of sole.

Fried Parsley

large bunch of parsley, divided into sprigs
frying oil

Wash the parsley and dry in a cloth. Heat the oil to about 185°C/360°F. Drop in the parsley and fry for 25 secs, until bright emerald green and so crisp that it is quite brittle. Drain on soft paper and serve as a garnish with fried *goujons* of sole.

August

Cappuccino Ice

Banana and Passion Fruit Ice

Honey and Ginger Ice

Mixed Currant Ice

Blood Orange Sorbet

Grapefruit and Redcurrant Sorbet

Pear and Blackcurrant Ice

Melon Sorbet

Pineapple and Champagne Sorbet

Chocolate Ice Cream

Strawberry Ice Cream with Raspberry Sauce

Cucumber and Mint Ice

Iced Ayran

Melon with Purée of Exotic Fruits

Passion Fruit Sorbet

Pineapple Sorbet

Mango Fool

Tropical Fruit Salad

Green Fruit Salad

Guava Jelly

Mango Chutney

Hot Mango Mousse

Pavlova with Exotic Fruit

Risotto Verde

Sole à L'Indienne

Curried Fish

Grilled Boned Leg of Lamb

Tempura

Caponata

Tapenade

Preserved Lemons

Salat Meschoui

Chicken with Green Olives

Braised Beef with Olives

Veal with Green Olives

Salade Niçoise

Salad of Orange, Olives and Watercress

My first experience of homemade ice cream was as a child towards the end of the war. Once a week I used to go to dancing class, and sometimes stay to lunch, in a country house where they made the most wonderful blackcurrant ice cream, despite food rationing, which struck me as unlike anything I had ever tasted. The only ice cream I had come in contact with until then was the chalky white Walls ice, made at that time with every sort of substitute, and sold in thick slabs, sandwiched between two wafers. Even that I liked, just as I liked the Walls ices we had later, when I went to boarding school. By then Walls had introduced a second flavour, laughingly called strawberry...

My next revelation in terms of ice cream came on my first trip to visit my grandparents in the United States in the summer of 1947, when I was just thirteen. I was overwhelmed by the drug stores, where you could sit at a counter at any time of the day and order ice cream sodas and sundaes, malted milk and milk shakes, by the score. My grandmother was almost bed-ridden by that time, but every now and then she would get dressed very smartly, with hat and veil, to be driven down to the local drug store. There Earl, the chauffeur, would buy a strawberry ice cream soda which she would eat in the back of the car, before driving home again. Another memorable event took place in New York, where I shared a quart of strawberry ice cream with a cousin, for breakfast. This caused quite a culture shock, after twelve years of eating porridge for breakfast - with salt instead of sugar - and I can still remember it clearly, with chunks of strawberry embedded within it.

Returning to the US recently for the first time in ten years, I was able to assess the ice creams from a more detached viewpoint. At first they still seemed rather wonderful, but the very things that I had loved as a child soon began to pall. They seemed to have grown even richer and sweeter, with Haagen-Dazs chocolate ice cream as the ultimate, while my tastes have moved in another direction. I am still a sucker for ice cream, but now I crave the fresh, fruity ices of northern Italy, with their clear flavours and bright colours unmasked by too much cream. They are like a cross between an ice cream and a sorbet, and I have yet to learn how they are made. My favourites are the ices of Genoa, in particular those of a seafront café in Boccadasse. I also love Venetian ices, especially the ones served in Florian in Piazza San Marco, and those served in Floka, in Athens.

In Greece and Italy, ices are considered as something to eat in a café, between meals, rather than as a dessert. In England, however, they have remained firmly rooted as part of the structured meal, apart from summer holidays in seaside resorts. After an initial success, the spread of Dayville ice cream parlours a few years back did not last long, for the English have never really become addicted to ice cream as the Americans have. Sorbets, on the other hand, have grown in popularity, but only at the upper end of the market. This is partly because they fit in well with modern cuisine, and because they make an appropriate end to a meal in a good restaurant.

I enjoy sorbets in this context, but I never feel the same craving for them that I do for real ice cream. A carton of sorbet can rest undisturbed in my freezer for weeks, which is not the case with ice cream. Frozen yoghurt on the other hand has no appeal for me, for it lacks the very thing I love, and which is after all the whole point of ice cream: the flavour and texture of real cream. Accordingly, I have worked on making a series of ice creams using a mixture of cream and yoghurt, thus lowering the fat content considerably, yet retaining some of the creaminess of the classic ice cream. Those who want a richer version can simply double the cream and omit the yoghurt. Since many excellent varieties of ice cream and sorbet can now be bought, I have concentrated on some more unusual combinations of flavours.

Anyone making their own ice cream is well advised to do it shortly before serving, and not attempt to store it, at least not for long. This applies especially to sorbets which are never as good again. Most flavours diminish, while others grow stronger, upsetting the balance. It is often difficult, especially with sorbets, to regain the right consistency. This is very marked in those with a high water content, which seem to change in a flash from a solid block of ice to a puddle, with no intermediate stage. Cream ices can be stored for a time, although their flavour decreases in the end, but their texture does not alter much. Commercial ice creams should also be eaten as fresh as possible, and for this reason they should always be bought from shops with a quick turnover. I have eaten New England ice cream the same day it was made, and the difference was remarkable.

Tropical fruit has an exotic appeal, both visual and symbolic, that acts strongly on Anglo-Saxons. These strange and intriguing fruits, ranging in size from the large mangoes, pawpaws and guavas, pomegranates and persimmons, to the smaller passion fruit and kiwi fruit, and the tiny lychees, kumquats and Cape gooseberries, come as a welcome contrast to our own home-grown apples and pears. Yet apart from the pineapple, and the avocado pear which we tend to treat as a vegetable, they have not been generally adopted by the British public. Although we are happy to eat tinned lychees and mango chutney in Indian restaurants, we seem wary of buying the fruits in their fresh state.

Perhaps their strongest appeal is that of sight and smell, almost all of them mouth-watering shades of pink, orange and pale green, often contrasting delightfully with the outer skin, and having a strong fragrance - especially the guava. To be honest, their taste often comes as something of a disappointment, as most of them combine a sweet rich flavour with a curious bland texture, not unlike the avocado. Others, like the passion fruit, are so richly endowed with seeds as to be almost unmanageable. But their qualities should not be overlooked, for they can be made into ravishingly pretty dishes, ideal for serving in small quantities at the end of dinner.

Probably the best-known tropical fruit is the mango, and this may have helped to put people off as it is a curiously difficult fruit to eat. It must first be skinned and then the flesh cut away from the stone, even when fully ripe, which results in a lot of messy juice and pulp. It is the best loved fruit in India, where about 5 million tons a year are produced. They have a strange heavy taste and can be made into a fool with lime juice and yohurt, but I prefer them cooked when still green, to make the best of all chutneys for eating with curries.

Far more delicious, in my opinion, is the pawpaw, or papaya. These are best simply skinned and cut in cubes, then sprinkled generously with lime juice and chilled for two or three hours before eating. They are also good in a mixed fruit salad. Guavas are a strange fruit, very sweet, with a pervasive aroma and rich in vitamin C. I sometimes include them in a mixture of tropical fruit, but by far the best way of using them is to make guava jelly, which is delicious when eaten with cream cheese and water biscuits. Passion fruit, with their funny wrinkled skins, have a much more appealing tart flavour but their great disadvantage is a multitude of tiny seeds which are almost impossible to separate from the flesh. Luckily I don't mind them, like the pips in raspberry jam, but if you do, the only answer is to sieve them, which then produces a small amount of pulpy juice which is good for adding to a fruit salad or making into sorbets. Kiwi fruit, or Chinese gooseberries as they were originally called, are simplicity itself to eat. They are also extremely pretty when cut, the few black seeds contrasting with their pale green flesh. They can be skinned and sliced and eaten in salads, or with yoghurt, or simply cut in half and eaten with a teaspoon. I like to mix them in a salad with other pale green fruit: honeydew melon, pineapple, and lime juice.

Prettiest of them all, is the little lychee with its bumpy pink rind opening to reveal a pearly-white fruit with a luscious sheen, shaped like a small bird's egg. These are excellent both when added to a mixed fruit salad and when eaten alone in a thin syrup flavoured tartly with fresh lime juice. Many of these tropical fruits make exquisite sorbets, rather than ice creams, as they are too rich for mixing with cream and egg yolks. They are also good cut in cubes and mixed with scoops of tart fruit sorbets: raspberry, lemon and lime.

The original wild pomegranate, like the Seville orange, was bitter. Years of cross-breeding have produced the sweet version that we buy in the shops today. Too sweet for my taste, I like to use them purely as decoration, for they are a remarkably pretty fruit and can be kept for weeks without losing their colour. I encountered the bitter pomegranate for the first time in the south of Spain. It is sad that we cannot buy these outside Spain as they give one of the best fruit juices I have ever drunk, a beautiful dark crimson in colour.

The juice of the sweet pomegranate is used commercially to make grenadine, a sweet dark red syrup much loved in France. Those with a very sweet tooth may like it poured over vanilla ice cream, but I much prefer it in cocktails. My favourite is the Monaco which is made with equal quantities of lager and fizzy lemonade, with a dash of grenadine, mixed over ice cubes in tall glasses.

The concept of a desert island has been fostered in recent years by Desert Island Discs, by cartoons in *The New Yorker*, and by films like *Castaway*. But it must have existed long before any of these, perhaps even before Defoe wrote *Robinson Crusoe* in 1719. It has probably been handed down ever since men first set sail in boats, and shipwrecks became another hazard to be overcome. For most people, it conjures up a double image: on the one hand, an escape from reality, and on the other, the ultimate test of survival. How many of us could exist totally alone?

I've been compiling and revising my desert island lists for years: books, paintings, records and food. Each time I find myself stuck in an airport, on a train or at a health farm - anywhere where there is enforced idleness and a dearth of good food - I revise my list of desert island dishes. Because I should hate to grow sick of my favourite foods, eating them day after day, I decided I would limit myself to one good meal a week, and that for the rest of the time I would exist on whatever the island had to offer: fish, birds' eggs, leaves, fruit and nuts. (Ben Gunn lived for three years on Treasure Island on goats, berries and oysters.) Therefore I haven't included much fish or fruit - or any goat - in my list. And I decided that each dish would be served with an appropriate wine or with vodka, in the case of caviar.

My desert island lies in the Indian Ocean, with a marvellous climate and semi-tropical vegetation. There are fresh-water springs, fish to catch, and exotic fruit and coconut palms in abundance. This earthly paradise is enhanced by my choice of luxury. This crystallized when I received a letter from a friend in Goa, describing the place where she had her meals. 'The Sunset Beach Café has a wide verandah, shade, good food, fairy lights at night and lots of travellers to talk to.'

I visualize a shady café built out over the water on stilts, made of slatted wood, with coconut matting for shade, facing due west, and with an inexhaustible supply of Nastro Azurro beer. Here I would make my way each evening to sit drinking beer and watching the sun set, and here, once a week, a magnificent meal would materialize.

If I were allowed a book, I would take Sri Owen's *Indonesian Food and Cookery*, for this is full of fascinating and relevant information, with drawings of all the edible plants, and diagrams of how to make dishes out of bamboo leaves.

These are my chosen dishes, at the time of writing, for they are liable to change from day to day:

1. *Blinis* with oscietra (caviar), with a carafe of iced vodka, as served at Caviar Kaspia in Paris.

2. A plate of Parma ham, cut paper thin, with a glass of Sauvignon Blanc, as served in any good restaurant in Parma or Bologna.

3. *Crevettes grises*, the tiny grey-shelled shrimps which only exist in the northern hemisphere, boiled for a moment and served hot, with a chilled bottle of Muscadet, as at Les Vapeurs, a jolly brasserie on the seafront at Trouville.

4. *Risotto verde* with white truffles, and a Piedmontese white wine like Arneis, as served in Del Cambio, the elegant eighteenth-century restaurant in Turin.

5. *Spaetzle* with meat sauce, as served in The White Chimney Sweep restaurant in Vienna. *Spaetzle* are like a cross between small dumplings and *gnocchi*; they are usually served with a meat or game dish, but I like them best with a sauce from a *ragoût* or a goulash. They would be accompanied by a good Beaujolais: Fleurie or Chiroubles.

6. Chicken in a pastry case, halfway between a tiny pie and a huge *vol-au-vent*, as cooked by Nico Ladenis in his Shinfield days, and served with a California Zinfandel.

7. *Boeuf Braise à la mode de chez nous*, the best of all braised meat dishes, as cooked by the Moët & Chandon chef at the Château de Saran, near Epernay, served with Cabernet Sauvignon.

8. A salad of mixed green leaves, the youngest and freshest imaginable, as served at Chez Panisse, Berkeley, California.

9. Bread and butter pudding, served warm, with vanilla ice cream, as it was made by Anton Mosimann during his years at The Dorchester.

10. Mixed fruit ices such as one only finds in Italy or Greece, halfway between a sorbet and an ice cream. Among the best I've ever eaten are those in a café overlooking the sea, on the outskirts of Genoa; in Florian in the Piazza San Marco, Venice; and in Floka, the café a few doors from the Hotel Grande Bretagne, in Athens.

I like to think that I could be reasonably happy, although lonely, leading a simple and solitary life. I might revert to childhood occupations, building elaborate tree houses, and making castles in the sand. And each evening I would spend happily in the Sunset Beach Café, wondering what to eat on the following Sunday.

Like many other aspects of life in the Mediterranean world, the olive dates back to prehistoric times. Ever since the dove returned to the ark from its second flight with an olive leaf in its beak, as a sign that the floods had abated, it has served as a symbol of forgiveness. It was well known to the Ancient Egyptians and the Phoenicians, and much valued for its precious oil; visitors to Knossos, in Crete, will remember the beautiful amphorae in which the oil was stored. The olive first grew on the northern shores of the Mediterranean, probably in and around Greece. The northern limit of its growth is used to define the northern border of the Mediterranean world; to the south, it is bordered by the northern limit of the palm tree (as grown in clumps, not isolated instances). The spread of the olive tree round the shores of the Mediterranean was already under way in pre-Christian times, and was accelerated by subsequent colonization. The Greeks took the first olives to Provence some 2,500 years ago, while the Phoenicians brought them to Tunisia. When the Romans conquered Carthage and the Phoenicians in the second century BC, they planted olive groves throughout Tunisia, a legacy which persists today.

The olive tree is ideally suited to withstand the rigours of the Mediterranean climate, which imposes a pattern of growth quite foreign to our experience. The dormant period is during the long dry summer, and this creates two periods of growth, the first in spring, and the second in autumn, continuing to a lesser degree through the winter, at least in the mild coastal areas. Only a plant like the olive, with its deep tap roots and small glossy leaves, can withstand the long drought. Although we think of the olive as a small tree, in some coastal areas it grows to a considerable height; I have seen them in Tunisia over sixty feet high. It also grows to an immense age, 300 years being considered comparatively young. It starts to bear fruit around the sixth or seventh year, but does not reach its full potential - some twenty to forty kilos - until about twenty-five years old.

Many people are confused about the different coloured olives: although there are some sixty different varieties of olive tree, the green and the black olive come from the same tree, and are the same fruit at different stages of ripeness. The olive starts green, changes gradually through tan to brownish red, and finally a glossy black. After this point, it loses its shine and starts to shrivel on the tree. At no stage can it be eaten straight from the tree; for it is a bitter fruit and only made palatable by processing, which includes soaking in brine. The best olives are grown for two main purposes: for eating, as aperitifs or in cooked dishes, and for making into oil. Different varieties of olive are used for each of these purposes, grown in different regions, and harvested at different times. In Spain, for instance, one of the largest exporters of olives, the best 'table olives' are grown within a fifty-kilometre radius of Seville, while the olives for oil are harvested a month later, depending on the weather. Spain exports huge quantities of stuffed green olives. These are the small green olives stuffed with what appears to be a piece of red pepper, but is in fact a strip of paste made from red peppers and gelatine. (This enables the olives to be stuffed by machine.) Other more interesting stuffings are also available, but in much smaller quantities; some are stuffed with peeled almonds, others, even better, with anchovy fillets, but both of these must be done by hand which makes them much more expensive to produce. The small green Spanish olive is called a *manzanilla;* larger, but less delicate in flavour, is the queen olive. Both these can also be bought in jars, unstuffed, either with stones or pitted. Most olive fanciers believe that the black Kalamata olives from Greece are best for eating; they can be bought in tins but are very expensive. Sad to say, the cultivation of the olive tree is declining everywhere, for financial reasons. For one thing, the olive does not lend itself to mechanization. It grows on hillsides difficult for machines to negotiate, it is costly to fertilize, and both the pruning and the harvesting must be done by hand. These facts, taken in conjunction with the growing popularity of cheap corn and seed oils, has led to a grave decline in the olive industry. The same land can be used for growing vines, which are cheaper to maintain and adaptable to modern methods of farming; furthermore, the demand for wine grows constantly. In Italy, in recent years, the government has accelerated this trend by offering subsidies to encourage farmers to switch from olives to vines, with sad results. No longer is Tuscany the land of olive groves as it was when I first visited it. More and more hills are covered with vines, and even these are no longer pretty, for they are now grown on wires supported by concrete posts. The result of all this is that olive oil is growing steadily more expensive, and the time will surely come when it becomes a luxury product, available only in expensive restaurants and speciality food shops. And the olive tree, for many of us a symbol of the Mediterranean, with its silvery leaves, rounded shape, and gnarled boughs, will be seen only in travel posters.

ICES AND SORBETS

Cappuccino Ice

This is a low-fat version of a delicious ice cream I ate on holiday in Rhode Island, USA.

2 eggs and 2 yolks
30 ml/2 tblsps castor sugar
10 ml/2 tsps Nescafé Gold Blend
150 ml/¼ pt double cream
300 ml/½ pt strong black coffee, freshly made and chilled
150 ml/¼ pt mild yoghurt (Danone, Chambourcy, etc.)
40 g/1½ oz bitter chocolate

Beat the eggs and yolks with the sugar and Nescafé. Heat the cream until almost boiling, then pour onto the eggs, beating continuously. Stir over hot water for 6-8 mins, until slightly thickened, then cool quickly by standing in a sink half full of cold water. Stir often while it cools to prevent a skin forming. When it has reached room temperature, blend in a food processor with the liquid coffee and yoghurt. Pour into your machine and start freezing as usual. Meanwhile, cut the chocolate into small chips and shavings, using a small sharp knife. When the coffee ice is half frozen, stir in the chocolate chips and continue as before. Serves 4-5.

For a richer ice, more like the original, use an extra 150 ml/¼ pt double cream and omit the yoghurt, and increase the Nescafé to 20 ml/4 tsps.

Banana and Passion Fruit Ice

2 bananas, peeled and cut in chunks
150 ml/¼ pt mild yoghurt (Danone, Chambourcy, etc.)
30 ml/2 tblsps castor sugar
4 passion fruit, halved
juice of 2 limes
1 egg white, beaten

Put the bananas in the food processor with the yoghurt and sugar. (Don't use Greek yoghurt for this as the flavour is too strong.) Blend to a smooth purée, then scoop out the insides of the passion fruit and add with the lime juice. Purée again briefly, without decimating the seeds, then freeze as usual, folding in the beaten egg white half-way through. Serves 3-4; can easily be made in double quantities, to serve 6. An excellent and unusual flavour.

Honey and Ginger Ice

300 ml/½ pt semi-skimmed milk
1 vanilla pod, halved and split
2 eggs and 2 yolks
15 ml/1 tblsp vanilla sugar
30 ml/2 tblsps Greek honey (clear)
30 ml/2 tblsps ginger syrup (from a jar of
preserved ginger)
150 ml/¼ pt mild yoghurt (Danone, Chambourcy, etc.)
150 ml/¼ pt double cream, partly whipped
2 pieces preserved ginger (45 ml/3 tblsps chopped)

Put the milk in a small pan with the vanilla pod. Bring slowly to the boil, remove from the heat and leave, covered, for 20 mins. When the time is nearly up, beat the eggs and yolks with an electric hand beater, add the sugar and beat again. When the 20 mins is up, remove the vanilla pod and reheat the milk, adding the honey and ginger syrup. When almost boiling, pour onto the eggs and beat all together. Stand the bowl over a pan of simmering water and stir until it has slightly thickened; cool quickly by standing the bowl in a sinkful of cold water, stirring as it cools. Then blend in the food processor with the yoghurt and cream. Freeze as usual, adding the chopped ginger half-way through. Serves 6. For a simpler honey ice, omit the ginger syrup and ginger, and increase the honey to 60 ml/4 tblsps.

Mixed Currant Ice

350 g/12 oz blackcurrants, fresh or frozen
350 g/12 oz redcurrants, fresh or frozen
60 ml/4 tblsps sugar
150 ml/¼ pt mild yoghurt
150 ml/¼ pt double cream, partly whipped
2 egg whites, beaten

Cook the currants separately, putting each into a heavy pan with 30 ml/2 tblsps sugar. If using fresh currants, add 30 ml/2 tblsps water; if frozen, add no water. Heat them gently until the sugar has melted (and the currants thawed, if frozen); don't cook them. Cool, then push both lots through a medium food mill. This will hold back most of the pips; to eliminate every one, use a fine food mill. Put them in a food processor with the yoghurt and cream. Process until blended, then freeze as usual. When half frozen, blend again in the processor, adding the egg whites, beaten until thick and foamy, but not yet stiff. Continue freezing. Serves 6-8.

Blood Orange Sorbet

This makes an unusual and delicious sorbet, one of those special dishes that cannot be made to order, but only when blood oranges appear in the shops. Like all sorbets, it is best made shortly before serving.

12-14 blood oranges
50 g/2 oz sugar
1 egg white, beaten

Take thin strips of peel from 2 of the oranges and put in a small bowl. Squeeze the juice and measure it; you will need 450 ml/¾ pt. Put the sugar in a small pan with 130 ml/¼ pt winter. Bring to the boil and cook gently until the sugar has dissolved, then pour onto the strips of peel and leave to cool. Then pour through a strainer onto the orange juice, stirring to mix. Tip into an ice cream machine, or ice trays, and freeze as usual. Serves 4.

Grapefruit and Redcurrant Sorbet

2 pink grapefruit
450 g/1 lb redcurrants (fresh or frozen)
75 g/3 oz sugar

Thinly pare the peel from ½ grapefruit and cut in thin strips. Squeeze the juice of all the grapefruit. Put the currants in a pan with the grapefruit peel and the sugar. If using fresh currants, add 30 ml/2 tblsps water; if frozen, they will not need water. Cook gently, until the sugar has melted, 2-3 mins at most. Cool, then blend in a food processor with the grapefruit juice. Strain and freeze. Serves 4-5. This is an exquisite sorbet, with a beautiful colour.

Pear and Blackcurrant Ice

700 g/1½ lbs pears, Comice or similar
30 ml/2 tblsps sugar
175-225 g/6-8 oz blackcurrants
22 ml/1½ tblsps eau-de-vie, eg. Myrtilles, Poire, Framboise, etc.
1-2 egg whites (optional)

Peel the pears and core them; cut in eighths. (The round pears from China or Japan are not suitable.) Put them in a pan with the sugar and 60 ml/4 tblsps water. Bring to the boil and cook gently, covered, adding the currants half-way through. When pears are soft, push the contents of the pan through a medium food mill and leave to cool. Later, stir in the *eau-de-vie* – any flavour works well – and freeze. If egg whites are used, beat until stiff and fold into the ice half-way through the freezing process. Serves 4-6, depending on whether egg whites are included. If to be eaten immediately, I would leave them out, as the flavour is intense and delicious. If made in advance, beaten egg whites help to keep a good consistency.

Melon Sorbet

1 small ripe melon, peeled
225 g/8 oz green grapes, seeded
45 ml/3 tblsps sugar
6 passion fruit, halved
juice of 1 lime
1 egg white, (optional), beaten until thick

Cut the melon in chunks and put in the food processor with the seeded grapes. Process until reduced to a mush, then push through a medium food mill to catch the grape skins. Put the sugar in a small pan with 60 ml/4 tblsps water and boil until it has melted and the syrup has slightly reduced, then cool. Scoop out the inside of the passion fruit and add to the melon purée, together with the lime juice and the sugar syrup. Process briefly, just long enough to blend without destroying the seeds of the passion fruit. Freeze as usual. This delicate ice should be served soon after making, for its flavour and texture are equally fragile. A thickly beaten egg white may be incorporated half-way through the freezing to increase the amount. I prefer it without. Serves 6 with egg white, 4-5 without.

Pineapple and Champagne Sorbet

1 ripe pineapple, peeled and cored
15 ml/1 tblsp sugar
juice of 1 blood (or ordinary) orange
¼ bottle champagne (200 ml/7 fl oz)

Cut the pineapple in chunks and process in a food processor, then start to push through a medium food mill. Stop for a moment, when only a little of the juice has filtered through the mill, and put it in a small pan with the sugar. Heat gently, until the sugar has melted, then leave to cool. When the pineapple has all been milled, put it back in the food processor with the sugar syrup, orange juice, and champagne. Process briefly, then freeze as usual. This is truly delicious with a subtle flavour. Serve in small glasses; enough for 6.

Chocolate Ice Cream

75 g/3 oz Chocolat Menier
300 ml/½ pt milk
2 eggs, plus 2 extra yolks
65 g/2½ oz castor sugar
300 ml/½ pt double cream

Break the chocolate in small bits and put in a small pan with the milk. Heat slowly, until the chocolate has melted, then set aside. Put the eggs and extra yolks into a bowl and beat them with an electric whisk for 2 mins. Reheat the chocolate milk and pour, boiling, onto the egg. Continue to beat for another 2 mins. Then set the bowl over a pan of simmering water and stir constantly until it has very slightly thickened; this may take about 7 or 8 mins. Once this happens, remove from the simmering water and stand the bowl in a sink half full of cold water and stir now and then as it cools, to prevent a skin forming. When it has reached room temperature, whip the cream lightly, then fold into the chocolate mixture. Pour into an ice cream machine, or ice trays, and freeze as usual. Serves 6.

Strawberry Ice Cream with Raspberry Sauce

675 g/1½ lb strawberries
75 g/3 oz castor sugar
300 ml/½ pt double cream

raspberry sauce:

200 g/8 oz raspberries
30 ml/2 tblsps castor sugar
15-30 ml/1 -2 tblsps double cream

Put the strawberries in a food processor with the castor sugar and reduce to a purée. Then push through a fine food mill to catch the seeds. Whip the cream until thick but not stiff, and fold into the purée. Pour into an ice cream machine, or ice trays, and freeze as usual.

The raspberry sauce should be made 1-2 hours beforehand. Process the raspberries, then push through a fine food mill. Stir in the sugar and a drop of cream, then chill for 1-2 hours, until ready to serve. The sauce may be served separately, in a jug, or poured over the ice cream in a large glass bowl. Serves 6.

Cucumber and Mint Ice

This is a savoury ice made with yoghurt instead of cream. It is very refreshing in hot weather, served as a first course. Because of its high water content, it does not keep its texture, so is best made shortly before serving.

24 large mint leaves
2 cartons Greek yoghurt
1 cucumber, peeled
1 egg white, beaten

Chop the mint leaves coarsely and put in a food processor with the yoghurt. Put the rest of the mint leaves in a small pan with 300 ml/½ pt water. Bring slowly to the boil, then turn off the heat and stand, covered, for 20 mins. Then strain and cool. Add to the yoghurt mixture in the processor and process again, until smoothly blended. Turn into a bowl and stir in the grated cucumber, then freeze as usual, in an ice cream machine, or in ice trays. Halfway through the freezing process tip back into the food processor, adding the beaten egg white. Process briefly, then continue freezing as before. Serve the same day as made. This is good served inside hollowed out tomatoes, or on crisp leaves of Little Gem lettuce, or in halved avocados, or simply in small glasses, garnished with tiny sprigs of mint. Serves 6-8.

Iced Ayran

This iced drink is based on the chilled yoghurt that is widely drunk throughout the Mahgreb, the Middle East, and India. It is called *kefir* in Morocco, *ayran* in Turkey, and *lassi* in India. In these hot countries it is mostly drunk in the cafés, rather than with a meal, but it goes well with curried or with light vegetarian or salad meals.

15 large ice cubes, crushed
3 cartons Greek sheep's milk yoghurt
2.5 ml/½ tsp sea salt
15-22 ml/1-1½ tblsp thinly sliced mint

Crush the ice cubes by wrapping them loosely in a clean teacloth, then hitting them with a hammer. Put the crushed ice into a food processor with the yoghurt. (I prefer sheep's milk yoghurt for this dish, but it is not essential.) Add the sea salt and process briefly, just until blended, then pour into tall glasses which have been chilled for an hour or two. Scatter the shredded mint over the top before serving.

Variation:

Make as above, then instead of pouring into chilled glasses freeze as if making ice cream. Serve in small glasses, with the shredded mint scattered over it. Or, skin ripe beefsteak tomatoes and cut them in half, scoop out the seeds, and fill with the iced *ayran*. Scatter the sliced mint over the top and serve as a first course. Serves 4 as a drink, or 6 as an ice.

EXOTIC FRUIT

Melon with Purée of Exotic Fruits

2 ripe mangoes
6 passion fruit
4 limes
1 small honeydew melon, or ½ large one

Peel the mangoes and cut the flesh away from the stones. Discard the stones and put the flesh in the food processor or blender with the flesh and seeds of the passion fruit. Add the juice of the limes and process, or blend. Pour through a fine food mill to get rid of the seeds. Cut the melon in small cubes and put in large wine glasses. Pour over the purée and chill for 2 hours. Serves 4-6.

Passion Fruit Sorbet

12 passion fruit
4 large oranges
2 limes
100 g/4 oz sugar
100 ml/4 fl oz water
2 egg whites

Cut the passion fruit in half and scoop out the pulp with a teaspoon. Rub it through a medium food mill, keeping back the seeds. Squeeze the juice of the oranges and limes and add to the passion fruit. Heat the sugar with the water in a heavy pan until dissolved, then boil until reduced to 150 ml/¼ pt thin syrup. Cool slightly, and mix with the fruit juices. Pour into the ice cream machine and freeze until mushy – about 1 hour. Whip the egg whites until fairly stiff, and fold into the semi-frozen ice. Continue freezing until set. Serves 4.

Pineapple Sorbet

1 large ripe pineapple
100 ml/4 fl oz water
100 g/4 oz sugar
4 medium oranges
15 ml/1 tblsp lime juice
(when available)
2 egg whites

Cut the top and bottom off the pineapple, and slice it thickly. Remove the central core from each slice and cut off the rind. Cut the flesh in cubes and purée in a food processor or blender. Then push through a nylon or hair sieve. You should have about 300 ml/½ pt of juice. Melt the sugar with the water in a heavy pan. Boil until reduced to 150 ml/¼ pt thin syrup, then cool. Squeeze the oranges to make about 300 ml/½ pt of juice. Mix with the pineapple juice, the cooled sugar syrup and the lime juice. (If limes are not available, use 5-10 ml/1-2 tsps lemon juice to sharpen the flavour very slightly.) Mix well, pour into the ice cream machine and freeze for about 1 hour, until mushy. Tip into a bowl and fold in the stiffly beaten egg whites. Continue freezing in the machine. Serves 5-6.

Mango Fool

1 large ripe mango
1 lime (about 30 ml/2 tblsps juice)
300 ml/½ pt yoghurt

Peel the mango and cut the flesh off the stone. Put it in the blender or food processor with the lime juice and yoghurt. Blend until smooth, then pour into 3-4 small glasses and chill for 2-3 hours before serving. This is rather a startling colour, but tastes good.

Tropical Fruit Salad

2 guavas
4 kiwi fruit
8 lychees
2 passion fruit
2 limes
castor sugar to taste

Peel the guavas and cut in small cubes. Peel the kiwi fruit, cut in half and then in quite thick slices. Peel the lychees, cut in half and remove the stones. Mix all together in a bowl. Cut the passion fruit in half and spoon over the other fruit. Squeeze the juice of the limes and mix with the fruit, adding castor sugar to taste. Chill well before serving. Serves 4. Like all dishes of exotic fruit, this looks best served in glass bowls.

Green Fruit Salad

1 small honeydew melon
½ large pineapple
4 kiwi fruit
juice of 2 limes

Cut the melon in cubes. Slice the pineapple thickly, remove the centre cores and cut in chunks. Skin the kiwi fruit and cut in slices. Mix all together lightly in a glass bowl and pour over the juice of the limes. Chill well before serving. Serves 4. An Ogen melon can be substituted for the honeydew, although I prefer to keep all the fruits pale green if possible.

Guava Jelly

900 g/2 lbs guavas
about 450 g/1 lb sugar
1 lime

Wash the guavas and cut in quarters. Put them in a pan with cold water to come level with the fruit. Bring to the boil and boil for 30 mins, crushing the fruit now and then against the sides of the pan with the back of a wooden spoon. Pour into a jelly bag and leave overnight to drip. On no account try to hurry it up by stirring, or the jelly will be cloudy. Next day, measure the juice and put in a heavy pan adding 450 g/1 lb sugar and the juice of 1 lime to every 600 ml/1 pt of liquid. Bring to the boil and cook slowly until the sugar has dissolved, then increase the heat and boil hard until setting point is reached – about 20 mins. Then skim off the scum that has formed on the surface, and spoon into hot sterilized jars. Cool and cover. This makes only 700-800 g/1½ -1¾ lbs but guavas are never cheap, and it is a delicacy worth making even in small quantities. Delicious eaten with cream cheese and water biscuits.

Mango Chutney

2 green mangoes (about 550-700 g/
1¼ – 1½ lbs)
40 g/1½ oz sea salt
750 ml/1¼ pts water
225 g/8 oz soft brown sugar
300 ml/½ pt white wine vinegar
25 g/1 oz root ginger, chopped
2 cloves garlic, crushed
5 ml/1 tsp ground chilli
5 cm/2 in piece cinnamon stick
50 g/2 oz chopped almonds
50 g/2 oz raisins

Peel the mangoes and cut the flesh from the stones. Chop the flesh and put in a bowl. Cover with the sea salt and pour over the water: leave for 24 hours, then drain. Boil the sugar with the vinegar until it has dissolved, then add the chopped ginger, crushed garlic, chilli powder and cinnamon stick. Boil for 5 mins, then add the chopped mango and continue to boil gently until thick, about 15 mins, adding the chopped almonds and raisins for the last 5 mins. Stir frequently while boiling. Cool and discard the cinnamon before spooning into jars. Keep for at least 2 weeks before eating. Serve with curries of all sorts.

Hot Mango Mousse

3 ripe mangoes, stoned and skinned
75 g/3 oz fromage blanc
60 ml/4 tblsps lime or lemon juice
2 large eggs, separated
Raspberry Sauce (see page 138)
15 ml/1 tblsp vodka

Cut the mango in chunks and put in the processor with the *fromage blanc* and fruit juice. Process till smooth, then add the lightly beaten egg yolks and process again. Tip into a bowl and fold in the stiffly beaten egg whites. Pour into small greased soufflé dishes and bake for 35 mins at 180°C/350°F/gas mark 4.
While they cook, make the Raspberry Sauce (see page 138), omitting the cream, and adding a dash of vodka. Serve the hot mousses still in their dishes, with the cold sauce handed separately. Serves 6.

Pavlova with Exotic Fruit

5 egg whites
225 g/9 oz castor sugar
5 ml/1 tsp white wine vinegar
15 ml/1 tblsp cornflour, sifted
450 ml/¾ pt double cream, lightly
whipped
350 g/12 oz mixed fruit, weighed after
stoning: mangoes, strawberries, kiwis, and
passion fruit etc.
22 ml/1½ tblsp vanilla sugar, or castor
sugar (optional)

An old bread board, or chopping board, makes an ideal surface for your pavlova. Otherwise, use a flat metal circle laid on a baking sheet. On no account line them with foil or paper; simply rub with butter and dust with flour, then mark a large circle in the flour. Beat the egg whites until stiff, then start to add the sugar gradually, while continuing to beat. When most of the sugar has been added, fold in the rest by hand, using a metal spoon. Continue to beat by hand until the mixture is smooth as silk. Then stir in the vinegar and cornflour, mixing briefly. Pile onto the circle, making a gentle hollow in the top. Bake for 10 mins at 140°C/275°F/gas mark 1, then a further 30 mins at 110°C/225°F/gas mark ¼. Then turn off the oven and leave the pavlova in the cooling oven for at least 45 mins. Leave to cool completely on its board, or metal ring. If using a circle it covers completely, it can stay on it, simply laying it on a china platter. Otherwise, lift it carefully with two fish slices and slide it onto a china dish. Don't worry if it breaks, as it can always be reassembled under the cream. Whip the cream lightly, adding sugar, or vanilla sugar, if you like. Prepare the fruit, cutting the stoned mango in chunks, halving the strawberries, slicing the kiwis, halving and seeding the grapes, and scooping the pulp and seeds out of the passion fruit. Mangoes, strawberries, and kiwis make a good mixture, with some passion fruit pulp spread over the surface. Only assemble the pavlova shortly before serving. Pile the cream lightly on the meringue, and lay the fruit on the cream. Serves 6-8.

DESERT ISLAND DISHES

Risotto Verde

This is my approximation of the delicious *risotto* served in Del Cambio.

100-150 g/4-5 oz spinach
25 g/1 oz butter
15 ml/1 tblsp olive oil
2 shallots, finely chopped
225 g/8 oz arborio rice
750 ml/1¼ pts chicken stock
sea salt and black pepper
grated Parmesan

Put the spinach through a juice extractor, to get about 50 ml/2 fl oz spinach juice. Heat the butter and oil in a sauté pan or deep frying pan, and cook the shallots for 3 mins. Add the rice, and stir for 2 mins, while you heat the stock almost to boiling point. Now add 300 ml/½ pt of the hot stock and cook gently, stirring often, until it has almost all been absorbed. Then add another 200 ml/7 fl oz and continue to cook over a moderate heat. When this too has been absorbed, add half the remaining stock, reheated until almost boiling. When this also has cooked away, the rice should be almost tender. Stir in the spinach juice, and cook a few mins longer. If still not quite tender, add the rest of the stock and cook until this has disappeared. The *risotto* should be quite moist. Season with sea salt and black pepper, and tip into a warm serving dish. Serve immediately, with a bowl of grated Parmesan on the table. It takes almost exactly 15 mins to cook, from the moment the stock is first added to the rice. Serves 4 as a first course, or 3 as a main dish.

Note: When white truffles are in season, and you are lucky enough to get hold of one, slice it paper thin over the top of the finished risotto, and omit the Parmesan.

Sole à l'Indienne

3-4 Dover sole, lemon sole, or plaice, skinned and filleted, with their bones, skins, etc
½ onion, sliced
1 small carrot, sliced
½ leek, sliced
1 stalk celery, sliced
½ bay leaf
2 stalks parsley
sea salt and black pepper
300 ml/½ pt dry white wine
45 ml/3 tblsps desiccated coconut
12 g/½ oz butter
3 shallots, chopped
1 small dessert apple, Granny Smith, or Cox, peeled, cored and chopped
1 tomato, skinned and chopped
1 small clove garlic, finely chopped
7.5 ml/1½ tsps mild curry powder
150 ml/¼ pt double cream
5 ml/1tsp flour
5 ml/1 tsp sweet fruit syrup (optional)
10 ml/2 tsps lemon juice

Put the fish bones, skins, etc. in a pan with the flavouring vegetables, herbs, salt and black pepper. Add the white wine and enough water just to cover. Bring to the boil and simmer for 25 mins, then strain. You will need just under 600 ml/1 pt. Measure 300 ml/½ pt of the strained stock and pour it over the desiccated coconut in a bowl. Stand for 30 mins then drain, squeezing the desiccated coconut which you then discard. Melt the butter and cook the shallots until they soften and start to turn colour. Add the chopped apple, then the tomato and garlic. Stir in the curry powder and cook for 1 min, stirring. Add the strained coconut milk and simmer gently for 10 mins. Towards the end of the time, heat the remaining fish stock in a pan. Cut the fish fillets into diagonal strips about 2.5 cm/1 in across. Poach them in the fish stock for 2 mins, then remove from the heat. When the sauce has finished cooking, mix 15 ml/1 tblsp of the cream with the flour to make a smooth paste. Drop this by degrees into the sauce, stirring constantly, then simmer gently for 3 mins. Then add the rest of the cream, the fruit syrup (if you have it; if not, reduce the lemon juice to 5 ml/1tsp), and the lemon juice. Drop the strips of fish into the sauce and reheat. Simmer altogether for 1 min, then serve, with boiled rice. Serves 4.

Curried Fish

1 leek, sliced
1 carrot, sliced
1 stalk celery, sliced
3 stalks parsley
1 bay leaf
5 ml/1 tsp sea salt
6 black peppercorns
700 g/1½ lbs haddock fillet
45 ml/3 tblsps desiccated coconut

curry sauce:

40 g/1½ oz butter
2 onions, finely sliced
2 cloves garlic, finely chopped
15 ml/1 tblsp mild curry powder
1.25 ml/¼ tsp ground turmeric
1.25 ml/¼ tsp ground cumin
1.25 ml/¼ tsp ground coriander
a pinch of ground chilli
50 g/2 oz ground almonds
juice of 1 lime, or ½ lemon
15 ml/1 tblsp redcurrant jelly
60 ml/4 tblsps plain yoghurt
30 ml/2 tblsps sliced almonds

Simmer the sliced vegetables in 1¾ pts water for 30 mins, adding the herbs, sea salt and black peppercorns. Cut the fish in large pieces and add to the pan; poach gently for 12 mins. Then remove the fish and boil up the liquid to reduce until well flavoured; you will need 600 ml/1pt. Put the desiccated coconut in a bowl and pour 300 ml/½ pt of the boiling fish stock over it; leave for 20-30 mins then pour through a strainer, squeezing with the back of a wooden spoon to express all the coconut milk. Flake the fish, removing the skin. Then make the sauce: melt the butter and cook the sliced onions gently until golden, adding the chopped garlic towards the end. Stir in the curry powder and spices and cook for 4 mins. Add the ground almonds and cook for another 2-3 mins. Pour on the remaining 300 ml/½ pt fish stock and simmer for 15 mins. Stir in the lime (or lemon) juice, the fruit jelly and the strained coconut milk. When all is blended, add the yoghurt, and do not allow to boil again. Add the fish and reheat gently. Pour into a serving dish, scatter the sliced almonds over the top and serve with boiled rice. This can also be made in advance and reheated, or served cold. Serves 4.

Grilled Boned Leg of Lamb

This is best cooked over an open fire, but can be done under a gas or electric grill. Ask your butcher to 'butterfly' the leg for you, as for a barbecue. This involves boning it, then splitting it in a rectangular slab of meat roughly even in thickness.

One 2 kg/4½ lb leg of lamb, butterflied

marinade:

45 ml/3 tblsps olive oil
juice of ½ lemon
freshly ground black pepper
a few sprigs thyme, rosemary and marjoram or oregano

Two hours before cooking, lay the lamb, skin side down, in an oval dish and rub all over with the oil and lemon juice. Sprinkle with black pepper and strew the herbs over it. Leave for 2 hours before cooking. About 1 hour before cooking, start to build up the fire so that you will have a glowing source of heat. Lay a rack over the fire – this must be arranged before the fire is lit – and lay the meat on it, skin side down. Cook for about 7-8 mins, then turn and cook another 7-8 mins. The meat will shrink alarmingly, but don't panic. When the time is up, push to one side of the fire to keep warm, covered loosely with foil. Allow to rest for 15 mins before carving, while you eat your first course. Then cut it in neat slices, fairly thick, slightly on the diagonal. This is also delicious cold.

To cook under a domestic grill, allow about 12 mins on each side. Serves 6. This is very good indeed served with simple accompaniments like fruit jelly, sauté potatoes, and a green salad.

Tempura

Tempura is a fabulous dish, festive yet adaptable. It is best made for a few people, for it is a lot of work.

12 giant prawns, uncooked
200 g/8 oz monkfish, filleted
1 aubergine
1 green pepper
1 Spanish onion
4 small courgettes
4 sprigs broccoli
100 g/4 oz button mushrooms
frying oil

dipping sauce:
100 ml/4 fl oz chicken stock
60 ml/4 tblsps soy sauce
60 ml/4 tblsps mirin, or sweet vermouth, or sweet sherry
15 ml/1 tblsp wasabi, (Japanese horseradish), or grated daikon
15 ml/1 tblsp grated root ginger

batter:
180-200 ml/7-8 fl oz iced water
100 g/4 oz white bread flour

First prepare the main ingredients. Shell the prawns, leaving on the last joint of the shell and the tail, and discarding the vein down the back. Cut the monkfish in strips 4 cm/2 in by 1.5 cm/3/4 in. Cut the aubergine in slices 0.25 cm/1/8 in thick. Alice the whole pepper in 0.5 cm/1/4 in rings, and cut the whole onion into 0.25 cm/1/8 in slices. Divide a few of these into rings, choosing 8 perfect ones, and use the rest another time. Cut the courgette into thick strips, and the broccoli into florets. Slice the mushrooms thickly. To make the dipping sauce merely mix the chicken stock, soy sauce and mirin, or vermouth or sherry. Pour into 4 tiny bowls and set one at each place. Divide the *wasabi* and ginger between 4 small dishes, making a little pile of each, and set by the bowls. Mix the batter by hand, in a rather cavalier fashion. It must not be done thoroughly; in Japan they use a single chopstick. Beat the egg, add the iced water, continuing to beat, then mix in the sifted flour quickly and lightly. Have a wok or deep pan half

filled with oil heated to about 180-190°C/360-380°F. Dip each prawn in batter, shaking off the excess, and drop into the hot oil. Do not crowd them. Cook for a couple of mins, then lift out and drain on soft paper before transferring to a hot dish. They will not brown; the batter covering should stay pale, and rather patchy. Fry the vegetables in groups, without crowding them. When all are done, serve immediately, on a large platter, with chopsticks. Serves 4.

OLIVES

Caponata

450 g/1 lb aubergines
salt and black pepper
1 small onion
about 150 ml/1/4 pt olive oil
3 stalks celery, chopped
225 g/8 oz tomatoes, skinned and chopped
12 green olives, stoned and chopped
15 ml/1 tblsp capers, drained
15 ml/1 tblsp sugar
30 ml/2 tblsps white wine vinegar

Cut the unpeeled aubergines in cubes about 1 cm/1/2 in square. Put them in a colander and sprinkle with salt; weigh down lightly and leave to drain for 30 mins. Cook the onion gently in 30 ml/2 tblsps oil in a sauté pan. When it starts to colour, add the celery. A few minutes later add the tomatoes; cook slowly until thickened, adding the olives, capers, pepper, sugar and vinegar. Heat the remaining oil in a broad pan. Dry the aubergine cubes and fry until soft and golden brown. Lift out with a slotted spoon and add to the other vegetables. Mix well, pour into a shallow dish and leave to cool. Serve at room temperature. Serves 4 as a first course.

Tapenade

100 g/4 oz black olives, stoned
100 g/4 oz capers, drained
50 g/2 oz anchovy fillets, soaked in
45 ml/3 tblsps milk
50 g/2 oz tunny fish, drained
7 ml/1/2 tblsp mustard powder
150 ml/1/4 pt olive oil
22 ml/1 1/2 tblsps brandy
black pepper
a pinch of ground mace or nutmeg
6 hard-boiled eggs, halved

Put the olives, capers, drained anchovy fillets, tunny fish and mustard powder in the food processor. Process until a smooth paste. Turn into a bowl and stir in the oil gradually, then add the brandy, pepper and spice. To serve, spread on a flat dish and lay the halved eggs on it, cut side down. Serves 4.

Preserved Lemons

These preserves come from Tunisia, where they are called *limons*, and are much used in delicious oily dishes of grilled green and red peppers, tomatoes, and black olives, like *salat meschoui*.

6 lemons, preferably organic, with thin skins
45 ml/3 tblsps sea salt

brine:
225 g/8 oz coarse salt
2.4 litres/4 pts water

With a sharp knife, cut the lemons almost into quarters, stopping about 1 cm/1/2 in from the bottom, so the four pieces are still joined together. Remove any obvious pips, and rub the sea salt into the cut surfaces. Pack into a stoneware jar, or crock. Make the brine by dissolving the coarse salt in a little boiling water, then making up to 2.4 litres/4 pts with cold water. Allow to cool completely, then pour over the lemons so that they are completely covered. Ideally, they should be held down with a small china or glass plate, or a piece of wood which has been boiled, so that they are kept submerged. Cover the jar and leave for at least 10 days before using. They will keep for 6 months, or even longer. To serve, rinse off the brine and cut in thin slices. They may be served alone, on a small plate, with hors d'œuvres, or included in a dish of mixed vegetables.

Salat Meschoui

This is a marvellous Tunisian dish, far superior to *ratatouille* to my mind, for each individual vegetable has been grilled beforehand, making it much easier to digest, and adding a subtle smokey flavour. The preserved lemon, or *limon*, also adds an unusual piquant tang.

700 g/1 1/2 lb large, ripe tomatoes
3 large cloves garlic
1 Spanish onion
350 g/12 oz green peppers
1 celery heart, plus leaves
1/2 preserved lemon (see above)
15 ml/1 tblsp capers
juice of 1/2 lemon
sea salt and black pepper
2.5 ml/1/2 tsp ground coriander
30 ml/2 tblsps extra virgin olive oil
8-10 black olives

Stick the ripe tomatoes on skewers and grill them, either under the grill or over a gas flame, or in front of an open fire or barbecue, which is best of all. When the skins have blackened and blistered evenly all over, remove and leave to cool. Repeat these with the garlic cloves, the onion, and the green peppers. When all are done, and cool enough to handle, scrape away the charred skin with a small knife, and remove the seeds of the tomatoes and the peppers. Chop all the vegetables together by hand, to a fine hash. Chop the celery, including the leaves, and the preserved lemon, and mix all together, adding the drained and rinsed capers. Put the lemon juice in a soup plate and add a little sea salt and black pepper, and the ground coriander. Add the olive oil and beat with a fork until blended. Mix with the hashed vegetables, then spoon into a shallow dish and scatter the black olives over the top. Serve soon after cooling, at room temperature, or chilled, as you prefer. Serves 4 as a first course, with crusty French or Italian bread, or pitta bread.

Chicken with Green Olives

30 ml/2 tblsps olive oil
25 g/1 oz butter
1.6 kg/3½ lb chicken
1 large onion, sliced
1 head fennel, sliced
2 green peppers, cut in strips
2 red peppers, cut in strips
sea salt and black pepper
2 pckts saffron
175 ml/6 fl oz white wine
175 ml/6 fl oz chicken stock
24 green olives, stoned

Heat the oil and butter in a casserole and brown the chicken all over. Remove it and put the sliced onion in the pan. Cook slowly for 4 mins, then add the sliced fennel, then the peppers. Cook gently for 5 mins all together, then replace the chicken and sprinkle with salt and pepper and saffron. Heat the wine and stock together and add to the pan. Lay the chicken on its side, cover the pan, and cook for 45 mins, either on top of the stove or in the oven at 170°C/325°F/gas mark 3, turning the bird over half-way through. Then turn it breast up, add the olives to the pan, and cook for another 20 mins, or until tender. To serve, lift out the bird and carve into joints: spoon the vegetables into a shallow dish and lay the chicken joints on them. Pour over some of the juice. Serve with pasta, or boiled rice, or steamed couscous. Serves 4.

Braised Beef with Olives

60 ml/4 tblsps olive oil
1 large onion, coarsely chopped
50 g/2 oz unsmoked bacon, chopped
2 cloves garlic, finely chopped
2 stalks celery, sliced
1.1 kg/2½ lbs rolled topside of beef
30 ml/2 tblsps brandy
100 g/4 oz young carrots, thickly sliced
225 g/8 oz tomatoes, skinned and coarsely chopped
200 ml/7 fl oz stock

200 ml/7 fl oz red wine
sea salt and black pepper
1 bay leaf
3 stalks parsley
3 sprigs thyme
1 strip dried orange peel
16 black olives

Heat 45 ml/3 tblsps oil in a heavy casserole and cook the chopped onion gently. After 2-3 mins, add the chopped bacon, then the chopped garlic and the sliced celery. Stew all together gently for 5 mins, then lift out with a slotted spoon. Put another 15 ml/1 tblsp oil in the pan and brown the meat, turning on all sides. Warm the brandy in a large spoon, set light to it, and pour over the beef. When the flames have died down, put the fried vegetables back in the pan, and add the sliced carrots and chopped tomatoes. Heat the stock and wine together and pour on, adding sea salt, black pepper, bay leaf, parsley, thyme and orange peel. Cover closely and cook for 3½ hours at 160°C/310°F/gas mark 2-3. Then add the olives and cook for a further 30 mins. To serve, carve the beef in thick slices and lay in a shallow dish. Take as much fat as possible off the surface of the sauce, spoon the vegetables and olives over the meat, and pour the sauce over all. Serve with noodles and a green salad. Serves 6.

Veal with Green Olives

45 ml/3 tblsps olive oil
1 large onion, sliced
2 stalks celery, sliced
1 green pepper, cut in strips
1 head fennel, sliced
900 g/2 lb stewing veal, cut in cubes
seasoned flour
225 g/8 oz tomatoes, skinned and cut in quarters
300 ml/½ pt chicken stock
150 m/¼ pt white wine
1 bay leaf
1 piece dried orange peel
sea salt and black pepper
grated ginger
24 green olives, stoned

Heat the oil and cook the onion, celery, pepper and fennel slowly for 5 mins, stirring often. Dip the veal in seasoned flour and add to the pan. Stir round until lightly coloured, then add the tomatoes, and cook for a further 2 mins. Heat the stock and wine and pour on, adding the bay leaf, orange peel, salt and pepper and grated ginger. (I use whole roots of dried ginger, grating them as needed; alternatively use ground ginger.) Cover and simmer for 1½ hours, then add the green olives and cook another 30 mins. Serve with boiled rice and a green salad. Serves 5-6.

Salade Niçoise

a few lettuce leaves
225 g/8 oz tomatoes, cut in quarters
175 g/6 oz string beans, boiled and cooled
225 g/8 oz large mild onion, cut in rings
225 g/8 oz tunny fish, drained
3 hard-boiled eggs, halved
10 black olives, rinsed
4 large leaves basil, cut in strips
sea salt and black pepper
1.25 ml/¼ tsp Dijon mustard
90 ml/6 tblsps olive oil

Line a bowl with lettuce leaves and pile the cut tomatoes in it. Cover with the string beans and the sliced onion. Flake the drained tunny fish and pile in the centre, with the halved eggs round the edges of the bowl. Add the olives and scatter the basil over all. Mix the salt, pepper and mustard with the olive oil and pour over the salad, tossing thoroughly. Serves 4, as a substantial first course or a light main dish.

Salad of Orange, Olives and Watercress

This is an excellent salad to serve with cold duck. Young spinach leaves, called *pousses* in France, can be substituted for the watercress.

2 bunches watercress, or 4 handfuls young spinach leaves
3 small oranges, or blood oranges
30 ml/2 tblsps chopped shallots
a pinch of sea salt
15 ml/1 tblsp lemon juice
15 ml/1 tblsp orange juice
60 ml/4 tblsps olive oil
freshly ground black pepper
8-10 black olives, stoned (or not, as you prefer)

Pinch the tender sprigs off the watercress, discarding the tough stalks. (Or, discard the stalks of the spinach). Wash and shake dry, then pat in a cloth. Pile in a wooden bowl. Peel the oranges with a sharp knife, taking away every last scrap of white pith. Cut across into round slices and lay over the watercress. Scatter the chopped shallots over all. Put a pinch of sea salt in a small bowl and add the fruit juices. Beat well, adding the olive oil. Once it is blended, pour over the salad and toss gently, grinding some black pepper in as you do so. Finally, scatter the black olives over all and serve, with cold roast duck, or after a game dish. Serves 4.

September

In medieval times, dishes called grand sallets were made with complex mixtures of different ingredients: chicken, pickled or salt fish, hard-boiled eggs, raw, cooked and pickled vegetables. These were massed together in a great mound, and garnished with edible flowers. By the late eighteenth century, a derivation of these dishes had become popular: this was called salamagundy. As described in *The Art of Cookery Made Plain and Easy* by Hannah Glasse, published in 1871, it is assembled in a novel way, with all the different components laid out in small dishes. The garnish of flowers, usually nasturtiums or violets, remains as before.

The use of flowers in food, either for flavouring or as a decorative garnish, is no modern idea, but one that was common practice in England for hundreds of years. During the fourteenth and fifteenth centuries, many flowers were included in the herb gardens of monasteries and private houses, for use in the kitchen, dispensary, and for strewing. The most usual were roses, lilies, border carnations (gillyflowers), lavender, violets, nasturtiums and marigolds.

In the East, orange flowers and jasmine have been used as flavourings for centuries, as have rose petals in Turkey and Iran. In Central European countries, elderflowers are still picked in June, dipped in batter, and deep fried. In Italy and the South of France, courgette flowers are sold in the markets, for stuffing with rice or cheese, and frying in batter. It is only in England that the use of flowers has lapsed, except for a few isolated cases, so rare as to seem almost symbolic, like the sprig of borage in Pimm's. Almost the only real use of flowers that has survived is thanks to the Women's Insistute, in rural areas, where wines are still made with cowslips, primroses, elderflowers and dandelions.

In the past, the English used flowers as much for their flavour as for decorative effect. Marigolds were dried and added to *bouquets garnis*, for flavouring beef stews and broths.

(Dried marigolds can be bought or grown and dried at home. Only the Pot Marigold, *Calendula officinalis*, should be used, not the French or African Marigold, *Tagetes patula* or *Tagetes erecta*.) Dried marigolds were also used as a cheaper substitute for saffron - itself a flower, but a very expensive one, since only the pistils of the crocus are used. Nasturtium seeds were pickled and used like capers: the flowers were preserved in a chutney-like sauce.

The petals of roses, violets, and primroses were crystallized, for adding to cakes and sweet dishes.

In France, on the other hand, flowers seem to have been used mainly for decoration, both of dishes and the table, apart from their health-giving properties. In *Savouring the Past* Barbara Ketcham Wheaton gives a description of the wedding feast of the illegitimate daughter of Louis XIV to the Prince de Condi, in 1680. The table was decorated with nineteen openwork baskets in silver and silver gilt, filled with anemones, hyacinths, jasmine, tulips and orange leaves - no mean feat for the middle of January. One hundred years later, the great mustard firm of Maille was making sixty-five different vinegars, flavoured with fruit, flowers, and herbs. One made with elderflowers sounds irresistible.

The first time I saw flowers actually on my plate was in the 1960s, at a restaurant called Parkes, in Beauchamp Place, where they were used lavishly, and with dramatic effect. I was somewhat startled by the exotic appearance of the dishes - a typically English reaction. I still however prefer flowers used as an intrinsic part of a dish, rather than merely as a decoration.

Even the use of flowers as flavouring, however, seemed strange at first. I was put off by the memory of dishes flavoured with orange flower water, and rose water, with their perfumed taste that I find hard to like. But the use of fresh flowers gives quite another effect. One of my friends used to flavour an apple jelly with lavender; another showed me how to make elderflower fritters, and I was converted. The great appeal of such dishes is that they cannot be simulated. They can only be made at the right time of year, with ingredients that have been picked in the garden, or gathered in the fields. This is what gives them their particular magic, and makes them memorable.

The use of flowers in food seems to be coming back into fashion. Some supermarkets now sell cartons of mixed salad leaves which include the flowers of nasturtium and borage, inviting a revival of the Elizabethan Salad. At Hediard, in the Place de la Madeleine, jars of flower-petal jelly can be bought, made with the blooms of roses, jasmine and orange blossom. They also sell jars of crystallized lilac blossom in different colours, also red rose petals, violets and mimosa: an ideal present for anyone who likes decorating cakes.

146

The history of the domestic duck in England over the past fifty years differs only slightly from that of the hen. Before the war, ducks were kept largely for the table, both for the sake of their eggs, and for the occasional bird. Immediately after the war the number of duck kept in this country fell, since the spread of broiler houses and battery farms altered the British attitude towards poultry. Unlike hens, ducks and geese do not lend themselves to intensive farming, and people began to feel that it was uneconomic to keep birds that didn't show a larger profit. So the old breeds started to die out, just as they did in the case of hens.

They reached their lowest ebb in the sixties, and it was not until the early seventies that the old breeds began to regain their popularity. This was linked, in part, with a growing nostalgia for the countryside, and the old customs. The British Waterfowl Association was formed and it promoted a campaign to clean up village ponds throughout the country, and restock them with ducks and geese. Poultry shows and exhibitions began to spread all over the country, and a new national interest was born. While in *The Poultry Book* by Wingfield & Johnson, first published in 1853, only eight breeds of duck are mentioned, now there are over twenty, many with colour variations. Whereas only four breeds of geese were listed in 1853, now there are nine.

A leading figure in the British waterfowl world is Tom Bartlett, vice-president of the British Waterfowl Association, who has been breeding ducks and geese since 1937. He has probably done more than anyone else in this country to promote the old breeds, and to protect them from dying out. He delights in introducing newcomers to his birds, encouraging their interest, and guiding their enthusiasm in the right direction. At Folly Farm, near Bourton-on-the-Water, in Gloucestershire, Tom has over 2,000 birds, many of them living on a series of fresh-water ponds fed by springs. Folly Farm is open to the public and draws 10,000 visitors a year. Tom sells 800 pairs of duck a year; these are to be kept live, not for killing and eating.

Ducks are a more attractive choice for the potential breeder than hens. For one thing, the lines have been kept pure, whereas with chickens you tend to get throwbacks. And ducks have kept their value, unlike chickens which have become seriously underpriced in recent years.

I find ducks more appealing than chickens. I like their stance, their gait, and their expression. Ducks are predominantly well-disposed towards humans, and adapt themselves amazingly well to human company. As Tom Bartlett says: 'You can keep them in a large garden, and they don't damage the plants, they will rid the garden of slugs and snails, they will all lay before nine o'clock in the morning, and they will go to bed when you tell them!'

He relates how a lady recently brought five Call ducks over to Folly Farm sitting on the back seat of her car. When she opened the car door they jumped out and waddled off to join the 800 other ducks for a dip in the big lake. After lunch, their owner put her fingers in her mouth and whistled three times, whereupon five small ducks clambered out of the pond, waddled back to the car park, and got into the car. Geese also become very attached to their owners. I remember a young man some years ago telling me how he had a pair of Canada geese and one had died, whereupon the other adopted him as her mate. She followed him everywhere, even flying after his car when he went out to dinner, sitting on the bonnet until he emerged from his friend's house, then flying back home after him.

The friendly little Call duck is almost my favourite: adorable in appearance, it looks just like the rubber duck we used to put in the bath. It comes in various colours, but I like the pure white best, with its pale yellow bill. It is one of the easiest ducks to keep, but it is very noisy, with a constant loud quack. (Only ducks quack; drakes merely clear their throats.) Its noisy behaviour is what gave the Call duck its name, for it was used as a decoy, to 'call' in the wild birds when out shooting.

My other favourite is the Indian Runner, with its comic stance. It looks like a hock bottle on legs, standing almost upright, leaning forward at an angle of eighty degrees. The Indian Runner comes in eight different colour variations and was brought back from Malaysia by a sea captain from the Borders, who proceeded to give Indian Runners to many of his neighbours. They are enchanting birds, and very good layers. For this reason they were used in the breeding of the popular Khaki Campbell. Unlike most ducks, the Indian Runners make good mothers. (For some strange reason, only the small ducks make caring mothers.) Another attractive small bird is the Black East Indian duck, with its glossy green sheen, and the White Crested duck, with its topknot worn like a knitted beret on the back of its head. Some of the larger birds are also very appealing, like the German Pekin, which has an upright stance similar to the Indian Runner. The glossy black Cayuga duck lays black eggs; the Khaki Campbell lays white eggs, while the white Campbell lays blue eggs. Unlike hens, there are few miniaturized breeds of duck.

Over half of the world's population relies on rice for its staple diet. Rice grew in India 5,000 years ago, but it did not reach Europe for several thousand years, brought by the Arab invaders in the eleventh century. It must have reached England by 1400, for it appeared in dishes at the wedding feast of Henry IV, in 1399. Rice flour figures frequently in a fifteenth-century English cookery book. Yet rice itself never became very popular in England, except as rice pudding. During the days of the Raj, many of the British living in India grew to like rice, and the Indian dish of lentils and rice called *khichri* evolved into the popular English breakfast dish, kedgeree.

According to some estimates, there are as many as 10,000 varieties of rice - more than 1,000 in India - yet only a few reach Britain. For the most part they fall into two categories: long-grain and short-grain. The two main varieties of long-grain rice available here are Basmati rice from Pakistan, and Carolina rice from the USA (not necessarily from Carolina). As a general rule, long-grain keeps its grains separate, while short-grain sticks together. Each has its own virtues. Basmati rice is best used for curries and other Indian dishes, for Iranian pilavs and most Middle Eastern dishes. It can be used for Chinese and South-East Asian dishes, although many cooks use Carolina rice for these.

Carolina rice, as typified by Uncle Ben, is the rice most widely bought in the UK. It has little intrinsic character of its own, yet is immensely adaptable and almost impossible to spoil. It can be used for virtually any type of rice dish and can even be used for puddings. The USA is now the world's largest exporter of rice, since the Eastern rice-growing countries use most of theirs for home consumption. However, long-grain rice is also grown in most of China, South-East Asia and the Middle East. The Chinese grow a short-grained rice as well, and a round glutinous rice, used mainly for sweet dishes. Short-grained rice is also grown in Japan, where they like a sticky rice, easily eaten with chopsticks.

Italian short-grained rice, grown in the Po Valley, is the basic food - as opposed to pasta - of northern Italy. The excellent Italian *superfino* rice can be bought here, from Italian shops; there is also a white *cristallo* or golden *arborio*, both ideal for *risottos*. I also use this rice for *paella* since it is similar to the variety grown in Valencia and to my mind superior.

Brown rice is rice that has been milled once only, thus retaining its outer casing, or bran, which contains most of its mineral content. After its second milling the rice becomes white, or 'pearled'; during the process more than half the vitamin and mineral content is lost. From a health point of view we should always eat brown rice. It is an extremely balanced and complete food, ideal for a day's eating prior to a fast, or as an interim before returning to a normal diet after fasting, or simply as a rest for the system once a week. Like all whole-grain and unrefined foods, it is not easy to digest for those who are not used to it.

Wild rice is an anomaly since it is not, strictly speaking, a rice at all but a sort of grass. It is a luxury food, rare and highly priced. It grows mainly in the eastern states of North America, where only the Indians are allowed to harvest it. They gather it by canoe from the swamps. It also grows in Taiwan, China and Japan. It is even richer in food value than brown rice but is so expensive that it is mostly used in small quantities: as a stuffing for game birds, or mixed with white or brown rice for economy.

Rice can be grown under water or on dry land; the former method is more usual. In ideal conditions near the Equator, in places like Bali, rice can be grown all year round. In southern China it is harvested twice a year four months after sowing. One of the most beautiful sights I have seen was rice growing on the terraces of western Szechuan, near the Tibetan border. Here, in enchanting countryside of unreal beauty, every spare inch has been terraced into ricefields, following the contours of the land. At every level, climbing the slopes of the rounded hills, lie crescent-shaped fields filled with trapped water reflecting the sky. From a gastronomic point of view, however, rice in China is disappointing. It is used largely as a filler; the poor eat rice - and little else - three times a day, while at banquets rice is hardly seen. Neither does rice in Japan have much appeal for Western palates, for here it is cooked without salt and served in a bland, somewhat gluey mass.

Some of the most delicious rice dishes must be those of Azerbaijan, in the Caucasus. Here excellent pilavs are made: fillings of meat, mushrooms, dried fruit and nuts are enclosed between two layers of rice and steamed. For Turkish pilavs the rice is often flavoured with saffron and cooked with pine nuts and raisins. Sweet dishes of rice and rose water are also popular in Turkey. The Greeks make a creamy rice pudding called *risogallo*, flavoured with the elusive mastic, the resin of a species of pine tree grown on the island of Chios. Italian *risottos* are among my favourite dishes; *risotto Milanese* is one of the simplest, made with chicken stock and saffron and served as the traditional accompaniment to *osso buco*. Best of all, in autumn, is a *risotto* served with grated white truffles scattered over it.

The Gentle Art of Cookery is a classic, unique among cookery books in its powers of evocation. Written in 1925, it conveys a sort of natural magic, a sense of things unsaid. This was Mrs Leyel's first book, written in conjunction with Miss Olga Hartley.

Most food writers err on the side of the prosaic, writing with one hand in the flour bin, as Paul Levy once remarked of a colleague. Hilda Leyel, on the other hand, was a master at conveying the magical side of cookery, its essence of romance and mystery. Her book has many admirers, including Elizabeth David, who wrote the introduction for the paperback edition. Surprisingly undated, despite the fact that it was written so many years ago, the preface states: 'The book has been made as modern as possible; there are a great many recipes for cooking vegetables and fruit, because the tendency of today is to eat less meat.' In 1925? Certainly, the main part of the book is given up to fruit and vegetables, with special chapters on almonds, chestnuts, mushrooms, and flower recipes. One chapter is called 'Food from the Arabian Nights', another 'The Alchemist's Cupboard'. Nor are these purely fanciful, for Mrs Leyel was a fund of knowledge about the East, and about alchemy.

She must have been a remarkable figure. The daughter of a house master at Uppingham, she left school early to work in the theatre, and married, at seventeen, a Swedish theatrical manager called Carl Frederick Leyel. In 1934 she was prosecuted for organizing The Gold Ballot to raise money for ex-servicemen and hospitals. She was acquitted, having helped to legalize lotteries for charity, and raised £350,000; for this she was made a Life Governor of three eminent London hospitals. She then proceeded to study herbalism, in particular the work of the seventeenth-century herbalist, Nicholas Culpeper. In 1925 she published The Gentle Art of Cookery, and the following year The Truth about Herbs. In 1927 she opened the first Culpeper shop, selling herbal medicines, foods and cosmetics. The same year she started the Society of Herbalists, later to become the Herb Society, to promote the practice of herbalism in Britain. In 1941 both the shops and the Society - indeed the future of herbalism - were threatened by the proposed Pharmacy and Medicines Bill. Mrs Leyel, aided by some influential friends, got an amendment passed, enabling herbalists to continue their practice, although within limits. (One of the friends who helped her, and who later took on the Herb Society, was Lady Meade-Fetherstonhaugh, owner of Uppark, whose success in the restoration of the eighteenth and nineteenth-century fabrics by natural methods was legendary.)

In 1947 she published the first of the Culpeper Herbals, a huge body of work which only ended with her death ten years later. These six books: Herbal Delights, Compassionate Herbs, Elixirs of Life, Heartsease, Green Medicine and Cinquefoil, are an astonishing tribute to her breadth of knowledge. Quite unlike the old-fashioned herbals, they are a fascinating mixture of information on such obscure plants as durian, ginseng, and mastic - none of which I had even heard of ten years ago - quotations ranging from Cardinal Newman to Willa Cather, and some appealing recipes for such things as Green Almond Tarts, Vine Leaf Fritters, and Rose Petal Sandwiches. Now sadly out of print, they have as many as fourteen different indices ranging from Turkish to Sanskrit.

Yet it is not knowledge alone that conveys a sense of magic. I would guess it is also due to three other things: a way with words, a sense of the past, and a feeling for the unknown. Magic, as defined by the Oxford English Dictionary, is 'produced by enchantment'. Natural magic, which seems particularly appropriate to Mrs Leyel's work, is 'that which does not involve recourse to the agency of personal spirits', thus removed from any taint of witchcraft, or the occult. Some of Mrs Leyel's appeal lies in the fact that she was a true alchemist. Alchemy was a medieval science, a forerunner of chemistry as it were. It constituted the search for the alkehest, a universal solvent capable of transmuting base metals into gold, and the panacea, a cure for all illness. Linked with herbalism, alchemy was tinged with romance, not unlike the search for the Holy Grail. Elizabeth David, herself a master of evocative writing, sees The Gentle Art of Cookery as 'yet another manifestation of the English love affair with Eastern food'. Much of the magic connected with food comes from the East, from Turkey, Persia, and the Middle East, where myth and legend are interwoven with kitchen lore. An Iranian friend tells me of a traditional dish among her family: the first snow of winter, eaten with honey, as a dessert. This is to me pure magic, enhanced by the realization that it can have virtually no sustenance whatsoever.

Another writer who bears witness to Eastern magic is Claudia Roden, in her classic, Middle Eastern Food. In this case, nostalgia for her homeland gives the book its potency, as Mrs Roden conjures up scenes from her childhood in Cairo with all the passion of a true exile. She describes eating ful medames with a group of relations, all exiles from Egypt, in a one-room flat in Paris. 'Ceremoniously, we sprinkled the beans with olive oil, squeezed a little lemon over them, seasoned them with salt and midst. Delicious ecstasy! Silently, we ate the beans whole and firm at first, then we squashed them with our forks and combined their floury texture and slightly dull, earthy taste with the acid tang of the lemon, mellowed by the olive oil; finally, we crumbled the egg, matching its earthiness with that of the beans, its pale warm yellow with their dull brown...'

Traditional English dishes have their own power, as we find in such books as Dorothy Hartley's *Food in England*, and Florence White's *Good Things in England*. Here the magic is summoned up by ancient recipes, dishes using wild foods gathered in the fields or woods, with the familiar thread of folk lore running through them. Such things as Easter Ledge Pudding, made with wild herbs and barley, or a bargee's dinner, cooked in a bucket on the tow-path - things far removed from the modern world of supermarkets and launderettes, of synthetic cake mixes and pot noodles.

Stuffed Eggs with Nasturtiums

6 large eggs
sea salt and black pepper
30 ml/2 tblsps soured cream
30 ml/2 tblsps chopped chives
15 ml/1 tblsp chopped dill
15 ml/1 tblsp chopped chervil
12 nasturtium leaves
6-8 nasturtium flowers

Boil the eggs for 12 mins; cool and shell. Cut them in half lengthwise and scoop out the yolks. Mash them with a fork, adding salt and pepper to taste. Stir in the soured cream and chopped herbs, then pack into the egg whites, mounding them up. Lay them on a bed of nasturtium leaves and scatter the flowers among them. Serves 4, as a first course.

Fried Courgette Flowers 1

These flowers are simply dipped in batter and deep fried. If picking them in your own garden, be careful only to pick the male flowers until the fruit has formed, after which time the female flowers also may be picked.

batter:

100 g/4 oz flour
a pinch of salt
30 ml/2 tblsps sunflower oil
150 ml/1/4 pt warm water
1 egg white, beaten
frying oil
24 courgette (or marrow) flowers

garnish:

2 lemons, cut in quarters

Make the batter a little ahead of time, either in a food processor or by hand. Sift the flour and salt into the food processor, then add the oil. Process, adding the water through the lid. Stand for 1 hour if convenient. Process again just before using, then pour into a bowl and fold in the stiffly beaten egg white. Have a deep pan, or a wok, half full of oil. Heat it until approximately 180ºC/360ºF. Then dip the flowers in the batter, scrape off excess on the side of the bowl, and drop into the hot oil. Cook for 2-3 mins, turning them over once. Drain on soft paper and serve immediately, piled loosely on a hot dish, with lemon quarters. Serves 4, as a first course.

Fried Courgette Flowers 2

These flowers have been filled with a little rice and spinach stuffing, not unlike a *risotto*, before frying. Batter as before.

stuffing:

1 medium onion, chopped
22 ml/1½ tblsps olive oil
1 small clove garlic, finely chopped
50 g/2 oz rice
225 g/8 oz spinach
sea salt and black pepper
40 g/1½ oz freshly grated Parmesan
1 egg and 1 yolk, beaten together
frying oil
20 courgette flowers

garnish:

2 lemons, cut in quarters

First make the batter. Cook the onion in the oil until it starts to colour, then add the garlic and cook for another min, then set aside. Cook the rice in lightly salted boiling water until just tender; drain. Drop the spinach into lightly salted boiling water and cook for 4 mins; drain well, squeezing out excess moisture, then chop. Reheat the onion, add the rice and cook for 1-2 mins, then remove from the heat and stir in the chopped spinach. Mix well, adding salt and pepper to taste, grated Parmesan, and beaten egg. Leave to cool. A little later, heat some oil to 180ºC/360ºF. Beat the batter once more and fold in the egg white. Spoon a little of the stuffing into each of the flowers, folding over the petals to enclose it. Then dip each one in batter and drop into the hot oil. Fry them for about 4 mins, turning over once. Then drain on soft paper while you cook the next lot. Don't try to do too many at one time. Serve as soon as possible, with cut lemons. Serves 5-6.

Stuffed Courgette Flowers

12 courgette flowers
60 ml/4 tblsps olive oil for frying

stuffing:

250 g/9 oz fresh Ricotta cheese
salt and freshly ground black pepper
3 grates of nutmeg
1 bunch chives, chopped
1 egg, beaten
60 ml/4 tblsps freshly grated Parmesan

batter:

2 eggs
50 g/2 oz flour
60 ml/4 tblsps cold water

First make the batter. Beat the eggs, stir in the flour evenly then gradually add the water to make a smooth consistency. Put it aside.
Meanwhile, clean the flowers carefully: gently wash and dry the outside, and make sure there are no insects inside. Prepare the filling by thoroughly mixing together the Ricotta, salt, pepper, nutmeg, chopped chives, beaten egg and grated Parmesan cheese. Use spoonfuls of the mixture to fill the flowers. Then dip the flowers into the batter and proceed to fry in hot oil until

golden brown. Drain on kitchen paper briefly before serving. Serves 4.

Elder Flower Fritters

This delicate dish can only be made in late May or early June, when the elder blossoms are out. Pick the young heads only, shaking them well; do not wash them. These fritters are very popular in Central Europe – Austria, Poland and Czechoslovakia, where they are served either as a vegetable dish or, sweetened, as a dessert.

Version 1

18 elder flowers
frying oil

batter:

100 g/4 oz flour, sifted
a pinch of salt
30 ml/2 tblsps sunflower oil
150 ml/1/4 pt tepid water
1 egg white, beaten

Make the batter an hour in advance. Sift flour and salt into a food processor or large bowl. Add the oil gradually, while processing, or beating with an electric beater, or by hand. Then add the water slowly, continuing to process or beat until you have a smooth cream. Stand for 1 hour, then process or beat again. Fold in the stiffly beaten egg white just before serving.
Have a deep pan or wok half filled with oil to approximately 180ºC/360ºF/gas mark 4. Dip each flower head in the batter, shake off the excess, and drop into the hot oil. Do not crowd them; only do a few at a time. Cook for 2-3 mins, turning once, then lift out and drain on soft paper. Then fry another batch, and transfer the first lot to a warm dish. When all are done, serve immediately, as a vegetable, or as a first course. If serving as a vegetable they go best with dry dishes like chicken, lamb or veal, grilled chicken wings or lamb cutlets, or escalopes of veal. If serving alone, add some lemon wedges. Serves 6.

Version 2

If serving as a dessert, add 10 ml/2 tsps castor sugar to the batter. Sprinkle the fritters with castor sugar before serving, with lemon wedges. Serves 6.

Golden Risotto

1.4 kg/3 lb pumpkin
4 shallots, chopped
50 g/2 oz butter
350 g/12 oz risotto rice
900 ml/1½ pts chicken stock
sea salt and black pepper
freshly grated Parmesan

garnish:

8-10 courgette or marrow flowers, deep fried, or 4 marigolds

Make the pumpkin purée in advance:
Discard the rind and seeds, and cut the pumpkin into cubes about 4-5 cm/1½ -2 ins square. Place them in a steamer over boiling water and cook, covered, until soft, about 10 mins. Then purée in a food processor, or push through a medium food mill. Turn into a clean pan and cook gently, over very low heat, for 10 mins, stirring often, to dry out the purée. At the end you should have 450 ml/¾ pt of fairly thick purée.

When ready to make the *risotto*, cook the chopped shallots gently in the butter in a broad pan. When they start to soften and colour, add the rice. Stir around until it is coated with butter, then add the pumpkin purée and stir to mix well. Cook gently for 1-2 mins, then pour on half the heated stock. Add salt and pepper, cover the pan, and cook gently until almost all the stock is absorbed. Then add the remainder, cover again, and simmer until the rice is cooked and all the stock has been absorbed. Turn out onto a round dish to serve, surrounded with deep fried courgette or marrow flowers. As a simpler garnish, use the flowers uncooked, or alternatively, scatter the petals of the marigolds over the surface of the dish. Serve as soon as made, with a bowl of freshly grated Parmesan. Serves 4 as a main dish or 5-6 as a first course.

Creamed Rice with Marigolds

100 g/4 oz short grain rice
600 ml/1 pt milk
1 vanilla pod
30 ml/2 tblsps vanilla sugar or
castor sugar
200 ml/7 fl oz double cream
4 pot marigolds, petals only

Put the rice in a buttered dish with the milk, vanilla pod, and vanilla (or castor) sugar. Cook for 2 hours at 130°C/250°F/gas mark ½. Remove and leave to cool. Then remove the skin and the vanilla pod. Warm the cream gently with the marigold petals, then fold it into the cooked rice. Turn into a serving dish and chill for 2-3 hours before serving. Serves 4. This goes well with a dish of stewed apricots, fresh or dried, cooked with vanilla sugar.

A Tart of Flowers

This is based on a 16th-century recipe from *Good Things in England* by Florence White. It was made with borage, marigolds or cowslips. I tested it with elderflowers, in season at the time of writing, and it was delicious.

pastry:
175 g/6 oz flour
75 g/3 oz butter

2.5 ml/½ tsp castor sugar
a little iced water

filling:
300 ml/½ pt single cream
8 marigolds, petals only, or 3 elderflowers
3 large egg yolks
50 g/2 oz castor sugar
1 large egg white, stiffly beaten

Make the pastry, roll out, and line a 20.5 cm/8 in pie tin. Bake blind, weighed down with beans, for 8 mins at 190°C/375°F/gas mark 5, then take out and turn the oven down to 180°C/350°F/gas mark 4.

Heat the cream slowly with the marigold petals or elderflowers. When hot, but not yet boiling, remove from the heat and stand, covered, for 10 mins. Then beat the egg yolks with the sugar, reheat the cream and pour through a strainer onto the eggs, beating well. Fold in the stiffly beaten egg white and pour into the pastry case. Bake for 20 mins or until puffy or golden brown. Serve as soon as possible. Serves 4. Six sprigs of borage, flowers only, or 8 cowslips can be substituted for the marigolds or elder flowers.

RARE BREEDS OF DUCK

Lentil Soup with Duck Skin

for the stock:
½ duck
1 onion, halved
1 leek, halved
1 carrot, halved
1 stalk celery, halved
150 ml/¼ pt dry white wine
sea salt and 6 black peppercorns

for the soup:
25 g/1 oz butter
15 ml/1 tblsp olive oil
1 carrot, sliced
175 g/6 oz lentilles de Puy, or green lentils, washed
sea salt and black pepper

Start one day in advance. Remove the skin from the duck breast and put aside. Put the rest of the duck in a pressure cooker. Add 1.2 litres/2 pts of cold water and bring slowly to the boil, skimming now and then. When the surface is clear, add the flavouring vegetables (keeping back the best part of the leek and celery), the wine, sea salt and black peppercorns. Bring back to the boil, screw down, and cook for 1 hour under pressure (or 3 hours in an ordinary pan). Then strain, cool, and chill overnight.

Next day remove all the fat from the surface of the stock.

You should have at least 1 litre/¾ pt. Slice the tender, (or white) parts of the leek and the celery that you reserved from the stock. Cook them in the butter and oil for

3 mins, then add the sliced carrot and cook for another 3 mins before adding the lentils. Cook gently altogether for 4 mins, while you heat the stock. Then pour it on and bring to the boil slowly, adding sea salt and black pepper. Half cover the pan and cook gently until the lentils are soft, about 35 mins. Then leave to cool for a little, and purée in the food processor. Tip into a bowl and leave for a few hours if possible, for the flavours to develop. Shortly before serving, cut the duck skin in thin strips, paring away most of the fat from the inside. Fry them gently in a non-stick pan, until they have rendered most of their fat and become crisp, then drain them on soft paper. Reheat the soup and serve in bowls with the strips of duck skin laid over it. Serves 4-5.

A simpler version of this soup can be made by buying a smoked *magret de canard*. Remove the skin, pare away the fat, and fry the skin as above. Then use as a garnish for a lentil soup made with a good game or chicken stock. The smokey taste of the skin is excellent with the lentils.

Fresh Foie Gras, Poached

This is the old way of cooking a whole *foie gras* wrapped in a cloth, as practised in the south-west of France. Whereas formerly this was usually the liver of the goose, it is now often made with the duck's liver, which is slightly less expensive. I am indebted to Mme. Gracia, proprietress of a famous restaurant in Gascony, Auberge à la Belle Gasconne, in Poudenas, for the recipe. Fresh *foie gras* can be bought at French *boucheries* in London. They weigh between 450 g/1 lb and 790 g/1¾ lb.

Start several days before you plan to eat it. Make about 5 pts good stock with veal bones, poultry, vegetables and seasonings. It must be very well flavoured; you may add a little sherry, port or brandy. Leave to cool, then chill overnight. Sprinkle the *foie gras* with salt and black pepper and leave in a cool place overnight.

Next day, remove the fat from the surface of the stock and divide in half. Put one half in a bowl, and the other in a saucepan just broad enough to hold the *foie gras.* Scald a piece of cloth in boiling water, leave to cool, then wring it out and roll the *foie gras* in it, twisting the ends like a cracker. Tie tightly with string at either end. Lower the bundle into the cold stock in the saucepan – there must be enough stock to cover it – and heat until it starts to simmer. Keep at this temperature for 30-35 mins, depending on size. Try not to let it ever reach a full boil. When the time is up, lift it out of the pan carefully, for it will be very soft, and lower it into the bowl of cold stock and leave to cool. When it has cooled completely, lift it out and unwrap it. Transfer it very carefully into a rectangular china dish; one holding about 900 ml/1½ pts will do nicely. Cover it loosely with a piece of foil and place a small board or dish about the same size and shape on the foil. Lay about 675 g/1½ lb in weights on the board and leave for a few hours. Then remove weights, board and foil, and flood the *foie gras* with melted duck or goose fat, or clarified butter. This provides an airtight seal, so that the dish can be kept for 2 or 3 weeks under refrigeration. (It should in any case be kept for 2-3 days before eating.) Keep the stock; it will make an excellent consommé. Serve the *foie gras* in its dish, with warm toast. (No butter.) Toasted *brioche* is especially delicious, as is a sweet, or semi-sweet wine. Many people serve a very sweet wine like Sauternes, but I prefer a Vouvray Demi Sec, or an Alsatian Vendange Tardive Gewürztztraminer. A *foie gras* weighing 675 g/1½ lb will feed eight; it should be served cold, soon after taking out of the refrigerator, and is best cut with a knife kept standing in a jug of hot water.

Roast Gressingham Duck

This recipe also works well with a larger French or English duck, allowing 18 mins per 450 g/1 lb roasting time in all.

1 Gressingham or Croisé duck (about 1.1 kg/2½ lbs)

glaze:
15 ml/1 tblsp clear honey
15 ml/1 tblsp fruit jelly (crab apple, rowan, redcurrant etc)
30 ml/2 tblsps bourbon whiskey, Southern Comfort or port
juice of ½ orange
juice of ½ lemon

Prick the duck all over with a sharp skewer and lay upside down in a rack in a roasting pan. Roast for 20 mins at 200°C/400°F/gas mark 6. During the last 5 mins, put the ingredients for the glaze in a small bowl over a pan of simmering water and heat until the honey has melted and the ingredients have blended. When the 20 mins are up, turn the duck right side up and spoon some of the glaze over it. Return to the oven and roast for another 25 mins (or 18 mins per 450 g/1 lb in all), basting 2-3 times with the rest of the glaze. When the time is up, remove from the oven and keep warm for 5-10 mins before serving. Cut in half to serve, using poultry shears to cut through the carcase – ducks have much larger bones than chickens – and remove the backbone entirely, keeping it for stock. Serve with baked potatoes which have been cooked in the oven at the same time as the duck, then puréed and put

back in the skins, or new potatoes in their skins, and an orange and watercress salad. Serves 2.

These little duck are also very good cold, cooked as above then left to cool at room temperature for a few hours, then served with a dish of lentils, also at room temperature, and a green salad.

Smoked Duck with Lentils

1 pckt (2 breasts) smoked magrets de canard
2 bunches large spring onions, sliced
45 ml/3 tblsps olive oil
2 cloves garlic, finely chopped
2.5 ml/½ tsp black peppercorns
2.5 ml/½ tsp black mustard seeds
5 ml/1 tsp sea salt
2.5 ml/½ tsp ground coriander
225 g/8 oz green lentils, cooked
100-175 g /4-6 oz brown lentils, when available, cooked
2 x 2.5 cm/1 in pieces root ginger, juice of
zest of 1 lime
juice of 2 limes
45 ml/3 tblsps chopped coriander
frying oil

Cook half the sliced spring onions in the oil for 2-3 mins, then add the garlic and cook for another 2 mins, stirring. Crush the peppercorns and mustard seeds roughly in a mortar and add to the onions and garlic. Cook for 1 min, then add the sea salt and ground coriander; cook for another 1-2 mins, stirring. Then stir in the drained (cooked) lentils and cook gently for 5 mins, stirring now and then. (If you can't get any brown lentils, use 350 g/12 oz green lentils. Don't add orange lentils as they will spoil it.) Now remove from the heat and stir in the juice of the ginger, which you have crushed in a garlic press, the finely chopped zest and juice of the limes, and the rest of the spring onions (uncooked). Leave to cool, then stir in the coriander.

Take the skin off the *magrets*, removing most of the fat, then cut it (the skin) in strips about 3 mm/⅛ in wide. Drop the little strips into a small frying pan half full of hot oil and fry for 1-2 mins, until they are crisp and golden. Then lift them onto soft paper to drain, leave to cool. Shortly before serving, cut the *magrets* into slices about 3 mm/⅛ in thick, slightly on the diagonal. Lay them on one half of a large platter, and pile the lentils on the other half. Scatter the crisp strips of duck skin over the lentils; serve as a first course or light main dish, at room temperature. Serves 4-6.

If serving as a main course, accompany it with a watercress (or *mâche*) and tomato salad, and hot pitta bread. If smoked magrets are unobtainable, grill fresh *magrets*

as for Magrets de Canard aux Pommes Sautées (see below). The skin may be left on, or removed and cut in strips for frying, as above.

Magrets de Canard aux Pommes Sautées

Magrets de canard are boneless breasts of duck; they can be bought in vacuum packs, or cut off the whole bird, either by the butcher, or at home. French *magrets* are often about twice the size of English ones, since the French ducks may have been specially fattened to enlarge the liver for *foie gras*.

700 g/1½ lb waxy potatoes, peeled and cut in 2 cm/¾ in cubes
100 g/4 oz duck or goose fat, or 100 ml/4 fl oz olive oil
4 magrets (from 2 ducks)
15 ml/1 tblsp sunflower oil
sea salt and black pepper
22 ml/1½ tblsps finely chopped parsley

Dry the cubed potatoes in a cloth. Heat the fat (or oil) in a heavy pan. When it is very hot, put in the potatoes, spreading them evenly. Cover the pan and cook for 20 mins, keeping it covered for the first 15 mins, turning them over once or twice. During the last 5 mins, turn them frequently to brown evenly, then lift them out and drain on paper. While they are cooking, heat the grill and rub the *magrets* on both sides with sunflower oil and the sea salt and pepper. Grill them, skin side up, for 6-8 mins, depending on how plump they are. (English ones will probably take 6 mins; French ones 8 mins.) Then turn them over and grill on the other side, allowing 4-5 mins. Remove from the heat and leave to cool for a few moments while you finish the potatoes.

To serve, carve the *magrets* in slices about 0.5 cm/¼ in thick, on the diagonal. Reassemble them, then lay them on individual (warm) plates, with a pile of sauté potatoes beside it. Sprinkle the potatoes with chopped parsley. Serves 4. This exquisite dish needs only a green salad to accompany it.

Cassoulet

This is a simple version of a cassoulet, based on one I ate at the Relais Gascon, a small restaurant in Albi. This is a useful dish in that it uses the wings, legs and fat of the duck, leaving the *magrets* (breasts) free for another dish. It can also be made in double quantities for a party, and can be kept for 3-4 days in the refrigerator (before its final browning) before serving.

450 g/1 lb dried haricot beans, French or Italian for preference
1 onion, sliced

1 carrot, sliced
1 stalk celery, sliced
3 cloves garlic, unpeeled
1 bay leaf
3 stalks parsley
225 g/8 oz salt pork, or streaky bacon, in one piece
350 g/12 oz coarsely cut sausages, smoked or unsmoked, ie. Toulouse
2 duck legs, jointed (4 pieces)
2 duck wings
sea salt and black pepper
50-75 g/2-3 oz soft white breadcrumbs
30-45 ml/2-3 tblsps melted duck fat, or lard

Italian or Greek beans make a better substitute for French beans than English ones. Italian sausages are also a good substitute for Toulouse sausages, if you can get them. Preserved duck (or goose) can be used instead of fresh duck.

Soak the beans for 4 hours, then drain. Put them in a deep pan with the onion, carrot, celery, garlic, bay leaf and parsley. Cut the rind off the salt pork and cut into small squares, then cut the rest of the pork into thick strips. Put the rind squares into the pot with the beans and cover generously with cold water. Bring slowly to the boil, skim once or twice, then lower the heat and simmer gently for 45 mins, half covered. While the beans are cooking toss the salt pork strips in a heavy frying pan for 2-3 mins, until browned all over, then remove them. If using unsmoked sausages, cook them in the pork fat for a few mins, until partly browned outside and half-cooked within. (If using smoked sausages this will not be necessary.) Then cut each sausage in half or, if using a length of sausage, into 6.5 cm/2½ in lengths. Grill the duck joints for 5 mins on each side, saving the fat that runs into the grill pan. When the beans have finished cooking, strain them, reserving their liquid. Discard the carrot, celery, bay leaf and parsley. Peel the garlic and mash it to a paste. Stir this back into the beans, adding sea salt and plenty of black pepper. (Not too much salt because of the salt pork.) Tip half of the beans into an earthenware casserole – it doesn't need a lid – and cover with the strips of salt pork, chunks of sausage and joints of duck. Cover with the rest of the beans then pour over 300 ml/½ pt of their cooking liquid. Cover the surface of the beans with breadcrumbs – the shape of the dish will determine how much you need – then dribble the melted duck fat (or lard) over the crumbs, having added the fat from the grill pan. Bake for 1½ hours at 170°C/325°F/gas mark 3. The crust should be crisp and golden brown, the beans soft and melting. Serves 4-6 as a main course.

Duck Terrine

1 duck
350 g/12 oz unsmoked streaky bacon, in 1 piece, rind removed
350 g/12 oz fatty pork (belly, throat or boned spareribs)
350 g/12 oz pie veal
22 ml/1½ tblsps green peppercorns
2 large cloves garlic, crushed
15 ml/1 tblsp sea salt
2.5 ml/½ tsp ground mace
200 ml/7 fl oz dry white wine
45 ml/3 tblsps brandy

garnish:
3 small bay leaves
a few juniper berries

Put the duck upside down on a rack in a roasting tin. Roast for 25 mins at 200°C/400°F/gas mark 6. Then remove and leave to cool. Cut the bacon, pork and veal in pieces and chop in the food processor, or put through a mincer. Mix all together in a large bowl. Cut the flesh off the half-roasted duck, reserving the carcass for making soup. Chop the duck meat by hand, in neat dice, and mix with the other meats in the bowl. Add the green peppercorns, garlic, salt and mace, then stir in the wine and brandy and mix thoroughly. Cover and set aside for an hour or two, if possible, to allow time for the flavours to develop. Arrange the bay leaves and juniper berries in the bottom of a 900 g/2 lb terrine mould, or loaf tin. (Alternatively, you can use long thin strips of bacon fat, cut off the whole piece after removing the rind.) Pile in the duck mixture, smoothing it evenly with a palette knife. Stand it in a roasting tin half filled with hot water and cook, uncovered, for 1¾ hours. Remove it and leave to cool, then cover loosely with a piece of foil. Find a small board or dish roughly the same size and shape as the terrine and stand it on it, weighed down with two 675 g/1½ lb weights. Leave overnight in a cool room, then remove the weights and store in the refrigerator. This is best made 1-2 days before eating, but it will keep for 1 week under refrigeration, or 3-4 weeks if sealed, after cooling, with a thick layer of melted duck or goose fat, or lard, or clarified butter. Turn out on a flat dish to serve, with toast, unsalted butter, and small gherkins. Serves 8-10.

RICE

Rice and Vermicelli Pilav

In Turkey, broken vermicelli is often mixed with rice to make an interesting pilav.

50 g/2 oz vermicelli
100 g/4 oz butter
175 g/6 oz Italian rice, arborio
or cristallo
600 ml/1 pt chicken stock
sea salt and black pepper

Break the vermicelli into small pieces. Melt half the butter in a sauté pan and cook the vermicelli for 5 mins, stirring constantly, until pale golden. Add the washed and drained rice and stir around for another 3-4 mins. Heat the stock and add to the pan with the remaining butter, sea salt, and black pepper. Boil for 1 min, then stir, and lower the heat as much as possible. Cover and cook gently for 15 mins, until the stock is completely absorbed and the rice cooked. Turn off the heat, cover the pan with a cloth under the lid, and stand for 20 mins in a warm place before serving. Serves 4-5.

Nasi Goreng

An Indonesian form of fried rice, often found in Holland as a result of the Dutch colonization of the East Indies. This is a simplified version which makes a light meal for one or two people.

about 225 g/8 oz freshly cooked rice, boiled or steamed
2 shallots, sliced
30 ml/2 tblsps light oil
1-2 chilli peppers, de-seeded and finely chopped
2 rashers bacon, chopped
50 g/2 oz shelled shrimps or prawns
1 smallish endive, sliced
2 eggs, fried

Ideally, this should be made with rice cooked 2-3 hours beforehand and left to cool. Cook the sliced shallots in the oil, preferably in a wok, adding the chopped chilli. Toss for 1-2 mins, before adding the chopped bacon and tossing again for 1 min. Add the shrimps or prawns and sliced endive and toss for another min. Finally add the cooked rice and toss everything together. Divide between 2 hot plates and top each one with a fried egg. Serve immediately; serves 2. This can easily be made in half quantities, for 1 person.

Fesenjan

1 duck, cut in quarters
1 large onion, chopped
25 g/1 oz butter
2.5 ml/½ tsp ground turmeric
sea salt and black pepper
22 ml/1½ tblsps flour
100 g/4 oz chopped walnuts
150 ml/¼ pt tomato juice
10 ml/2 tsps brown sugar
150 ml/¼ pt fresh lime juice, or lime and lemon juice mixed
300 ml/½ pt chicken stock
1 medium aubergine, cut in thin slices, salted and drained

frying oil
16 cardamoms, shelled and crushed, or 5 ml/1 tsp ground cardamom

Trim the duck pieces with a sharp knife, removing all flaps of fatty skin and pieces of bone. Cook the chopped onion in the butter until it is golden, adding the turmeric. Sprinkle the duck with salt, pepper and flour, shaking off any excess, and add to the pan. Brown the joints all over, adding the chopped walnuts towards the end. Mix the tomato juice with the sugar and lime juice. (If possible, use lime juice only, or mostly lime juice. If limes are not available and lemon juice alone is used, add an extra 5 ml/1 tsp sugar.)

Pour the fruit juices over the duck and mix; add the stock and mix again. Cover the pan and cook gently for 30 mins, turning the duck pieces once or twice. Meanwhile, dry the aubergine slices in a soft cloth and fry in hot oil briefly, until golden on each side. Drain on soft paper. When the 30 mins is up, lay the aubergine slices over the duck and cook for another 10 mins. Then stir in the crushed or ground cardamoms, and cook for a further 5 mins. Lift out the duck and lay on a hot dish covered with the aubergine. Keep warm. Let the pan cool for a few minutes, then skim all the fat from the top of the sauce. Spoon some of it over the duck, and serve the rest in a sauceboat. Serve with Chelou (see below), or plain boiled rice. A chicken or two partridges can be substituted for the duck. In Iran, this dish is made with pomegranate juice; the mixture of tomato juice, lime juice, and brown sugar is the best approximation I can find. Serves 4.

Chelou (Persian Rice)

300 g/10 oz long grain rice
2 litres/3½ pts water
22 ml/1½ tblsps sea salt
50 g/2 oz butter

I find this best made with Carolina rice; if using basmati, wash it well and soak for 2-3 hours. Bring the water and salt to a boil and shake in the rice, well-drained if it has been soaking. Try to keep the water boiling steadily. Allow 10 mins for Uncle Ben's and 8 mins for basmati. (It should be about three-quarters cooked, still with a hard core in the centre of each grain.) Drain, and rinse in tepid water. In a heavy pot, preferably one with a rounded bottom, melt half the butter and add 15 ml/1 tblsp hot water. Swirl it round the bottom and sides of the pan, then let it collect in a pool at the bottom. Spoon in 3-4 large spoonfuls of the drained rice and mix with the melted butter. Make a layer of the rice, then spoon in the rest on top of it. Melt the remaining butter and dribble it over the surface of the rice. Cover with the lid wrapped in a cloth, with the corners folded back over the top. Cook over very low heat for 35 mins, then put the pot on a cool surface for 5 mins before serving. To serve, spoon out the rice on to a dish then remove the crust at the bottom, invert it, and lay it over the rice. It doesn't matter if it breaks into small pieces; simply scatter them over the rice. If the crust has not worked, and the rice seems hard and burnt, simply leave it in the pan and just serve it from within the pan: it should be perfectly tender and separate.

Lamb Pilav

This is a dish from the Caucasus, the part of Russia bordering Iran, where lamb is often cooked with tart fruit and served with rice.

450 g-700 g/1-1½ lb lamb, free from bone (buy ½ a boned shoulder)
1 large onion, chopped
25 g/1 oz butter
15 ml/1 tblsp oil
1 pckt saffron
225 g/8 oz slightly sour plums or damsons
30 ml/2 tblsps raisins
100 ml/4 fl oz sour plum juice
50 ml/2 fl oz chicken stock
sea salt and black pepper
6 sprig onions or 6 sprigs watercress

Cut the lamb in neat cubes. Cook the onion in the butter and oil until it becomes golden, then add the meat and brown it on all sides. Add the saffron and mix, then the plums or damsons, stoned and cut in pieces, the raisins, plum juice, and stock. Add sea salt and black pepper, cover the pan, and simmer gently for 40 mins, stirring occasionally. Pile on to a hot dish and scatter chopped spring onions or watercress over the top. Serve with saffron rice pilav, or Chelou (see above). Serves 3-4.

Saffron Pilav

Soak one packet saffron in 15 ml/1 tblsp hot water. Boil the rice as before and, after draining, tip it back into the saucepan and mix with the saffron water. Then mix with the melted butter and continue as for Chelou (see above).

October

Alice Toklas and Gertrude Stein met in 1907 in Paris. Alice, aged thirty, had arrived that day with her friend Harriet Levy from their home in San Francisco. They went in the afternoon to call on their friends, Michael and Sarah Stein, Gertrude's brother and sister-in-law. There they met Gertrude, who had come to live in Paris three years earlier and was sharing a studio with her brother Leo. All the Steins were keen collectors of modern art: Sarah influenced by Matisse and Gertrude by Picasso. The Stein collection was later to form the nucleus of the Museum of Modern Art in New York.

Alice and Gertrude became friends almost immediately, and three years later, when Leo left the apartment in the rue de Fleurus, Alice moved in with Gertrude. She did not return to San Francisco until she accompanied Gertrude on a lecture tour of the United States in 1937, by which time her father had died and she had become estranged from her brother. The story of her life with Gertrude Stein is moving, often hilarious, and strangely impressive. Theirs was an existence dedicated to things of the intellect, and the arts. They lived together in France for thirty-six years, refusing to leave despite two world wars and the occupation. In March 1915 they did leave Paris for Majorca, driven out by the shortage of food and fuel, but they regretted their departure, and returned the following year. Alice knitted throughout the war, taught by Madame Matisse. In 1916 Gertrude ordered a Ford to be sent out from the USA; they had it converted into a truck, and spent the last two years of the war ferrying medical supplies around France for the American Fund for French Wounded, an organization similar to the Red Cross.

In 1933 *The Autobiography of Alice B Toklas* by Gertrude Stein was published. It has been puzzling librarians ever since. Should it be listed as biography or autobiography? Is the author Toklas or Stein? The ambiguity of the title is symbolic of their relationship. While Gertrude Stein was no slouch at creating deliberate confusion, Alice was a past master at mixing fact with legend. Reading the account of Alice's youth, the strands become more and more confused. Miss Toklas's father must have been an unusual man but I find it hard to believe that he displayed the sort of lateral thinking and inverted patterns of speech that we have come to associate with Gertrude Stein herself. At one point he instructs his daughter: 'A hostess should never apologise for any failure in her household arrangements, if there is a hostess there is insofar as there is a hostess no failure.' On another occasion, Alice's brother went riding with a friend, and one of the horses returned riderless to the hotel. When the

friend's mother started to make a scene, Mr Toklas said to her: 'Be calm, Madam, perhaps it is my son who has been killed.'

The Autobiography of Alice B Toklas gives a fascinating picture of life in Paris before the First World War, depicting the lives of many of the major painters of the time. Gertrude Stein's greatest friend – one of the few that Alice accepted without jealousy – was the twenty-three-year old Picasso then living in Montmartre with his mistress Fernande Olivier – 'always beautiful but heavy in hand'. One of Alice Toklas's duties was to sit with the wives of the great men who came to talk with Gertrude Stein. She often planned to write her memoirs, which she intended to call *Wives of Geniuses I Have Sat With*. She commented wryly, 'Fernande was the first wife of a genius I sat with and she was not at all amusing.'

Gertrude Stein's friendship with Picasso was a very different matter. Alice describes how they would sit for hours, knee-to-knee on two low chairs, discussing ideas, and how Picasso would say '*Expliquez-moi cela*' and '*Racontez-moi cela*'. For, as Alice states, Gertrude Stein 'understands very well the basis of creation and therefore her criticism and advice is invaluable to all her friends.' She also understood painters, and described a lunch party she gave for them: 'You know how painters are, I wanted to make them happy so I placed each one opposite his own picture, and they were happy so happy that we had to send out twice for more bread...'

Many of the painters were living in great poverty, for their work was not yet received with any sort of favour by the public at large. But they showed great courage in refusing to compromise, and the loyalty of their wives was often heroic. 'Matisse had at this time a small Cézanne and a small Gauguin and he said he needed them both. The Cézanne had been bought with his wife's marriage portion and the Gauguin with the ring which was the only jewel she had ever owned. And they were happy because he needed these pictures.' Some years later, when most of them had become successful, Braque said, with a sigh and a smile, 'How life has changed we all now have cooks who can make a soufflé.'

During the Second World War they stayed at their summer house at Bilignin, near Belley, ignoring pleas from their friends in the USA to leave France. Alice spent most of the war reading cookery books, dreaming of meals she would cook once the war was over. In 1943 the shortage of food became so acute that they were forced to sell one of their favourite paintings, Cézanne's *Portrait of Madame Cézanne*. 'We ate the Cézanne,' Alice commented. Their existence must have been hard; at one point their house was reclaimed by its owner, their landlord, and they were forced to move to another nearby. Here they had a series of troops billeted on them: first Germans, then Italians, then more Germans.

In 1946 Gertrude Stein died. Alice Toklas lived for another twenty-one years, filling her time as best as she could, writing cookery books and memoirs. But the point had gone out of her life. It seems as if it was only in the context of Gertrude Stein that she flourished; left alone, she seemed diminished in every way. The two women could hardly have been more different, in appearance and temperament, but they complemented each other admirably. Gertrude Stein was probably the more lovable, an innovator with a formidable intelligence, immense vitality and a big heart. Alice Toklas was also intelligent, but in a different way: more subtle then Gertrude, and highly sophisticated, she was adept at manipulating people and events. She was more conventional in her tastes and was a passionate admirer of Henry James. And, although deeply interested in modern painting, she lacked Gertrude Stein's immediate understanding of what the painters were trying to achieve. She seemed content to remain in the background, devoting herself to housekeeping, cooking, gardening, needlework, and looking after Gertrude Stein. Often dismissed by outsiders as Miss Stein's mousy companion, she seems in some ways to have been the more dominant of the two. Anyone who threatened their relationship was liable to be summarily dealt with, as Hemingway found to his cost.

The Alice B Toklas Cook Book was published in 1954, when the author was seventy-two. I remember reading it soon after publication, when I was twenty and teaching myself to cook. It was an uneasy period for the English, trying to adapt to peace time; although the war had been over for nine years, rationing had only just ended. I remember being taken aback by the richness of the dishes in the *Toklas Cook Book*; I chose two of the more restrained recipes, curry sauce and peaches *glacées*, which I often used to make. Re-reading it recently, I was stunned to learn that Alice Toklas wrote it during an attack of jaundice, as a celebration of the food she was no longer allowed to eat. Also, perhaps, as a nostalgic reminder of the years with Gertrude Stein. In 1958 she produced another cookery book, *Aromas and Flavors of Past and Present*, published in the USA. This was edited by Poppy Cannon, food editor of *House Beautiful*, a strange choice, for the two women had little in common. Poppy Cannon prefaces the recipes with such comments as 'deliriously delicious', and suggests using canned condensed soups as substitutes for the Toklas stocks and *fumets*. It must have been a stormy partnership, for Poppy Cannon's ingenuous enthusiasm often invokes acid retorts from Miss Toklas. Her suggestion that we should 'cream the world for our tables', combining Russian soups with French desserts, Chinese vegetables with American steaks, is greeted with 'How incongruous'. None the less, Poppy Cannon did a good job, for the recipes in this little book are infinitely more practical than those in *The Alice B Toklas Cook Book*, although none are perhaps quite so 'deliriously delicious' as the one for hashish fudge, contributed by a friend, in the first book.

Alice Toklas was a purist, with a passion for detail. I find myself warming to her accounts of how she laid the breakfast trays at Bilignin, and to her strictures to her readers. In *Aromas and Flavors of Past and Present*, she admonished them: 'You mustn't be afraid to serve things on their own...but of course there is bread on the table...' She knew how to appreciate both the extravagance of rich food, and the joys of simplicity. Although Miss Toklas served elaborate dishes when entertaining, in the evening she preferred to eat very simply: a *bouillon*, a vegetable and a fruit compote...

Perhaps the strongest trait in her make-up was perversity. When aroused in conflict with a totally disparate character, like Poppy Cannon, this emerges as crushing, acid and destructive. Yet when experienced in the context of Gertrude Stein, whose 'otherness' was loved and esteemed, then her perversity appears at its best, witty and gently mocking. Driving around New York, on the lecture tour in 1937, they found the lights in Times Square announcing 'Gertrude Stein has arrived in New York'. 'As if we didn't know it,' Alice remarked. On the very first page of *The Autobiography* is a typically provocative statement that sums her up: 'I like a view but I like to sit with my back turned to it.'

Harvest festival time seems an appropriate moment to reassess the importance of grain in our diet. One of the most difficult things about moving over to a healthy programme is giving up the old meal structure based on meat, fish and eggs. If we can only accept grain as the linchpin of our diet, things will fall into place more easily.

For anyone changing to a completely vegetarian diet, it is vital to replace the animal protein. Vegetable protein is not 'less good', but is it incomplete. In order to acquire the balanced protein that one might find in steak, for instance, it is necessary to combine two or more foods. If grain is to be the main source of protein, it must be complemented – not necessarily even at the same meal – by another food such as dried vegetables and/or yoghurt. A good example would be the Middle Eastern *megadarra*, in which rice and lentils are cooked together, often served with yoghurt. Once this balance is understood – and even those of us who still eat fish, poultry and game should have an awareness of this – planning meals is easy.

It does help to set down a pattern, even if we do not always stick to it. My breakfast consists of orange juice, unsweetened muesli and two oatcakes. I eat raw food at midday, either salad or fruit with yoghurt. In the evening, I have a cooked meal based on a grain dish, with two or three cooked vegetables. If I have had fruit for lunch, then I have green salad with my evening meal. If I have salad for lunch, I end my evening meal with fruit or yoghurt. Except when I am trying to lose weight, I also have tea, which consists of two slices of wholemeal bread, piled with mustard and cress, sprouting lentils or mung beans. I therefore eat a dish derived from grain three or four times a day. The protein this provides is balanced by sprouting seeds, yoghurt or dried vegetables cooked with the grain. This is my pattern when I am alone. If I go out, or have a friend in, we usually have fish, calves' liver, free-range poultry or game. This may sound rigid and limited but, if you crave variety, there is probably a different grain dish for each day of the month, and their wholesome nutty flavour grows on one. Even if you are living alone, grain dishes are surprisingly practical. I tend to cook 8 oz of brown rice, buckwheat, cracked wheat or couscous at a time. I eat a 2 oz serving straight away, storing the remainder in the refrigerator to use as the basis for my meals over the next couple of days. Often I prepare four small pudding basins with lightly cooked vegetables at the bottom, then filled with cooked grain, an idea that I took from Ken Lo's *Healthy Chinese Cooking*. I keep the bowls covered with foil in the refrigerator. To serve, I simply steam them and turn them out on to individual plates. Accompanied by two freshly cooked vegetables – chicory braised with orange juice, steamed courgettes or broccoli, tomatoes baked with ginger and garlic, poached spring onions – these savoury little puddings look very appealing.

Cracked wheat, buckwheat, millet and couscous are delicious fried. After boiling, mix with chopped onion and herbs, and bind with egg beaten with *fromage blanc*. Shape into little round patties or large flat cakes, fry until brown in the minimum of oil in a non-stick pan and serve with plain yoghurt, or a yoghurt and cucumber sauce, with grilled tomatoes or a mixed salad. *Polenta* and semolina can be left to get cold after cooking, then cut in strips and fried, finished off in a grill pan to give them a striped appearance. *Burghul* (cracked wheat) and couscous make good salads, such as *tabbouleh*. Soak the *burghul* in water, or steam the couscous, dress with olive oil and lemon juice, and mix with chopped parsley and mint. When you are cooking for a family, the most useful dishes are probably the grain casseroles. Fill a fireproof dish with layers of cooked grain, sliced cooked vegetables and yoghurt, with a topping of breadcrumbs, chopped nuts, wholewheat crumble or toasted sesame seeds. This may be prepared in advance and baked for forty-five minutes – or even left in a pre-set oven – before being served with more yoghurt and a green salad.

For a party, wild rice may be mixed with white or brown rice in a ring mould, turned out and filled with wild mushrooms. For every day, brown rice may be combined with ordinary field mushrooms. *Risotto*-type dishes may be made with cracked wheat, with brown rice and lentils, or brown rice and wholewheat *vermicelli*.

'*Faire bien la soupe!*' That's what mothers teach their daughters in south-west France. If France is a nation of soup-*eaters*, the south-west is the land of soup-*lovers*. Soup is often eaten more than once a day, and very often a fine, rich soup will constitute an entire evening meal...

Soups are one of the most versatile foods, with a range that stretches from the grandest occasion to the simplest family meal. They are widespread in their appeal; what may have originated as food for the peasants working in the fields, like *gazpacho*, may well in later years become a favourite food of the rich, its very austerity proving a virtue. When a young Brandolini married a Faucigny Lucinge in Paris a few years ago, the bridegroom's family sent along their chef to prepare one of his favourite dishes for the wedding breakfast. This was none other than *pasta e fagioli*, a thick soup of pasta and dried beans, once the food of the poorest Italian family.

Soups are variations on a theme, classic dishes of the sort one returns to with pleasure, especially at the onset of winter. They fall into four or five main groups: consommés, with or without a garnish; smooth creamy soups, based on a *béchamel;* vegetable purées; fish soups; and thick soups, almost like stews of meat or poultry, dried or fresh vegetables, with additions of rice, pasta or bread. As a general rule, the smoother the soup, the more elegant the dish. There are few more delicate dishes than a well-made consommé, especially when it contains a few tiny ravioli, or soup dumplings. These may be filled with finely chopped game or crabmeat, puréed spinach and ricotta, or pumpkin. Bought *tortellini* can be used, but homemade pasta is softer and more fragile, even if simply cut in strips, or small shapes. A garnish of slivers of spring onions and fresh ginger gives an oriental flavour to this pretty soup.

Smooth soups made almost like a sauce are no longer as popular as they once were, but one or two are worth preserving. My favourite is a curried cream of chicken, garnished with chopped chicken breast, which may be served hot or cold. Oddly enough, the only place I find this, apart from my own home, is in old-fashioned men's clubs. The Knickerbocker Club, in New York, serves a delicious chilled *Crème Sénégale*, while I ate a good hot version at Boodles, where it is called mulligatawny, which is misleading, since this is not usually made with chicken. The only other smooth soup I like is *vichyssoise*, but this belongs in the third category, for it is simply an ultra-smooth vegetable purée. This is best made in a blender – rather than a food processor – for ultimate smoothness,

unlike most vegetable purées, which are best left slightly lumpy. A variation of textures can be achieved by simply mashing with a fork, pushing through a coarse food mill, or giving them a quick whirl in a food processor. Winter vegetables are ideal for making purées, especially the root vegetables like parsnip, celeriac, Jerusalem artichoke, turnip, carrot and swede. The leaf vegetables also make good soups, often combined with potato to give consistency. Cabbage soup is one of my favourites, while watercress and spinach are also good.

Fish soups deserve a category to themselves for they vary widely, ranging from the Mediterranean *bouillabaisse* to the American chowder, and *bisques* of lobster and crab. But the most extensive range is the last, for every country has its own range of hearty soups. These are survival food, often the linchpin of the Mediterranean diet during the long fasts imposed by the Catholic, Orthodox and Islamic Churches. *Minestrone* is a typical example, with all its regional variations. In some parts of Italy rice is included, in others pasta, while in some places it is made with vegetables alone. In Milan, according to Marcella Hazan, it is often eaten cold the next day, while in Florence it is reheated and served over freshly cooked purple cabbage, piled on thick slices of country bread. In Liguria it is made with green vegetables only, and *pesto* is stirred in before serving.

Some of the best soups are seasonal, in that they depend on a combination of vegetables which only coincide briefly. Such a one is the Niçoise *soupe au pistou*, which should be made with fresh pink and white haricots, before drying, combined with green string beans and peas, in early summer, while the Tuscan bean soup is incomparable when made with the fresh *borlotti* beans before they have been dried. It comes into its own again a couple of months later when made with the first of the dried beans and the new season's olive oil, added at the table.

Even quite basic soups can be transformed by an appropriate garnish. Fried noodles add crunch to a purée of root vegetables, while fried cubes of potato coated with sesame seeds are good with a leek or celery soup. Crisp curls of fried duck skin are wonderful scattered over a smooth lentil soup, especially when it has been made with duck stock. Tiny broad beans, skinned and split, look pretty laid in a circle on a purée of peas, or of leeks. Mustard and cress makes an elegant and unusual garnish, scattered over an oriental version of chicken noodle soup, but the simplest garnish of all, and hard to beat, is coarsely chopped parsley, added at the very last moment, and sprinkled in generous quantities.

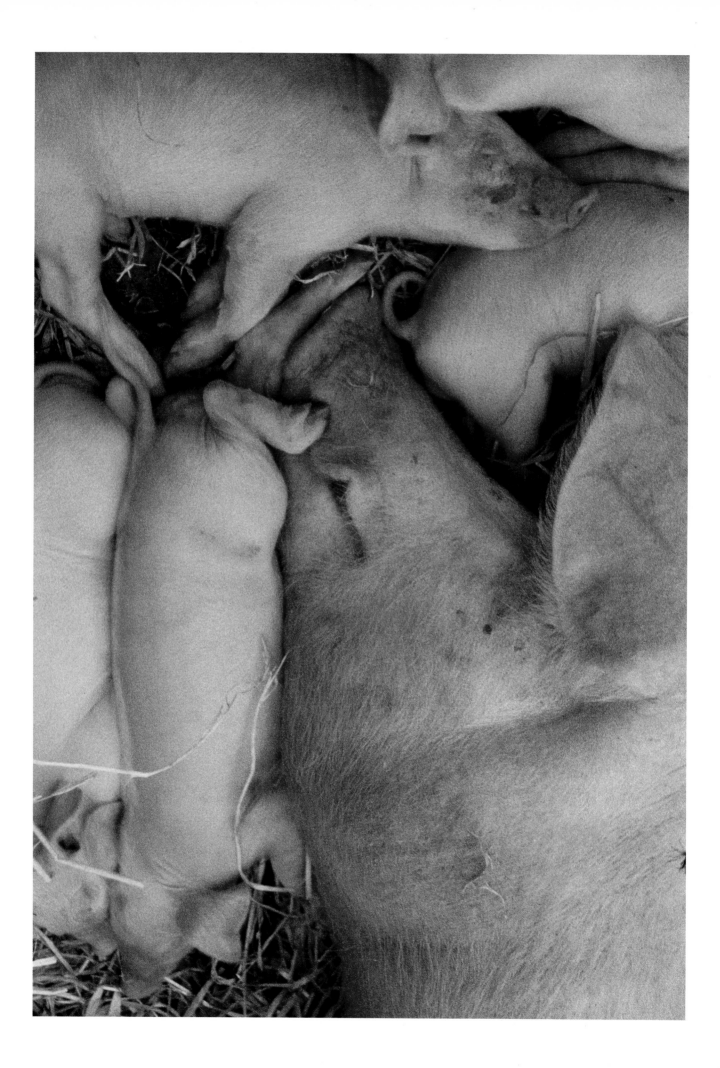

Organic farming today represents only 1 per cent of farms in the UK, but this figure is growing steadily. On the Continent, it stretches from 1 per cent in France to 3 per cent in Germany and Denmark. It is not yet clearly understood by most people what the term 'organic' really means, and I am constantly irritated by shops who claim that their meat is organic when I know that it is not. To be fair, most of these claims arise through ignorance or confusion rather than dishonesty, but the sooner this becomes illegal practice the sooner the public will learn the difference. The term organic may only be used of produce, be it meat, vegetables, fruit or grain, that has been grown in accordance with the rules of any organic certification scheme recognized by UKROFS (the government backed United Kingdom Register of Organic Food Standards). The largest of these is the Soil Association.

Organic farming is based on certain principles which must be adhered to strictly in order to satisfy the inspectors, who make annual visits. This entitles the producer to display one of the organic symbols on his produce. As organic farmer Sir Julian Rose explains: 'The crucial definition of organic farming as opposed to conventional farming is that it relies entirely on the fertility of the land.' Central to the structure of the organic farm is the rotation system, which restricts pests without resorting to chemical pesticides, and increases fertility, aided by natural fertilizers like (organic) farmyard manure and calcified seaweed. In the case of livestock, growth stimulators, hormones, and the routine use of antibiotics are banned, although sick animals may be given antibiotics to avoid suffering. (The animal then ceases to be organic, in terms of meat or milk, until a statutory period has passed, when it reverts to its former status.) Animal feed must be mainly composed of organic matter. (Soil Association standards demand a minimum of 45 per cent organic matter, 45 per cent 'in transition' – this means grain grown on land in the process of conversion to full organic practice – and 10 per cent from another source.)

Converting a conventional farm to organic practice can take ten years or more, depending on the degree of intensity with which it has been farmed. Hill farms in Wales and Scotland are easy, for hill land has never been treated with chemicals. Dairy farms are also comparatively easy, but with an intensive farm previously given up to producing just one crop, or animal, it is a lengthy and expensive business. First the water supply must be cleaned, then the hedgerows replaced. The organic system only works with mixed farming; this makes the rotation system practicable, and the cereals supply food for the animals, who in turn fertilize the land. Both cows and sheep are relatively easy to farm organically, since they feed themselves by grazing for most of the year, but both pigs and poultry are more demanding in that they must be fed every day. (Primitive pigs in Third World countries can fend for themselves, like the wild boar, but the modern pig has been so bred for massive meat production that it cannot support itself on grass alone.) Organic grain for animal feed is very hard to get, unless you grow it yourself, since most of it is milled into flour.

The Soil Association has been the backbone of the organic movement ever since it started, just after the war. Until the 1930s, all farming was organic, for chemical fertilizers and pesticides were not yet readily available. With their development in the mid 1930s, a few enlightened individuals like Lady Eve Balfour, together with Doctors Scott-Williamson and Pearse, joint founders of the Peckham Health Centre, joined forces to found the Soil Association in 1946. Its aim, then as now, was to establish and maintain a healthy balance between the soil, plants, animals and man, without resorting to the use of chemicals. Sadly, their achievements were largely ignored by the government who chose to back the development of agro-chemicals, and urged the farmers to go all out to produce an abundance of cheap food. As organic farmer Bill Reynolds comments sadly: 'Now all we've got is cheap rubbish.' Not to mention diseased animals, and an impoverished countryside.

Julian Rose farms 300 acres on his family estate near Reading. When two farms that had previously been let fell vacant in 1975, he decided to convert them to organic practice. He chose to do this slowly, and registered with the Soil Association in 1985. His farm is mixed, with dairy produce at its centre. (The livestock was originally introduced to consume the surplus of the skim milk; now this sells as well as other milk, and the animals see less of it.) In 1989 he led a whirlwind campaign to stop the government banning unpasteurized milk. (Its sale had already been restricted, since 1985, to farm-gate sales and milk rounds.) In just three months the campaign was successful, and green top (unpasteurized) milk was restored to its former status. Julian Rose's own organic unpasteurized cream is reknowned, surely the best I have ever tasted.

His dairy herd consists of sixty Guernseys. It is a 'suckler herd', which is unusual in dairy herds; this means the calves run with their mothers, or 'nurse cows', for five months. (In most dairy herds the calves are weaned at four days.) For beef, he crosses Guernseys with Aberdeen Angus, North Devon, Hereford bulls. At 2½ years, the cattle are ready for slaughter, or for sale to other organic farms. The slaughter is carried out at a local abattoir who are sympathetic to organic principles, and are prepared to treat his animals according to Soil Association regulations. In addition to dairy produce and eggs, Julian Rose sells beef, pork, lamb, turkeys and chickens.

Less rigorous than organic farming, but still in a different league from conventional farming, is Conservation Grade. These farmers differ from the organic lobby in that they permit the use of certain listed chemicals, and they have their own requirements regarding animal feed. (All components must be grown on Conservation Grade land.) For some farmers, this is a stage en route to full organic practice, but for others like Jonathan Blackburn of The Pure Meat Company it is an end in itself. He takes a pragmatic view, and believes that organic food may soon cost more than most people are prepared to pay. His 300-acre farm is situated in wild hilly land overlooking Moreton Hampstead, in Devon. 'At the turn of the century, there were thirty men working on the farm. Now I've got two pensioners, terrific fellows. One works half-time, the other three-quarters.'

Jonathan Blackburn raises red English cattle for beef and veal, Welsh mountain sheep, pigs and geese. He specializes in veal, raised by humane methods. (The calves stay with their mothers, out of doors, until they are killed at eight months.) This is more like young beef than the veal we are used to. It lacks the tenderness and pallour of the best Dutch veal but that, of course, is achieved by methods that most of us find unacceptable. They also sell mutton, which is proving more and more popular. In a recent mail order 'package', 80 per cent of their customers chose mutton as their main joint.

For an unbiased assessment of the meat market, I spoke to David Lidgate, whose family have been butchers for 130 years. His main objective is to get the best possible quality meat for his customers, whether it is organic or not. And while he approves wholeheartedly of organic and Conservation Grade farming, he claims that at present their meat rarely comes up to his standards. He believes that taste and texture are all important, and that these depend on an unbroken chain of factors: breed, feed, treatment, transport to slaughter, method of slaughter, transport to point of sale, and craftsmanship, ie butchery. 'You can have everything: right breed, right feed, right husbandry, right transport, right slaughter, then they chill it too quickly, and it's finished.' His preferred beef is Aberdeen Angus, raised on the Black Isle in the Moray Firth.

Julian Rose believes that exercise is all-important for flavour, since this affects the quality of the fat, which in turn affects the taste. When an animal is allowed to roam freely, unsaturated fat forms around the muscle, while animals that are cooped up put on saturated fat. And by being allowed to wander, the animal will find for itself a variety of food which adds to the flavour of the meat.

Since becoming organic Julian Rose has been struck by three things: the increased level of wildlife on his farm, the improved fertility rate, and the overall health of his animals. 'I've only had to give one pig one injection in six years, and I've given nothing to the chickens.' (He has 1,000 hens.) He believes that organic farming could prove the answer to many of the problems the EC are trying to solve. It would produce 20 per cent less food, which is exactly what is needed, given the current food surplus; it would sort out the worst effects of pollution caused by the use of agro-chemicals, and it would ensure that wildlife could return to its natural habitat.

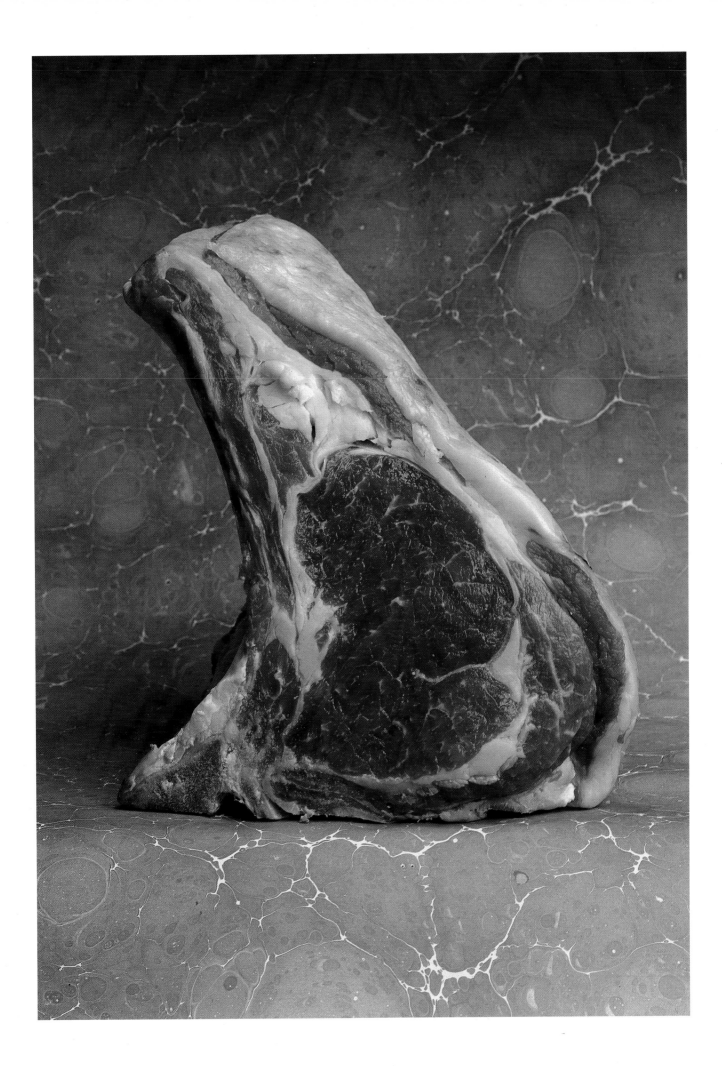

GRAIN

The Grains

WHEAT: Whole wheat is not practical for ordinary cooking purposes, since it requires long cooking and a strong digestion. Cracked wheat is the grain broken by rolling. It must be cooked, not just soaked, before eating, and is good for making *risottos*, casseroles, croquettes or steamed-in-a-bowl. *Bulgur*, also called *burghul* or *pourgouri*, is another form of cracked wheat, but the grain is broken by boiling, so it is pre-cooked. Use for dishes like *tabbouleh* which only require soaking. It can also be cooked as above. Kibbled wheat is a coarse form of cracked wheat which needs longer cooking. Semolina is wheat that that has been ground to varying degrees of fineness, slightly thicker than flour. Wholewheat semolina is more nutritious than white, being less refined. Both can be used to make gnocchi. Couscous is semolina that has been rolled into little pellets. Formerly done by hand, this is now done by machine and pre-cooked. Usually served steamed, with a chicken or vegetable stew, it is also excellent steamed-in-a-bowl, made into patties and dry-fried, or served cold, as a salad.

RICE: Brown rice comes in two forms, short-grained and long-grained. Both are good in different ways; I slightly prefer the short one, with its nutty flavour. Both can be used in many ways: steamed-in-a-bowl, in casseroles or timbales, in croquettes or *risottos*, in salads, or mixed with lentils.

WILD RICE: Not a true rice but the seed of a wild grass that grows in swamps, in the USA and the Far East. Even more nutritious than brown rice, it can be mixed with brown or white rice, served in a timbale, and boiled, or steamed-in-a-bowl. It makes excellent stuffing for poultry and game, or for fish.

BUCKWHEAT: Not strictly a grain but the seed of a plant related to rhubarb. A staple food in Russia, buckwheat is highly nutritious and delicious. It can be bought roasted or plain – roasted is better. It cooks quickly and can be served with fried onions and yoghurt, steamed-in-a-bowl, or made into patties and dry-fried.

CORN: *Polenta* is corn meal, similar to semolina. It can be served boiled, with dishes of game or vegetables, or shaped like a cake and cut in wedges, with a thick tomato sauce. It is also good cold, then cut in shapes and dry-fried, finished off in a grill-pan.

BARLEY: Pot barley is the most nutritious form, but it needs lengthy cooking before it becomes palatable. Pearl barley is slightly less nutritious, in that it has been partly refined, but much quicker to cook. It can

be mixed with brown rice, or added to vegetable soups, or cooked in a casserole.

MILLET: An unusual grain, well worth trying. It is rich in nutrients, and quick to cook. I like it made into a flat cake and deep-fried, with a yoghurt and cucumber sauce. It is also good in casseroles, in croquettes, or steamed-in-a-bowl.

OATMEAL: Oatmeal is rolled or flaked into varying degrees of fineness, and in some cases pre-cooked. Apart from an occasional dish of porridge, I use it differently from the other grains. It is excellent in baking, in bread, biscuits and oatcakes, also in muesli, and as a coating for grilled herrings.

Basic Ways to Cook Grain

BROWN RICE: Wash rice and put in a pan with twice its volume of water. Bring to the boil, cover, and simmer gently for about 40 mins, until all the water is absorbed.

WILD RICE: Wash grain and put in a pan with three times its volume of water. Bring to the boil and simmer gently for 45 mins, until the grain is tender and all the water absorbed.

CRACKED WHEAT: Measure the grain, put in a pan and add twice its volume of water. Bring to the boil, cover the pan, and simmer gently for 15 mins, or until all the water is absorbed.

BULGUR: Cook as for cracked wheat, or for serving cold, in salads, simply soak in cold water for 45 mins, then squeeze out the water with your hands.

BUCKWHEAT: Buy roasted buckwheat and put twice its volume of water in a pan. Bring to the boil, add the buckwheat and bring back to the boil. Boil briskly for 1 min, then lower the heat as much as possible, cover the pan, and cook very gently for about 14 mins, or until all the water is absorbed.

COUSCOUS: Put the couscous in a bowl and pour the same volume of cold water over it. Leave for 10 mins, then steam over vegetable stock (or water) for 30 mins.

MILLET: Measure the grain and put twice its volume of water into a pan. Bring to the boil and shake in the millet. Cover the pan and simmer gently for 25 mins, or until all the water is absorbed.

POLENTA: Measure the *polenta* and put four times its volume of water in a pan. Heat it and shake in the *polenta*, stirring. Bring to the boil stirring constantly, then simmer for 15 mins, or 5 mins if pre-cooked, stirring now and then.

POT BARLEY: Measure the grain, and wash it well. Put it in a pan with three times its volume of water. Bring to the boil, then cover and simmer gently for 1 hour. Or cook for 15 mins in a pressure cooker.

PEARL BARLEY: Wash the grain, and put in a pan with twice its volume of water. Bring to the boil, cover, and simmer gently for about 35 mins, until the water is absorbed.

Buckwheat Steamed-in-a-Bowl

225 g/8 oz buckwheat
225 g/8 oz small carrots, sliced
225 g/8 oz spring broccoli, sliced
30 ml/2 tblsps sunflower oil
Maggi Liquid Seasoning, or soy sauce

Add the buckwheat to 600 ml/1 pt very lightly salted boiling water. Bring back to the boil and boil briskly for 1 min, then cover and simmer as gently as possible for 14 mins, by which time all the water should have been absorbed. Boil the carrots for 2 mins. Boil the broccoli stem for 2 mins adding the flower sprigs half-way through. Mix the carrot and broccoli and put in the bottom of 4 small bowls, lightly oiled. (They should hold 300 ml/½ pt.) Dribble a little oil over them, and a few shakes of Maggi Liquid Seasoning, or soy sauce. Cover with the buckwheat, adding a little more oil and seasoning sauce. Cover the bowls with foil and set aside; they can be kept for several days in the refrigerator. To serve, steam for 10-12 mins over boiling water, then turn out on warm plates. Serve with braised chicory, baked or grilled tomatoes, leaf spinach, and yoghurt. Makes 4 bowls.

Variations:

A useful basic recipe, it can be varied in countless ways. It is also a good way of using small amounts of expensive ingredients, such as wild rice. Any cooked grain, or mixture of grains, may be used. The best vegetables for using parboiled, alone or mixed, are leeks, carrots, spring onions, broccoli, leaf spinach, broad beans, peas. Onions, fennel and mushrooms are best cooked first in a little oil; in this case, omit the sunflower oil added in the bowl.

Millet Cake

150 g/5 oz millet
1 bunch spring onions, sliced
45 ml/3 tblsps sunflower oil
30 ml/2 tblsps chopped coriander
1 large egg, beaten
30 ml/2 tblsps fromage blanc, or Jockey

Bring 300 ml/½ pt very lightly salted water to the boil and shake in the millet. Bring back to the boil, cover the pan, and simmer for 25 mins, or until all the water is absorbed. Turn the millet into a bowl. Cook the sliced spring onions (best of the leaves as well as the bulbs) in 30 ml/2 tblsps sunflower oil for 2-3 mins, then stir into the millet. Add the chopped coriander and mix well. Beat the egg and *fromage blanc* together, then stir into the millet. Put the remaining 15 ml/1 tblsp oil in a non-stick frying pan, heat it gently, then tip the millet into the pan, spreading it evenly with a palette knife. Cook over gentle heat for about 12 mins, then put under the grill for 3-4 mins to cook the upper surface. Turn out on a flat dish to serve, cut in wedges. Serves 4, with a yoghurt and cucumber sauce and grilled tomatoes.

Variation:

The mixture can be made into croquettes, like Couscous Croquettes (see below).

Millet Casserole

100 g/4 oz millet
1 large onion, or 2 leeks, sliced
25 g/1 oz butter
30 ml/2 tblsps sunflower oil
2 heads fennel, sliced
225 g/8 oz courgettes, sliced
225 g/8 oz tomatoes, roughly chopped
black pepper
30 ml/2 tblsps chopped coriander
300 ml/½ pt (225 g/8 oz) Greek yoghurt
45 ml/3 tblsps toasted sesame seeds

Shake the millet into 300 ml/½ pt boiling water, lightly salted. Bring back to the boil and simmer for 25 mins, covered, until all the water is absorbed. Cook the sliced onion in the butter and oil until it starts to soften, then add the sliced fennel and cook for another 5 mins. Add the sliced courgettes and cook for another 5 mins, then add the tomatoes and cook for 6-8 mins, until all is nicely softened and moist. Add a little black pepper and stir in the chopped coriander. Put the cooked millet in the bottom of a heatproof (lidded) casserole and pile the cooked vegetables and their juices over it. Spread a thick layer of Greek yoghurt over them, and scatter the toasted sesame seeds over the surface. Bake, covered, for 35 mins at 180°C/350°F/gas mark 4. Or, prepare in advance and bake for 45 mins. Serves 4, with a green salad.

Variations:

This basic grain casserole can be made with any cooked grain, and different mixtures of vegetables: allow 350 g/12 oz cooked grain and 700 g/1½ lbs vegetables.

Couscous Croquettes

175 g/6 oz couscous
vegetable stock
½ bunch spring onions, sliced
45 ml/3 tblsps sunflower oil
1 large egg, beaten
30 ml/2 tblsps fromage blanc, or Jockey
30 ml/2 tblsps chopped coriander

Soak the couscous in 225 ml/8 fl oz cold water for 10 mins, then steam for 30 mins over vegetable stock. Leave to cool. Cook the sliced spring onions in half the oil for 2 mins, then stir into the couscous. Beat the egg with the *fromage blanc* and chopped coriander, then stir into the couscous. Form into large round patties, shaping them lightly. Heat the remaining oil in a non-stick frying pan and cook the croquettes until golden on both sides. Serve with chopped avocado and tomatoes, and a salad of lettuce hearts. Makes 8 croquettes, serves 4.

Wild Rice with Wild Mushrooms

50 g/2 oz wild rice
50 g/2 oz white long-grain rice
50 g/2 oz buckwheat
4 shallots, chopped
60 ml/4 tblsps olive oil
3 cloves garlic, finely chopped
350 g/12 oz wild mushrooms, or 175 g/6 oz wild mushrooms and 175 g/6 oz field mushrooms
120 ml/8 tblsps flat parsley leaves, coarsely chopped
sea salt and black pepper
Maggi Liquid Seasoning, or soy sauce
150 ml/¼ pt soured cream
150 ml/¼ pt yoghurt
45 ml/3 tblsps pine kernels

Cook the 3 grains as usual, separately. Long grain brown rice may be used instead of white, but I prefer white for this dish as it is lighter and prettier. Mix the 3 cooked grains and put in an oiled casserole (one holding 1.1-1.4 litres/2-2½ pts is best). Cook the chopped shallots in the olive oil, adding the garlic after 2 mins. Cook for 1 min, then add the wild mushrooms, cut in large pieces. (If using some field mushrooms, add them after 3-4 mins.) Cook gently, tossing frequently, until the mushrooms have softened. This will probably take 6-8 mins. Then add the parsley leaves, a little sea salt and black pepper, and remove from the heat. Add a dash of Maggi Liquid Seasoning, or soy sauce. Tip over the rice, spreading evenly. Mix the soured cream and yoghurt and spread over the mushrooms. Toast the pine kernels in a dry frying pan for a few moments, just until they are straw-coloured, then scatter them over the top. Cover with a lid, or foil, and bake for 35 mins at 180°C/350°F/gas mark 4. (Or 45 mins if prepared in advance.) Serve with a green salad.

Variations:

Pack the mixture of cooked grains into an oiled ring mould and leave in a low oven, 100°C/200°F/gas mark ¼, for 20 mins, or until ready to serve. Turn out on to a flat dish, and pour wild mushrooms into the centre, serving the rest separately. Serve the soured cream and yoghurt as a sauce, and omit the pine kernels. Cheaper versions of both dishes may be made by using brown rice alone, with field mushrooms.

SOUPS

Game Consommé with Ravioli

This delicious soup can be made with the remains of roast game eked out with raw chicken joints, using the flesh for the ravioli and the carcasses and chicken joints for the consommé.

consommé:

2 carcasses of game birds
450-700 g/1-1½ lbs chicken wings, or joints
1 large onion, roughly chopped
2 leeks, roughly chopped
2 carrots, roughly chopped
2 stalks celery, roughly chopped
1 bay leaf
3 stalks parsley
sea salt and 10 black peppercorns
300 ml/½ pt dry white wine

filling for ravioli:

150 g/5 oz pheasant, grouse, etc. cooked or raw, chopped
25 g/1 oz good smoked ham, chopped
1 clove garlic
sea salt and black pepper
30 ml/2 tblsps chopped parsley
1 egg, beaten
225 g/8 oz fresh pasta, in thin sheets

garnish:

1 small leek, white part only, or ¼ heart of green cabbage
1 small carrot
18-24 large leaves watercress

Make the consommé a day or 2 in advance. Put the carcasses and chicken joints into a deep pan and cover with about 2 litres/3½ pts cold water. Bring slowly to the boil, skimming as it reaches boiling point. When the surface is clear, add the vegetables, herbs, seasonings and wine. Bring back to the boil and cook for 3 hours or 1 hour under pressure. Strain and leave to cool, then chill overnight. Next day remove the fat from the surface, and boil up until reduced to about 1.4 litres/2½ pts, adjusting seasoning. Set aside. Next make the ravioli. Put the game trimmings into a food processor with the chopped ham and garlic. Process until it is evenly minced, fairly finely. Turn into a bowl and stir in the seasoning, chopped parsley, and beaten egg. Use to make ravioli as usual. You will probably have between 30 and 40; freeze half for another day. Shortly before serving, reheat the soup and prepare the garnish. Cut the white part of the leek into 4 cm/1½ in sections, then cut each one into very fine strips. (Or, if using cabbage, shred it in very thin slices.) Cut the carrot in fine strips like the leek. Just before serving, drop the ravioli into the simmering consommé and poach for 2½ -3 mins, adding the leek (or cabbage) and carrot for the last minute. When the time is up, lift out the ravioli and vegetables with a slotted spoon, and divide between heated bowls, allowing 2-3 ravioli for each one. Scatter 3 leaves watercress over each one, pour on the soup and serve immediately. Serves 6-8. Note: Domestic or wild duck, or even guinea fowl, may be substituted for game.

Ginger Consommé with Crabmeat Ravioli

consommé:

900 g/2 lbs raw chicken joints, or
2 carcasses
1 piece knuckle of veal, or veal bones
1 large onion, roughly chopped
1 large leek, roughly chopped
1 large carrot, roughly chopped
2 stalks parsley, roughly chopped
1 bay leaf
3 stalks parsley
sea salt and black peppercorns
300 ml/½ pt dry white wine

filling for ravioli:

900 g/2 lbs cooked crab (in shell), or
225 g/8 oz crabmeat, white and brown mixed
8 spring onions, bulbs only, finely chopped
1 cm/½ in square root ginger, finely chopped
sea salt and black pepper
30-45 ml/2-3 tblsps chopped coriander
225 g/8 oz fresh pasta, in thin sheets

garnish:

4 spring onions, cut in 4 cm/1½ in sections
8 thin slices peeled root ginger
6-8 small sprigs coriander

Start 1-2 days in advance.
Put the chicken and veal in a deep pan and cover with about 2 litres/3½ pts cold water. Bring slowly to the boil, skimming off the fat that rises to the surface. When it is clear, add the chopped vegetables, herbs and seasonings and wine. Bring back to the boil and cover the pan. Simmer for 3 hours, or cook for 1 hour under pressure. Strain and leave to cool, then chill overnight. Next day, remove the fat from the surface and boil up to reduce until you have 1.1-1.4 litres/2-2½ pts good flavoured consommé. Adjust seasoning to taste. Then make the ravioli. Extract the crabmeat from the shell and claw; shred the white meat and mix it with the brown in a bowl. Add finely chopped spring onions and ginger, salt, pepper and chopped coriander, and mix well. Use to make ravioli in the usual way. This will make 30-40

ravioli; half can be frozen for another occasion.
Shortly before serving, reheat the soup and prepare the garnish. Cut the sections of spring onions into very thin slivers. Just before serving, drop the ravioli into the simmering stock, adding the sliced ginger. Poach gently for 2½ -3 mins. (Test one in advance to determine cooking time.) Add the spring onions for the last 30 seconds. When the time is up, lift the ravioli with a slotted spoon, and lay in heated soup bowls, allowing 2-3 for each bowl, and adding some ginger and spring onion to each one. Pour the consommé into the bowls, and lay a sprig of coriander in each one. Serve immediately. Serves 6-8. Alternatively, the soup can be served in a large tureen, and spooned into bowls at the table.

Vegetable Consommé with Pumpkin Ravioli

This can be made without meat.

consommé:

1.1 kg/2½ lbs shin of beef, or skirt
1 piece knuckle of veal
some beef or veal bones
1 large onion, cut in quarters
2 bay leaves
1 large leek, roughly chopped
2 large carrots, roughly chopped
3 stalks celery, roughly chopped
225 g/8 oz tomatoes, roughly chopped
1 small head fennel, roughly chopped
1 small bunch watercress, roughly chopped
sea salt and 12 black peppercorns
juice of ½ lemon, or to taste

filling for ravioli:

900 g/2 lbs pumpkin
25 g/1 oz Ricotta
½ beaten egg
15 ml/1tblsp grated Parmesan
8 large leaves basil, when available
sea salt and black pepper
225 g/8 oz fresh pasta, in thin sheets

garnish:

1 large tomato, skinned
6-8 small sprigs basil, when available, or
24 leaves watercress

Start the consommé a day or 2 in advance. Put the beef, veal, and bones in a deep pan and cover with 2.3 litres/4 pts cold water. Bring slowly to the boil, skimming constantly when scum starts rising to the surface. When all is clear, add the onion and bay leaves and bring back to the boil. Cook for 3 hours or 1 hour under pressure, strain and leave to cool. Chill overnight. Next day remove fat from the surface and pour the soup into a clean pan. Add the vegetables, salt and peppercorns and bring slowly back to the boil. Half cover the pan and cook gently for 1½

hours, then strain. Boil up until reduced to about 1.4 litres/2½ pts, adding sea salt, black pepper, and lemon juice to taste.
The pumpkin purée can also be prepared a day in advance. Cut the pumpkin into cubes about 4 cm/1½ ins square, discarding rind and seeds, and steam over boiling water until soft, about 10 mins. Purée in a food processor, or push through a medium food mill. Then dry out in a heavy pan for about 10 mins, stirring often, until you have about 300 ml/½ pt fairly thick purée. Set aside.
On the day of serving, put the purée in a food processor with the Ricotta, beaten egg, Parmesan, and basil, when available, adding sea salt and black pepper to taste. Process until you have a smooth paste, then use to fill ravioli, as usual. You will have between 30-40, so freeze half for another time.
Shortly before serving, reheat the soup and prepare the garnish. Cut the outside flesh off the tomato in slabs, leaving the pulpy interior intact. Cut the flesh into strips, or neat dice, and put some in each soup bowl. Poach the ravioli for 2-3 mins in the simmering stock, then lift into the soup bowls with a slotted spoon, allowing 2-3 for each bowl. Pour the soup over them, and add the sprigs of basil, or watercress. Serves 6-8.
Note: For vegetarians, simply make a light vegetable stock using vegetable trimmings – onion skins, carrot tops, leek ends, celery tops, etc – and substitute for the meat stock, then proceed as above.

Mixed Mushroom Soup 1

300 ml/½ pt lentil stock (or 75 g/3 oz green or brown lentils)
12 g/½ oz dried porcini
350 g/12 oz flat mushrooms
900 ml/1½ pts game or chicken stock
sea salt and black pepper
5 ml/1 tsp flour
150 ml/¼ pt crème fraîche, or soured cream

garnish:

100-175 g/4-6 oz wild mushrooms: chanterelles, ceps, etc
2 shallots, chopped
25 g/1 oz butter
22 ml/1½ tblsps olive oil
2 cloves garlic, finely chopped
60 ml/4 tblsps roughly chopped parsley

Make the lentil stock by cooking 75 g/3 oz lentils in 600 ml/1 pt lightly salted water until they are tender, then drain, reserving the lentils for another dish. This should yield about 300 ml/½ pt stock. Soak the dried *porcini* in 300 ml/½ pt hot water for 20 mins, then drain, reserving the liquid. Chop the dried mushrooms quite finely, and the fresh mushrooms fairly coarsely.

Heat the chicken and lentil stock, adding the dried mushroom liquid. Put in the chopped mushrooms, fresh and dried. Bring to the boil, add sea salt and black pepper, and simmer until the mushrooms are soft, about 20 mins. Stir the flour into the *crème fraîche*, or soured cream, and add to the pan slowly, stirring well.

Simmer for another 3 mins then set aside to cool slightly. Process in a food processor, then return to the clean pan and reheat while you make the garnish.

Wipe the wild mushrooms and slice thickly. Cook the shallots in the butter and oil for 2 mins, then add the garlic and cook for another min. Add the wild mushrooms and cook, stirring often, until they have softened. This may take from 4-6 mins. Then stir in the chopped parsley and cook for a moment longer. Put the mushroom soup into bowls and spoon some of the wild mushroom garnish into the centre of each one. Serves 6.

Mixed Mushroom Soup 2

When wild mushrooms are not around, the above recipe may be adapted as follows:

Remove the stalks from the fresh mushrooms, and divide the caps into 2 equal piles. Reserve half for the garnish, slicing them fairly thickly. Sauté them with the chopped shallots and garlic, as you would do with the wild mushrooms, but adding 10 ml/2 tsps ground coriander.

Mixed Root Vegetable Soup, with Fried Noodles

4 medium leeks
1 large potato
1 head celery
2-3 small turnips
3 small parsnips
350 g/12 oz Jerusalem artichokes
3 stalks parsley
1 bay leaf
1.1 litres/2 pts chicken stock
sea salt and black pepper
50 g/2 oz butter
50 ml/2 fl oz double cream

garnish (optional):

50 g/2 oz fine egg noodles
frying oil

Scrape or peel all the vegetables and chop coarsely. Put them in a large pan with the herbs and cover with cold water, lightly salted. Bring them to the boil and cook for 10 mins, half covered. Strain off the water and discard. Pour on the cold stock and bring to the boil. Cook for 10 mins, then set aside to cool. Purée in a food processor, then return to the clean pan. Shortly before serving, reheat the soup, adding sea salt and black pepper to taste. If serving with the noodle garnish, this may also be prepared in advance. Break them into pieces about 5 cm/2 ins long, and cook as usual in boiling salted water. Drain well, then spread out on a cloth to dry thoroughly. Heat some oil to about 160°C/320°F; you only need about 5 cm/2 in depth. Fry the noodles a few at a time, just until they turn pale straw-coloured and crisp, then lift out and drain on kitchen paper. Shortly before serving, reheat the soup, stirring in the butter and cream, and adjust the seasoning. If using the noodle garnish, pour it into bowls and scatter the fried noodles over the top. Serves 8-10.

Potato Soup with Sesame Seeds

2 leeks, sliced
40 g/1½ oz butter
550 g/1¼ lbs waxy potatoes, sliced
900 ml/1½ pts chicken stock, heated
sea salt and black pepper
300 ml/½ pt creamy milk, or milk and cream mixed

garnish:

30 ml/2 tblsps sesame seeds, toasted

Cook the sliced leeks in the butter for 4 mins, stirring now and then. Add the sliced potatoes and stir around for 1½ mins, then add the heated stock. Bring to the boil, add salt and pepper, and simmer gently, half covered, for about 15 mins, or until the potatoes are soft. Heat the milk and add to the pan, stir to mix well, and adjust seasoning. Do not purée; simply serve as it is, in bowls, with some toasted sesame seeds sprinkled over the surface. Toast sesame seeds by heating in a dry frying pan over gentle heat. Shake the pan once or twice, and remove from the heat as soon as they have changed colour. Serves 6.

Chicken Soup with Beansprouts

900 ml/1½ pts good chicken stock
175 g/6 oz beansprouts, rinsed
1 bunch spring onions, trimmed
75 g/3 oz small mushrooms, caps only, sliced
75 g/3 oz Chinese egg noodles, broken in small pieces
100 g/4 oz cooked chicken, chopped or shredded
10 ml/2 tsps light soy sauce
sea salt and black pepper
Maggi Liquid Seasoning (optional)

garnish:

1 basket mustard and cress

Heat the stock until it reaches boiling point. Add the beansprouts, whole spring onions and mushrooms, bring back to the boil, and cook for 3 mins. Drop the egg noodles into boiling water, remove from the heat, and stand for 5 mins, then drain and add to the soup with the shredded chicken. Cook for 2-3 mins, then remove from the heat. Stir in the soy sauce, sea salt and black pepper, and a dash of Maggi Liquid Seasoning. Spoon into bowls and scatter mustard and cress over the top. Serves 4.

Note: For a light main dish in a bowl, double the amount of noodles.

ORGANIC MEAT

Roast Saddle of Lamb

This is a truly wonderful joint, rarely seen nowadays. It should be carved in long rectangular strips, parallel to the backbone. Allow roughly 450 g/1 lb per head

2.7 kg/6 lb saddle of British lamb
45 ml/ 3 tblsps virgin olive oil
15 ml/1 tblsp lemon juice
freshly ground black pepper
fresh herbs (optional)
4 sprigs rosemary, in winter or
6 sprigs each tarragon and chervil, in summer
300 ml/½ pt meat or chicken stock, heated

Little need be done to this before putting it in the oven. With old-fashioned breeds like Welsh mountain lamb, where the layer of fat is thin, I rub it all over with olive oil and lemon juice a couple of hours before cooking. Sometimes I scatter herbs over it, rosemary in winter, or a mixture of tarragon and chervil in summer. Lay on a roasting rack and cook for 1¼ hours for a small breed, like the Welsh mountain sheep, or 1½ hours for a normal breed. (The weight has little to do with the length of cooking time, since this usually indicates the length of the joint rather than the thickness, which is what determines the time it takes to cook.) The oven should be moderate: 180°C/350°F/gas mark 4. It doesn't need basting, since it is completely covered with fat. When the time is up, move the meat onto a carving platter and cover loosely with two thicknesses of foil and a heavy towel. Rest for 15-20 mins before carving. Pour off the fat in the tin and set it over a moderate heat. Pour on the heated stock and scrape all the bits of sediment into the juices. Let it all bubble away and reduce slightly for 3-4 mins, then strain into a sauceboat. Carve the saddle lengthwise in slightly wedge-shaped pieces about 0.5 cm/¼ in thick on the outside, tapering slightly as they meet the bone. If they are very long, cut them in half before laying on the plate. Serves 6, with mint sauce and redcurrant jelly.

A leg of lamb or a shoulder can be cooked in exactly the same way, allowing 2 hours for a leg, and 1½-1¾ hours for a shoulder.

Again, the thickness must be the deciding factor in calculating the cooking time, and the shoulder is a shallow joint, especially with small breeds of sheep.

Grilled Sirloin Steak

This is my favourite steak, the equivalent of the French *entrecôte*.

2 sirloin steaks (200-225 g/7-8 oz each)

Heat a cast-iron grill pan for 2-3 mins, until very hot. Grease the ridges lightly with a small piece of fat from the steak. Lay the steak across the ridges and cook quite briskly for 2-2½ mins. Then slide a small spatula under them and turn them over. Cook for another 2-2½ mins, depending on their thickness, and your taste. Serve immediately, on hot plates, either alone, or with parsley butter. Accompany them with a potato purée and green salad, and some good Dijon mustard. Serves 2.

Boiled Leg of Mutton with Caper Sauce

Mutton has not been much in evidence for some time, but it is steadily gaining popularity in the west country. With the Welsh mountain sheep, and the Shetland and Soay breeds that are becoming popular, a leg is no longer the massive joint it once was. This is one of the best ways of cooking it, and I am grateful to Caroline Blackburn of The Pure Meat Company for the recipe.

1 leg of mutton, trimmed of excess fat
1.4-1.7 litres/2½-3 pts light meat or chicken stock
1 stalk celery
1 medium onion, halved
3 carrots, halved
20 black peppercorns

Start 1 day in advance. Place the leg in a large saucepan or casserole. Cover with stock, add the vegetables and peppercorns and bring slowly to the boil. Simmer for 2 hours, leave to cool overnight.
Next day, remove any excess fat from the top of the pan and discard the vegetables. Bring slowly back to the boil, and simmer for another hour. You can add some fresh root vegetables for the last 30 mins. Any mutton left over can be kept in the stock in a cool place overnight. Reheat thoroughly just before serving. Serves 6-8, depending on the breed.

caper sauce:
25 g/1 oz butter
20 g/³/4 oz flour
2.5 ml/½ tsp dry mustard
salt and black pepper
30 ml/2 tblsps capers, drained
7 ml/½ tblsp caper juice
15 ml/1 tblsp double cream

Melt the butter in a pan, add the flour and mustard, and mix well. Add 150 ml/¼ pt stock from the mutton and season well with salt and pepper. Simmer for 2-3 mins. Add the capers plus their juice. Simmer a few moments more, then add cream just before serving.

Braised Oxtail

first day:
2 oxtails, cut in 5 cm/2 in sections
40 ml/2½ tblsps flour
salt and black pepper
30 ml/2 tblsps olive oil
25 g/1 oz butter
2 cloves garlic, finely chopped or crushed
30 ml/2 tblsps tomato purée
1 large onion, halved
1 large carrot, halved
1 stalk celery, halved
1 bay leaf
3 stalks parsley
750 ml/1¼ pts beef stock
150 ml/¼ pt red wine

second day:
2 medium carrots, cut in thick strips
2 small turnips, cut in thick strips
2 stalks celery, cut in thick strips
1 parsnip, cut in thick strips
1 leek, cut in thick strips
40 g/1½ oz beef dripping, or fat from the stew
30 ml/2 tblsps chopped parsley

Start 1 day in advance. Trim excess fat off the oxtail. Season the flour with salt and pepper, and coat the oxtail sections with it, shaking off any excess. Heat the oil and butter in a casserole and brown the oxtail on all sides, transferring them to a plate as they are done. Add the garlic and tomato purée to the casserole, replace the meat, and add the halved vegetables and herbs. Heat the stock and wine together and pour over the meat; bring to the boil, adding more salt and pepper. Cover the pan and cook for 4 hours at 150°C/300°F/ gas mark 2. Take out of the oven and leave to cool overnight.
Next day, remove the fat from the surface of the stew and reserve. Lift the meat onto a shallow earthenware dish and discard the flavouring vegetables and herbs. Keep warm while you cook the fresh vegetables. Take 40 g/1½ oz of the fat from the stew, or a good beef dripping, and heat in a sauté pan. Put in all the vegetables cut in strips about 4 cm/1½ ins long, like thick matchsticks. Cook them gently in the fat for 8 mins then add 300 ml/½ pt of the oxtail stock. Bring to the boil, and simmer gently for 15 mins.
When they are done, scatter them over the surface of the oxtail, adding the remainder of their stock, and the rest of the oxtail stock. Put back in the oven for another hour at 180°C/350°F/gas mark 4, basting from time to time with the juices. The surface of the dish should acquire a slightly crisp, browned surface as the meat juices caramelize in the heat of the oven. Sprinkle with chopped parsley before serving with boiled potatoes and a green salad. Serves 6.

Grilled Breast of Lamb

1 breast of lamb
1 onion, sliced
1 leek, sliced
1 carrot, sliced
75 g/3 oz butter
sea salt and black pepper
1 large egg, beaten
dry white breadcrumbs
22 ml/1½ tblsps olive oil

Ask your butcher to leave the breast of lamb flat, not to roll or tie it. Cook the sliced onion, leek and carrot in 25 g/1 oz butter in broad pan for 5 mins, then lay the folded breast of lamb over them, and add 600 ml/1 pt hot water. Add salt and pepper and bring to the boil, then simmer, covered, for 1¾ hours. Remove the lamb and cool a little.
When just cool enough to handle, slide out the bones using a small sharp knife. Cut the meat in strips about 2.5 cm/1 in wide, and dip them first in beaten egg and then in breadcrumbs. They can now be left for several hours, or even overnight, or grilled straight away. Lay them on the rack of the grill pan and baste with the remaining 50 g/2 oz butter, melted and mixed with the oil. Grill the meat strips for 5 mins on each side, basting once or twice while they cook. They should be crisp and brown all over. Serves 3-4.

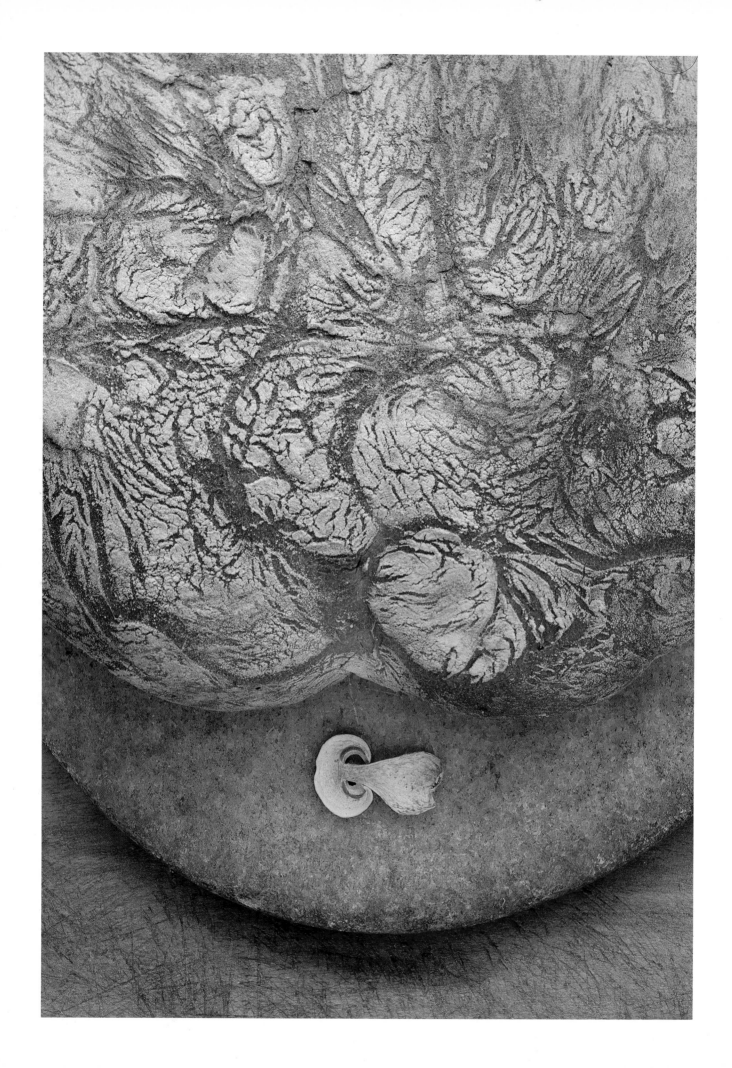

November

The English are a curious mixture of insecurity and complacency, and this is nowhere more apparent than in the realm of food. Ever since Elizabeth David's first book was published, a few years after the war, we began a love affair with 'foreign' food that has gone on ever since. It must be remembered that in 1950, when *A Book of Mediterranean Food* was published, food rationing was still in force. This, combined with the post-war currency regulations, had deprived us of everything foreign, including food and wine, sight-seeing, sun-bathing, swimming in warm seas, and many other delightful things.

This delight in the food of the northern Mediterranean countries has never left us; it merely moves around through the different regions. To start with, it was French Provençal, and restaurants with names like Le Matelot sprang up in London, with fishing nets and strings of garlic incorporated in the decor. Some years later, it reached the Middle East; at present, it seems firmly rooted in northern Italy. I love Tuscan food as much as anyone else, but I would rather eat it in Italy, or in a good restaurant like The River Café, or at home with Italian friends. It seems to me slightly incongruous that tomato and mozzarella salad should have replaced the prawn cocktail as our favourite first course, while *pesto* has become a national dish.

None of this would matter, were it not for the sad fact that in the meantime we have neglected our own foods. And this is a pity, not only for us, as consumers, but also for the thousand or more small food producers throughout the UK. With little encouragement from the government, they have worked to supply us with an impressively varied range of goods. These include such traditional things as haggis and Bath chaps, Cumberland sausages, rare breeds of sheep and pig, and fallow and roe deer. Others have come up with such unusual products as air-dried ham, smoked venison, wheat wafer biscuits, cheeses made with ewes' or goats' milk, wild boar, and guinea fowl eggs. Some, like Matthias Luethi, specialize in growing miniature vegetables for some of the best restaurants; others organize a team of hunters to gather wild mushrooms, or edible seaweed. There are those who farm *gigas* oysters or salmon, trout or small scallops, while others catch eels and elvers in the Severn and its tributaries. Many producers grow unusual salad leaves and herbs which formerly had to be imported; others make their own wine, or fruit liqueurs, or cordials.

With all this wealth of native products to draw on, surely it is time to abandon our passion for foreign food, and concentrate on reviving British food? I do not necessarily mean the old clichés like steak and kidney pudding and jam roll, good as they are, for the English tradition has a far greater potential than this. There is no reason why an innovative chef should not work with British produce as his base of reference.

Instead of serving red mullet with a pepper *coulis*, why not work with our own shellfish to produce a British *plateau des fruits de mer?* Or make our own potted shrimps, or cod's-roe paste? We could serve a selection of our own smoked fish with a creamy horseradish sauce; or smoked game or poultry, without resorting to such things as Parma ham. We could work on the English fish pie, as Mosimann has done with the bread and butter pudding, to produce a superlative version.

Bearing Mosimann in mind, it occurs to me that it has been the foreign chefs who have given English food what little attention it has received. Our two great food writers since the war, Elizabeth David and Jane Grigson, were both singularly unappreciative of English food. Both wrote books about it in the end, but it did not figure high on their list of priorities. In *The Observer Guide to English Cookery*, Jane Grigson acknowledges her debt to Guy Mouilleron in this respect: 'It was Guy Mouilleron, when he was at the Café Royal, who told me not to be quite so ashamed of our cooking, there were some good ideas and good recipes that he had taken up and adapted with great success.... More recently, Anton Mosimann ticked me off for my poor opinion of bread and butter pudding, and converted me.'

It is partly thanks to Anton Mosimann and his protégés that we see as much English food in our restaurants as we do. The Dorchester still serves only English food in the Grill Room, just as they did in Mosimann's day, while he continues to serve his version in his club, Mosimann's. It is the grandest and most expensive restaurants that do English dishes justice, while the humblest pub now loses its head, and offers a lengthy list of such inappropriate dishes as *chile con carne* and lasagne. Yet Bibendum serves fish and chips with sauce tartare, black puddings, and steamed ginger pudding. The Connaught has never failed to serve 'British plain cooking done well,' as Tom Jaine comments in *The Good Food Guide*, while Le Caprice and the Ivy both continue to serve good English food.

Game has recently acquired a new significance. For not only is it one of our traditional foods, much esteemed by gourmets and foreigners, it now has a healthy image that endears it to food purists. Game is, for the most part, a wild food, free from hormones and chemicals except for those which escape into the atmosphere and are unavoidable. Wild game birds live free, without suffering the indignities of battery farming and slaughter houses. Like all creatures that are free to roam at will, and are constantly exercising their muscles, their fat is unsaturated, unlike that of animals or birds that are kept cooped up. And, by being free to feed where they will, they enjoy a varied diet that adds immeasurably to their flavour.

The food values of grouse, pheasant and partridge are higher in minerals, especially iron and calcium, than poultry, and they are much lower in saturated fat. Pigeon is higher still in iron, but lower in calcium. Game is expensive to buy, but during its short season it makes good sense to enjoy it often, both as a treat, and as a health food. Grouse are shot from August 12th to December 10th; partridge from September 1st to February 1st, and pheasant from October 1st to February 1st. Snipe, woodcock and wild duck are in season from November until March, while wood pigeon may be shot all year round. Some game birds are now farmed, which means that they can be bought all year round, but these are not organic, since they are fed artificially and reared in captivity. In some cases, farming does improve the product, for I find little comparison between the tender succulence of the farm-raised squab and the tough gamey flesh of the wild pigeon.

There are many light and delicious ways of treating game, more in keeping with its healthy image than the old pies and terrines, and without all the elaborate accompaniments of the roasted bird. Tender young game birds are good taken off the bone and lightly browned in sunflower oil, then braised briefly with a few sliced vegetables, their juices made into a sauce with *crème fraîche* or *fromage blanc*. Alternatively, after browning, they can be wrapped in a cabbage leaf and steamed, before serving with an egg and lemon sauce, like the Greek *avgolemono*. They may also be laid on a bed of celery stalks and steamed, with chopped tar-ragon added to the slightly thickened sauce. The breast fillets may be removed from grouse, partridge or squab and treated like *magrets de canard:* grilled and served warm, with a *salade tiède*, or a dish of wild rice and slightly caramelized vegetables. The carcasses can then be used to make an excellent stock for adding to sauces, or a lentil soup. A grouse can be used to make a good sauce for fresh pasta, even more delicious when combined with some wild mushrooms, like the golden girolles, or oyster mushrooms. Used in this way, game takes on a new character, no less luxurious, but light and healthy.

For those who prefer their game in more traditional ways, there is much to be said for braising rather than roasting. Few things are more delicious than a well-hung bird, perfectly roasted and served with game chips, gravy, bread sauce and fried breadcrumbs. But for the home cook this is very ambitious, except perhaps for two people, and I prefer to adopt an easier alternative. In the past, I have been put off braised game birds by the age of the birds that were considered suitable for this method of cooking. Young birds, on the other hand, respond excellently to braising, while potentially dry birds like pheasant are even improved. The timing is no longer so vital as in roasting, and only the simplest of accompaniments are necessary, or even desirable. The same method works well with all game birds, also guinea fowl, adapting the timing accordingly. Instead of gravy and bread sauce, a good sauce can be made by enriching the cooking juices with some sour cream, or *crème fraîche*. Braised fennel, celery, or red cabbage can be cooked in the oven at the same time as the birds, while a creamy potato purée is made on top of the stove.

Another advantage of braising is that the remains of the dish make a most excellent soup that varies each time it is made. The combination of the braising vegetables and their juices with scraps of game and the remains of the sauce make a wonderful soup. The carcasses can be used to make game stock, best of all mediums for making soups of fresh root vegetables, or dried vegetables like lentils or haricot beans. Game is indeed a versatile food that adapts well to modern methods of cooking as well as the old-established *cuisine de terroir*, for it has a basic character and strength that are hard to spoil.

The range of English puddings is enormous, and the variations almost limitless. Take steamed puddings for a start. These may be made with suet, or with fat; with breadcrumbs or with flour, or with a mixture of both; they may be flavoured with fresh or dried fruit, with jam, syrup or marmalade, with ginger, chocolate or coffee. The same mixture may be baked instead of steamed, although those made with suet are usually steamed, at least in part. Then there is the variation in shapes. Most steamed puddings are made in pudding basins, covered with a lid of domed or pleated foil to allow for expansion. Some, however, like castle puddings, are made in small individual shapes, using dariole moulds, like tiny sandcastles. Apple dumplings are unique in that they stand alone, without a container, either on a baking sheet or in a steamer.

Then we come to the bread pudding. Apple Charlotte is a prime example of this; there is also a simpler version invented by an old friend of mine, which she calls apple sandwich. Another surprisingly good bread pudding is *pain perdu*, or eggy bread, its less appealing English name. This is simply fingers of dry white bread dipped in beaten egg and fried in butter. The other great bread-based pudding is toffee pudding, in *The Constance Spry Cookery Book*, a staple of the old English country houses: very rich but totally irresistible.

Apples are probably the best of fruits for winter puddings, since their juicy tartness complements the bland tastes and textures of suet, sponge and bread so admirably, and their season seems planned with this in mind. Pears make excellent tarts, and hard pears like Conference are unbeatable when baked slowly in red wine and sugar. Quinces should not be forgotten, for these unusual fruit have a singular flavour and aroma. They mix well with apples and with pears, although they need much longer cooking. In *Chez Panisse Cooking: Taste and Techniques*, Lindsay Shere recommends adding a sliced poached quince to the raw apples in the tart. If, however, you choose to add a quince to the recipe for apple hat, it may be added raw, since the long cooking demanded by the suet will work perfectly. Quinces may also be mixed with cooking pears in the recipe given for baking in red wine. Rice puddings are rarely seen nowadays, which I find sad. One that I had only ever read about until recently

turns out to be surprisingly delicious. Called *tête de nègre*, it consists of a mould of creamed rice, with an egg custard replacing most of the cream, chilled overnight in a rounded pudding basin, then turned out and masked with a dark chocolate sauce which sets to a hard shell on contact with the chilled rice. A 'turban' of whipped cream is piled on top, just before serving. This would also be pretty made on a small scale, using small muffin tins, or tiny bowls. It is quite a lot of work, but fun.

Most simple English puddings need a sauce, and often cream as well. Many of the steamed puddings are good served with a complementary sauce to intensify their flavour. This applies to marmalade puddings, treacle puddings and chocolate puddings. Castle pudding has no intrinsic flavour of its own, and is usually served with a sauce of warmed golden syrup sharpened with lemon juice. The fruit puddings, like apple hat and apple Charlotte, are best served with a custard sauce, or thick cream. Some people serve both together, which is my idea of true luxury. This gave me the idea of combining the two: I now make a custard sauce which I serve warm, with about one-third of its volume of lightly whipped cream folded in just before serving.

It's odd how food goes in fashions. I don't mean the great sweeping waves, like *cuisine minceur*, but the individual dishes. Almost all the best restaurant meals I had over one six-month period ended with one of two things: either an almond tart or a lemon tart. Yet out of my 150 cookbooks, I could only find about three recipes, and none of them were exactly what I had in mind. At the pre-opening celebrations of Bibendum a wonderful almond tart was one of the three desserts on offer. I had it again some weeks later, at the oyster bar downstairs, and a version of it at The River Café, cooked by Rose Gray, who got the recipe from Simon Hopkinson, chef at Bibendum. Rose has altered it slightly, in that she usually incorporates fruit in the form of raspberries, peaches, pears or apricots, either in the almond filling or beneath it.

The lemon tart I have in mind is similar. The best I've had was at Harvey's, at the close of a memorable meal cooked by the brilliant young chef, Marco Pierre White. Recently I spied two handsome lemon tarts while interviewing Alistair Little in his kitchen, but alas, by the time I came to eat there, they had all gone.

It seems that, with the possible exception of Holland, we are the only country in Europe which chooses to ignore mushrooms. Like most Anglo-Saxons I was brought up to believe that the only edible mushroom was the field mushroom, and that all the others were poisonous things called toadstools. And this, despite the fact that we lived in north-east Scotland, where the woods are carpeted with golden chanterelles...

Wild mushrooms are especially valued in northern countries like Russia, Finland, Norway and Sweden, where the choice of winter vegetables is few, and in central European countries like Germany and Poland, also in France and Italy. In China, Tibet and Japan they are also highly prized. Yet in the United States and Canada their popularity is almost nil.

In the USSR the mushroom season is short, but very prolific. Special trains leave Moscow at midnight, taking the mushroom hunters to spots on the edge of the forests, where the search for mushrooms is highly organized. The hunters can sell their find if they wish, or engage themselves for paid working holidays, picking, washing and drying the wild mushrooms. According to Lesley Chamberlain in her book, *The Food and Cooking of Russia*, the three most popular mushrooms in the USSR are ceps, morels and chanterelles. As Nabokov writes scathingly in his autobiography *Speak, Memory:* 'It is however to the...lowly and ugly agarics (field mushrooms) that nations with timorous taste buds limit their knowledge and appetite, so that to the Anglo-American lay mind the aristocratic boletes (ceps) are, at best, reformed toadstools.'

One man who has done more than anyone to promote wild mushrooms in Britain, through his Neal Street Restaurant, books and television appearances, is Antonio Carluccio. When he first came to the UK in 1975, Antonio was amazed by the lack of interest in wild mushrooms. He lost no time in finding productive hunting grounds within reach of London, but rarely met another hunter. Today, wild mushrooms in their various forms – fresh, preserved and dried – together with white truffles from Piedmont, form the linchpin of many of his dishes at his restaurant. His own special favourites are *porcini*, or ceps (*Boletus eculis*), and honey fungus (*Armillaria mellea*). His favourite funghi dishes are *risotto con porcini* and *polenta con funghi*.

When I lunched with him at Neal Street, I started with a *ragoût* of wild mushrooms – followed by *brandelli*. These are made with scraps of freshly made pasta speckled with powdered dried *porcini* mixed into the dough, served in a pile like thin pancakes, in a cream sauce flavoured with white truffles. It was a fabulous meal, full of the flavours of autumn.

Possibly because I did not learn to distinguish them as a child, I do not feel confident enough to gather wild mushrooms unless accompanied by an expert. This would not apply in most European countries, where professional identification of wild mushrooms is laid on automatically each season, as a service to the public. In France, the chemists' shops stay open on Sunday for the purpose, since this is the great day for forays in the woods, while professionals inspect the wild mushrooms on sale in the markets. In Norway, according to Alan Davidson in *A Kipper For My Tea*, 'a mushroom control point is established at the railway station in Oslo during the season, so that mushroom hunters returning from their excursions can have their harvest checked.' Without these useful aids, I am restricted to buying wild mushrooms in the shops, something which has only recently become possible. They are expensive, but only a small amount is needed, and for some dishes they can be mixed with cultivated mushrooms. There are six main varieties to be found: ceps, chanterelles (*Cantharellus cibarius*), morels (*Morchella esculenta*), oyster mushroom (*Pleurotus ostreatus*), *pieds de mouton* (*Hydnum repandum*), and *trompettes des morts* (*Craterellus cornupiodes*). With the exception of the chanterelles which are brought down from Scotland in summer and early autumn, most of the others come from Rungis wholesale vegetable market in Paris. Wild mushrooms and game have a strong affinity, in that both are genuine wild foods, sharing the same season, and both resist attempts to raise them commercially. The cultivation of wild mushrooms is still in its infancy. So far, the most successful results have been achieved with the oyster mushroom, and with the *shiitake* and *enoki*, which are now widely farmed, both in their native Japan and throughout Europe.

Apart from the beautiful *ovolo* (*Amanita caesarea*), which only exists in Tuscany, my favourite mushroom is the apricot-coloured chanterelle, with its firm texture and delicate flavour. Its season stretches from mid July (in Scotland) to early December (in the south of England). I love to use it alone, or mixed with oyster mushrooms or brown caps. Other inspired accompaniments are shallots, garlic, game stock, fresh noodles, buckwheat and sour cream.

The best mushrooms for drying are the ceps (usually called *porcini* when dried), morels, *trompettes des morts*, and *shiitake*. Especially good, but very expensive, are the dried morels, as they keep their distinctive shape and their flavour becomes concentrated.

Steak and Kidney Pie

675 g/1½ lb best stewing steak cut in 2.5
cm/1 in cubes
225 g/8 oz ox kidney cut in small pieces
seasoned flour
40 g/1½ oz beef dripping, or butter
2 medium onions, sliced
2 medium carrots, sliced
salt and black pepper
450 ml/¾ pt beef or chicken stock

suet dough:

225 g/8 oz self-raising flour, sifted
a pinch of salt
100 g/4 oz shredded suet

Dip the beef and kidney in seasoned flour, shaking off the excess. Heat the dripping (or butter) in a casserole and cook the sliced onions for 3 mins, stirring them about. Then add the carrots and continue to cook gently for another 3 or 4 mins, until they are all lightly coloured. Then lift the vegetables out with a slotted spoon and brown the meat. When all is nicely browned, replace the vegetables and pour on the heated stock. Stir till blended, then bring to the boil, adding salt and black pepper. Cover the casserole and cook gently for 2 hours, either on top of the stove or in a low oven, 170°C/325°F/gas mark 3. Shortly before the time is up, sift the flour into a bowl, adding the salt. Cut in the suet with the blade of a knife, adding just enough cold water to make it all cling together. Form into a ball, knead briefly, then roll out until about 1.5 cm/½ in thick. When the beef has finished cooking, transfer the contents of the casserole to a rectangular pie dish. Cut 4 long strips of pastry about 2.5 cm/1 in wide and lay them along the dampened rim of the pie dish, to make a base for the pastry lid. Damp the top surface of the strips, and lay the pastry over the surface of the dish, pressing down the edges to seal firmly. Trim the edges and decorate if you wish. Bake for 30-40 mins at 190°C/375°F/gas mark 5, until golden brown. Serves 4-5.

Shoulder of Lamb with Herb Crust

1 shoulder of lamb

herb crust:

50 g/2 oz dry breadcrumbs
2 cloves garlic, crushed
30 ml/2 tblsps chopped parsley
sea salt and black pepper

Calculate the cooking time, allowing 30 mins per 450 g/1 lb. Lay the shoulder on a rack in a roasting tin and roast it for ¾ of the total time at 180°C/350°F/gas mark 4. Shortly before the time is up, prepare the herb crust by mixing the ingredients in a bowl. Take the lamb out of the oven and press the crust mixture all over the surface of the skin. Put back in the oven and continue roasting until the time is up, basting once or twice with the fat in the tin. When the time is up, take it out of the oven and leave it for 15-20 mins in a warm place, covered loosely with a piece of foil. Serves 4-5.

Eve's Pudding

450 g/1 lb cooking apples, peeled, cored
and thickly sliced
100 g/4 oz castor sugar
75 g/3 oz unsalted butter, at room tem-
perature
100 g/4 oz self-raising flour, sifted
2 eggs, beaten

Put just enough water in a heavy pan to cover the bottom. Add the sliced apples and 40 g/1½ oz sugar and cook gently until soft. Then turn them into a buttered soufflé dish holding about 900 ml/1½ pts. Cream the butter with the remaining 75 g/3 oz sugar, in a food processor or by hand. Fold in the sifted flour and beaten eggs in alternate spoonfuls, or process, until blended. Spoon over the apples so that they are completely covered. Bake for 30 mins at 180°C/350°F/gas mark 4, until golden brown and puffy. Serve soon after taking out of the oven, with a jug of thick cream. Serves 4.

Bread and Butter Pudding Homemade

This simple old-fashioned pudding is exceptionally delicious when served warm, with homemade vanilla ice cream.

75 g/3 oz dry white bread, crusts removed
approx. 25 g/1 oz unsalted butter
20 g/¾ oz raisins
300 ml/½ pt milk
150 ml/¼ pt single cream
3 eggs
75 g/3 oz vanilla sugar, or castor sugar

Slice the bread and spread each slice with butter. Cut each slice in half diagonally, then lay them in a buttered fireproof dish that will hold about 600 ml/1 pt. Scatter the raisins between each layer and over the top. Heat the milk with the cream in a small pan. Beat the eggs with an electric hand beater or wire whisk, adding the sugar. When the milk is about to boil, pour it onto the eggs, continuing to beat. Then pour through a strainer onto the bread. Bake for 40-45 mins at 160°C/325°F/gas mark 3, until the custard has set and the top is crisp and golden brown. Serves 4. At its best about 45 mins after coming out of the oven. Serve with thick cream, or ice cream.

Salmis of Game with Celery and Tarragon

2 grouse or 4 partridge or squab
22 ml/1½ tblsps sunflower oil
675 g/1½ lbs chicken wings, or jointed
rabbit (if using partridge or squab)
1 onion, halved
1 carrot, halved
½ bay leaf
sea salt and 8 black peppercorns
150 ml/¼ pt dry white wine, or 75 ml/
⅛ pt vermouth
6 stalks celery
10 ml/2 tsps cornflour
30 ml/2 tblsps fromage blanc
30 ml/2 tblsps chopped tarragon

If using grouse, cut the breasts and wings off the carcasses to make 4 pieces. Use the carcasses to make a stock with the flavouring vegetables, herbs and seasoning, wine or vermouth, and 750 ml/1¼ pts water. If using partridge or squab, simply cut them in half and make a stock with rabbit or chicken wings. Strain the stock after making, cool quickly, and remove any fat from the surface. Put it in the bottom part of a steamer and bring to the boil. Cut the stalks of celery into strips about 7.5 cm/3 ins long by 0.5 cm/¼ in wide; lay them in the top part of the steamer with the cut-up birds lying on them. Cover and cook over the boiling stock for 15 mins, then set aside, covered, to keep warm. Measure about 340 ml/12 fl oz of the stock, and re-heat in a small pan. Mix the cornflour in a cup with 15 m/1 tblsp cold water, then stir into the measured stock. Boil gently for 2-3 mins, stirring, then remove from the heat and cool slightly. Pour into a food processor, add *fromage blanc* and tarragon, and process briefly, until smooth. Tip back into the pan and reheat gently, without allowing it to boil. To serve, lay the celery sticks in a shallow dish with the game lying on them. Spoon a little of the sauce over them, and serve the rest in a jug. Fresh noodles make an excellent accompaniment to this delicate game dish. Serves 4.

Fresh Pasta with Game Sauce and Wild Mushrooms

1 grouse, or ½ pheasant
½ onion, sliced
1 small carrot, halved
½ stalk celery
¼ bay leaf
sea salt and 6 black peppercorns
60 ml/4 tblsps vermouth
1 medium onion, coarsely chopped
60 ml/4 tblsps sunflower oil
1 medium carrot, coarsely chopped
1 stalk celery, coarsely chopped

5 ml/1 tsp flour
2 shallots, finely chopped
1 large clove garlic, finely chopped
225 g/8 oz wild mushrooms: girolles, ceps,
or oyster mushrooms, when available
45 ml/3 tblsps chopped flat parsley
450 g/1 lb fresh tagliatelle

Cut all the flesh off the bird and cut in cubes. Make a stock with the carcasse, flavouring with vegetables and herbs, seasonings and vermouth, and 450 ml/¾ pt water. Strain and cool, then remove any fat. Cook the coarsely chopped onion in half the sunflower oil for 6-8 mins until it has started to soften. Meanwhile, parboil the carrots and celery in the stock for 5 mins, then drain them, and add to the onion. Cook for 2-3 mins, then add the chopped game. Stir until lightly coloured and cook for another 2-3 mins. Then stir in the flour and cook for another min, stirring. Pour on 225 ml/8 fl oz of the hot stock and stir until blended. Simmer gently for 5 mins, then set aside in a warm place. Shortly before serving, bring a large pan of lightly salted water to the boil. Stew the shallots gently in the remaining 30 ml/2 tblsps sunflower oil in a sauté pan, adding the garlic after 1 min. After another min, add the wild mushrooms, cut in large pieces, and cook for 6-8 mins, stirring now and then until they have softened, adding the parsley towards the end. Cook the pasta for 2-3 mins and drain in a colander. Tip into a large shallow bowl, and pour the game sauce over it. Lift lightly to distribute the sauce, then spread the wild mushrooms over the top. Serve immediately, with a green salad. Serves 4.

Game with Salade Tiède

2 grouse or 4 partridge or squab
15 ml/1tblsp sunflower oil
8 small leaves radicchio
1 small head chicory
8 small leaves batavia, or curly endive
8 rosettes mâche
15 ml/1 tblsp lemon juice
15 ml/1 tblsp white wine vinegar
30 ml/2 tblsps walnut oil
30 ml/2 tblsps sunflower oil
sea salt and black pepper

Cut the breast fillets off the birds, reserving the rest for a pasta sauce, or a soup. Rub them on both sides, leaving the skin on, with a few drops sunflower oil. Half an hour before serving, heat the grill and cook the fillets for 2-3 mins on each side, then set aside to cool slightly. Wash and pat dry the leaves, and lay 2 of each slightly on one side of 4 plates. Mix the dressing, and spoon a little of it – you may not need it all – over the leaves. Then cut the warm fillets into diagonal slices about 0.5 cm/¼ in thick, and lay them beside the salad.

Serve as soon as possible. Serves 4, as a first course.

Wild Rice and Vegetables

50 g/2 oz wild rice
50 g/2 oz white long grain rice
100 g/4 oz young carrots, sliced
1 bunch large spring onions, bulbs only
12 g/½ oz butter
15 ml/1 tblsp olive oil
50 g/2 oz fennel, sliced
sea salt and black pepper
15 ml/1 tblsp chopped tarragon

Put the wild rice in a pan with 600 ml/1 pt lightly salted water. Bring to the boil and cook for 30 mins, then add the white rice and cook for another 15 mins, or until both are tender. Drain well. Parboil the sliced carrots in a little water for 5 mins, then drain. Cook the whole spring onions in the butter and oil in a lidded sauté pan, adding the fennel half-way through. When they are golden, stir in the drained carrots and cook all together until slightly sticky and almost caramelized. Then stir in the drained rice and cook for 2-3 mins more. Finally, remove from the heat and add sea salt and black pepper to taste, and the chopped tarragon. Serves 3-4, as a side dish. This makes an excellent accompaniment to roast game or a roast guinea fowl, or grilled breasts of game birds.

WINTER PUDDINGS

Tête de Nègre

This unusual pudding dates back to the thirties. This version is based on an Ambrose Heath recipe. It is quite lengthy to make, but both pretty and delicious.

75 g/3 oz Patna rice
450 ml/¾ pt milk
3 egg yolks
50 g/2 oz vanilla sugar
300 ml/½ pt double cream

chocolate sauce:
75 g/3 oz Chocolat Menier
50 g/2 oz butter

Drop the rice into boiling water to cover, and cook for 10 mins; drain well. Heat 300 ml/½ pt milk, shake in the rice, and cook for another 10 mins, then drain off any remaining milk.
Make a custard by beating the egg yolks with the vanilla sugar. (If you don't have any, flavour the milk by infusing with half a vanilla pod for 20 mins.) Then heat the remaining 150 ml/¼ pt milk until it is just about to boil and pour it onto the egg yolks, beating constantly.
Stir this custard into the rice, mixing well and then leave to cool. Afterwards, stir in 30 ml/2 tblsps of the cream and turn it into

a pudding basin which you have rinsed with water, and which it fills nicely.
Chill for several hours to set, or overnight. Later, make a chocolate sauce by grating the chocolate into a bowl over boiling water, adding the butter in small bits and 15 ml/1 tblsp water. Once completely melted, beat well. Unmould the pudding onto a flat dish and pour the chocolate sauce carefully over the top, so that it is totally covered. The hot sauce will set immediately on contact with the cold rice to form a delicious thin shell. This may be chilled again before serving, or not.
Just before serving, whip the remaining cream lightly and pile on top, like a turban. Serves 4-5.
Note: This would also look pretty made in individual moulds, so long as they are rounded. Small teacups would probably work well. In this case increase the chocolate sauce by half as much again.

Apple Hat

This is an apple suet pudding, in which quinces can be incorporated at will. Simple but very good.

15 g/½ oz butter
225 g/8 oz self-raising flour
a pinch of salt
100 g/4 oz shredded suet
4 Granny Smiths, or other crisp dessert apple
60 ml/4 tblsps brown sugar
grated rind of 1 lemon
1 quince (optional)

Grease 1.1 litre/2 pt pudding basin. Sift the flour with the salt. Cut in the suet with the blade of a knife, and mix lightly. Stir in enough cold water to make a firm dough, and cut in 2 pieces. Roll out ¾ of it and use to line the greased bowl. Peel, core and slice the apples, and put them in the lined bowl, sprinkling with the brown sugar and lemon rind.
When quinces are available, add one, also peeled, cored and sliced, mixing it with the sliced apples.
Roll out the remaining suet to make a lid and lay over the top of the bowl, damping the edges to seal, and trimming. Cover with a piece of foil, doming it slightly to allow for expansion, and tie with string round the rim. Place in a steamer over boiling water and cook for 2-3 hours. Serves 5-6. Serve with custard sauce, or cream.

Apple Charlotte

There are many recipes for Apple Charlotte, but this is my favourite. I have based it on one in Constance Spry's *Come into the Garden Cook*, which was published in 1942.

194

900 g/2 lb cooking apples, peeled, cored, and thickly sliced
100 g/4 oz sugar
100 g/4 oz butter
juice of ½ lemon
30 ml/2 tblsps apricot jam
approx 8 thin slices dry white bread, crusts removed.

Put the sliced apples in a heavy pan with the sugar, 25 g/1 oz butter, and 60 ml/4 tblsps water. Cook gently, covered, until soft. Then uncover the pan and continue to cook, uncovered, over low heat until you have a thick purée. Stir in lemon juice and the apricot jam; set aside.

Cut the bread to fit a mould or soufflé dish about 7.5 cm/3 ins deep. Melt the remaining butter, and dip the slices of bread in it so that they are coated on both sides, then replace them in the dish. Fill the lined dish with the apple purée, and cover with a lid of more bread dipped in butter, cut to fit nicely into the top of the dish. Bake for 35-40 mins at 180°C/350F/gas mark 4, or until the top layer of bread is crisp and golden brown.

Turn out onto a flat dish and serve, fairly hot but not scalding, with a jug of thick cream. Serves 4-6.

Marmalade Pudding

100 g/4 oz white breadcrumbs
100 g/4 oz shredded suet
100 g/4 oz castor sugar
30 ml/2 tblsps marmalade, chopped
1 egg, lightly beaten

marmalade sauce:

60 ml/4 tblsps marmalade, chopped
30 ml/2 tblsps orange juice

Mix the breadcrumbs, suet and sugar. Mix the marmalade and the beaten egg together, and stir into the pudding. Turn into a greased pudding basin holding about 900 ml/1½ pts, and cover with some foil, tied with string. Steam over boiling water for 2 hours, then unmould and serve with marmalade sauce. Put the marmalade and orange juice in a small pan, add 30 ml/2 tblsps water, and heat gently. Turn into a sauceboat to serve with the pudding. Serve with a jug of thick cream as well. Or, if you prefer, combine the two by stirring 150 ml/¼ pt double cream into the marmalade sauce. Serves 4-5.

Creamy Custard Sauce

This is a fabulous sauce. If you like real vanilla ice cream, you will particularly like this.

½ vanilla pod
300 ml/½ pt milk
3 egg yolks
37 ml/2½ tblsps vanilla or castor sugar
150 ml/¼ pt double cream

Put the vanilla pod in a small pan with the milk. Bring slowly to the boil, then remove from the heat, cover the pan, and stand for 20 mins.

When the time is up, reheat the milk gently and start beating the egg yolks with the vanilla sugar, or castor sugar. When the milk is just about to boil, pour onto the egg yolks, still beating continuously. Then stand the bowl over a pan of simmering water and stir constantly, until the sauce has thickened slightly; this may take 6 or 7 mins.

Remove the bowl and stand it in a sink partly full of cold water to cool quickly. Stir often as it cools to prevent a skin forming. While it is cooling, whip the cream until just thickened without being solid. When the custard is warm, take it out of the sink and fold in the whipped cream.

This is at its most delicious served while still slightly warm, but it is good at any temperature. It is excellent served with puddings of all sorts: steamed and baked puddings, crusty bread and fruit puddings. Serves 4-6.

Jam Sauce

I based this recipe on a mixed jam sauce that often used to be served in the thirties. It is very good indeed with dishes like castle puddings.

60 ml/4 tblsps raspberry jam
60 ml/4 tblsps redcurrant jelly
15 ml/1 tblsp orange juice
15 ml/1 tblsp lemon juice
7 ml/½ tblsp brandy

Warm the jam and the jelly together over low heat, until melted. Then push them through a small food mill into a clean pan. Heat again, adding the fruit juices and brandy, but remove from the heat well before it reaches boiling point.
Serve warm, or fairly hot.

WILD FUNGHI

Spatchcocked Quail with Mushrooms and Polenta

6 quails
75 ml/5 tblsps olive oil
juice of 1 lemon
5 ml/1 tsp each of chopped thyme, rosemary and oregano
knob of butter
1 clove garlic, crushed and finely chopped
450 g/1 lb wild mushrooms or a mixture of cultivated ones such as oyster and brown-cap, sliced
1.1 litres/2 pts chicken stock
200 g/7 oz coarse polenta (cornmeal)
150 ml/ ¼ pt game or chicken stock
a handful of sultanas soaked in grappa or brandy (optional)
salt and freshly ground black pepper

Using kitchen scissors, cut along one side of the backbone from the tail to the neck. Open out the bird and lay it on a flat surface breast upward. Press down on the breast with the palm of your hand to flatten the bird. Make a small slit in the bottom flap of skin and ease the legs through to keep the bird in a tight neat shape. Mix 60 ml/4 tblsps of the olive oil, lemon juice and herbs with some salt and pepper, then rub this into the quails. Leave for at least 1 hour.

While the quails are marinating, prepare the mushrooms and *polenta*. Heat the butter and remaining oil in a heavy frying pan; add the garlic and cook gently to soften without colouring. Stir in the mushrooms, salt and pepper and sauté until the mushrooms are cooked. Set aside. Bring the 1.1 litres/2 pts of chicken stock to the boil, add the *polenta* in a slow steady stream, stir with a wooden spoon until the *polenta* is cooked and comes away from the sides of the pan (about 35 mins). Heat the game stock in a small saucepan and add the sultanas. 10 mins before the *polenta* is ready grill the birds. Place a small mound of *polenta* in each dish, make a well in the centre and fill with some mushrooms and a half quail. Pour some stock and sultanas around the edge.

Note: you can get away with one quail per person because the *polenta* is so filling. Serves 6.

Chanterelles in Pastry Cases

These little tarts may be filled with a mixture of chanterelles and wild mushrooms, the proportions depending on availability and cost. They may of course be made with chanterelles alone, or the chanterelles may be replaced by ceps.

pastry:

175 g/6 oz plain flour
50 g/2 oz wholemeal flour
a pinch of salt
100 g/4 oz butter, cut in bits
2.5 ml/½ tsp lemon juice
60-75 ml/4-5 tblsps iced water

glaze:

1 egg yolk, beaten
15 ml/1 tblsp milk

filling:

3 shallots, chopped
60 ml/4 tblsps olive oil
350 g/12 oz chanterelles
100 g/4 oz field mushrooms
sea salt and black pepper
a few shakes Maggi Liquid Seasoning (optional)
90 ml/6 tblsps chopped flat parsley

Make the pastry as usual, wrap in floured clingfilm, and chill for 20-30 mins. Then roll out and line 6 small round tins. Chill again for 10 mins, then weigh down with foil and beans and bake for 5 mins at 200ºC/400ºF/gas mark 6. Remove the foil and beans, brush with egg yolk beaten with 15 ml/1 tblsp milk, and bake for another 5 mins, or until lightly coloured. Set aside. Shortly before serving, reheat the pastry cases for 5 mins at 170ºC/325ºF/gas mark 3. Cook the chopped shallots in the oil for 2 mins, then add the chanterelles and cook for 10-12 mins, adding the field mushrooms after 4 mins. Remove from the heat, add sea salt and black pepper and a dash of Maggi Liquid Seasoning, and stir in the chopped parsley. Spoon into the warm pastry cases to serve. (If preferred, the mushrooms may be already assembled in the cold pastry cases and all reheated together; allow 10 mins at 180ºC/350ºF/gas mark 4.) Serves 6 as a first course, or as part of a spread of dishes.

Buckwheat Crêpes with Wild Mushrooms

This is best of all made with ceps or chanterelles, but may be made with a mixture of wild and cultivated mushrooms. Buckwheat flour can be bought at health food shops. If unobtainable, substitute wholemeal bread flour.

batter:

75 g/3 oz white bread flour
75 g/3 oz buckwheat flour, or wholemeal bread flour
1.25 ml/¼ tsp sea salt
2 eggs
300 ml/½ pt milk and water, mixed

filling:

1 shallot, finely chopped
15 ml/1 tblsp olive oil
12 g/½ oz butter
1 clove garlic, finely chopped
450 g/1 lb ceps or chanterelles, or mixed wild mushrooms, cleaned and cut in large pieces
sea salt and black pepper
60 ml/4 tblsps chopped flat parsley

sauce:

25 g/1 oz butter
15 ml/1 tblsp flour
200 ml/7 fl oz chicken stock
150 ml/¼ pt crème fraîche, or soured cream
sea salt and black pepper

Make the batter as usual, either in a food processor or by hand, and set aside. Then make the filling. Cook the shallot in oil and butter until pale golden, adding the garlic half-way through. Then add the mushrooms and cook until softened, about 8 mins. Then remove from the heat

and stir in the chopped parsley. Then make the sauce. Melt butter, add flour, and cook for 1 min, stirring. Then add heated chicken stock, stirring, and *crème fraîche*, or soured cream. Add salt and pepper to taste and simmer for 4 mins. Set aside.

Beat the batter once more, and use to make 6 x 15 cm/6 in thin *crêpes*. Have a broad heatproof bowl well greased and lined – or partly lined – with buttered greaseproof paper. Lay a *crêpe* in the bottom, cover with a layer of the mushrooms and another *crêpe*. Repeat the process until all the *crêpes* and fillings are used, leaving the last *crêpe* uncovered. Wrap foil over the bowl and place in the oven at 170ºC/325ºF/gas mark 3 for 20 mins. Then remove from the oven and turn out on a shallow dish. Reheat the sauce and pour some over the *crêpes*; serve the rest in a sauceboat. Serves 6 as a first course, or 4 as a main dish.

Wild Mushroom Salad

A delicious way of using a relatively small number of chanterelles.

225 g/8 oz chanterelles, cleaned
2 shallots, chopped
45 ml/3 tblsps olive oil
75 g/3 oz thinly sliced smoked back bacon, cut in strips
100 g/4 oz mixed green leaves, or mâche, or watercress
45 ml/3 tblsps chopped flat parsley, or coriander

dressing:

65 ml/4 ½ tblsps extra virgin olive oil
22 ml/1½ tblsps balsamic vinegar, or white wine vinegar

Leave the chanterelles whole, except for the very largest, which may be torn in half lengthways. Cook the chopped shallots in the oil until pale golden, then add the chanterelles. Cook all together gently for about 10 mins, then set aside to cool. Fry the bacon until crisp, then drain on soft paper. Wash and dry the salad leaves and pile in a large bowl. Dress with olive oil and vinegar, toss well, then scatter the chanterelles and bacon over the top. Sprinkle the parsley (or coriander) over all and serve. Serves 3-4 as a first course, or 2 as a light main dish.

Wild Mushroom Sauce

This makes the most of a small amount of wild mushrooms, whether gathered in the woods or bought.

15 g/½ oz dried porcini
300 ml/½ pt chicken stock
150-225 g/6-8 oz wild mushrooms: ceps, chanterelles, oyster mushrooms, pieds de

mouton, trompettes des morts, etc.
sea salt and black pepper
60 ml/4 tblsps crème fraîche, soured cream, or fromage blanc
30 ml/2 tblsps coarsely chopped flat parsley

Soak the dried mushrooms in half the stock for 1 hour then drain, reserving the stock. Chop the dried mushrooms and set aside. Wipe the fresh mushrooms, chop the caps coarsely and slice the best part of the stalks thickly. Put them in a pan with both lots of chicken stock (300 ml/½ pt in all). Bring to the boil and cook gently, half covered, for 10 mins. Then add the chopped *porcini* and cook for a further 5 mins. Remove from the heat, adding salt and black pepper, and cool for a little. Then put in the food processor with the *crème fraîche* (or soured cream, or *fromage blanc*), and process briefly, stopping before it becomes smooth. Then pour into a clean pan and reheat gently. Serves 4, with egg noodles, vegetable timbales, rice dishes, etc.

Wild Mushroom Butter

Another useful way of using small amounts of precious wild mushrooms. Best of all when made with *trompettes des morts*, ceps or chanterelles, this is also good made with *pieds de mouton*, oyster mushrooms and *shiitake*. It makes exquisite sandwiches, and can also be used like *maître d'hôtel* butter, on grilled veal chops, steaks, and noodles. Also freezes well.

150 g/6 oz wild mushrooms: trompettes des morts, ceps, chanterelles, etc, roughly chopped
150-225 g/6-8 oz unsalted butter
1 clove garlic, finely chopped
10 ml/2 tsps lemon juice
sea salt and black pepper
a pinch of cayenne

Cook the roughly chopped mushrooms in 25 g/1 oz butter for 10-12 mins, until soft, adding the garlic half-way through. Cook, then weigh and purée in a food processor, adding an equal weight of unsalted butter cut in bits. Add lemon juice, sea salt, black pepper and cayenne to taste. Pile into a small jar and chill. Spread on thin slices of unbuttered bread, or make into sandwiches to accompany a green salad. Alternatively, form into rolls, wrap in foil, and cut in thick slices to serve over veal chops or steaks, or grilled fish. Or stir into freshly cooked fettucine. May be frozen in a covered container, or wrapped in foil.

December

The concerns of the Englishwoman in the days leading up to Christmas have probably not changed radically over the last 400 years. Although the giving of presents at Christmas did not occur in Elizabethan and Stuart times, the preparation of the traditional dishes went on as always. In 1617, Lady Anne Clifford, at that time married to the third Earl of Dorset, writes in her diary of there being 'great housekeeping all this Christmas at Dorset House'.

It is interesting trying to trace the history of our traditional Christmas dishes – when they first appeared, how they developed, when they first became associated with Christmas... It soon becomes clear that not only the food has changed, but the nature of the holiday itself. It is not until the nineteenth century that the 'Christmassy' nature of the occasion becomes familiar, with the emphasis on the family, especially the children, as opposed to the indiscriminate entertaining of all and sundry that went on in earlier times, at least in the great houses. Prince Albert is generally credited with having brought this about, but there are indications that the movement towards a cosy family holiday had already started, well before Queen Victoria's accession. In 1819, Lady Palmerston, at that time married to Lord Cowper, writes to her brother, describing Christmas at Panshanger: 'I have exerted myself manfully, or I might rather say womanfully, to make the dear children pass a Merry Christmas. We have had Snapdragon and games of all sorts every night...' The holiday ended with a New Year's ball, an annual event, where children and grown-ups danced together. In 1829, Princess Lievan, the wife of the Russian Ambassador was among the party, and she introduced the Cowper children to the German custom of Christmas trees and presents. Three trees, one for each child, were set in pots on a large table, lit with coloured candles and surrounded with presents. In Germany, they were told, it was customary to do the same for grown-ups, but at Panshanger it was confined to the children. If only it had stayed that way...

It is hard to ascertain which of our Christmas foods was the first to be recognized as especially appropriate, for reports differ, and even contradict each other. The turkey seems to have reached England by 1540, but references to it in the sixteenth century are unreliable, for the name had previously been given to the guinea fowl. When Thomas Tusser, writing in the 1570s, describes the turkey as 'Christmas husbandlike fare, the farmer's Christmas dinner', it is hard to know which bird he was referring to. In any case, it is not until the nineteenth century that we find turkey accepted as an indispensable part of our Christmas dinner. Nor did plum pudding become known as Christmas pudding until Victorian times, although the dish dates back to earliest records. Mincemeat was another of our oldest dishes, originally composed of a mixture of meat – usually beef or tongue – with dried fruit. Now, as with the plum pudding, only the suet remains as a reminder of the meat.

Once the roast swans and peacocks of medieval times had been out-dated, roast beef and mince pies seem to have become the most usual part of Christmas fare. In 1666, Samuel Pepys describes sitting down to his Christmas dinner of 'some good ribs of beef roasted, and some mince pies'. He also mentions that his wife had been up until 4 am seeing to the making of the mince pies. Five years later, in his book, *The Accomplisht Cook*, Robert May gives a lengthy menu for Christmas Day which includes turkey and roast beef, together with mince pies and a host of other dishes. A century later, in 1773, Parson Woodforde records his Christmas dinner at New College, Oxford. The first course consisted of two cod, boiled, with fried soles and oyster sauce, a roast sirloin of beef, pea soup, and orange pudding; this was followed by a pair of wild duck, a shoulder of lamb, salad, and mince pies.

In 1835, in *The Art of Dining*, Thomas Walker describes an unusually simple Christmas meal, citing it as perfect, which he had enjoyed with two friends. It consisted of just three things: crimped cod, woodcock and plum pudding. 'Just as much of each as we wanted and accompanied by champagne.' A contemporary critic, Abraham Hayward, protested, declaring that 'roast beef and roast turkey are indispensable on Christmas Day'. When *Great Expectations* was published in 1861, readers must have vicariously enjoyed Pip's Christmas dinner – a leg of pickled pork (basically a ham before it has been smoked) with greens, a pair of chickens, stuffed and roasted, a large mince pie and a plum pudding. Towards the end of the century, Francatelli, at one time chef to Queen Victoria, gives a suggested menu for Christmas Day that includes roast turkey with braised ham, plum pudding and mince pies, and fifteen other dishes.

In the north of England, Scotland and Ireland, a roast goose has always been more popular than turkey. There is a good description of a Christmas meal in *The Dead*, a short story by James Joyce, published in 1914. The meal consists of a roast goose at one end of the table, with a ham and a round of spiced beef at the other. A carver sits at each end, and a dish of hot floury boiled potatoes is handed round. This is followed by dishes of jelly, custard and blancmange, with figs, raisins and almonds.

'Beef is the soul of cookery,' Carême once said, and I am totally in agreement. The bull is a noble animal, and it is not for nothing that roast beef has been a symbol of England for centuries. (The fact that the best beef comes from Scotland, and has done for hundreds of years, is another matter.) English beef cookery has a strength and character all of its own, and owes nothing to foreign influence. A standing wing rib, or a sirloin complete with undercut, is both a marvellous sight and one of the few gastronomic delights that does not seem to have deteriorated in recent years. I can think of no adult in their right mind who would not welcome this as an alternative to roast turkey at the Christmas feast. Even the traditional English accompaniments – Yorkshire pudding, English mustard, horseradish sauce and clear unthickened gravy – cannot be improved upon, while a traditional plum pudding to follow will add the seasonal touch.

When I lived in Scotland as a child, our Sunday joint was invariably a roast sirloin, being my father's favourite food. We loved it even more cold and, once before going unwillingly on holiday, one of my sisters was heard moaning plaintively, 'I just don't know how I'll manage without cold roast beef'.

In those days, the sirloin always came with its undercut intact, nestling up against the bone, basted with its marrow and protected by the flap of rib ends folded over it, and deliciously moist. Nowadays there is such a demand for fillet steaks that butchers tend to remove the undercut and sell the sirloin on its own, which makes a much less splendid joint.

I much preferred the older fashion, for a slice of undercut served with a thinner slice of the rarer sirloin made a most delicious combination. A whole roast fillet always seems rather an effete joint; it is too soft somehow, and lacking in character. Possibly because it is often treated in a rather decadent way, smeared with *pâté de foie* and wrapped in pastry, it has come to symbolize the food of the ultra-rich. Even fillet steaks do not appeal to me; I far prefer a sirloin steak, which comes halfway between the rump and fillet in price, and is to me more desirable than either, in flavour, texture, and appearance.

My first choice of a joint for roasting, on a less lavish scale than sirloin or standing ribs, would be a rolled joint from either of these two prime cuts. A particularly nice looking joint is the French *contre filet*, or *faux-filet*. This is the same cut of meat as our rolled sirloin, but is trimmed and tied differently to give a neat compact shape, ideal for carving. Whenever possible meat should be cooked on the bone, which contributes both fat and flavour. In the case of beef, however, this is only possible on a very large scale, as a rib roast consisting of two bones would make a thin dry joint. An American friend of mine compromises by getting the butcher to bone and roll the meat, then to tie it back on the bone. In this way he feels that he retains some of the benefits, yet has at the end a compact joint, easy to carve.

Many of the old English beef dishes are rarely seen nowadays, and some of them are well worth reviving. Beef olives are one; thin slices of tender beef beaten out even thinner with a mallet, then rolled round small handfuls of bread and onion stuffing, flavoured with herbs. They are neatly tied with string, then braised with sliced carrots and onions in a meat gravy, and served on a bed of mashed potatoes. Steak and kidney pudding is good on a cold winter's day; a lighter version is the lesser known and strangely named sea pie, which consists of stewed beef with onions and carrots topped with a lid of suet pastry. A popular dish in men's clubs used to be marrow bones; the cut ends were sealed with puff pastry, and the bones boiled standing upright and served wrapped in a napkin. The marrow was extracted by each diner armed with a narrow silver spoon, and eaten with toast. Beef marrow was also served as a savoury, either cooked in the above fashion then spooned on to rounds of toast, or extracted from the bones before cooking and poached, then sliced and served on toast.

Most butchers now have so little demand for marrow that bones can often be had free for the asking. This is an amazing waste of precious material, for beef marrow is the richest and most easily digested of all fats, perfect for feeding invalids and children. It adds succulence to a *risotto*, or can be made into delicate dumplings mixed with chopped chervil. Alternatively, it can be used as dripping, for frying potatoes, onions, bread, meat stews, and for a myriad other uses.

In terms of food values, beef is by far the most valuable of meats. It is richer in protein and minerals than mutton, the only comparable mature meat which is not often seen nowadays, and very much richer in iron, calcium and vitamin B than lamb, pork or veal.

Opinions differ about the best beef. It is generally thought to be that from Aberdeen Angus bullocks, aged four to five years. Some people think the Belted Galloway, another Scottish animal, produces even better beef, and in smaller, more convenient joints.

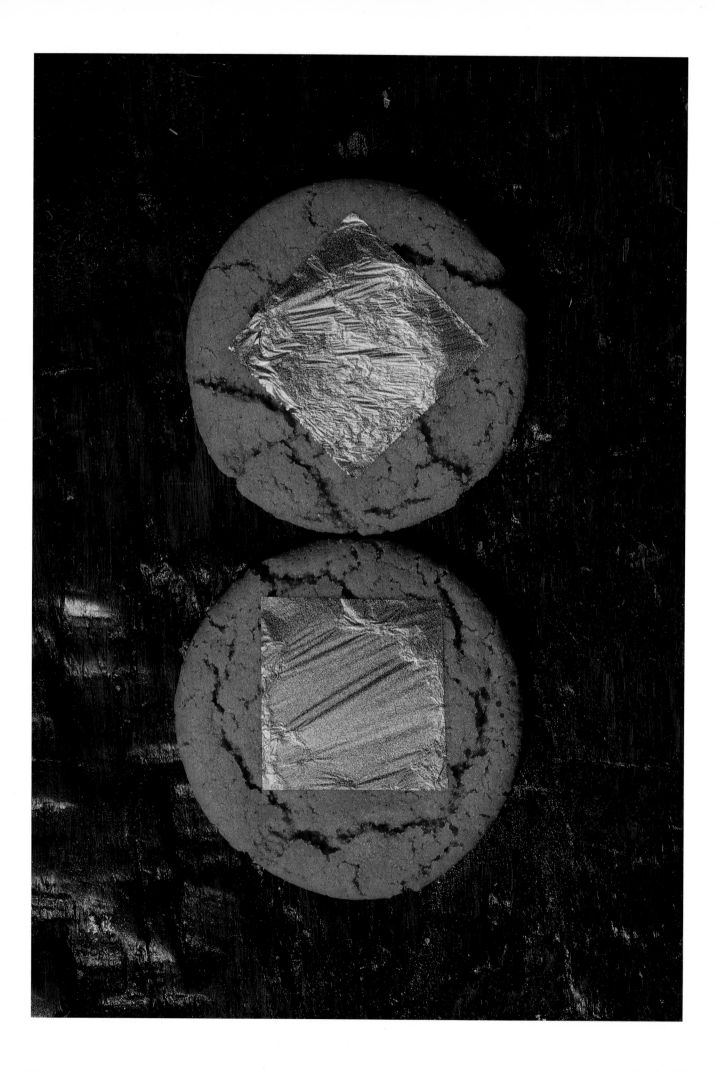

Gilt gingerbread must be one of the earliest of golden presents, at least in Britain, for the gilding of gingerbread cakes and biscuits dates back to Tudor times, or earlier. A fifteenth-century recipe sounds remarkably like the French *pain d'épices:* flavoured with honey, saffron and cinnamon, as well as ginger, it was often gilded, or decorated with cloves and small bay leaves to simulate tooled leather. Gilding cakes and biscuits is done by laying a thin layer of pure gold leaf over the surface immediately after baking. Although it is bought in artists' stores, pure gold leaf is edible. It comes in the thinnest of small square sheets, interleaved with paper. Both gold and silver leaf are used in India to decorate dishes for special occasions; a pilaff of rice, sweet or savoury, is often garnished with little strips of gold and silver. Silver leaf can be bought in some Indian shops.

Gingerbread biscuits, often gilt, were the traditional fairing, the gift bought by young men for their girls at country fairs. Fairings varied: although gingerbread seems to have been constant, the recipe and shape differed. In Norfolk and Lincolnshire, the gingerbread was pale in colour, almost white, and was made into puffy round biscuits. In Hampshire, it was baked in moulds to make gingerbread men and gilded, while in Derbyshire, the men were not gilt, but had coloured hats and sugar buttons. In some parts, figures of kings and queens were made, with gilded crowns; in others, figures of the saints were made to celebrate the saint's day. In Cornwall, a traditional fairing consisted of gingerbread biscuits, caraway comfits, candied sticks of angelica and macaroons. But fairings were not always edible, any small trinket or piece of clothing, preferably sparkling, served the same purpose, and thimbles, ribbons, or pieces of lace were often given. The fairings at an early eighteenth-century fair are described by John Gay, author of *The Beggar's Opera:* 'Now pedlars' stalls with glittering toys are laid, the various fairings of the country maid: Long silken laces hang upon the twine, and rows of pins and amber bracelets shine...'

Country fairs played an important part in English rural life, both for trade and entertainment. Fairs and markets were quite separate. The fair took place once a year, for conducting trade on a large scale. The market happened regularly, once a month or even weekly, and was for trading on a small scale. Many fairs had Christian origins, but some dated to pre-Christian times. They were usually held on hilltops. Fairs associated with saints' days lasted three days: the vigil, the feast itself, and the morrow. A number were known as Becket fairs, being linked to the canonization of Thomas à Becket, not only at Canterbury itself, but at nearby towns. Most of the country fairs received their charters in the thirteenth and fourteenth centuries – over 3,000 were granted in the thirteenth century alone. Charters were granted by the sovereign, either to the church, or to the citizens of a town, or to a noble family. In medieval times, both fairs and markets were usually held on holy days, but this was prohibited in the mid-fifteenth century, except for the four Sundays in harvest time, and Saturday became the accepted day.

According to T F G Dexter, in *The Pagan Origin of Fairs,* 'Fairs in medieval times and later had two sides: a business side, selling and genuine trade, and a pleasure side, represented by the booth, the mountebank, and the acrobat...' At three-day fairs, the first day was reserved for commerce, on the second day the gentry came, while the third was given over to entertainment and revelry. The range of amusements was wide, especially in the more sophisticated London fairs, and sounds somewhat startling. Freak shows, both human and animal, competed with wild beasts, jugglers and acrobats, with fire-eaters and sword-swallowers; while the public entered into contests of wrestling, weight-lifting, even shin-kicking. Bear-baiting and cock-fighting also took place along with fortune-telling and the like. In his diary, Samuel Pepys records many visits to Bartholomew Fair in the mid sixteenth century, with vivid descriptions of the performing animals: a horse which 'told' money, the dirt, and inevitably the young women, for fairs were also popular haunts of prostitutes.

Bartholomew Fair, at Smithfield, was the main London fair, based on the sale of cloth. Stourbridge was undoubtedly the greatest of country fairs. It was held near the monastery of Barnwell, two miles from Cambridge; started under Queen Elizabeth I, it originally lasted for several weeks, from Barthelmas in August until Michaelmas, in late September. Its main commodities were wool and hops, and merchants came from as far afield as Venice and Genoa, Ghent and Liège, Spain, Gascony, and Norway. As well as the goods for sale, there were food stalls. Defoe describes 'coffee houses, taverns, brandy shops, and eating houses, innumerable and all in tents or booths...' At Weydon Fair, in Wessex, Hardy described the frumenty which led Michael Henchard to the disastrous act which was to wreck his life. It was not the frumenty itself, 'the mixture of corn in the grain, flour, milk, raisins, currants, and whatnot', that led him to his downfall, but the rum with which it was laced. Baked warden pears were sold hot at the Great Michaelmas Fair at Bedford, while Colchester oysters were always sold at Stourbridge.

Most fairs were based on the sale of one main commodity. Horse fairs were important in Yorkshire,

Yarmouth had a herring fair which lasted forty days, while Nottingham Goose Fair, where more than 20,000 geese were sold, still takes place today. (In *The Land of England*, Dorothy Hartley relates how the gooseherds used to drive their geese over cool tar, or damp clay, and then over sand, to harden their feet for the long trek over hard roads from the marshy land of the Fens to the city of Nottingham.) Also intriguing are the 'Mops' – Statute Fairs, or Hiring Fairs – which provided a sort of primitive labour exchange where potential employers and employees met to agree on a hiring contract. Those seeking service grouped and dressed themselves according to their trade: shepherds carrying crooks, grooms with sponges, maids wearing white aprons and carrying mops or brooms. More sinister were the instances of wives being put up for sale by their husbands, as in *The Mayor of Casterbridge*, where Susan Henchard is sold to a sailor for five guineas. (The last recorded instance took place in Sheffield in 1877, where a man sold his wife for five shillings.)

Sad to say, trade fairs diminished in importance over the years, while the hiring fairs disappeared completely. Up until the nineteenth century, the serious side of the fair was dominant, and it was only when trading was concluded that the entertainments took over. But with the growth of machinery and mass-production, the spread of transportation and communications, country fairs inevitably lost much of their point. For a time, the pleasure side took over, but without the balance of genuine commerce this soon degenerated into rowdy scenes of rioting and drunkenness. The fairs became meeting places for thieves and their accomplices, and became notorious. A series of acts of parliament gradually succeeded in prohibiting many of the fairs, and rendering others innocuous.

Country fairs still exist, but they are shadows of their robust forebears. Some are based on sales of livestock, produce, and agricultural machinery; others are pure fun-fairs. Yet every now and then a hint of the past lingers, and that odd eerie quality of English medieval life surfaces.

An enjoyable way to learn more about caviar is to spend a day in Paris, visiting Caviar Kaspia, in the Place de la Madeleine, and Petrossian, near Les Invalides. There are few nicer things on a rainy day than to sit in the elegant restaurant above the shop at Caviar Kaspia, sampling their caviar with *blinis*. The restaurant is small and pretty, with Russian porcelain and glass lining the walls. The *blinis* here are made with plain flour: soft, light, almost frothy, pale gold with crisp brown edges, spattered with little holes. They are deftly served, spread with a little melted butter – not more than a spoonful – and a dollop of *crème fraîche*. The caviar is served in its jar, surrounded with packed ice. With the *blinis* comes vodka in tiny glasses, filled to the brim, or in a frosted carafe. There is also the best toast I have ever eaten, with unsalted butter, and halved lemons for those who want them. Purists prefer caviar served without, and I agree. Such things as onion and hard-boiled egg are not to be thought of. There should be a Bateman cartoon: 'The man who asked for chopped onion at Caviar Kaspia...'

All this deliciousness costs less than you might expect. I ate two *blinis* with 30 g of oscietra, an excellent caviar not often seen in Britain, halfway between beluga and sevruga in price, together with a glass of vodka and coffee for a very reasonable price, and it kept me happy through a long day, the only food I ate for fourteen hours. Caviar is immensely sustaining, the best source of energy I know. French tastes in caviar differ radically from the British. Whereas 80 to 85 per cent of caviar sold in the UK is beluga, in France the situation is reversed, with oscietra and sevruga accounting for 80 to 85 per cent. The British have always eaten beluga, and are loath to change their ways, despite the fact that beluga is now less than 5 per cent of the world's annual catch, and correspondingly expensive. (Another difference is that while the British appear almost reluctant to be seen consuming caviar in public, and prefer to eat it at home, the French have no such qualms.)

Caviar sold in Europe comes generally from three fish, all members of the Acipenser family of sturgeons. These are prehistoric fish, with skeletons of bone and cartilage combined, and a form of armour-plating. Largest and rarest is the beluga, which can weigh over a ton and live for over 100 years. It is a slow, sluggish fish, living on plankton, and seems an anomaly in the twentieth century. It produces large eggs, usually grey in colour, with a delicate, almost nutty flavour. Beluga is the most expensive of all caviars, owing to its rarity; the very finest is called Royal Beluga.

Next in size is the oscietra, the true sturgeon, which yields a smaller roe, roughly halfway between beluga and sevruga both in size and in price. It ranges from darkish brown to gold in colour, and has a distinctive and delicious flavour. It is hardly sold in Britain but is very popular in France, and in the USA. Both the beluga and the oscietra are also prized for their flesh, which is often smoked. The least expensive caviar is sevruga, but it is no less good than the others, simply more abundant. It has small grey-black eggs, with an excellent flavour.

Pressed caviar is something quite distinct. (Until the discovery of refrigeration, in the 1890s, all caviar was pressed, since it keeps better than in egg form.) It is made from a mixture of roe, normally beluga and oscietra, which is drained by hanging in muslin bags, then packed tightly into tins. The result is a highly concentrated food – it takes 1.3 kg of loose caviar to make 1 kg of pressed. I find it very strong, redolent of the old joke about 'fish jam', but some caviar enthusiasts love it, including many Russians. It is especially suited for eating with *blinis* or baked potatoes.

If you are fortunate enough to acquire some beluga, it should be served very simply. Still in its tin, packed round with ice, it is best eaten with toasted white bread, crusts removed, and unsalted butter. Vodka makes the best accompaniment, better by far than champagne or white wine. Less expensive caviar – oscietra, sevruga or pressed – is delicious eaten with *blinis*, with melted butter and *crème fraîche*, or sour cream. But these ways of treating caviar only work if you have enough; 25 g a person is the absolute minimum. With small amounts it pays to be more adventurous....Try serving it with dollops of *crème fraîche* on baked potatoes, or alone, on scrambled eggs. Both eggs and potatoes make good foils for caviar, especially when pressed, since their blandness offsets its salty tang. For those with deft fingers, *Michel Guèrard* for filling empty eggshells with scrambled egg, and shaping a little mound of caviar in the top part of the shell, reforming the egg in its egg-cup. Anton Mosimann gives a recipe for Royal Beluga mixed with cream, poured over an *oeuf en cocotte*. I had a delicious dish once with Anton: tiny potatoes baked in their skins, scooped out, and filled with sour cream and chives, topped with caviar. The world's best caviar comes from the Caspian Sea. Ninety per cent of the catch is Russian, and most of it is consumed in Russia. (From 1929 until 1954, all the caviar was made by Russia, who had the concession to make it even on the Iranian shore.) Sturgeon used to abound in the large rivers of northern Europe, in the Atlantic, and especially in the Great Lakes and big rivers of the USA. In Lake Michigan, the catch of sturgeon in 1880 was about 2,000 tons, but by 1920 this had dwindled to almost nothing. The few that survive are now protected and attempts are being made to farm them.

The sturgeon lives in salt water but, like the salmon, returns to the rivers to spawn. Here it is caught, in the river mouth, as soon before spawning as possible, since only the mature eggs make good caviar. The roe is removed immediately, without allowing it to come in contact with the blood, for it should not be washed. After being freed from all membrane, it is carefully sieved, then lightly salted, roughly 3 to 4 per cent salt to caviar. This is a highly skilled process, both in the handling of the eggs, which must not be damaged or broken, and in the judging of the proportions. The caviar is then packed in large tins holding 1.8 kgs. The tin divides in half, and each half is closely packed. The halves are then sealed with a broad rubber band, forming an almost hermetic seal. The tins must be kept at a temperature of between 0 and -2 degrees centigrade; the salt content prevents the caviar from freezing at this temperature. Caviar must on no account be frozen.

This is how Russian caviar reaches the UK, in large blue tins with a picture of sturgeon, and only the words *Caviar Malossol* – Russian for slightly salted. The tins are coded as to the contents, but this can only be read by the importer. The lack of clear information as to whether the tin holds beluga or sevruga is often a puzzle for the individual. (Smuggled caviar is inevitably sevruga, but buying caviar from unauthorized sources is a risky business, since it has rarely been kept at the correct temperature, and could well be dangerous.) The tins are then opened by the wholesaler – Grivan Products and W.G. White are the two largest in the UK – before being repacked for distribution. The caviar in small glass jars has been heated, which prolongs its shelf life, but all caviar should be kept at the temperature indicated. Once a tin has been opened, the contents start to deteriorate, although it can be kept under refrigeration for several days without risk. But to be enjoyed at its best, it should be consumed as soon as opened. (I remember my mother telling me how she once bought a shoebox full of caviar for my father – it must have been cheaper in those days – when he was suffering from tuberculosis in a sanitorium in Switzerland, and how he kept it in the snow on his window sill. I see now that he probably hit on the ideal temperature, purely by chance.)

ENGLISH CHRISTMAS

Roast Turkey

A roast turkey has been the central point of our Christmas dinner since the days of Queen Victoria. I wrap the breast in buttered cloth to prevent it drying out during the long cooking.

4.5-7.75 kg/10-15 lb turkey
sea salt and black pepper
1 or 2 stuffings
1 small onion, peeled
200 g/8 oz butter

Remove the giblets, liver, etc. Sprinkle the inside of the bird with sea salt and black pepper, and stuff both cavities. The neck cavity is easily closed, using the neck flap of skin. Either sew up the main cavity after stuffing, or push in a small peeled onion and tie the legs tightly around it. Rub the surface of the bird with butter, and sprinkle with salt and pepper. Lay on a rack in a roasting tin. Melt the remaining butter, and dip a clean piece of linen in it; part of an old sheet, or a teacloth will do. Lay this over the breast of the bird. Roast for 25 mins per 400 g/1 lb at 180°C/350°F/gas mark 4. Half an hour before the time is up, remove the cloth and baste frequently. When the bird has finished cooking, remove from the oven, cover loosely with foil and a thick towel, and rest for a while before carving.

Bread Stuffing

This is my favourite stuffing for the body of the turkey, with a chestnut stuffing for the crop. This makes enough to stuff a 5.5 kg/12 lb turkey.

300 g/12 oz shallots, finely chopped
100 g/4 oz butter
300 g/12 oz soft white breadcrumbs
37 g/1½ oz chopped parsley
sea salt and black pepper

Sauté the chopped shallots slowly in the butter until golden, then add the breadcrumbs and stir around until well mixed. Remove from the heat and stir in the chopped parsley. Season well with lots of sea salt and freshly ground black pepper. Leave to cool before using.

Chestnut Stuffing

560 g/1¼ lb chestnuts
200 ml/7 fl oz milk
225 g/8 oz pork belly
225 g/8 oz lean pork
100 g/4 oz shallots, chopped
60 ml/4 tblsps chopped parsley
1 large clove garlic, finely chopped
15 ml/1 tblsp brandy
7 ml/½ tblsp sea salt
freshly ground black pepper
a pinch of ground mace

This makes a fairly rich stuffing, enough to fill a large chicken or capon, or the neck of a turkey. Best made a day before using and kept in the refrigerator. First shell the chestnuts. With a small sharp knife, make a small nick in the flat side of each chestnut. Put them in a pan and cover with cold water. Bring to the boil, simmer for 1 min, then remove from the heat. Lift out 3 or 4 nuts at a time and cut off the shells, removing the inner skin at the same time. When this becomes difficult, reheat the pan until almost boiling and continue as before.

When all are done, cook them in the milk for 12 mins, then drain and leave to cool. Then chop them coarsely. Chop or mince the pork, either by hand or in a processor or mincer. In a large bowl, mix the chopped pork with the chopped nuts, shallots, parsley, and garlic. Then add the brandy, sea salt, black pepper and mace. Mix well, then fry a small ball and taste to check the seasonings. Adjust accordingly.

Spiced Beef

Spiced beef was popular at Christmas, in days gone by, if not for Christmas Day itself, then on the days that followed. It used to be made with saltpetre, but this is now illegal.

2.3-2.7 kg/5-6 lb beef: topside, round, or rolled brisket
5 ml/1 tsp ground mace
5 ml/1 tsp coarsely ground black pepper
25 g/1 oz juniper berries, roughly crushed
10 ml/2 tsps ground cloves
½ small nutmeg, grated
1 ml/⅛ tsp cayenne
87 g/3½ oz dark brown muscovado sugar
200 g/8 oz Maldon sea salt

Mix all the spices and seasonings except the salt and rub the beef all over. Lay it in an earthenware crock with a lid, if it will fit. Otherwise put it in an oval dish and cover with foil. Leave it for 3 days, then scatter half the salt over it, and rub it again with the spices and salt mixed. Put back in the crock, or dish, and leave it for another 12 days, turning it every day. On the 4th day add half the remaining salt, and on the 8th day add the rest.

On the 12th day (after 15 days in all), wipe off the spices and rinse the meat briefly under the cold tap. Put it in a casserole to fit as closely as possible and add 300 ml/½ pt water. Cover with 2 sheets of foil and the lid and cook for 45-50 mins per 400 g/1 lb in the bottom of the oven at 140°C/275°F/gas mark 1. When it is cooked, take it out and leave to cool for 2-3 hours. Then take it out of its pot and lay on a flat surface. Weigh down with a board with 3 x 800 g/2 lb weights on it,

and leave overnight. Next day, remove the weights and wrap the beef in foil and keep in the refrigerator. It will keep for 10-14 days if replaced in the refrigerator after use. To serve, cut in thin slices and serve with baked potatoes and a green salad.

Christmas Pudding

This is the pudding I always make at Christmas; it is unusual in that it contains neither sugar or flour.

700 g/1½ lb seedless raisins,
halved if large
225 g/8 oz mixed candied peel, chopped
225 g/8 oz glacé cherries, halved
100 g/4 oz blanched almonds, chopped
350 g/12 oz shredded suet
350 g/12 oz soft white breadcrumbs
8 eggs, beaten
150 ml/¼ pt Guinness
90 ml/6 tblsps brandy

Mix the dried fruit, candied peel, cherries, almonds, suet and breadcrumbs in a large bowl. Stir in the well-beaten eggs, the Guinness and the brandy. Leave overnight, or for a few hours. Then pack the mixture into 2 buttered pudding basins holding about 1.1 litres/2 pts each; be careful not to fill them too full. There should be at least 2.5 cm/1 in at the top, to allow the pudding to swell. Add charms at this stage. Cover with buttered foil, wrap each bowl in a piece of cloth, tying the 4 corners in a knot over the top, to use as a handle. An old sheet can be torn up for this purpose. Have a large pan of boiling water; measure the amount first, so that it comes half-way up the sides of the bowls. Stand them on upturned saucers, or small tins. Cover and boil steadily for 6 hours. Check every hour or so, adding more water from a kettle as needed. When ready, lift them out and leave to cool. Unwrap and discard the cloth, replacing with a clean piece. Store in a cool place until Christmas Day, then boil again, as above, for 4-5 hours. To serve, turn onto a flat dish, stick a sprig of holly in the top, and flame with 45 ml/3 tblsps brandy, warmed in a soup ladle, and set alight.

Brandy Butter

100 g/4 oz unsalted butter
100 g/4 oz castor sugar
45-60 ml/3-4 tblsps brandy

Cream the butter and sugar in a food processor, then add the brandy slowly through the lid, while continuing to process. Taste after adding 45 ml/3 tblsps, adding more, very gradually, if required. Pile into a small dish and chill in the refrigerator until needed. Can be made several days in advance. Rum, or even whiskey can be substituted for the brandy, if preferred.

BEEF

Boiled Brisket of Beef

1.4 kg/3 lb salted brisket, or silverside
12 black peppercorns
1 large onion, halved
3 cloves
1 large carrot, halved
1 leek, halved
1 stalk celery, halved
1 bay leaf
3 stalks parsley

Cover the beef with cold water, unsalted, and bring slowly to the boil, skimming off the scum that rises to the surface as it approaches boiling point. When all that remains is a few bubbles, add all the other ingredients, cover the pot and simmer gently for 1½ hours or 30 mins per 450 g/1 lb. When the time is up, remove the beef and throw away the stock as it will be too salty to use. Serve with freshly boiled carrots and leeks, and suet dumplings. Any left over salt beef makes excellent sandwiches, on rye bread.

Boiled fresh beef is also good, and more adaptable, in that it can be re-heated in various ways, and its stock is delicious. Cook as above, but use hot water instead of cold, and add 5 ml/1 tsp coarse salt. Fresh vegetables can be added to the pan and cooked with the beef for the last 30 mins. Serve with a *salsa verde*.

Grilled Steaks

My favourite steak is a sirloin (called *entrecôte* in France) weighing 200-225 g/7-8 oz. I cook it either over the fire, or on a small black cast-iron ridged pan made by Le Creuset, which makes black stripes on the meat. Serve with parsley butter, or just with a good mustard.

Beef Miroton

This is a wonderful way of serving re-heated boiled fresh beef – do not try to use salt beef. When making boiled fresh beef I always buy a large joint, and save the stock to make a *miroton* the following day.

approx. 450 g/1 lb cold boiled beef (un-salted)
450 g/1 lb onions, thinly sliced
50 g/2 oz butter
45 ml/3 tblsps flour
450 ml/3/4 pt beef stock (from boiling the beef)
sea salt and black pepper

Cut the beef in small, neat slices, discarding all the fat. Cook the sliced onions slowly in the butter, until they are soft and transparent but not brown. Add the flour and stir for 1 min. Pour on the heated stock gradually, stirring until it is blended smoothly into the sauce. Add salt and pepper to taste, and simmer gently for 15 mins, covered, stirring now and then. Finally, add the little slices of beef, folding them gently into the sauce. Remove the pan from the heat and leave for 5 mins, covered, for the beef to warm through. On no account let it boil again after adding the meat. Serves 4, with boiled potatoes. This is not an elegant dish, but nothing could be better for a family meal.

Parsley Dumplings

50 g/2 oz self-raising flour
a pinch of salt
12 g/1/2 oz butter
1 large egg
15 ml/1 tblsp chopped parsley

Sift the flour with the salt. Cut in the butter in small bits. Beat the egg and stir in the chopped parsley. Add to the flour. Beat until smooth. (Alternatively, this can be very quickly done in a food processor.) Drop teaspoonsful onto the top of the simmering beef stock, or, if there is not enough room, cook separately in a shallow lidded pan half full of boiling salted water. Cover the pan and boil gently for 10 mins, turning once. Serve immediately, or leave in the pan with the heat turned off for up to 10 mins. (Suet dumplings are the correct orthodox accompaniment to boiled beef, but I prefer this lighter version.)

Parsley Butter

1 clove garlic
75 g/3 oz butter
30 ml/2 tblsp chopped parsley
15 ml/1 tblsp lemon juice
sea salt and black pepper

Pound the chopped garlic in a mortar until well crushed. Add the butter at room temperature, cut in small bits. Pound again, until amalgamated. Add the parsley and pound away, adding lemon juice and salt and pepper to taste. Chill in the refrigerator for 1-2 hours, then form into a roll, and cut in thick slices. Alternatively roll into balls. Serve with grilled steaks. Serves 4.

Horseradish Sauce

When fresh horseradish is not available, try to get a German brand of bottled horseradish, made either by Koch or Scandia, in small glass or plastic jars.

22-30 ml/1½-2 tblsps freshly grated horseradish, or 80 g/3½ oz Koch or Scandia Horseradish
150 ml/1/4 pt soured cream, or crème fraîche, or fromage blanc, or double cream
sea salt and white pepper
5-10 ml/1-2 tsps lemon juice (optional)

Stir the grated horseradish into the cream. If using double cream, whip it lightly first. You can use a mixture of cream and *fromage blanc*, if you wish. Add salt and pepper to taste, and a dash of lemon juice if it needs it. (Soured cream or *crème fraîche* are better without.) Serves 4-5.

Roast Sirloin of Beef

For a large joint, there is nothing to beat a sirloin on the bone, but for smaller joints the boned and rolled sirloin is more appropriate. Ask the butcher to give you the bones, and one or two extra ribs if he has them.

1.6 kg/3½ lb rolled sirloin
150 ml/1/4 pt red wine, or meat or chicken stock

Heat the oven to 220°C/425°F/gas mark 7. Lay the ribs in a roasting tin like a primitive roasting rack; if cut up into singles, simply lay them flat. Lay the joint on them and put in the oven. Allow 20-22 mins per 450 g/1 lb for medium rare beef; adjust according to your taste. After 20 mins lower the oven to 180°C/350°F/gas mark 4. During the rest of the cooking, baste every 20 mins with the fat in the tin. When the time is up, transfer the meat to a carving platter and cover loosely with 2 layers of foil and a towel. Pour off the fat in the roasting tin, leaving the juices behind, and set it over a moderate flame. As the juices start to bubble. scrape them together with a metal spoon, so that all the caramelized bits blend with the juices. Add the red wine, or the heated stock, and let it all bubble together for 3 or 4 mins, then strain into a sauceboat and keep warm. Let the meat rest for at least 15 mins, preferably 20, before carving. Serves 6.

GILT FAIRINGS

Steamed Ginger Pudding

125 g/4½ oz flour, sifted
a pinch of salt
5 ml/1 tsp bicarbonate of soda
5 ml/1 tsp ground ginger
125 g/4½ oz shredded suet
50 g/2 oz soft white breadcrumbs
2 eggs
90 ml/6 tblsps golden syrup
90 ml/6 tblsps treacle

Sift the flour into a large bowl with the salt, bicarbonate of soda, and ginger. Mix in the suet and the breadcrumbs. Beat the eggs lightly, warm the syrup and treacle, and stir both together into the dry ingredients. Tip into an oiled pudding basin holding 900 ml/1½ pts; it must not be more than ¾ full. Cover with greased foil, tie down, and steam for 2½-3 hours. Turn out to serve, either with custard sauce, or with a jug of warmed golden syrup, and a bowl of whipped cream. Serves 6-8.

Ginger Apple Crumble

900 g/2 lbs cooking apples, peeled and cored
60 ml/4 tblsps granulated sugar
30 ml/2 tblsps lemon juice
30 ml/2 tblsps water

crumble:

100 g/4 oz plain flour, sifted
15 ml/1 tblsp ground ginger
50 g/2 oz butter, cut in small pieces
50 g/2 oz light brown sugar

Pile the apples in a buttered baking dish, sprinkle with sugar, and add lemon juice and water. Sift the flour with the ginger into a bowl. Rub in the butter, as if making pastry, and mix in the sugar. Spread over the apples, level off with the back of a spoon, and bake for about 40 mins at 175°C/350°F/gas mark 4, until the top is lightly coloured. Serve warm, about an hour after cooking, with custard sauce or whipped cream. Serves 4-6.

Sticky Gingerbread

This is a really dark treacly gingerbread, delicious at tea-time, sliced and spread with butter.

225 g/8 oz flour, sifted
2.5 ml/½ tsp bicarbonate of soda
5 ml/1 tsp ground ginger
a pinch of salt
100 g/4 oz treacle
100 g/4 oz golden syrup
100 g/4 oz butter, cut in pieces
100 g/4 oz dark brown sugar
2 eggs, lightly beaten
30 ml/2 tblsps milk

Sift the flour into a large bowl with the bicarbonate of soda, ginger, and salt. Make a well in the centre. Warm the treacle, syrup, butter and sugar until melted; do not overheat. Pour into the well and mix with a wooden spoon. Then stir in the lightly beaten eggs, and the milk. Mix thoroughly, then tip into a 1.1 litre/2 pt loaf tin which you have lined with buttered foil or greaseproof paper. Smooth the surface, and bake for 1 hour at 160°C/325°F/gas mark 3. Remove from the oven, cool slightly, then remove the foil and

leave to cool completely on a wire rack. When cold, wrap in a cloth, and if possible, store in an airtight tin for 1 to 2 days, before eating. Serve sliced, with butter for tea.

Puffy Gingerbread

This is a very good gingerbread, less rich than the sticky one, and more adaptable. It is best made in a shallow tin and cut in squares rather than sliced. It can be served cold, for tea, or warm as a pudding. It is delicious combined with apple purée.

125 g/5 oz flour, sifted
2.5 ml/½ tsp bicarbonate of soda
2.5 ml/½ tsp baking powder
4 ml/¾ tsp ground ginger
1.5 ml/¼ tsp ground allspice
1.5 ml/¼ tsp ground cinnamon
a pinch of salt
1 egg, lightly beaten
45 ml/3 tblsps golden syrup
45 ml/3 tblsps treacle
40 g/1½ oz dark brown sugar
75 g/3 oz butter, cut in bits
30-60 ml/2-4 tblsps milk

Sift the flour into a large bowl with the soda, baking powder, spices, and salt. Stir in the beaten egg, warm the syrup, treacle, sugar and butter until the butter has melted; do not overheat. Stir into the flour, and add enough milk to make a thin mixture just capable of pouring. Pour into a shallow tin, ie. one 15 cm/6 ins square and 4 cm/1½ ins deep. It must not fill it by more than half. Bake for about 35 mins at 175°C/350°F/gas mark 4, until puffy and firm in the centre, and lightly coloured – but not yet brown – round the edges. Cool on a wire rack before serving, cut in squares and serve straight from the tin.

Variation:

In a broad china dish, make a thick layer of sieved apple purée. Cover with the gingerbread mixture, remembering the dish must not be more than half full, and bake as above. Serve warm, with custard sauce or thick cream, as a dessert. Serves 4-5. Also easily made in double quantities, either as a cake or combined with apples.

Ginger Biscuits

This is a good biscuit for gilding, as it is easily made in different shapes.

100 g/4 oz flour, sifted
2.5 ml/½ tsp bicarbonate of soda
2.5 ml/½ tsp ground ginger
40 g/1½ oz brown sugar
25 g/1 oz butter
60 g/2½ oz golden syrup or treacle, or half and half
15-30 ml/1-2 tblsps milk

Sift the flour with the bicarbonate and ginger. Warm the sugar, butter and syrup

(or treacle); do not overheat. Stir into the dry ingredients, adding a little milk if necessary, to achieve a good consistency. Chill for 30 mins to firm, then roll out thinly and cut with tin moulds into the desired shapes; stars are particularly pretty for gilding. Alternatively, the dough can be simply broken off in small pieces, rolled into balls between the hands, and slightly flattened to make ginger nuts. Lay on a greased baking sheet and bake for 8-10 mins for rolled biscuits, and 15 mins for nuts at 180°C/350°F/gas mark 4. For a large number, simply double the quantities. If making in advance, keep the mixture in the refrigerator or freezer, and bake on the day you plan to eat them.

Ginger Thins

These are exquisite biscuits, lacy thin, for eating either at tea-time or with a dessert. They are delicious with a cold apple purée, or with ice cream, or fruit fools, but they are a bit thin for gilding.

100 g/4 oz flour, sifted
4 ml/¾ tsp ground ginger
100 g/4 oz butter, cut in pieces
100 g/4 oz light brown sugar
15 ml/1 tblsp golden syrup
15 ml/1 tblsp treacle
30 ml/2 tblsps cream

Sift the flour with the ginger and rub in the butter. Add the sugar and rub all together lightly. Warm the syrup and treacle (use double quantities of one if this is simpler), and stir in the cream. Mix with the dry ingredients, beating well with a wooden spoon until well mixed. Drop in small teaspoonsful on to a greased baking sheet, leaving 5 cm/2 ins between them. Bake for about 8 mins at 175°C/350°F/gas mark 4, until cooked in the centre and lightly coloured – but not burnt – round the edges. Remove from the oven and leave to cool for 2-3 mins before lifting with a palette knife onto a flat surface. They will become crisp on cooling. If used for serving with dessert, you may prefer to make larger biscuits, using a heaped teaspoonful of dough, and leaving more space between them. As they cool, lay them over a greased rolling pin so that they harden in a curved shape, like *tuiles d'amandes*. They are best eaten on the day they are made, but the dough can be made in advance, and kept in the refrigerator or the freezer. It must be brought back to room temperature before use.

How to Use Gold and Silver Leaf

There are two kinds of leaf, transfer on waxed paper and loose leaf. Transfer is best for decorating hard dry surfaces like biscuits and chocolate. If the surface is very dry, it needs to be brushed lightly with water, but this is not necessary if the surface is in any way sticky. Cut the leaf to the desired shape and size, press gently onto the surface of the food by rubbing the back of the waxed paper.

Sheets of loose leaf come bound into small books and interleaved with tissue. They need very careful handling: they are more delicate than transfer and crease easily. To separate the sheets, cut the binding of the book. Always use the inter-leaving tissue to work the leaf, never touch it with your fingers. Holding the tissue, turn the loose leaf over into or onto the food being decorated. Loose leaf is ideal for rice and aspic recipes.

CAVIAR

Boiled Eggs with Caviar

This is an adaptation of 2 recipes, one by Michel Guèrard and one by Jean and Pierre Troisgros. In the Guèrard recipe the empty egg shell is filled with scrambled eggs mixed with a little cream (or *fromage blanc*), finely chopped onion and chives. The top part of the shell is filled with caviar and replaced. In the Troisgros recipe, the egg is simply served soft boiled, but with the top part of the shell filled with tiny brown shrimps, tossed in butter with a chopped shallot.

4 large eggs
50 g/2 oz sevruga, or black lumpfish roe

Drop the eggs carefully into boiling water and cook for 4½ mins. Remove them and cool for a second under the cold tap, then put them in egg cups and slice off the pointed end of the shell with a saw-edged knife. Empty it out and fill with caviar, then replace over the bottom part of the egg. Serve immediately, with toasted white bread and unsalted butter.

Scrambled Eggs with Caviar

8 eggs
sea salt and black pepper
4 thick slices white bread
40 g/1½ oz butter
60 ml/4 tblsps fromage blanc, or Jockey
22 ml/1½ tblsps chopped chives
30 g/1¼ oz sevruga,
or 50 g/2 oz black lumpfish roe

Beat the eggs in a bowl, adding sea salt and black pepper. Keep the seasoning very light. Toast the bread, remove the crusts, and shape into circles. Keep warm. Melt 12 g/½ oz butter in a heavy pan and scramble the eggs as usual, taking them off the heat just before they have completely set. Butter the toast and lay a piece on each of 4 hot plates. Spoon the scrambled eggs onto the toast, and put a spoon-

ful of *fromage blanc* on top of each. Sprinkle with chopped chives, and put a dollop of caviar on the top. Serve at once. Serves 4, as a first course, or light main dish.

Stuffed Eggs with Caviar

6 eggs
90 ml/6 tblsps fromage blanc, or Jockey
sea salt and black pepper
45 ml/3 tblsps chopped chives
30 g/1¼ oz sevruga
or 50 g/2 oz black lumpfish roe

Boil the eggs for 12 mins, cool quickly, and remove the shells. Cut them in half horizontally and scoop out the yolks. Mash them with a fork, then beat in the *fromage blanc*, salt and pepper and chopped chives. Mix about half the caviar with the egg yolks, keeping back about 6 coffeespoonfuls. Fill the egg whites with the mixture, then put the reserved caviar on top. Serves 3-4 as a first course, or canapé, with drinks.

Baked Potatoes with Caviar

These make a delicious first course, or hot canapé, with drinks. Small potatoes, about 50 g/2 oz each, baked in their skins. Most of the inside is scooped out, and the centre filled with soured cream and chopped chives, topped with caviar. Anton says 'the quantity is left according to your budget.' My suggestions below. Even tiny potatoes take a long time to bake; allow 40-45 minutes at 200°C/ 400°F/gas mark 6. Allow 2 per person.

8 small potatoes, about 450 g/1 lb in all
75 ml/5 tblsps soured cream
30 ml/2 tblsps chopped chives
approx. 50 g/2 oz sevruga

Blinis

Blinis are usually made with plain flour nowadays, even in the USSR, but a proportion of buckwheat flour may be used.

350 g/12 oz plain flour
100 g/4 oz buckwheat flour
20 g/¾ oz fresh yeast
600 ml/1 pt milk
2 large eggs, separated
2.5 ml/½ tsp sea salt
15 ml/1 tblsp sugar
40 g/1½ oz butter, melted

Sift the flours through a coarse sieve into a large bowl. Put the yeast in a bowl, add 475 ml/16 fl oz lukewarm water, and stand in a warm place for 10 mins. Then stir it into the flour, mixing well with a wooden spoon. Cover with clingfilm, or a cloth, and stand in a warm place for 1-1½ hours, until it has doubled in bulk. Then heat the milk to blood heat and stir into

the yeast batter, stir in the lightly beaten egg yolks, salt, sugar, and melted butter. Beat well, then cover again and put back in a warm place for another 30 mins. Beat thoroughly, cover, and put back to rise for a final 30 mins. When the time is up, beat the egg whites until stiff and fold into the mixture. Allow to stand for 10-15 mins, while you prepare the griddle, or use 2 or 3 small frying pans. Heat the griddle (or pans) well, and grease lightly. You can use a lump of suet wrapped in muslin, on the end of a fork, or a cut potato dipped in melted butter, or a pastry brush. Make little cakes about 10-15 cm/4-6 ins wide; you can do 2 or 3 at a time on a griddle, turning them once, and stacking in a warm place once they are done. Serve flat, with a little jug of melted butter, a bowl of *crème fraîche* or *fromage blanc*, and the accompaniment of your choice. If this is caviar, serve it still in its tin (or jar), set in a bowl of cracked ice. Other fish eggs may be turned out if you prefer, while smoked salmon is best served flat, cut in *blini*-sized pieces.

Buckwheat Pancakes

These are made without yeast, easier by far than traditional *blinis*.

batter:
150 g/5 oz white bread flour
100 g/4 oz buckwheat flour
2.5 ml/½ tsp sea salt
3 eggs
450 ml/¾ pt milk and water, mixed

If making by hand, sift the flours through a coarse sieve with the salt, into a large bowl. Make a well in the centre and break in the eggs. Start to beat them into the flour, using a wire whisk, and adding the milk and water at the same time. Continue to beat until all the liquid is incorporated, and the whole smoothly mixed. Leave for an hour, if convenient, then beat again. If using a food processor, simply sift the flour with the salt into the container, adding the eggs and a drop of the milk and water. Process, adding the rest of the milk and water through the lid. Leave for 1 hour, if convenient, then process again.

To make the pancakes, heat a frying pan and grease it lightly. Make small pancakes about 10-12.5 cm/4-5 ins wide, and stack them in a warm place until ready to serve. Lay them on a platter to serve, with a bowl of *crème fraîche* or *fromage blanc*, and caviar or other fishy accompaniment. Enough for 6; this is a good way of using scraps of smoked salmon.

THE PHOTOGRAPHS

Cover
Vegetable lily pond. Computerized at Apex Graphics.
London 1990

Page 1
Quinces, pomegranates and grapes.
Milan 1983

Page 2
Spartan apples in a Chinese bowl.
London 1983

Page 5
Quinces in a silver bowl.
Istanbul 1984

Page 6
Homage to Claude Monet. Computerized on the Quantel System.
England 1989

Page 8
Blue cabbage leaf.
England 1984

Page 11
Chillies and peppers on Patna rice.
London 1988

Page 12
Garlic from Fauchon.
Paris 1986

Page 15
A Leek from Enton Hall.
England 1984

Page 16
Poulet de Bresse, champignons de Paris, hare, asparagus and pigeon.
Paris 1989

Page 18
Savoy cabbage leaf.
Paris 1987

Page 23
Tournedos of beef with paupiettes of beef and veal.
Paris 1989

Page 24
Miniature vegetables on full sized red cabbages.
London 1988

Page 26
Pacific oyster, 'crassostrea gigas'.
Cornwall 1988

Page 29
Pacific oysters, winkles, mussels, queenies, native oysters, whelks and clams.
Scotland 1986

Page 30
Live lobster from H J Brunning.
London 1989

Page 33
Handmade wholewheat spaghetti.
London 1986

Page 34
Kneaded dough.
London 1987

Page 36
Poilâne sourdough bread, Normandy butter, salt-cured pig snout, tail and ear.
Paris 1989

Page 41
Cold water crust raised pie.
London 1985

Page 42
Red Snappers.
London 1990

Page 45
Parrot fish.
London 1990

Page 46
Sprouting beans.
London 1987

Page 49
Waxy salad potatoes: Pink Fir Apple, Romano and Sieglinde.
Devon 1990

Page 50
Silver Sebright bantam cock.
Devon 1990

Page 52
A Devon maund of potatoes.
Devon 1985

Page 57
A five-toed Dorking fowl.
Devon 1990

Page 58
Spring shoots.
Devon 1985

Page 61
Lamb from Toatley Farm's Friesland/Dorset milking flock.
Devon 1990

Page 62
A collection of eggs commonly eaten before the days of conservation.
London 1976

Page 65
Coriander leaves, flowers, stalks and seeds in the patterns of a Berber carpet from the Atlas mountains.
Devon 1990

Page 66
Curds and whey.
Devon 1983

Page 68
A mature cheddar from J Green, Mulberry Farm, West Pennard, Somerset.
Devon 1985

Page 75
A potting shed.
England 1984

Page 76
Greenshaft peas from Bridgerule.
Devon 1986

Page 79
Peas in flower on Delabole slate.
Devon 1986

Page 80
Fish wife with lobster, native oysters, whitebait and bladderwrack face, whiting shoulders, scallops, herrings, trout and mackerel arms, eel and clam basket, smoked cod skirt.
London 1977

Page 83
Steamed vegetables.
London 1990

Page 84
Culinary herb knot with soot, gravels, pebbles and coloured sands.
Devon 1980

Page 86
Thirty-six common garden herbs.
Devon 1980

Page 93
Vegetable lily pond. Computerized at Apex Graphics.
London 1990

Page 94
Asparagus.
London 1984

Page 97
After Arcimboldo – reversible Summer and Winter face.
Devon 1979

Page 98
Salmon, trout, sardine and sprat in a bowl by Clive Bowen.
London 1984

Page 100
Peppers, chillies and onions in raspberry vinegar.
London 1989

Page 102
Tuscan extra virgin olive oil.
London 1989

Page 104
Fennel on Cornish granite.
Devon 1988

Page 109
An onion from Appledore.
Devon 1986

Page 110
Woman in a lumpfish hat dressed in plums and blueberries.
Paris 1989

Page 112
Strawberries and clotted cream on Rex Whistler's Clovelly china and chintz.
Devon 1988

Page 115
Soft fruit on a sea kale leaf from the walled garden at Hope End, Herefordshire.
England 1987

Page 117
Mango mousse with passion fruit in an English tea bowl c.1810.
London 1986

Page 118
Plaice drying in the sun at Skaagen.
Denmark 1986

Page 120
Homage to Alfred Wallis, St Ives.
Cornwall 1988

Page 125
After Arcimboldo.
London 1978

Page 126
Devonshire clotted cream from Bearah Farm with an organic strawberry.
Devon 1988

Page 129
Sorbet face with strawberry lips after Benito's Vogue cover 1929.
London 1987

Page 130
Tropical fruit and sugar cane.
London 1980

Page 133
A native beauty in cocoa. After Gauguin.
London 1988

Page 134
Spanish olives grown near Seville.
London 1979

Page 136
Tomatoes from the Chelsea Flower Show.
London 1982

Page 143
Rose petal tart at Clovelly Court.
Devon 1988

Page 144
Rainwater drop on a nasturtium leaf.
Devon 1989

Page 147
Salamagundy, an eighteenth-century salad.
London 1987

Page 148
Aylesbury duck.
Devon 1990

Page 150
'Bowl of rice' in chinese characters made from wild, brown and pudding rice and chopsticks.
London 1982

Page 152
Old fashioned herbs and reliable garden remedies: nasturtiums and marigolds, borage, dandelion and wild strawberries.
Devon 1985

Page 155
Oranges, lemons, kumquats, limes, clementines, mandarins and a pink grapefruit.
London 1981

Page 161
Suffolk smokehouse with trout, mackerel and salmon.
England 1977

Page 162
House built of chocolates from Belgium, France and England.
Paris 1987

Page 164
Cubist collage of halibut, Gertrude Stein and Alice B Toklas.
London 1984

Page 167
Pasta nymph with tagliatelle.
London 1984

Page 168
Unripe wheat.
England 1986

Page 170
Spaghetti collage soup tureen.
London 1981

Page 172
Landrace sow and litter, Devon County Show.
England 1990

Page 175
Wing-rib of hay-fed Angus Beef.
London 1990

Page 181
Salt cod, carp, frog legs, poutargue (waxed roe of grey mullet) and a pike.
Paris 1989

Page 182
A Pugliese loaf with dried funghi porcini.
Italy 1988

Page 184
A Mammoth Improved onion from W Robinson and Sons Ltd, Forton, Lancashire.
England 1990

Page 187
Partridge, woodcock, pheasant and pigeon.
England 1986

Page 188
Quince in carved wooden bowl.
London 1988

Page 191
Oyster mushrooms and a chanterelle on pine needles.
New Forest 1989

Page 192
Ham, pork pies and a salted pig's tail from the Auvergne.
France 1989

Page 197
Pumpkin, potatoes, shallot and peas from the Rue Mouffetard market.
Paris 1989

Page 198
Chocolate sponge with icing sugar stencil.
London 1989

Page 201
Christmas pudding with china pudding moll and silver charms.
London 1983

Page 202
Spiced beef with juniper berries and cooking pot.
Devon 1984

Page 204
The gilt on the gingerbread.
London 1985

Page 207
Canapes and quail eggs.
London 1988

Page 208
Caviar figure on ice.
London 1986

Page 211
Sugar loaf, princess meringues, Alsatian Kugelhopf and patisserie.
Paris 1989

218